Political Marketing

Political Marketing is the first comprehensive textbook to focus on political marketing, and introduces students to how candidates, parties, elected officials and governments around the world utilise marketing concepts and tools to win elections and remain in office.

Drawing on the latest theoretical work and providing the broadest collation of international political marketing research available, this text:

- Examines a wide range of political marketing topics, including the rise of the political consumer, market intelligence and segmentation, opposition research, e-marketing, direct mail, market-orientation and strategy, internal marketing, product redevelopment, branding, local political marketing, marketing in government, delivery and global knowledge transfer.
- Analyses the implications of political marketing for democracy – are we happy to be 'citizen-consumers'?
- Features over forty case studies written by international specialists in over 20 countries, and practitioner perspectives from those currently engaged in political marketing.
- Illustrates theories with clear examples integrated with topical discussion points, and provides essay and applied assessment suggestions in each chapter.

Presented in a clear and engaging style, this textbook offers sophisticated understanding of this exciting new area. Written by a leading expert in the field, it is essential reading for all students of political marketing, parties and elections, and comparative politics.

Jennifer Lees-Marshment is Senior Lecturer in Political Marketing at Auckland University and was founding chair of the UK PSA Political Marketing Group. Her books include *Political Marketing and British Political Parties* (1st edn 2001, 2nd edn 2008), *The Political Marketing Revolution* (2004), *Political Marketing in Comparative Perspective* (2005, co-editor) and *Current Issues in Political Marketing* (2005, co-editor).

Political Marketing

Principles and applications

Jennifer Lees-Marshment

LONDON AND NEW YORK

First published 2009
by Routledge
2 Park Square, Milton Park, Abingdon, Oxon OX14 4RN

Simultaneously published in the USA and Canada
by Routledge
270 Madison Avenue, New York, NY 10016

Routledge is an imprint of the Taylor & Francis Group, an informa business

© 2009 Jennifer Lees-Marshment

Typeset in Times New Roman by
Florence Production Ltd, Stoodleigh, Devon

British Library Cataloguing in Publication Data
A catalogue record for this book is available from the British Library

Library of Congress Cataloging in Publication Data
Lees-Marshment, Jennifer.
  Political marketing: principles and applications/Jennifer Lees-Marshment.
     p.cm.
  1. Campaign management. 2. Political campaigns. 3. Marketing—Political
aspects. I. Title.
  JF2112.C3L44 2009
  324.7′3—dc22   2008054937

ISBN 10: 0–415–43128–X (hbk)
ISBN 10: 0–415–43129–8 (pbk)
ISBN 10: 0–203–87522–2 (ebk)

ISBN 13: 978–0–415–43128–6 (hbk)
ISBN 13: 978–0–415–43129–3 (pbk)
ISBN 13: 978–0–203–87522–3 (ebk)

This book is dedicated to my son,
James Paul Lees-Marshment,
who was with me every day
I spent writing it,
even if he didn't know it at the time.

Contents

Case studies and contributor details

1.1 George W., the Marlboro Man and the Messiah: how voters view politics from a consumerist perspective
Dave Brown is a Lecturer/Creative Director in Advertising Creativity at the Auckland University of Technology. His research focuses on the persuasion industry, politics and the promotion of sustainable consumption. Email address: dave.brown@auckland.ac.nz

1.2 The explosive outcome of treating the electorate as customers
Richard Scullion is a Senior Lecturer specialising in marketing communications and is writing up his thesis comparing consumer and political choice practices and experiences at the London School of Economics. He is co-editor of two books, including *Voters or Consumers: Imagining the contemporary electorate* (Cambridge Scholars Publishing, 2008). Email address: rscullio@bournemouth.ac.uk

2.1 An application of Lloyd's product concept: the UK Conservative Party in 2001
Tim Sansom is a Ph.D. research student at the University of Leicester, England. His research has focused on modern British political communication, and his thesis concerns the marketing strategies of the Conservative Party between 1966 and 2001. Email address: t.sansom@yahoo.co.uk

3.1 The Lees-Marshment POP-SOP-MOP model applied to UK Labour, 1983–97
Jennifer Lees-Marshment is Senior Lecturer at Auckland University, and her research focuses on how parties use political marketing strategy and market-orientation. Her earlier work on UK politics broadened the concept of political marketing, from selling to the design of political products. See for example *Political Marketing and British Political Parties* (Manchester University Press, 2001, 2008) and *The Political Marketing Revolution* (Manchester University Press, 2004). More recent research is comparative, for example *Political Marketing: A Comparative Perspective* (co-edited with D.G. Lilleker, Manchester University Press, 2005); in addition to this textbook, in progress is a second comparative collection, *Global Political Marketing* (co-edited with J. Stromback and C. Rudd, forthcoming) and a monograph, *The Political Marketing Game*, forthcoming), featuring interviews with practitioners in the UK, US, New Zealand and Australia. For more information see www.arts.auckland.ac.nz/staff/index.cfm?P=8779. Email address: j.lees-marshment@auckland.ac.nz

3.2 The re-launch of the APRA Party in a new political era in Peru
Pedro Patrón Galindo is Chief of the Press Department at PR Agency Solsona Comunicación, Barcelona, and Ph.D. candidate in Political Science at the Universidad Autònoma de Barcelona, Spain. Email address: pepatron@hotmail.com

3.3 Principle versus patronage: The Lees-Marshment method and political marketing in Japan
Bryce Wakefield is completing a Ph.D. at the Political Studies Department of Auckland University. His research focuses on political culture and defence policy in Japan. Email address: bwak003@ec.auckland.ac.nz

3.4 The strategy of the British Liberal Democrats
Stephen Barber is Senior Research Fellow at the Global Policy Institute at London Metropolitan University and author of *Political Strategy: Modern politics in contemporary Britain*. Email address: s.barber@global-policy.com

4.1 Bye-bye Belgium? Reputation and competitive positioning in the historic 2007 federal election and formation period
Dave Gelders is Lecturer in Government Communication and Political Marketing at the Leuven School for Mass Communication Research and the Public Management Institute, K.U. Leuven. His research focuses on public sector marketing and the relationship between media and politics. Email address: dave.gelderssoc.kuleuven.be

4.2 The Finnish case: strategic positioning of a niche party – the Swedish People's Party
Susanne Jungerstam-Mulders is Research Manager at the Department of Social Welfare and Health Care at the Novia University of Applied Sciences, Vasa, Finland. Her research focuses on a variety of themes related to party politics, political systems and welfare policy issues. Email address: susanne.jungerstam@novia.fi

4.3 Market positions of Polish political parties in 2007
Wojciech Opioła is a Ph.D. candidate at the University of Opole, Poland. Email address: opiol1@wp.pl
Arleta Opioła is a Master of Arts in Journalism at the University of Opole, Poland. Email address: a.opiola@wp.pl

5.1 From the 'old' to the 'new' moderates: a Swedish case study
Jesper Strömbäck is Professor in Media and Communication and Lubbe Nordström Professor and Chair in Journalism at Mid Sweden University, where he is also Research Director at the Centre for Political Communication Research. His most recent books are *Handbook of Election News Coverage Around the World* (Routledge, 2008), co-edited with Lynda Lee Kaid, and *Communicating Politics: Political communication in the Nordic countries* (Nordicom, 2008), co-edited with Mark Ørsten and Toril Aalberg. Website: www.jesperstromback.com; email address: jesper.stromback@miun.se

5.2 The Hungarian Socialist Party winning young people
Balázs Kiss is Director of the Centre for Political Communications Research at the Institute for Political Sciences of the Hungarian Academy of Sciences. He also teaches political communications studies at the Eötvös Loránd University, Budapest. Email address: kiss@mtapti.hu

5.3 Political marketing strategy of Hillary Clinton in the 2008 Iowa and New Hampshire primaries
Daria Gorbounova holds a Bachelor's degree with a double major in Political Science and French from Auckland University. She was a 2007–08 Summer Scholar in Global Political Marketing for Dr Jennifer Lees-Marshment, researching political marketing in the

2008 United States presidential election, with a particular focus on Hillary Clinton. Email address: dariadash@hotmail.com

Jennifer Lees-Marshment is Senior Lecturer at Auckland University. Email address: j.lees-marshment@auckland.ac.nz

5.4 Branded American politics
Kenneth M. Cosgrove is Assistant Professor of Government and Director of Graduate Studies (Political Science) at Suffolk University in Boston, MA, US. His research interests focus on political marketing and its role in American politics. Email address: kcosgrov@suffolk.edu

5.5 Segmentation and brand development: an African perspective
Kobby Mensah is a Ph.D. candidate at the University of Sheffield, UK. His research is on forms and strategies in political branding. Kobby is an Associate Member of the Chartered Institute of Marketing (CIM), UK. Email address: jop05akm@sheffield.ac.uk

5.6 From database to relationship marketing: a case study of Fidesz
Zsuzsanna Mihályffy is Research Fellow at the Hungarian Academy of Sciences, Institute for Political Science, and Ph.D. candidate at Eötvös University, Budapest. Her research focuses on campaign communication in Hungary. Email address: zsmihalyffy@mtapti.hu

5.7 To thine own self be true: branding, authenticity and political leadership – the case of Don Brash
Jon Johansson is Lecturer in Comparative Politics at Victoria University of Wellington. His research focuses on political leadership and political psychology, as well as his own domestic politics in New Zealand. Email address: jon.johansson@vuw.ac.nz

5.8 ACT New Zealand and branding
Dr Chris Rudd is Senior Lecturer in the Department of Politics at the University of Otago, New Zealand. He is co-author of *The Politics and Government of New Zealand* (with G.A. Wood, University of Otago Press, 2004) and co-editor of *Sovereignty under Siege?* (with R. Patman, Ashgate, 2005), *Political Communications in New Zealand* (2004), *The Political Economy of New Zealand* (1997) and *State and Economy in New Zealand* (with D. Roper, Oxford University Press, 1993). Email address: chris.rudd@stonebow.otago.ac.nz

Geoffrey Miller is a Postgraduate student at the Department of Politics, University of Otago, Dunedin, New Zealand. Email address: geoffreymiller@gmail.com

6.1 Wasted on the young: marketing membership efforts by Plaid Cymru
Sue Granik is a UK Chartered Marketer and Visiting Lecturer in Human Resource Management at Birkbeck College, University of London, and the University of Westminster. At the time of her research she was under the age of 35.

6.2 Examples of internal blockage to market-oriented strategy: the UK Conservatives, 1997–2001
Jennifer Lees-Marshment is Senior Lecturer at Auckland University. Email address: j.lees-marshment@auckland.ac.nz

6.3 The problems of implementing medium-/long-term planning for political parties in Spain
Juan Ignacio Marcos Lekuona is Consultant on Governance/Management Systems and Professor of Political Marketing in the IDEC of the Pompeu Fabra University, Barcelona, and of Leadership Development in the University of Deusto, Bilbao and San Sebastian, Spain. His research and professional practice focuses on governance and political management. He is author of *Marketing Político: La Campaña Permanente* (2002), *Planes y Proyectos Políticos/Planes y Proyectos Estratégicos. Más sobre estrategias para el Mantenimiento/desarrollo de la Mayoria Electoral* (2004), *Del Marketing Político a la Gobernanza Eficaz* (2008). Email address: marcoslekuona@marcoslekuona.net

6.4 Resisting marketing: the case of the British Labour Party under Blair
Robin T. Pettitt is Lecturer in Comparative Politics at Kingston University, London. His research focuses on the role of party members and the impact of the political and media environment on the internal life of political parties. Email address: r.pettitt@kingston.ac.uk

7.1 Image supremacy? Lifting the veil in Belgium
Philippe De Vries lectures on Political Marketing in the Master's programme in Political Communication at the University of Antwerp, Belgium. His research focuses on aspects of candidate image and political personality. Email address: philippe.devries@ua.ac.be

Christ'l De Landtsheer is Director of the Political Communication Research Unit at the University of Antwerp, Belgium. She teaches several courses in the Master's programme in Political Communication. Her research focuses on psychological, technological and linguistic aspects of political communication. Email address: christl.delandtsheer@ua.ac.be

Soetkin Kesteloot is a Ph.D. student at the University of Ghent, Belgium. Her research focuses on the political marketing of Belgian political parties. Email address: soetkin. kesteloot@ugent.be

7.2 Czech Republic: Social Democrats strike back
Alexander Braun, MA, is Director of European Political Operations at Penn, Schoen and Berland Associates, specialises in polling and creating strategies for international political campaigns. He has worked on high-level international political clients, including leading parties and candidates in Britain, Estonia, Czech Republic, Slovakia, Thailand, Indonesia and the Philippines. He has also provided strategic communication advice for large corporations such as Microsoft, Procter and Gamble and MSNBC. Email address: abraun@ ps-b.com

Anna Matuskova is currently a Visiting Researcher at Columbia University, New York (awarded a Fulbright Scholarship). As the doctoral candidate in Political Science at the Masaryk University in the Czech Republic, she specialises in the fields of political marketing, electoral strategies, political campaigning and functions of political parties. As part of the doctoral study is teaching, she runs a course on the Theory of Political Marketing and, recently, a course on Election 2006: Electoral Marketing in the Czech Republic. She gained a grant for the development of political marketing from the Department of Education. Email address: matuskov@fss.muni.cz

7.3 UK MPs and the marketing of their websites
Nigel A. Jackson is Lecturer at Plymouth Business School, University of Plymouth and co-author of *The Marketing of Political Parties: Political Marketing at the 2005 British*

General Election (with D.G. Lilleker and R. Scullion, Manchester University Press, 2006). His research focuses on the impact of the Internet on political communication, and political PR. Email address: nigel.jackson@plymouth.ac.uk

7.4 ACT New Zealand Party and the limits of technological marketing
Gavin Middleton was Communications Manager for the ACT New Zealand political party from 2000 until 2007. Email address: gavinm@paradise.net.nz

7.5 Local political marketing: connecting UK politicians and voters
Darren G. Lilleker is Senior Lecturer in Political Communication and Director of Research for the Centre of Public Communication in the Media School, Bournemouth University. He has previously published on left-wing activism, political communication and political marketing in the UK and is currently researching interactive political communication via Web 2.0. Email: dlilleker@bmth.ac.uk

7.6 Canadian constituency campaigns
Alex Marland is Assistant Professor of Political Science at Memorial University St John's, Newfoundland, Canada (see www.mun.ca/posc). He researches and teaches Canadian politics, electioneering and political communications. Email address: amarland@mun.ca

7.7 Market-oriented political advertising in the 2005 New Zealand election
Claire Robinson was Head of the Institute of Communication Design and Associate Pro Vice-Chancellor of the College of Creative Arts at Massey University, New Zealand, at time of writing. Her research interests include political marketing and political communication, with specific emphasis on the visual communication of political messages. Email address: claire.robinson1@xtra.co.nz

7.8 Terminating politics as we know it: the political marketing case of the 'Governator'
David McCuan, Ph.D., is Associate Professor at Sonoma State University, studies California politics, electoral behaviour including campaigns and elections, and teaches courses in American politics. He is currently working on a book on the first political consultants in the United States, Whitaker and Baxter. Email address: david.mccuan@sonoma.edu

8.1 Unpredictable influences threaten government re-election: the effect of situational factors on the results of recent elections in Turkey
Umit Alniacik is a Ph.D. candidate at Gebze Institute of Technology, Turkey. Email address: ualniacik@gyte.edu.tr

8.2 Delivering in Greece: a threat or an opportunity for democracy?
Iordanis Kotzaivazoglou is Visiting Lecturer in Advertising and Communication at the Department of Advertising and Operations Management of the University of Macedonia, the Department of Marketing of the Technological Institute of Thessaloniki and the Department of Business Administration of the Technological Institute of Serres, Greece. His research interests focus on professionalisation of political communication, modern campaigning and social aspects of advertising dealing with stereotypes. Email address: ikptza@jour.auth.gr

Yorgos Zotos is Professor of Marketing at the School of Economics, Department of Business Administration of Aristotle University of Thessaloniki, Greece. His research interests are focused on social aspects of advertising dealing with stereotypes, and cross-country comparisons of perception and attitude formation. He has published articles in the following journals, among others: *European Journal of Marketing, Journal of Business Ethics, Psychological Reports, Journal of Current Issues and Advertising Research* and *Journal of Retail and Distribution Management.* Email address: zotos@econ.auth.gr

8.3 When politics becomes contractual: a case from Denmark

Jens Jonatan Steen is Master of Political Administration, Roskilde University, Denmark. His main research area is political pledges and contractual politics. He is Chief Editor of the political journal *Vision* and President of the Danish think tank Cevea. Email address: jjs@cevea.dk

8.4 After Blair ... the challenge of communicating Brown's brand of Labour

Jenny Lloyd is Senior Lecturer at the University of the West of England, Bristol, UK. The primary focus of her research is the interaction between political consumers and political brands. Email: jenny.lloyd@uwe.ac.uk

9.1 Top down or bottom up?

Dennis W. Johnson is Professor of Political Management at the George Washington University Graduate School of Political Management. He is author of *No Place for Amateurs: How political consultants are reshaping American democracy*, 2nd edn (2007) and editor of the *Routledge Handbook of Political Management* (2008). Email address: dwjgspm@gwu.edu

9.2 Learning from the master: the impact of New Labour on political parties in Denmark

Robin T. Pettitt is Lecturer in Comparative Politics at Kingston University, London. Email address: r.pettitt@kingston.ac.uk

9.3 International political product marketing

Jamie Turner is a student at Auckland University and a tutor in the Department of Political Studies. He is studying towards an LLB (Hons)/BA, with double majors in Political Studies and Economics. Email address: jamie.turner@xtra.co.nz

9.4 Political marketing in the rise and fall of Taiwan's New Party

Dafydd J. Fell is Senior Lecturer in Taiwan Studies at the Department of Political Studies of the School of Oriental and African Studies (SOAS), University of London. He has published numerous articles on political parties and electioneering in Taiwan. His first book was *Party Politics in Taiwan* (Routledge, 2005). In 2006 he co-edited *What has Changed? Taiwan's KMT and DPP eras in comparative perspective* (Harrassowitz). In 2008 he edited a four-volume reference collection titled *Politics of Modern Taiwan* (Routledge). Email address: df2@soas.ac.uk

9.5 Ideology matters: how political marketing influences the preparation process of election campaigns at Germany's federal state level

Melanie Diermann is Scientific Assistant and Chair for the Political System of Germany and Modern State Theories, Institute for Political Science, NRW School of Governance, University Duisburg-Essen, Germany. Email address: melanie.diermann@uni-due.de

9.6 How are Macedonian parties oriented?

Gordica Karanfilovska, MA, is a Ph.D. candidate at the Institute for Legal and Political Sciences of the Faculty of Law 'Iustinianus Primus' at Sts. Cyril and Methodius University,

Republic of Macedonia. Her research focus is on political marketing and political communication, public relations, election campaigns and product design in political marketing. Email address: gordicak@yahoo.com

9.7 The 'party of power' in Russian politics
Derek S. Hutcheson is Head of Subject in European Studies in the UCD School of Politics and International Relations, University College Dublin, Ireland. His research focuses on electoral politics in the post-communist region. Email address: derek.hutcheson@ucd.ie

10.1 Ideology, political marketing and the 2005 UK election
Heather Savigny is a Lecturer in Politics at the University of East Anglia. She is co-convenor of the PSA's Media and Politics Specialist Group and has just recently completed her first monograph *The Problem of Political Marketing* (Continuum International, 2008). Email address: h.savigny@uea.ac.uk

10.2 Political marketing in the 2006 Canadian federal election: delivering citizen or party needs and wants?
Daniel J. Paré is Associate Professor in the Department of Communication, University of Ottawa, Canada. His research focuses on socio-economic and policy issues arising from innovations in information and communication technologies. He is the author of *Internet Governance in Transition: Who is the master of this domain* (Rowman & Littlefield, 2003), and editor of the Canadian edition of the *Global Media Journal*. Email address: daniel.pare@uottawa.ca

10.3 Political marketing, democracy and terrorism: Ireland highlights the dangers
Sean McGough is Director of International Affairs at the Cuu Long Securities Corporation, HCMC, Vietnam. Email address: sbm743@hotmail.com

Tables

Boxes

Preface

Political Marketing: Principles and Applications is the first comprehensive introductory text in political marketing. It synthesises new and old literature from different disciplines and areas to provide a broad overview of study and practice around the world. It is led by existing research in the field and features the most recent work. While the majority of work called political marketing in the 1980s and 1990s focused on campaigns, this began to change around 2000. This text includes studies on the product, strategy, internal marketing, local political marketing, e-marketing, branding, stakeholder marketing, segmentation, marketing in government, international political marketing, consumerism and political marketing and democracy. While it does not cover every possible aspect of marketing that could be applied to politics, given inevitable gaps in existing literature, by bringing together new research hitherto unconnected or unnoticed, this book aims not just to help the study of existing work, but also to stimulate further research in political marketing. For further information about political marketing see www.political-marketing.org.

Jennifer Lees-Marshment, Auckland University,
New Zealand, 19 June 2008

Introduction

Political marketing is a growing area of academia, emanating from the two disciplines of marketing and political science. It offers a different way of viewing political behaviour, while raising new perspectives on classic questions in political science, such as the value of ideology and principle, the role of citizenship and the nature of democracy, yet within the context of the twenty-first century marketplace. It offers both potential for a new means of linking government and the governed, and fresh controversies as to the efficacy and value of elites consulting and responding to voter opinion.

As an area of practice, it includes polling, market research, databases, voter profiling, strategy, consulting, branding, communication, advertising, campaigning and delivery and is spreading rapidly throughout the world – this text contains over forty case studies from over twenty countries. It draws on existing literature in political marketing that has undergone a degree of peer review, discussion and debate and has taken into account the need to adapt marketing concepts to politics.

Like all fields of study, political marketing is always evolving and developing. The topics and aspects covered in this book reflect the literature available at the time of writing, in mid-2008. The book is organised into ten chapters:

- The political market and the rise of the political consumer
- What is political marketing?
- Political marketing strategy
- Understanding the market: market intelligence, consultation and participation
- Product development and branding
- Internal marketing: marketing to volunteers and the party
- Marketing communication and campaigns
- Marketing in government: delivering and staying in touch
- Global knowledge transfer
- Political marketing and democracy.

The order and separation of chapters and topics is not trying to suggest actual division and progression in practice or study. For example, marketing in government includes communication and strategy; organisations may conduct market intelligence before deciding on their strategy, and branding includes communication as well as product development. Each area overlaps.

These chapters include some, but not all, marketing concepts and tools, so a marketing scholar or student will find that a number of marketing models or theories do not appear. This is simply because political marketing literature has not yet covered all the areas that marketing covers. Regarding the communications chapter, for example, it could be argued that discussion of integrated marketing communication (IMC) within politics is essential in any up-to-date marketing text, but at time of writing no applied theory or empirical study in political IMC that could be used within a political marketing text existed. Additionally, the communications chapter only focuses on literature where marketing has been identified and is clearly adding something new beyond general political communication. This is a political marketing text, not a marketing, political communication or political science book, and any apparent gaps reflect gaps in the political marketing research literature. While this may be frustrating, as this is a textbook not a research book, it was only possible to reflect the existing state of the field, with the aim of stimulating further research to fill those gaps and include it in subsequent editions.

A thorough literature search across several databases identified over two hundred pieces of new and additional literature in a diverse range of journals and books, and included a search for conference papers available online. While every care has been taken to provide a balanced picture of the range of literature, given that my work on market-orientation has been utilised in empirical analysis and been the subject of debate, there are references to my own work. Furthermore, as the Lees-Marshment (2001) model offered a broad framework under which many different marketing aspects could be organised, and which indeed follows the natural logic of marketing theory, the chapter order or titles may seem similar to the MOP (market-oriented party) process, but this reflects the nature of marketing and politics more than any particular author. Any remaining bias is inevitable, given that I am the author of this text: no author can get rid of their own thinking altogether. Great care was taken to undergo an extensive literature search across several databases to identify all possible new work, and not one of the five reviewers identified anything missing from political marketing literature.

As for the case studies, all authors were invited to make their own choice regarding topics, theories and models. Authors were selected with the aim of encouraging the greatest possible variation in country, aspect and theory. A few use the Lees-Marshment model, but several use frameworks by other authors such as Butler and Collins, and most apply their own theory. Theoretical diversity has been encouraged, but, without being too prescriptive, I could not manufacture absolute equality in the number of times a particular model was used. Some authors declined a direct invitation to submit a case study that could have used their own model. The only other potential bias was the deliberate seeking of new authors who could broaden the range of material available to prospective students, and trying to reduce the UK bias criticised by reviewers of the original proposal. There are more political marketing authors in the UK than any other country, and so, while some significant authors are not authors of case studies, their existing published work has of course been discussed. Overall, the text provides a fair reflection of political marketing literature at time of writing.

As this is the first textbook in this area, it will aid teaching of political marketing by synthesising the broad range of research previously separated by different publication outlets, countries and disciplines. A student of marketing or political science can engage in numerous debates relevant to either discipline by studying political marketing, and this text will lay out the principles, theories, examples and scope to make the process as easy as possible.

The aims and objectives of any political marketing text and course would include to:

- appreciate how and why political marketing has developed over time, and its relation to party decline, increase in electoral volatility and so forth;
- comprehend the concept of political marketing: understanding that political marketing is not just about spin or election campaigns;

- understand how marketing may be used within the political environment, but also appreciate the differences between marketing business and marketing politics;
- learn about the difficulties in introducing marketing into politics, questioning the ethical issues arising from marketing politics, arguing the benefits marketing may bring to politics;
- gain knowledge about comparative political behaviour by utilising international case studies and learning about the global transfer of ideas and consultants;
- encourage broader thinking about the practice of modern-day politics;
- comprehend the potential and limitations of marketing politics, both practically and normatively;
- gain knowledge of another discipline, if from either marketing or political science;
- reflect on practical experience in politics, if appropriate.

The types of skill this text and a course in political marketing will develop include:

- intellectual agility and interdisciplinary understanding and analysis, by applying basic marketing concepts to political party behaviour;
- comparative analysis, by examining the use of political marketing in a number of countries and systems;
- balanced consideration, by learning about the different academic perspectives in the field of political marketing;
- debating skills, by discussing topical issues that arise from political marketing;
- critical analysis, through considering both the effectiveness and the democratic implications of political marketing;
- writing and reporting skills, including primary research skills, by completing assessed work;
- applied analysis, by reading and discussing the case studies and completing applied assessment.

For students of marketing, one of the challenges can be to understand politics quickly enough. In my teaching experience in management departments, this fear was proved unnecessary as the course progressed, but there are a number of books that could be utilised to give a quick guide to politics, such as *Politics: The Basics*, 4th edn, by Stephen D. Tansey and Nigel Jackson (Routledge, 2008). Other short cuts are introductory politics textbooks that have chapters on parties and elections in particular, and the Palgrave *Developments in British/American/German/French/Central and East European/West European/Russian Politics* series provides a quick read of recent issues in each country. For politics students, all the marketing understanding needed to grasp political marketing research is contained and explained within this book.

The first two chapters discuss the nature of the political marketplace and the rise of the political consumer and introduce the field of political marketing. The following Chapters 3–9 examine different aspects of the theory and practice of political marketing, including strategy, market intelligence, product development, branding, implementation, communication, campaigning, marketing in government and knowledge transfer across countries. The final chapter considers political marketing and democracy: both the problems and potential. In each chapter, the main theories, literature and examples are considered, along with appropriate case studies written by scholars around the world to illustrate the nature of political marketing in practice. Key questions for discussion, debates and tasks are within each chapter, as well as suggestions for written assessment, with further reading.

The completion of this book has been aided in a number of ways. I would like to thank Craig Fowlie at Routledge, for encouraging the book and suggesting the case studies, and the UK Political Studies Association for supporting the formation of a political marketing specialist group, which facilitated a growing network of political marketing scholars on which I drew to find case study authors. Auckland University provided a faculty research grant that funded research assistance and teaching buyout; and Jamie Turner and Daria Gorbounova took the positions of research assistants and carried out an extensive literature search. Daria also undertook comprehensive formatting work of the manuscript, and I am grateful for her reliability when I was pushing myself in the later stages of pregnancy to finish and submit the first draft before I went on leave. I would also like to thank the anonymous reviewers, some of whom devoted considerable time to providing detailed but also constructive suggestions for change. The reviews provided the most directly useable suggestions I've ever had on a manuscript, and this maximised their potential to further improve the value of the text.

I hope both lecturers and students will find it an appropriate foundation for exploring the many different aspects and issues involved in political marketing around the world, and that the text will be developed with further editions over time, as both the field and practice of political marketing expand. The field has come a long way since I first started writing on it a decade ago, when conventional wisdom classed political marketing as spin doctoring. *Political Marketing: Principles and Applications* will play an important role in ensuring it goes even further.

Dr Jennifer Lees-Marshment, Auckland University,
New Zealand, December 2008

1   The political market and the rise of the political consumer

Political marketing is a growing area of academic study. Although marketing has been used in politics in some form or other for a long time, it is only since the 1980s that it has become more commonly noted by academic and media commentators. In particular there has been a significant increase in the sharing of ideas, techniques, consultants and even product ideas across different countries since the 1990s.

This chapter will explore potential reasons for why this development has occurred. It will discuss how political behaviour such as voting and participation within political parties has changed, and how the attitude of voters towards political elites has become less predictable and more consumerist. The nature of the political marketplace – or environment – in which a political candidate or party has to interact has been transformed, affected by non-political changes such as the rise and development of telecommunications.

Politics is viewed by academic study as an activity that should be concerned with belief, principle, ideals and debate about how the world should be run – as well as winning elections and power. Marketing as a discipline, and indeed a practice, predominantly studies how businesses behave in a commercial world concerned with making profit and, while it has broadened to include consideration of how organisations achieve a range of goals, applying its concepts to politics raises many questions about ethics, value and consequences for democracy, which will be fully discussed in Chapter 10.

Consumerism is also a contentious topic. While the extent of such change is hard to measure, and literature on the political consumer limited, it is important to understand the different factors that both activate and influence the use of marketing in politics and gain an idea of the main normative concerns, before proceeding to examine the different ways marketing is used in the rest of the book.

The political marketplace

The political marketplace, which includes every aspect a candidate, party or government has to consider, as well as the more obvious aspects such as how voters behave, has changed significantly since the 1960s. A range of literature discusses a declining respect for, and confidence and trust in, authority, established institutions and politicians (see, for example, Norris's *Critical Citizens* (2005) and Pharr and Putnam's *Disaffected Democracies* (2000)). Box 1.1 provides an overview of the types of changes that have occurred.

Voters are now exposed to significantly more sources of information about politics, including more critical and independent reporting. Continual media coverage also provides an uncomfortable, unrelenting environment for political parties and politicians, especially in government. As Tony Blair, UK prime minister from 1997 to 2007, said in a speech to Reuters in his last year of power:

Box 1.1 Changes in the political marketplace since the 1960s

1   Party membership or registered support has declined in numbers and activity levels.
2   Party identification (a long-term attachment to a party, rooted in family history and background, akin to support for a football team) has declined in strength.
3   Participation in traditional politics has declined, with voting/turnout falling, while involvement in new movements or pressure groups has increased.
4   Youth, in particular, exhibits declining engagement with traditional politics.
5   Voting behaviour has become less predictable, with an increase in electoral volatility (where voters change which party they vote for from one election to the next); and there has been both a rise in independent voters (who base their vote decision on issues other than party identification) and a resurgence of value-based voting in the US.
6   Television and, now, the Internet have become the prime sources of political information.
7   The number and nature of media outlets and competition have vastly expanded and have become more commercial, competitive and questioning of elites.
8   Traditional bases of segmentation or cleavages in the electorate, such as class, geography and family background, have been eroded, while complex new electoral segments, such as those based on ethnicity, race, lifestyle, stage in the life cycle and age factors have emerged.
9   Voters are more critical of political elites and institutions.

When I fought the 1997 election – just ten years ago – we could take an issue a day. At the last election in 2005, we had to have one for the morning, another for the afternoon and by the evening the agenda had already moved on entirely ... a vast aspect of our jobs today – outside of the really major decisions, as big as anything else – is coping with the media, its sheer scale, weight and constant hyperactivity. At points, it literally overwhelms.

Indeed, new media outlets such as online discussions enable the voter to be part of the broadcast and make the news, not just watch it: see Discussion point 1.1.

Discussion point 1.1

Discuss how you decide what to think about politics. What sources of information are most relied on? What does this reveal about how voters form political opinions and therefore what politics should consider when using marketing?

Political parties in most countries have formal membership or official supporters, and this is a valuable means of generating long-term, loyal support as well as activists to go out on the ground in campaigns. But parties around the world have suffered from lower numbers, as well as a decline in their willingness to be active for the party. They also want more from their membership: see Practitioner perspective 1.1 and Discussion point 1.2.

These changes have eroded the link between people and political elites. Without such attachment, voters are more volatile – who they will vote for cannot be easily predicted; they are like buyers who will switch supermarkets easily instead of building a long-term relationship of loyalty and trust with their local grocery: see Discussion point 1.3.

Practitioner perspective 1.1

Membership attitudes today, particularly amongst young people, have evolved from the days when [being a member] was a form of social infrastructure. Today people want to feel they are involved in politics and that above all they have a right to be listened to – at the top.

(Archie Norman, a business executive appointed as the UK Conservative Party's
Chief Executive after the 1997 General Election, speaking in 1998,
quoted in Lees-Marshment 2001)

Discussion point 1.2

Drawing on personal experience, discuss whether and why you have been volunteers, and whether Norman's point about wanting to feel involved is true. To what extent did the candidates or parties you worked for ensure that you were 'listened to at the top'?

Discussion point 1.3

How do you decide to vote? List the different factors that influence you, and discuss which are more important.

While the extent of such changes varies between counties and, indeed, over time, with party identification continuing to influence voters and recent increases in participation in the 2008 presidential campaigns in the US, there are fewer guarantees in politics. Political elites even need to consider how to meet the needs of people who normally support them at every election, as these voters' behaviour has also changed. Furthermore, the recent resurgence of activity in the US could be argued to be a result of successful marketing: online social networking or e-marketing; use of market segmentation to reach potential participations; and galvanising, market-oriented campaigns by Democratic presidential nomination contenders; and effective Republican Party organisation.

Emerging new market segments such as young people, pensioners, women and ethnic groups present new challenges for candidates and parties. Such segments are distinctive in their lifestyles, attitudes, political participation and policies they desire. Parties therefore need to ensure they respond in different ways, with new understanding that traditional politics may not be able to help them with – but marketing may.

Furthermore, politics itself needs marketing: young people, as well as the general populace, are showing declining levels of voting turnout. While in newer democracies work may focus more on ensuring fair and free elections, in established democracies so work is being done to encourage people to vote: see Task 1.1.

For political parties, declining and unpredictable turnout has added a further variable for parties trying to calculate where best to expend their limited resources. Again, marketing can help with this, as it offers segmentation and direct marketing tools to help them identify potential supporters and get their vote out.

Task 1.1

The UK Electoral Commission organised a conference in June 2002 on turnout and asked what can be done to reverse the decline and by whom? They created television adverts, 'I don't do politics', for the 2005 election (see www.dopolitics.org.uk/). Look at the work being done by electoral commissions in different countries to boost turnout.

Indicative websites for electoral commissions around the world

UK Electoral Commission: www.electoralcommission.org.uk/

Australian Electoral Commission: www.aec.gov.au/

Elections New Zealand: www.elections.org.nz/

Tasmanian Electoral Commission: www.electoral.tas.gov.au/

Pakistan Electoral Commission: www.ecp.gov.pk/

US Electoral Commission: www.fec.gov/

Elections Canada: www.elections.ca/home.asp

Sweden: www.val.se/

Germany: www.bundeswahlleiter.de/e/index_e.htm

France: www.interieur.gouv.fr/

Hong Kong: www.eac.gov.hk/

Singapore: www.elections.gov.sg/

Romania: www.kappa.ro/guv/bec/ceb96.html

[See www.electoralcommission.org.uk/elections/Othercommissions.cfm for a full list.]

Furthermore, around the world, surveys indicate that voters are more critical of politicians, parties and government and less satisfied with their performance. Mortimore (2003) considered a range of qualitative and quantitative data on public attitudes towards politics in the UK and concluded that:

> The standing of politics is low. It affects public attitudes to politicians, political institutions, policies . . . politicians today are distrusted more than other professions or institutions . . . Public familiarity with politics and politicians is low, and familiarity with politicians at least is falling . . . Further, it has bred a public cynicism that weakens the political process and its democratic accountability. Democratic institutions need the participation of the public to claim any legitimacy; increasingly they are losing it. The need for the marketing of politics, as opposed to political marketing, is now an urgent one.

Pharr and Putnam (2000) argued that citizen disaffection was partly as a result of new public expectations and uses of information that have altered the criteria by which people judge their governments: see Task 1.2.

Overall, many changes have occurred that have facilitated the emergence of a new political market and that, not only influence the way the public view and evaluate political elites, but make their voting behaviour less predictable.

Task 1.2

Identify and examine data to consider to what extent the political market has changed in your country.

Sources of data: this will depend on where you live, but examples are the Eurobarometer, UK social attitudes survey, post-election survey, public opinion polls, academic studies of voting behaviour, political culture and public opinion.

Indicative factors to look for: party identification, party membership, participation, turnout, voting behaviour, media, political efficacy and satisfaction with government.

Older models of voting behaviour, such as *The American Voter* by Campbell *et al.* (1960), offer less explanation for election outcomes than in the past, as they rest on societal foundations such as that party identification was the main indication of vote. While there undoubtedly remain some loyal partisan voters, the market is more open, and elites have greater need to consider what it is that will attract public support, instead of relying on old attachments. Consumer behaviour in politics suggests that voters are more likely to choose on a more rational basis, as already argued by political scientists such as Downs (1957) and Key (1966).

Traditional politics in established democracies is less effective, while, in new democracies such as Brazil, Peru and the Czech Republic, where political allegiances and institutional cultures have yet to be created, there is the freedom to use marketing to create new support quickly, as no traditional behavioural patterns exist. There has also been a rise in consumerism, which will be discussed in the next section.

The political consumer

In reflection of the changes in political marketing, the public seems to act more like consumers. The rise of consumerism within the business sphere and then the public sector (e.g. government-funded health, education and local government) has gradually permeated the political arena (see Spring 2003, Lewis *et al.* 2005: 131–3). A number of political marketing scholars have discussed this change (see Walsh 1994: 63, Butler and Collins 1998: 3, Needham 2003, Scammell 2003, Lees-Marshment 2004, Lilleker and Scullion 2008). Political practitioners also show strong awareness of this change in public attitudes: see Practitioner perspective 1.2.

The rise of the political consumer is not just about how people vote, but the nature of their overall attitude to politicians, what they demand, how they want to be involved, how they question authority, how they want to be consulted and how they scrutinise lack of delivery. There is an increased desire for demonstrable improvements in performances: better schools, health care, and better services from the local council. Needham (2003: 7) argued that government itself has 'sought to import consumer values into the government–citizen relationship.' Consumerisation has a number of effects on politics: see Box 1.2 and Discussion point 1.4.

Practitioner perspective 1.2

Modern people are tired of being put into old fashioned political boxes. *Venstre* is today a broadly based party with voters in all groups . . . People do not think in terms of classes anymore but insist on being allowed to make the decisions that affect their lives by themselves. People no longer accept politicians saying 'we know what is best for you' . . . We live at the beginning of the 21st Century and I believe that . . . the answers to society's problems are not the same as the answers at the beginning of the 20th Century.

(Danish Prime Minister Anders Fogh Rasmussen, quoted by Pettitt in Case study 9.2)

The relationship between state and citizen has changed. People have grown up. They want to make their own life choices. In an opportunity society, as opposed to the old welfare state, government does not dictate; it empowers. It makes the individual – patient, parent, law-abiding citizen, job-seeker – the driver of the system, not the state.

(UK Prime Minister Tony Blair, party conference speech, 2004)

Box 1.2 Effect of consumerism on politics

1   Voters want a more tangible, rather than a rhetorical, product: hence the rise of pledge cards or contracts between the government and people.
2   Voters want more evident and instant delivery.
3   Voters prefer achievement to aspiration, and pragmatic effectiveness to moral principle.
4   Parties and politicians need to convey their governing capability.
5   Political promises needed to be costed and realistic.

Discussion point 1.4

To what extent are Fogh and Blair right about voters becoming more demanding and wanting to be empowered and drive the political system? What effects will an increase in consumerism have on politics?

Advantages of treating the voter like a consumer

Marketing can bring a number of benefits: it enables the politician to conduct research or gather market intelligence to understand voters' concerns more effectively. Data can then be used to inform campaign design, identify supporters/opposers/independents and, more broadly, to reconnect government with the governed. Marketing can provide a means for politicians and governments to listen to the public, which in turn can improve policy-making and implementation. Practitioner perspective 1.3 outlines many positive factors that strategists and market research professionals associate with their work in consulting the public.

Practitioner perspective 1.3

It is part of the democratisation of modern elections. Just as governments have changed, just as parties have changed, campaigns have changed. Democracy has changed. The institutions that used to be effective in mediating popular sentiment have atrophied . . . Politicians have always used various instruments to try to judge where the public stood. And now polls and focus groups are the best available means.

> (Stan Greenberg, an American pollster, on market intelligence,
> quoted by Gould 1998: 333)

I think politicians who say the public doesn't matter usually don't last that long. They don't. You know, because we don't live in a dictatorship, we can't function without them.

> (Gene Ulm, US public opinion professional,
> interviewed by Jennifer Lees-Marshment 2007)

The electorate is more demanding and is right to be so. It is up to us to meet the new challenge. I do not just see focus groups and market research as campaigning tools; increasingly I see them as an important part of the democratic process: part of a necessary dialogue between politicians and people, part of a new approach to politics.

> (Lord Phillip Gould, UK Labour strategist, 1998: 328)

Voters tend to be pretty rational, rational in a way that serves their interests. I think they tend to be pretty consistent . . . people are pretty true to their value system . . . The biggest danger for political parties is where they dismiss the feelings and the thoughts of the public.

> (Dr Matt Carter, PSB research and former UK Labour General
> Secretary, interviewed by Jennifer Lees-Marshment 2007)

You have to give the people who have elected you the benefit of the doubt. I can honestly say, hand on heart, I have never run qualitative research on anything with anybody where I haven't got a reasonable group of people together who can have a say on something, even if they don't really understand it . . . People are not stupid . . . You've got to give people more credit.

> (David Glover, Gravitas opinion research company of New Zealand,
> interviewed by Jennifer Lees-Marshment 2007)

Consumer behaviour can help check the behaviour of political elites. Case study 1.1 explores how Bush and Blair used certain symbolic tools to convey characteristics that would appeal to voters, but ultimately the impact of such effort was eroded both by time and the critical consumer.

Consumer citizenship can help hold governments to account in many ways. It can make government more responsive and encourage political leaders to renegotiate their relationship with the public. Consumerism can allow for ethical considerations. Ethical consumption shows awareness of the wider market and consumerism as a positive force. Slocum (2004: 767) notes how 'in the USA, personal wellbeing may be at the heart of much consumer action, but it is doubtful that people only think of themselves when they consider the safety of food, water, and other goods: they think of kids, family, and even community.' Consumers can care about issues.

Disadvantages of treating the voter as a consumer

There are a number of problems associated with treating the voter as a consumer and asking for their opinion about politics, as discussed by Lane (1991, 2000), Walsh (1994), Needham (2003), Slocum (2004), Lilleker and Scullion (2008) Savigny (2008) and Scullion (2008). Not only is measuring public opinions and views open to inaccuracy in terms of question wording, margin of error, biases and other methodological issues, but voters are criticised for being:

1   changeable in their opinion;
2   selfish, acting in their own interest, not that of the whole country;
3   led by media;
4   highly emotional, prejudiced and irrational;
5   short-term in focus;
6   lacking the necessary experience, knowledge and capacity to make appropriate judgements.

Environmentalism is a case in point. If governments tax business and individuals and ban certain products, it can cost individuals, but it is arguably good for the environment in the long-term, even if it hits the individual in the short term. Slocum (2004) studied a CCP (Cities for Climate Protection) campaign in the US. Climate change presented issues of scientific complexity and debate that made it hard to get people involved. The market had to be segmented according to differing levels of knowledge. At that time, climate change was viewed as something far removed from people's daily lives. Environmental groups have succeeded in placing environment awareness and positive behaviour on the agenda in recent years and through this raising the concept of citizenship. But it could be argued that politicians should have done much more about this sooner, because it was what the world *needed*, even if it wasn't what the public *wanted*.

The other problem with treating voters like consumers is that it threatens the notion of citizens and associated democratic values, such as collective obligation, community, the need for debate, discussion and exchange of ideas to obtain the best solution to problems and the allocation of resources according to principle, and the desire to change and improve conditions, rather than just meet market demand. Slocum (2004: 744) noted that what did succeed in the climate campaign were proposals that would save the public money, but this prevented a full discussion of non-material benefits to the whole community.

The debate on the consequences of political consumerism

Clearly, therefore, there are two sides to this argument. Political marketing scholars recently engaged in such a debate, and, in Box 1.3, Savigny (2008) and Scullion (2008) present opposing views that help us with this debate.

There are clearly arguments for and against treating the voter like a consumer. Case study 1.2 illustrates these issues empirically with a semi-fictional case about a local council that consulted citizens on the best recycling scheme.

Consider the lessons from Case study 1.2, as well as the points made in academic literature. Treating voters as consumers is a big area of discussion: see Debate 1.1.

Box 1.3 Scholars' debate on the pros and cons of treating the voter as a consumer in politics

Scullion: pro treating the voter as consumer	*Savigny: against treating the voter as consumer*
1 Citizenship can exist within a consumer culture.	1 The relationship between government and consumer is not straightforward.
2 Consumer sovereignty gives the public power, perhaps more power than as a citizen, which meets rather than erodes democratic ideals.	2 Referring to the public as consumers of politics can marginalise them from the process of politics.
3 Consumerism gives people a stronger voice, empowers them and increases their efficacy.	3 Individuals are not always able to pursue and maximise their own self interest.
4 The market is self-regulated, whereas traditional politics is rule-based.	4 It reinforces the new right emphasis upon markets as the best way to create solutions to societal problems.
5 Market populism is anti-elitist.	5 Politicians only consider consumer wants to suit their goals; political marketing satisfies the goals of politicians rather than the wants of the public.
6 It can encourage greater participation in politics, as people are asked to call government or other organisations to account; the market enables all to participate; it is non-discriminatory.	6 Politicians focus on those who will affect elections/support rather than everyone, alienating some consumers from the political process, and reducing participation.
7 Consumerism in politics can create avenues for the public to take on civic qualities, considering broader public issues and accepting responsibility to shaping their own lives.	7 Removing the notion of the citizen removes obligations as well as rights.

Source: adapted from Scullion (2008) and Savigny (2008)

Debate 1.1 Proposition: Voters should be treated as consumers

Task:

Hold your own debate, for and against this proposition. You can draw on Practitioner perspective 1.4 and Case studies 1.1 and 1.2 to help form your argument.

Instructions:

- Divide into two sides (with small groups within each side if the class is large), one for and against.
- Devise a list of points to support your side. Consider both practical (what is) and ethical (what should be) considerations.
- Present to the class.
- Open for debate.
- Hold a vote at the end.

Political consumer: a mixture of citizen and consumer

Applying consumerism to politics requires a combination of two disciplines and approaches. It can alternatively be argued that parties should not treat voters solely as consumers, but as both consumers and citizens (see Lees-Marshment 2008, Chapter 1). Scullion (2008) argues that the differences between the consumer and citizen can be minimised, and political consumers can come to expect a share of responsibility and blame when things go wrong, if they appreciate a link between their own choice and the outcome. This can enhance rather than detract from citizenship. This may need more consideration and time to work out in practice, but it is possible that, when consulting the public, values can still be integrated. Broader frameworks of discussion consultation (such as deliberative democracy frameworks) may produce more realistic demands, in the interests of the community not just the individual. Even if parties consult the public, they can still play the role of aggregating demands to ensure that decisions are taken for the collective good, not just the individual. Political marketing can be used as a balance between consumer demands and producer judgement.

This balance is becoming more important, and there is greater awareness of this among political elites. Phillip Gould, when interviewed ten years after UK New Labour's first election victory, had a more reflective perspective with the benefit of more experience and hindsight: see Practitioner perspective 1.4.

How this plays out in practice will be discussed in the rest of the book, while questions of ethics, values and normative implications will be considered in full in Chapter 10.

Practitioner perspective 1.4

It's absolutely crucial to listen in modern politics, but equally important to lead . . . you have to balance flexibility and resolution . . . The art of . . . modern politics is . . . being able to perfectly blend these two together and to make them work.

(Phillip Gould, interviewed by Jennifer Lees-Marshment 2007)

Summary

This chapter has explored how a number of changes in the political market have altered the way that voters respond to and judge political parties and candidates, so that voters are more demanding and questioning, and their behaviour is less predictable. Additionally, citizens appear to behave in a more consumerist manner. Such changes have encouraged parties and candidates to consider using marketing to help them achieve their goals. The next chapter will explore what political marketing is about: the foundations of political marketing, both as a practice and as a developing field of academic study.

WRITTEN ASSESSMENT

Essays
1   To what extent has the political market changed in recent decades, and how?
2   Explore the potential effects that the rise of the political consumer has on politics.
3   To what extent does the notion of the consumer threaten the notion of the citizen, and why does this matter?

Applied

1   Conduct a focus group of fellow peers/friends or family and ask them what they take into account when they vote, and consider what this tells you about the nature of political marketing.
2   Devise and carry out a survey to test and measure consumerist attitudes to politicians and government and whether these fit into the consumer or citizen category.
3   Interview local politicians/candidates: how do they view the electorate? What does this tell us about the extent of consumerism in your country?

Case study 1.1   George W., the Marlboro Man and the Messiah: how voters view politics from a consumerist perspective   *Dave Brown*

This case explores how consumerism can act as a check on elite political behaviour by examining how images and text are used as tools of positioning, but noting their ultimate limitations in preventing a fall in support for leaders over time. Visual cues in commercial advertising have influenced the way consumers see most forms of communications; this has infiltrated political communication. However, consumers digest and evaluate political packaging in the same way they do commercial products in the supermarket. This case examines how political leaders George Bush and Tony Blair tried to use communication to create the trust and credibility that the political consumer appreciates to generate support for the Iraq war, examining photographs that appeared prior to the invasion of Iraq as flashpoints connecting the politicians with potent symbols of religion, culture and power.

Analysis: communicating to the consumer

What we read and saw in the build-up to the invasion of Iraq was a continuing series of political pack shots and captions, all of which made references to iconic symbols that are part of western culture. These images were supported by statements that provided information packaged to convince the reader of the need for those in authority to act, which, from a consumerist perspective, sold the message.

The photographs have been sourced from local newspapers and magazines in New Zealand, as well as the Internet, and were used around the world in different media. They were selected because of their reference to iconic symbolism, which distinguished them from the stereotypical images of politicians that frequent the media daily. They are unusual in that they signify the power of association that goes beyond the familiar media 'photo opportunity'. They make reference to western cultural values that are translated through dress code, body language and location in a context that brings their credibility into question.

Image 1: George W. at Mt Rushmore

This picture appeared on many conservative websites, in particular www.freerepublic.com. The image was used as a photo opportunity that emphasised Bush's presidential status as he addressed the nation on issues of homeland and economic security. By positioning himself among the legendary past presidents honoured in the monument, Bush symbolically acquires their greatness. The photograph of President Bush was taken at Mt Rushmore in August 2002, almost one year after the 9/11 attack on the Twin Towers and the Pentagon. The picture is cropped so that George W. Bush appears as one with the four presidents carved in the famous Mt Rushmore monument – George Washington, Thomas Jefferson, Theodore Roosevelt and

Abraham Lincoln. The scale of his profile matches the scale of the carved images. And the angle of the photograph suggests a position of authority and historical significance.

Images 2 and 3: Welcome to Marlboro Country

Two photographs, appearing side-by-side in a September 2002 issue of the *New Zealand Herald,* feature George W. Bush and Tony Blair using identical body language, with Bush in the dominant role. Bush's pose is quintessentially western – the classic cowboy expression unique to America.

Both hands have thumbs tucked firmly into the front pockets of a pair of jeans held up by a silver Texan buckled belt. Countless cowboy images have appeared over decades in Hollywood movies and on television, which have cemented an unmistakable body language. Alongside Bush is a shot of Tony Blair with exactly the same swagger, but dressed in a traditional suit and tie. His thumbs are tucked in his belt for greater effect, but the pose is overtly similar to his cowboy partner.

Images 4, 5 and 6: The return of the Messiah

The next pictures, also taken from the *New Zealand Herald* (November 2002), display the connection Bush has with the moral crusade of western Christianity against evil. In image 4, Jesus prays to his Father, because the moment has come for him to complete the task that he and the Father set out to accomplish. Image 5 reveals the power of the cross as a symbol of Christianity. It appears with a missionary preaching in the days of the conquistadors in South America. Another photograph of Bush, image 6, is the most powerful picture in this study, because it is also the most symbolically graphic, as Bush gestures with the body language of a religious leader.

Images 7 and 8: Stand by your man

This is a shot of Bush and Blair marching in tandem to the podium of a White House press conference. We see the marching uniformity in their posture, their suits and their shiny shoes. The angle of the photograph suggests they are about to stamp their authority on world order. It is a statement of undoubted unity and confidence. This picture appeared in the *Listener*, a New Zealand current affairs magazine, in February 2003. The photograph was taken as both leaders were about to announce their decision to invade Iraq. The viewer responds to this image in a completely different framework to the cowboy photograph, because here the image is supported by a very serious message that relies on facts about the enemy that have been uncovered and leave no option but to attack.

Images 9 and 10: Good Guy – 2003

In the *Newsweek* cover of 18 November 2002, Bush assumed the pose of another, more recent American icon – the ace jet fighter-pilot so unforgettably etched in the American psyche through the Tom Cruise role in *Top Gun.* He also took advantage of the 'thumbs up' gesture to imply a certainty in his actions, and this gesture is repeated in the second photograph. By May 2003, the invasion of Iraq was going according to plan, with virtually no Iraqi resistance. So confident was Bush of military success, he 'co-piloted' a jet fighter that landed on an aircraft carrier in San Diego waters, changed from his flying gear into a business suit and then announced a cessation of operations, to imply total victory. In the background was a large banner with the words 'Mission Accomplished'. This was a photo opportunity for the media to project Bush as a military hero. But, because the image masked the reality, the product (Bush) was eventually rejected by the voting consumer, because it was full of fake ingredients. In other words, the modal cues lost their credibility.

Image 11: Bad Guy – 2006

Image 11 appeared in the New Zealand *Listener* soon after the decision was made to invade Iraq, at a time when Bush demonstrated the hubris of a leader with no doubt as to his destiny and his place in history: the Commander in Chief who is a decider and a War President. But in the context of the eventual outcome of his decisions, it appears more like a person who is desperate and is ready to gamble everything to succeed. What appears at first to be an image of ferocity and strength transforms into the very symbol of terror itself – a willpower with no control. The picture was taken during a speech made by Bush to a military audience and was used in articles that were both for and against the war.

Lessons for political marketing

The analysis of a number of photographs of George W. Bush and Tony Blair shows that politicians try to build trust and credibility in communications and suggests that certain techniques could possess considerable power.

However, political consumers demand the same quality checks that they ask for in supermarkets, not only by being less accepting of such communication but by demanding more rigorous scrutiny by the media, in the same way that products on the supermarket shelf that list ingredients are more carefully scrutinised. Subsequent to such communication, George W. struggled to maintain credibility both internationally and domestically, and Blair paid a similar price. While politicians often use communication to convey their product, visual tools have limited effect against a critical public. Every election offers 'new and improved' political candidates, who will compete for shelf space with their own pack shots and lists of benefits, but their popularity in the long term – or their shelf life – is affected by their ability to maintain consumer trust amid a cynical and questioning electorate.

Sources and further reading

The Bible, New Testament, John 17:1.

Bush, G.W. (2002). Speech at Mt Rushmore. December. Available online at www.whitehouse.gov.

—— (2006). News conference. December. Available online at www.whitehouse.gov.

Krugman, P. (2004). *The Great Unravelling*. New York: Norton.

Martin, M. (1968). *Le langage cinematographique*. Paris: Editions du Cerf.

Messaris, P. (1997). *Visual Persuasion*. London: Sage.

Penkrith, A. (2002). 'The Blair dossier'. *The Guardian*, September.

Schirato, T. and Webb, J. (2004). *Understanding the Visual*. Crows Nest, NSW: Allen & Unwin.

Scollon, R. and Scollon, S. (2005). *Discourses in Place*. London: Routledge.

Bad guy image: www.wikipedia.org

Kress, G. and van Leeuwen, T. (2000). *Reading Images: The Grammar of Visual Design*. London: Routledge.

George W. Bush military 'Cowboy' image: *New Zealand Herald*, September 2002.

Good guy image: *Newsweek* Magazine, November 2002.

Jesus praying: www.asheville-sda.com/jesus_praying_painting.jpg

Marching soldiers: www.army.mod.uk/img/staffords/1st_btln_desert_combats_marching.jpg

Marlboro Man advertisement: www.images.google.co.nz/marlboro+ads

'Messiah' image: *New Zealand Herald*, November 2002.

Mission Accomplished: AP Photo/J. Scott Applewhite.

Missionary with cross: www.traditiioninaction.org/Margil/AM003_Article2.htm

Mt Rushmore image: www.whitehouse.gov

Stand by your man image: *Listener* magazine (New Zealand), February 2003.

Case study 1.2 **The explosive outcome of treating the electorate as customers** *Richard Scullion*

This story is a mixture of faction and fiction, about what can happen when we treat the electorate as consumers. It is set in a seaside town in England, known for its mild climate – palm trees, trade winds and the warmest winter on record are the backdrop.

The recently elected Liberals were about to meet following the surprise election result. The councillors were feeling both excited and rather apprehensive – it was the first time they had been in power in forty years, so they were more comfortable and experienced in just opposing the council. Indeed, they had gained support by constantly pointing to the problems, failures and lost opportunities of those in power. Now, they had to suddenly decide how to make the decisions that would be implemented in government. Furthermore, they had criticised previous Conservative councils for adopting an elitist, out-of-date, 'we know best' attitude, and promised to let 'local voices prevail' if they ever got into power. They now had to turn this electoral 'promise' into reality.

Council members were nevertheless in a buoyant mood as they arrived for the meeting, and they fully expected the party to immediately start letting the local population have a far greater say in what the town council did. However, the council civil servants were highly sceptical of this 'loose talk' about direct democracy and consumer power and had prepared arguments to present to the politicians on how policy is complicated, it requires careful consideration, it has to take into consideration unintended consequences, and take a long-term perspective. They suggested that 'local voice' should mean ensuring that mechanisms were in place to hear and take into account public opinion, but not to decide policies by direct vote. As one of them said, 'Choosing which shop to frequent and what brand of toothpaste to buy is fine, since its immediate impact is on you and not the rest of your community.' However, the majority of the Liberal councillors were not convinced with this view.

After five hours of talks, a compromise was reached. The idea of letting local voice prevail was to be tried with a pilot scheme. The council was obliged by a European Union directive to implement recycling and 'green' friendly polices with regards to household waste. The council would therefore offer the local population the opportunity to vote on three different options as to which scheme to operate in their town: whichever won the most votes would become the official recycling/household waste policy of the council and be implemented as soon as possible. One of the options would be created by the Conservative opposition party as the start of a more co-operative approach – with less of the old-fashioned, 'ya boo' of party political bickering that the electorate seemed to dislike.

After a week of backroom negotiations, the format of the ballot paper and its options were agreed as follows:

> Your recently elected council wants you to let them know which of the following household recycling/waste management schemes you wish them to implement in the local area.
>
> 1   Provide three separate bins: one for recyclable material, one for non-recyclable and one for garden waste. Each will be collected on a three-weekly-cycle basis (one type of bin collected per week).
>
> 2   Provide one non-recyclable waste bin to be collected every fortnight, and set up twenty new recycling centres throughout the local area, allowing you to dispose of all recyclable material and garden waste.
>
> 3   Provide two bins: one for recyclable material, one for non-recyclable. No garden waste bin will be provided. Instead, we will also introduce a recycling incentive scheme.

Recycling monitoring officers will randomly check how the recycling bins are being used (measuring amount of non-recyclable waste thrown away). Those households consistently recycling more than 50 per cent of their waste will be refunded approximately 10 per cent of their council tax.

We will endeavour to implement a scheme closest to the expressed wishes of the local population. So please use this as an opportunity to make your views known.

Reaction to the different proposals was mixed:

- The local newspaper was balanced: it printed a full page on three consecutive days, outlining the case for each of the options.
- The Conservative opposition party favoured option 3 but was worried that as the last option, it would receive less support and so lobbied successfully for this option to appear in the Thursday edition of the local paper (highest circulation day).
- The Liberal Party official line did not express a preference, to enable the local voice to be heard first, but unofficially many members supported option 1 and spent more time talking to people about that option.
- The local supermarket chains collectively talked about how they would welcome, and be willing to part-fund, new recycling sites next to their shops, in effect lobbying for option 2.

Public discussion, such as letters to the local newspaper, indicated support for the idea of a vote but also widespread misunderstanding about what each option actually involved. In response to concerns the Liberal leader of the council made a statement that the voting paper would be amended so that it asked people to express preferences by writing 1, 2 and 3 against each option. In the event of a tie, second options would be counted to decide an overall winner.

The results were as follows:

Option 2:   18 per cent;
Option 3:   34 per cent;
Option 1:   48 per cent.

The council leader was elated. 'This is a turning point for local democracy,' he said, adding, 'others will look at what we have done and learn from this expression of the local will of the people.' Turnout had been just over 50 per cent, far higher than anticipated and far higher than at many local council elections, which helped the Liberal Party push for a speedy introduction of a new recycling scheme based on option 1.

Public opinion began to change as soon as the policy was implemented, however. Most of the letters in the press were against either the scheme or its apparent high costs. Many people moaned about the space three separate bins occupied and about the difficulty of remembering which bin to place out for collection. This sense of dissatisfaction was exacerbated by the fact that waste collectors were unable to empty bins that were put out in the wrong week because of the operating equipment required.

Opposition also emerged within the council. The Conservative opposition party suggested the ruling Liberals had not been sufficiently transparent about the knock-on consequences of each option. Even some Liberal Party councillors suggested they had rushed rather too eagerly into offering three options that were deliberately very different to each other, rather than offering quite similar but well-thought-out alternatives. Tempers were frayed in the council chamber, as July was proving to be the hottest month for years, and the air-conditioning system was not working. An opposition Conservative councillor shouted, 'you did it because you wanted to court popularity, and now look at you, the least popular council this town has ever had', across the floor of the council chamber.

In the streets, the temperature was about to rise even higher. There was panic in Wishart Gardens as a series of explosions ripped through this leafy suburb of the town at 2 a.m. By 7 a.m., the emergency services were overwhelmed in their efforts to respond to the fifty-seven calls made from across the town, all reporting sudden explosions. Daylight revealed the cause: bins with concentrated types of waste, having been exposed to very high temperatures for nearly three weeks, had generated a form of sulphuric fertiliser that, in contact with water vapour, had turned into an explosive device!

'Recycling scheme blows up in Councillor's face' was typical of the media response. The leaders of the town council appeared on national media, all in very defensive modes as they were criticised for being inept and unable to understand the real complexities of holding power. The Liberal Party's reputation was damaged. In response, one faction of the party wanted to accept this trial had failed and to recognise the great risks in following consumer choice in politics. Another faction argued that the problem was more one of implementation. The vast majority of the local population regarded the episode with a mixture of amusement and indignation, as it reinforced their opinion that they could not trust politicians. The episode of the exploding bins became a byword for local politics – a joke. Few appreciated that the joke was about them, the electorate, too.

This story combines fact and fiction in order to illustrate some of the dangers of simple transferability . . . from markets to public sphere. It was inspired by the author's research into the relationship between consumer and citizen choice-making, which can be read in Scullion (2005).

FURTHER READING

Bartle, John and Dylan Griffiths (2002). 'Social-psychological, economic and marketing models of voting behaviour compared'. In Nicholas O'Shaughnessy and Stephan Henneberg (eds), *The Idea of Political Marketing*. London: Praeger.

Butler, Patrick and Neil Collins (1998). 'Public services in Ireland: a marketing perspective'. Working Paper, Department of Public Administration, National University of Ireland, Cork, No. VII (August).

Campbell, Angus, Philip Converse, Warren Miller and Donald Stokes (1960). *The American Voter*. Chicago, IL: University of Chicago Press.

Clarke, John (2006). 'Consumers, clients or citizens? Politics, policy and practice in the reform of social care'. *European Societies*, 8(3): 423–42.

Downs, Anthony (1957). *An Economic Theory of Democracy*. New York: Harper.

Gabriel, Y. and T. Lang (2006). *The Unmanageable Consumer*. London: Sage.

Gould, Philip (1999). *The Unfinished Revolution: How the Modernisers Saved the Labour Party*. London: Abacus.

Key, V.O. (1966). *The Responsible Electorate: Rationality in Presidential Voting 1936–60*. Cambridge, MA: Harvard University Press.

Lane, Robert W. (1991). *The Market Experience*. Cambridge: Cambridge University Press.

—— (2000). *The Loss of Happiness in Market Democracies*. New Haven and London: Yale University Press.

Lees-Marshment, Jennifer (2004). *The Political Marketing Revolution: Transforming the Government of the UK*. Manchester: Manchester University Press.

—— (2008). *Political Marketing and British Political Parties* (2nd edn). Manchester: Manchester University Press.

Lewis, Justin, Sanna Inthorn and Karin Wahl-Jorgensen (2005). *Citizens or Consumers? What the Media Tell Us About Political Participation*. Maidenhead: Open University Press.

Lilleker, Darren (2003). 'Political marketing: the cause of an emerging democratic deficit in Britain?'. PSA Conference paper, available online at www.psa.ac.uk/journals/pdf/5/2003/Darren%20Lilleker.pdf.

—— and R. Scullion (eds) (2008). *Voters or Consumers: Imagining the Contemporary Electorate*. Newcastle: Cambridge Scholars Publishing.

Mortimore, Roger (2003). 'Why politics needs marketing'. *International Journal of Non-Profit and Voluntary Sector Marketing*, Special issue on 'Broadening the concept of political marketing', 8(2): 107–21.

Needham, Catherine (2003). *Citizen-Consumers: New Labour's Marketplace Democracy*. London: Catalyst.

—— (2004). 'The citizen and consumer: e-government in the United Kingdom and the United States'. In Rachel K. Gibson, Andrea Römmele and Stephen J. Ward (eds), *Electronic Democracy*. London: Routledge.

Norris, Pippa (ed.) (2005) *Critical Citizens*. Oxford: Oxford University Press.

Pharr, Susan and Robert Putnam (eds) (2000). *Disaffected Democracies: What's Troubling the Trilateral Countries?* Princeton, NJ: Princeton University Press.

Savigny, Heather (2008) 'The construction of the political consumer (or politics: what not to consume)'. In D. Lilleker and R. Scullion (eds), *Voters or Consumers: Imagining the Contemporary Electorate*. Newcastle: Cambridge Scholars Publishing.

Scammell, M. (2003). 'Citizen consumers: towards a new marketing of politics?'. In John Comer and Dick Pels (eds), *Media and the Restyling of Politics*. Thousand Oaks, CA: Sage, pp. 117–36. Another version is available online at http://depts.washington.edu/gcp/pdf/citizenconsumers.pdf.

Scullion, Richard (2005). 'Investigating electoral choice though a "consumer choice-maker" lens'. In D. Lilleker, N. Jackson and R. Scullion, *The Marketing of Political Parties. Political Marketing at the 2005 British General Election*. Manchester: Manchester University Press.

—— (2008). 'The impact of the market on the character of citizenship, and the consequences of this for political engagement'. In D. Lilleker and R. Scullion (eds), *Voters or Consumers: Imagining the Contemporary Electorate*. Newcastle: Cambridge Scholars Publishing.

Slocum, Rachel (2004). 'Consumer citizens and the cities for climate protection campaign'. *Environment and Planning*, 36: 763–82.

Spring, Joel (2003). *Educating the Consumer-Citizen*. Mahwah, NJ: Lawrence Erlbaum Associates.

Walsh, Kieron (1994). 'Marketing and public sector management'. *European Journal of Marketing*, 28(3): 63–71.

2 What is political marketing?

This chapter will explain how marketing can be applied to politics, its origins in marketing literature and subsequent development, along with the main debates and differences in the field. It will also outline the basics tenets of political marketing, which will be explored in greater detail in the following chapters. Like all areas of academic literature, there is a debate about what political marketing involves. It has also suffered from conventional views that it is nothing more than spin/media management or election campaigns, even though the marketing discipline offers a far broader array of concepts and ideas that can be applied to politics, and, in practice, a much broader range of marketing permeates politics. Although the chapter is primarily theoretical, it is important that this is considered as a basis for studying political marketing, given the different sources, points of view and disciplinary perspectives covered in the rest of the book.

How can marketing be applied to politics?

It is often wondered how marketing can be applied to politics when the two areas of practice (business and politics) and two disciplines (marketing and political science) seem so different. Indeed, there are a number of potential differences:

1 It is thought that politics should involve value over power, and be a moral undertaking.
2 There are more conflicting demands in politics/the market is much more complex.
3 The political product is intangible and more difficult to understand and create.
4 Products have symbolic value, and there is only a limited range available.
5 Consumers support one product simply to avoid another.
6 Volunteers make up the producers' labour force.
7 The political market does not always know what it wants.
8 Politics involves ideology.
9 The product is difficult to deliver.
10 There is a need for political leadership and professional judgement.
11 Politics is a much more long-term activity.

Additionally, political parties are supposed to serve a number of normative or ethical functions in society, such as:

1 providing the principle means of representation, serving to ensure there is an effective link between citizens and the government;
2 serving to aggregate and defend interests, bringing a variety of conflicting individual demands together, which aids governing;
3 facilitating political socialisation and mobilisation, bringing people into the system;

4   helping to create among voters a feeling of belonging and connection with government, which increases diffuse support for the system as a whole.

Marketing, however, is primarily viewed as being concerned with how organisations identify and respond to customer needs and wants in the way they design, produce and deliver their goods, and with what helps an organisation compete with its rivals to obtain a limited amount of consumer spending. Although it includes all areas of a firm's behaviour, not just the sales department, and is not just concerned with achieving profit, but also the satisfaction of all organisations and individuals involved in the transaction, the apparent ethos and certainly the language can appear at odds with politics. Maurice Saatchi, Executive Director of M&C Saatchi and former Co-chairman of the Conservative Party, discusses other differences between politics and business: see Box 2.1 and Discussion Point 2.1.

Box 2.1 Business and politics are worlds apart

Maurice Saatchi, 24 March 2008

The record seems to show that there is no similarity between politics and business. They are parallel universes with their own solar systems, time zones and laws of gravity . . . Noting public cynicism about politics, business critics say: 'Wouldn't we be better off with proper corporate governance procedures in politics – i.e. the chairman does this, the chief executive does that?'. Just as in business, all neatly codified for easy reference.

Brave souls have sought to implement such a logical structure in a political party. In Britain, the Conservative Party has done best, with a properly constituted board of directors, a majority of whom are non-executives and not paid party officials. But even that admirable structure could not stretch to the concept of a chief executive. When that was tried, the 'CEO' understandably felt he had some claim to power. He thought he was entitled to express political 'views'. The experiment soon stopped.

Business structures fail in politics because a political party is not just an organisation. It is a movement, at the top of which is a leader and a court. There, if the eye of the king alights on you, you are powerful. If the king's eye roams onto another, your strength ebbs away. No other power structure exists in politics.

Business critics note the number of political leaks to the newspapers and contend that this is a sure sign of mismanagement. At Procter & Gamble, for example, internal debate over whether the 'end benefit' of Ariel is 'whiteness' or 'stain removal' has gripped the minds of generations of executives. But you do not read about their deliberations on the front page of the *Daily Mail*. Nor does any division manager go into print to denounce one side of the argument. Why? Because 'political strategy' is hotly debated in every pub and living room in the country. 'Whiter Ariel?' is not.

Critics say politicians would make fewer mistakes if, like businesses, they conducted due professional diligence before they acted. But that is exactly what politicians do. They test concepts. They test statements. They test speeches. They test policies. They test phrases. Faces. And voices. They do pre-testing. Post-testing. Day polling. Night polling. National polling. Local polling. Nobody knows more about marketing breakthroughs in neuroscience than those running for office. All to no avail. There is no magic lamp that can lead you to the presidential desk in the Oval Office or the prime minister's chair at Number 10.

But if politics is not like business, what is it like? The record shows that the jury of public opinion is like the jury in a court of law: motive is all. The jury seeks motive and intent. It wants to see a motive and for it to be something 'good' in the moral sense. The proof comes from the masters of politics. When J.F. Kennedy was asked, as a presidential candidate, how he intended to defeat communism, he said it would take 'more than air power, or financial power or even manpower'. It would take 'brain power' that he defined as: 'The mastery of the inside of men's minds. So that people could see the splendour of our ideals.' President Ronald Reagan, who actually did defeat communism, told Americans they could only win if they: 'Never allowed themselves to be placed in a position of moral inferiority.'

. . . Here, then, is the crucial difference between business and politics. In business, the motive of the provider of the product is beside the point. In politics it is the whole point. It follows that politics is not a market and a political party is not a brand. As a party is not a brand, business disciplines do not apply. So next time you hear it said: 'If only politicians could be more businesslike', you can say that business has as much to do with politics as a cheese knife has to do with the man in the moon.

Source: excerpts from *The Financial Express*, accessed 15 May 2008

Discussion point 2.1

To what extent is Maurice Saatchi right that 'politics is not a market and a political party is not a brand. As a party is not a brand, business disciplines do not apply'? What are the most important differences between politics and business?

Nevertheless, there are similarities in what both disciplines study. What makes politics amenable to a marketing perspective is that it studies the relationship between elites (such as elected officials and political leaders) and the market, just as politics does. Politics studies the electorate and parties/candidates; volunteers and parties; audience and media. The two disciplines share common tenets: the aim to understand how an organisation or elite acts in relation to their market and vice versa. Marketing, among other things, provides tools and ideas about how an organisation can understand and respond to its market more effectively to achieve its goals. Politics also shares this idea of a political system that meets people's needs and demands: Jones and Moran (1994: 17) argue that British democracy 'means that the people can decide the government and exercise influence over the decisions governments take'. Political marketing is one of many potential ways of achieving this in an era of a critical, well-informed and consumerist mass franchise. The next section will explore how academic literature on political marketing has developed.

The origins of political marketing: broadening the concept of marketing

The basic notion that an area such as politics could ever use marketing was first suggested in the 1960s, most notably in a now-famous article by Kotler and Levy, who argued that marketing, previously confined to commercial and business organisations, could actually be used by all organisations, including non-profit, state, public sector and charitable ones:

The [marketing] concept of sensitively serving and satisfying human needs . . . provides a useful concept for all organisations. All organisations are formed to serve the interest of particular groups: hospitals serve the sick, schools serve the students, governments serve the citizens, and labour unions serve the members . . . Marketing is that function of the organisation that can keep in constant touch with the organisation's consumers, read their needs, develop 'products' that meet these needs, and build a program of communications to express the organisation's purposes.

(Kotler and Levy 1969: 15)

Like most new – and indeed the most ground-breaking and profound – ideas in academia, this aroused tremendous controversy within marketing: see Box 2.2 below for some examples.

Box 2.2 Objections to broadening marketing beyond business

Tucker (1974):

- The article is too simplistic: even the most careless reader of Kotler's article will have noticed that the old marketing myopia of seeing the world from the channel captain's seat continues. The organization is the marketer and the 'publics' are merely 'buyers.' This seems to have as its corollary the dictum that marketing theory need not consider the public except as marketing targets.
- Marketing literature will not gain anything by studying non-business organisations, because they are just too different to business: marketing is heavily concerned with economic rationality in terms of store location, advertising effectiveness, merchandise assortments, pricing policies, inventory management, sales territories, and the like. Relatively prompt and specific consumer satisfaction characterizes the great majority of transactions. In comparison . . . Political campaigns are so expensive that to regard the return as economic is to assume corruption more massive and more universal than even the cynic supposes. In all of these processes the 'consumer' must concern himself with distant and indefinite satisfactions.
- There will be little value from studying marketing in non-commercial organisations: marketing theory, which has fairly consistently looked at products, institutions, consumers, and various marketing practices from the standpoint of the marketing manager, is now splitting up under the force of its own growing sophistication and the irritation of contemporary problems. Kotler's suggestion that the traditional point of view be applied to nonmarketing institutions for the achievement of their goals is one possible new direction. But it does not promise much new theoretical development.

Luck (1969):

- If the definition is broadened to include nonbusiness, marketing will no longer be so clearly confined: 'if a definition were framed to meet the authors' contentions, marketing no longer would be bounded in terms of either institutions or the ultimate purpose of its activities.'
- No benefit will come from this: 'marketer's self image may be pleasurably inflated by claiming that political campaigns are just another part of marketing, but what progress is to be gained by such reasoning?'
- Marketing cannot be applied so broadly: 'it is more logically explained as a market transaction, and as a political party does not sell specific services, marketing cannot be applied so broadly.'

Arndt (1978):

- Arndt objected, on academic discipline grounds, that such 'a combined semantic and territorial expansion may threaten the conceptual integrity of marketing, add to the confusion in terminology, and widen the gulf between marketing theory and practice.'

"
"

Discussion point 2.2

Consider the objections to the argument to broaden the concept of marketing outlined in Box 2.2. To what extent are these valid and correct?

Nevertheless, new research applying marketing to a much broader range of organisations subsequently emerged. Marketing scholars applied marketing concepts to non-profit areas, including charities, churches, university recruitment, transportation and the public sector, as well as political candidates and parties (see Mindak *et al.* 1971, Zaltman and Vertinsky 1971, Shapiro 1973, Shama 1976, Kotler 1979, and Andreasen 1991). Within management science today there is significant research and teaching on non-profit marketing and new journals in the non-business field, such as the *International Journal of Non-Profit and Voluntary Sector Marketing*.

The marketing of politics is, however, a separate area of consideration, first because it links marketing to elections and therefore to government and the decision as to who ultimately controls the world; second because there is an older discipline, political studies or political science, that existed before the emergence of business, management or marketing research. Both disciplines have their own rules, norms and publishing outlets. Management studies scholars are not bound to utilise literature from political science, and consequently such work can be limited by not being truly cross-disciplinary: it somewhat inevitably neglects to incorporate traditional literature in political science. This is also true for political scientists, who will be less familiar with and less likely to use theories from marketing literature. Indeed, gaps in this textbook reflect how many areas of marketing theory have yet to be applied to politics. Scholars and practitioners may also reject the application of extensive marketing models created for business, because instinctive understanding from training and studying politics suggests they will not fit. Indeed, marketing scholars also note how different organisations and environments require concepts and strategies to be adapted if they are to be of value in understanding behaviour. Politics is different, and, while non-profit marketing literature is a useful area to consider, research specifically in political marketing has helped most to establish the field in its own right, and create appropriate frameworks and concepts with which to investigate this distinct phenomenon.

Political marketing: a 'marriage' of politics and marketing

However, because politics is different, it cannot simply be fitted into a marketing framework that stems from analysis of the business world. As Butler and Collins (1999: 55) note, 'to make progress in political marketing, scholars must draw from the disciplines of political science and marketing.' This is something that Scammell's (1999: fn 50) review of the field observed, noting that the 4Ps (product, pricing, promotion and place) 'need considerable stretching to make much sense in politics'. Political marketing is created by applying marketing concepts from business to politics, but not by simply imposing one over the other.

Lees-Marshment (2001b) called this process of combining the two disciplines a 'marriage', because political marketing literature needs to draw on both disciplines. Or, to put it another way, perhaps politics and marketing are the parents, and political marketing is the baby resulting from the marriage and so has some of its parents' traits but is its own separate entity.[1] As (Butler and Collins 1999: 55) noted later, conducting cross-disciplinary research is not easy: 'attempts to merge two diverse research areas are replete with problems of context, understanding and approach.' Lees-Marshment (2003) built on this concern to argue that, to make this marriage work, certain principles were needed: see Box 2.3.

While more recent work has been more comprehensive, the heritage of political marketing lies in research focused on political communication that concentrated on showing how parties sold themselves. Such work drew attention to political marketing and laid the foundations for future research.

Early political marketing communication literature

The most well-known literature in political marketing from the 1980s and 1990s is that of Niffeneger (1989), O'Shaughnessy (1990), Franklin (1994), Kavanagh (1995) and Scammell (1995), which focused on how political marketing might be used by parties, presidents and candidates in how they tried to sell themselves. It conveyed how awareness of the market, whether acquired informally or through consultants' expertise and market research, was beginning to influence party communication.

Box 2.3 Comprehensive political marketing: key principles from Lees-Marshment (2003)

1 **CPM applies marketing to the whole behaviour of a political organisation, not just communication.** Marketing is applied, not just to how parties campaign, but to what they try to sell in that campaign – their product, not just how that product is advertised. Marketing is applied to a party's leader, policy, organisation, members, candidates, symbols, activities and staff. Analysis carries from the beginning through to the end of an electoral cycle (not just the election campaign).

2 **CPM uses marketing concepts, not just techniques: the product, sales and market-orientation as well as direct mail, target marketing and market intelligence.** This book therefore considers the use of strategy and branding rather than just techniques.

3 **CPM integrates political science literature into the analysis.** Marketing is integrated and adapted to suit the understanding gained from traditional study of parties. The party's 'product' is therefore defined to include all the aspects of parties.

4 **CPM adapts marketing theory to suit the differing nature of politics.** Marketing is changed or adapted to suit what is already known about political parties. There is a synergy between the two disciplines. It does not simply take marketing and apply it as it is, even where it does not make sense. Work produced strictly from a management science perspective will fail by trying to fit politics into marketing, when the empirical reality is the other way round. It uses marketing to deepen the understanding of politics, to add to that already gained by existing traditional political science.

5 **CPM applies marketing to all political organisational behaviour: interest groups, policy, the public sector, the media, parliament and local government, as well as parties/elections.**

Developed political marketing work in communication and strategy

More innovative work in the 1990s attempted to utilise a greater range of marketing theory, such as Newman (1994, 1999), Butler and Collins (1996) and Wring (1996, 2002), who applied marketing concepts to political communication. Wring explored how political parties were using marketing in communication by applying the 4Ps to party campaigning, examining how the Labour Party developed a more communication-focused organisation in the 1980s and 1990s. Newman formulated a marketing model of campaign strategy for candidates. While both focused mainly on campaigns, Wring and Newman pioneered work to apply marketing more directly to politics and consider the influence of market intelligence on how candidates or parties campaigned. Newman also noted how marketing could influence policy, discussing a range of aspects within his book *Mass Marketing of Politics* (1999) and noting that, 'at the core of marketing is the belief that extensive research must be carried out to determine the needs and wants of the marketplace before a product or service is developed' (1999: 39). Butler and Collins (1996) created a model of how parties might compete against each other in a leader, follower, challenger and nicher categorisation. Lees-Marshment (2001) created a model of how parties might behave if they followed a product, sales or market-orientation, showing the difference between marketing the product, not just the presentation, and how MOPs might change their behaviour to suit voter demands, rather than try to change that demand.

Is political marketing still just about communication?

The short answer is no. Research also considers aspects such as a political market-orientation (Ormrod 2005), political product and branding (Lloyd 2005), internal marketing (Bannon 2005), membership marketing (Granik 2005), local political marketing (Lilleker and Negrine 2003), stakeholders (Hughes and Dann 2004a,b), branding (Cosgrove 2007), strategy (Barber 2005), e-marketing (Jackson 2005) and the market-orientation of political advertisements (Robinson 2004), among others that will be considered in this textbook. Other topics include network marketing, marketing of governors, minor as well as major parties, marketing at local council level, political contracts and delivery, market positioning, market-oriented candidates, relationship marketing, strategy, MPs' website marketing and internal product adjustment marketing.

The key difference is that political marketing is now seen as potentially affecting the way politicians, parties and governments behave, not just how they communicate that behaviour. Communication remains an important part of political marketing. But whereas twenty years ago the whole textbook might be expected to be about communication and campaigning, it is now only one chapter.

Definitions and scope

Political marketing is not just about communication, public relations or campaigning. It is much more than that. Parties are acting like businesses, using market intelligence to inform the design of the political product they offer, becoming market- (or voter-) oriented rather than focused on selling: see Box 2.4.

Definitions of political marketing vary, but almost all talk about the political organisation (whether it be the product on offer, the politician, the candidate, the government) and its relationship with, or to, the market (whether it be the public at large, citizens, or more specific such as members): see Box 2.5.

Box 2.4 Dispelling some myths about political marketing

Political marketing IS NOT ...	Political marketing IS ...
• just about political ads • just about political communication • just about campaigns • about spin-doctoring/media management	• about the design of the political 'product' • about how politicians and parties behave • about what they offer to the public • about how much this responds to what the public wants

Box 2.5 Political marketing definitions

Lock and Harris (1996)	As research: Political marketing is the study of exchanges between political entities and their environment and among themselves, with particular reference to the position of those entities and their communications. As an activity: Political marketing is concerned with strategies for positioning and communications and the methods through which these strategies may be realised, including the search for information into attitudes, awareness and response of the target audience.
O'Cass (1996a,b)	Political marketing is the analysis, planning, implementation and control of political and electoral programmes designed to create, build and maintain beneficial exchange relationships between a party and voter, for the purpose of achieving the political marketers' objectives.
Newman (1999: xiii)	Political marketing is the application of marketing principles and procedures in political campaigns by various individuals and organisations.
Lees-Marshment (2001a: 22)	Political marketing is about political organisations (such as political parties, parliaments and government departments) adapting techniques (such as market research and product design) and concepts (such as the desire to satisfy voter demands), originally used in the business world, to help them achieve their goals (such as win elections or pass legislation).
Henneberg (2002: 103)	Political marketing seeks to establish, maintain and enhance long-term political relationships at a profit for society, so that the objectives of the individual political actors and organisations involved are met. This is done by mutual exchange and fulfilment of promises.
Hughes and Dann (2004a)	Political marketing is a political communications [organisational] function and a set of processes for creating, communicating and delivering promises of value to customers, and for managing customer relationships in ways that benefit the political organisation and its stakeholders.
Lilleker (2007)	Political marketing is the reaching and influencing of decisions, and the formulation of strategies and creation of offerings that satisfy the needs and wants of a society that exchanges its own representative capacity for that satisfaction.

“
”

Discussion point 2.3

Discuss the differences between the definitions of political marketing in Box 2.5 and evaluate which makes the most sense.

Political marketing, despite the different definitions, is, at its most basic, the application of marketing academic theory to politics and the use of marketing activities in politics. For example, nearly all political parties and candidates conduct market intelligence in the form of polls or focus groups and use it to inform the way they campaign. However, not only do parties use marketing techniques to sell themselves and guide how they campaign, they also use marketing to decide what to offer to the public – what policies to adopt, which leaders to select, what professional advice to get, how to govern and how best to communicate delivery. As Newman (1999: 39) notes, 'marketing research is used by political leaders to shape policy. Bill Clinton and presidents before him have relied extensively on opinion polls to help determine the direction of their presidencies.' A wide range of marketing tools and concepts can be used in politics.

Marketing concepts to be used in politics

Often, marketing is just seen as a set of tangible, measurable tools or techniques, such as market intelligence, market segmentation, direct mail and targeting. However, while such tools are important, it should also be understood that all of these things – intelligence, research, direct mail – interact with each other. To be most effective, political marketing is not just about cherry-picking one or two bits from marketing; it is about an overall framework of interrelated activities that politicians can use to achieve a range of goals in a way they are comfortable with. Other concepts that marketing offers include, for example, customer management, consumer behaviour, competition management, relationship marketing, product development, product life cycle, e-marketing, public relations, internal marketing, integrated marketing communications and relationship marketing. Not all of them have been studied academically, and thus this book is limited to the literature available, but the main point is that a range of ideas are available to both academics and practitioners to use in politics.

Another important aspect of marketing is how study has depicted different activities as a 'marketing mix' or '4Ps' (McCarthy 1964) – product, pricing, promotion and place – which has in turn been expanded to be '7Ps' (product, price, promotion, place, packaging, positioning and people) (Booms and Bitmer 1981). The use of polls by parties, for example, exemplified by the stage of market intelligence, has become a notable area of study in political science. The marketing process does not leave it in isolation, however, but connects it to the communication and design of behaviour, and, as will be seen in this textbook, political marketing has produced its own models of the political marketing process. However, in marketing there are alternative views that will no doubt also be applied to politics in time.

There is a last, crucial, but difficult, point to explain: that is that marketing is much more a way of *thinking* than *doing*. The most important principle of marketing is what is called the market philosophy: a concept is less tangible and harder to 'see' or measure than actual tools or activities, although marketing academics have tried to quantify it. The marketing philosophy developed over time as businesses changed their behaviour from producing what they wanted, then trying to persuade the market to buy it by using sales techniques, to lastly finding out what the market wanted *before* developing a product it wants and that will satisfy the market, as well as the supplier's goals. It is now referred to as a market-/marketing-/customer-orientation.

Organisations that adopt the marketing philosophy will design their product to provide consumer satisfaction to achieve their goals. As Webster (1988: 32) observes, 'the product is not a given but a variable to be tailored and modified in response to changing customer needs.' A market-orientation is much more likely to satisfy its customers (see Levitt 1960: 50) and will stand a better chance of securing their long-term custom. Marketing strategy and branding also offer additional perspectives to capture the way organisations think and respond to their market.

Marketing theories direct themselves to how organisations can behave in relation to their market to help them achieve their goals, or how they fail to respond to their market and lose their customers. This basic direction is easily applicable to politics, where parties are constantly losing elections and looking for a means to help them win the next one. As with psychology, sociology and geography, marketing is another discipline within the social sciences that studies the interaction of human beings via organisations and therefore offers the potential to enrich or deepen political science understanding of parties and elections. For example, internal marketing can be linked to studies of party membership and candidate volunteers; product development to policy; implementation to party organisation; consumer behaviour to voter behaviour. Political parties can use political marketing to increase their chances of achieving their goal of winning general elections. They alter aspects of their behaviour to suit the nature and demands of their market. This book will therefore study a range of different aspects, from strategy through to government. Before that, though, the nature of the political product and market will be discussed.

What are organisations marketing? The political product

Politics can be viewed as a product. Not everyone likes this idea, because it brings with it connotations of commodification and consumerisation. There are a number of concerns about the applicability of the word product to politics, such as:

- The political product is not tangible: it is not a good that can be picked up off the shelves.
- The political product is also what parties achieve in government, which, as Lloyd (2005) notes, is both an outcome (e.g. decrease in the number of patients on hospital waiting lists) and a process (the way in which it is achieved).
- A party in opposition will also be judged on its ability to deliver its promised political product; therefore (perceived) delivery capability is an important characteristic.
- Even if parties deliver the product, voters are not always aware of, or credit them for, success.

Lees-Marshment (2001a) argues that the party product in the UK at least encompasses all aspects of party behaviour, which includes the leadership, members, staff, policies and symbols. However, Lloyd (2005) broadens the concept significantly by applying understanding from marketing literature: see Box 2.6 and an application to the UK Conservatives in Case study 2.1.

Box 2.6 The Lloyd concept of the political product

1   **Services offering**: the identification of the services (including policy) that the country/ electorate *really* needs (as opposed to what parties believe it needs), delivery of policy *and* the effective management of its implementation (involving appropriate management skills and expertise).

2   **Representation**: the way that all aspects of the political party, its policies and its members are represented to the electorate on a number of interrelated levels, from the political sector as a whole, through individual parties to individual politicians. It includes controlled and uncontrolled communication. For example, corruption or ineptitude on the part of one party has a trickle-down or trickle-up effect to the individual politicians or the political sector as a whole.

3   **Accommodation**: how parties understand and respond appropriately to the needs of the electorate, with their members, MPs and members of the government being accessible and open and the party encouraging participation at all levels across the community.

4   **Investment**: concerns the stakeholder-type relationship that the electorate has with its political representatives; it can be a direct financial payment in the form of subscriptions or donations to a political party or candidate, or a delayed financial 'investment', for example, likely changes in tax or welfare benefits; changes in the standard of living; or time and effort to participate. However, it also involves non-monetary investment, such as time, effort and emotion. Either way, electors expect to see a return, either tangible or intangible, and can end up feeling betrayed. Internal marketing can help ensure effective management of investment and returns by party members.

5   **Outcome**: the ability to deliver upon policy issues and election promises; a tangible measurement of performance by electors.

Source: Lloyd (2005: 41–3)

The political party product, however defined, is a complex and evolving being, which also varies from one electoral arena to another: see Discussion point 2.4. Ultimately, which characteristics are important depends on what voters' judge as an issue. It is more effective to examine a wide range of characteristics in relation to voter demands and therefore to marketing concepts.

To whom are organisations marketing? Political markets

The customer – or customer(s) – are complex in business, let alone politics. As with goals, the different markets a party considers are influenced by institutional features, such as the party's organisational structure and the electoral system, as well as the political culture and concept of party in the particular country. The most obvious market is voters – those people who will vote for or against the candidate or party in an election. However, it also includes

Discussion point 2.4

How might the political product differ when there is a single candidate campaigning, such as in a local, electorate, constituency or presidential election, as opposed to a political party?

electoral rules and members, competitors and potential co-operators, and indeed all stakeholders interested in, and with an investment in, the party or candidate (Lees-Marshment 2001a, Hughes and Dann 2004b, Ormrod 2005).

Why are organisations marketing? Goals of political marketing

In business, the goal of marketing is to help make profit, but how does this work in politics? The most obvious goal of political parties and candidates is to get elected – or re-elected. But politicians are often concerned with achieving additional goals such as:

- advancing a particular ideology, cause, policy or piece of legislation;
- changing the agenda in the media and public sphere;
- gaining support from new segments in the market;
- becoming a coalition partner in government;
- increasing the number and activity of volunteers;
- winning control of government; and
- believe it or not, wanting to make the world a better place!

Which goals dominate depends on the particular party, its electoral environment, the rules of the marketplace, its size, its philosophy and resources, and varies from one system or country to another. For major parties (i.e. those who win control of government with the largest share of the vote), the goal is to win enough votes in general elections to win control of government and do whatever is necessary to achieve this. Minor parties tend to be more interested in advancing a particular cause or influencing debate. And, of course, individual candidates are more interested in their particular seat than the overall party's success – even though the latter can affect the former. And once a party or candidate gets into power, the priority of goals can change again.

Box 2.7 collates such ideas and suggests a comprehensive list of potential characteristics involved in a party's product, goals and market.

Summary

Political marketing attracts significant attention from politicians, academics, journalists and the public. There is a common consensus that political marketing has notable importance in politics: those who study and comment on it can 'feel' its use in party politics, elections and policy-making, but also 'suspect' it may be in operation in wider fields: public services, local government, interest groups. It represents for marketing the triumph of an approach first originated in business; for politics, it suggests a significant transformation of the way the political world operates. Political marketing subjects politics – the arena of people power, philosophy and ideology – to the more consumer-like forces of business management and the market.

Political marketing is also somewhat controversial. Politics could become more responsive to citizen needs and demands, but it might also become consumer-led, which would override professional judgement, lack ideology and threaten the very essence of politics itself. The ramifications of this phenomenon may indeed be phenomenal: marketing could transform, or may already have transformed, the nature of politics as we know it. This makes it more exciting, but also more challenging for students. For students, this means, on one hand, they are going to be learning about a new, more flexible and reality-based academic field.

Box 2.7 A party's product, goals and market

Product	*Goals*	*Market*
1 Leadership/the candidate – e.g. their powers, image, character, support/appeal, relationship with the rest of the party organisation (advisers, cabinet, members, MPs), media relationship	1 Pursue a particular ideology, cause, of policy or piece of legislation	1 Electoral rules, boundaries and seat distribution that affected the importance of each vote
2 Members of the legislative (e.g. senators, MPs)/ candidates for election – e.g. their nature, activity, representativeness of society	2 Change the agenda/ general political debate	2 Any other part of the population with influence upon this electorate
3 Membership or official supporters – their powers, recruitment, nature (ideological character, activity, loyalty, behaviour, relationship to leader)	3 Change behaviour in society 4 Increase their support from the last election 5 Gain support from new segments in the market	3 Members or volunteers 4 Internal party figures – to ensure effective implementation 5 Voter segments 6 Competitors and potential co-operators
4 Staff: researchers, professionals, advisers etc. – their role, influence, office powers, relationship with other parts of the party organisation	6 Become a coalition partner in government with another party	7 Lobbyists 8 Lobby groups 9 Party donors 10 Media 11 Electoral commission
5 Symbols e.g. name, logo, anthem	7 Increase membership or involvement in their organisation	12 Unions 13 Voters who turn out 14 Party staff and
6 Constitution/rules	8 Ensure long-term electoral success, not just for one election	professionals, both internal and external
7 Activities e.g. meetings, conferences, rallies	9 Win control of government	15 Interest groups and think tanks
8 Policies: proposed, current and implemented	10 Change the world . . .	16 The public services 17 Professional organisations and groups
9 Services offering and delivery capability		
10 Representation of the electorate		
11 Accommodation of public needs and wants		
12 Investment the market makes into the candidate, party or government		
13 Outcome and delivery		

Discussion point 2.5

Discuss the product, goals and market characteristics listed in Box 2.7. Which are most important and why? Remember this can vary from one country to another, and over time.

On the other hand, they will have to develop more skills and objectivity than they might with fields located firmly within one discipline. Studying political marketing involves:

*   learning the basics of the other discipline;
*   utilising new journals in an unfamiliar discipline;
*   intellectual agility and a willingness to learn new concepts and language;
*   being prepared to take on new ideas.

The rest of the textbook will take readers through the main aspects of theory and practice, with case studies from different countries, presenting many questions to debate.

SUGGESTIONS FOR ASSESSED WORK

Essays

1   What is political marketing? Outline the major theoretical works and debates in the field.
2   Discuss what factors make up the political product, considering both theoretical concepts and empirical examples.
3   Explore and evaluate the nature and importance of the different markets or customers a political party, candidate or government needs to consider.
4   'The election campaign is the least important part of political marketing.' Explain and critique the validity of this statement, illustrating your argument with examples and theory.
5   Drawing on cases and theory, write a ten-point statement of 'political marketing principles': a list of the most important lessons and advice for how a political party should use political marketing.
6   Does political marketing really win elections? Support your answer with examples.

Applied

1   Analysing a recent election or campaign, discuss the relative importance of different characteristics of the product, different markets and different goals.

Case study 2.1 An application of Lloyd's product concept: the UK Conservative Party in 2001   *Tim Sansom*

By using Lloyd's political marketing framework, this account considers the British Conservative Party's attempts at initiating a product and communications strategy, following their landslide defeat to Tony Blair's New Labour government in the 1997 General Election. Following their eighteen years of power, the Tories, under the leadership of William Hague, were in a critically divisive state, which would hamper the effective implementation of what is called the 'political marketing process'. Therefore, it is remarkable that this party promoted any sort of product, given that the realities of opposition politics and the general political situation in 2001 hampered the effective communication of the offering.

The 'services' offering consists of the initial aspect of Lloyd's model, and this segment consists of a set of ideological beliefs and policies associated with the 'management of national security, social stability and economic growth'. Despite the criticisms from commentators, as well as serving and former Tory MPs, regarding the Conservatives' product for the 2001 General Election, the offering did contain a series of policies associated with the cited factors of a services contribution. For the 'management of national security and social stability', the Tories proposed firmer immigration controls, as well as a stronger emphasis on law and order. In terms of economic growth, the party offered a tax-cutting policy, as well as an assurance that Britain would not be involved in the European single currency.

Despite the promotion of these policies, the Conservatives could not effectively argue that they had the managerial skills to implement these measures. The tax-cutting ideas were compromised by suggestions that there was a more radical agenda to slash the tax burden, which would negatively affect public service provision. Furthermore, the previous retraction of Conservative economic policies, including the 'tax guarantee', also exacerbated the impression that the party's ideas were not resolutely endorsed, and the Tories did not possess solid economic policies. The 'save the pound' campaign was compromised by the public display of pro-European views within the party. In terms of the idea that dissident party members needed to suppress their views for the sake of effective political marketing implementation, it is probable that any opposition party would have struggled to reunite around a common concept within four years of such a catastrophic election result, which had left the Tories reeling since 1997.

The 'representation' aspect of Lloyd's model concerns the promotion of a suitably positive image. This component involves the communication of a sense of 'integrity, realism and the ability to be calm in a crisis'. The approach is undertaken within the controllable aspects of political activity, such as policy statements, and hopefully implied in the uncontrollable situations, such as unscripted television interviews. In the context of the Tories in 2001, the effective communication of this political marketing approach was made difficult for the party, owing to the historical 'spectre' of previous Conservative governments. In this particular election, the majority of the voters still held negative views associated with the Thatcher and Major governments. The idea of a potential William Hague-led administration possessing 'integrity' was compromised by the continual instances of 'sleaze' that had particularly occurred since 1992. The impression that the Conservatives would remain 'calm in a crisis' would also be compromised by memories of Black Wednesday, with the related measures such as 15 per cent interest rates in the face of a national economic crisis. The perspective of Tory realism was also disputed as a result of the media and public reaction to extreme negative campaigning that was conducted during the 2001 election.

The third aspect of the Lloyd framework concerns the need for a political party to demonstrate that they have listened, understood and accommodated the views of the electorate. Despite the internal party tensions, the Conservatives did try to commence some schemes to listen to the views of the electorate such as 'Listening to Britain' in the initial years of their opposition. A more inclusive strategy began to be discussed within the party under the concepts of 'Kitchen Table Conservatism' and 'Compassionate Conservatism'. The Tories were attempting to demonstrate that they did recognise the limits of the free market, the concept of well-funded public services and the general 'concerns of ordinary people'. As a result of the fledgling inclusive approach, the party 'traditionalists' disapproved of the apparent repudiation of Thatcherism, and the vehemence of this reaction forced the party to communicate a 'core' vote strategy, with habitual Tory policies such as tax cutting, that would attract their customary voters. It is easy to suggest that the Conservatives should have held their nerve by continuing to adopt a political marketing approach and promote an inclusive strategy, but as a result of the feverish internal party atmosphere, it is understandable that the party changed their approach. The opinion polls were continuously showing the Tories at about 32 per cent, and some surveys implied that the party would achieve an even worse result in a forthcoming election compared with the 1997 result.

The final two aspects of the Jenny Lloyd framework are closely linked to each other. The 'investment' aspect concerns what 'work' needs to be undertaken by the electorate to support the political party, such as a direct financial payment, and also less financially based factors, such as time and effort to participate in the voting process. In the 2001 election, the Conservatives portrayed the 'investment' of a vote for their party as a voice against the increasing European influence in British society, as well as to halt crime and improve education standards. Regardless of the form of investment, the electors will expect to see a return for their outlay, and the yield is covered in the 'outcome' aspect of the Lloyd framework. The political outfit should be seen to 'deliver upon these promises effectively, efficiently and ethically'. In the 2001 election, the Tories demonstrated how their particular policy agenda would impact on the electorate, but the disunited state of the party implied that there was no guarantee that the product could be developed intro reality.

Despite the intersections within the Lloyd framework, this strategy is a useful tool to understand the information that is contained within a political product. Regardless of whether the ideas and techniques can be linked to the trend in political marketing, or just the normal political process in action, Lloyd's ideas are a valuable contribution to understanding the different aspects of a political offering that is presented in an election campaign. However, these product frameworks have to be analysed in context for an understanding of the difficulties that a political party may have encountered during the product formation process. The Conservative Party did attempt to develop a politically marketed product and initiate a comparative communication strategy. The external political situation, the difficulties of opposition politics and the resultant inability to influence the political agenda meant that the effective marketing akin to the Lees-Marshment (2001) 'market-oriented' party model remained just a wishful aspiration.

Sources and further reading

Dermody, Janine and Richard Scullion (November 2001). 'An exploration of the advertising ambition and strategies of the 2001 British General Election'. *Journal of Marketing Management*, 17(9/10).

Lees-Marshment, Jennifer (November 2001). 'Marketing the British Conservatives 1997–2001'. *Journal of Marketing Management*, 17(9/10).

Lloyd, Jenny (2005). 'Square peg, round hole? Can marketing-based concepts such as the "product" and the "marketing mix" have a useful role in the political arena?'. In W. Wymer and J. Lees-Marshment (eds), *Current Issues in Political Marketing*. Binghamton, NY: Haworth Press.

Walters, Simon (2001). *Tory Wars*. London: Politicos.

NOTE

1 This analogy was suggested by one of the anonymous reviewers of this book, whom I would like to thank for their perceptiveness and help in communicating the principles of political marketing.

FURTHER READING

Arndt, Johan. (1978). 'How broad should the marketing concept be?'. *Journal of Marketing*, 42(1) (January): 101–3.

Baines, Paul R., Robert M. Worcester, David Jarrett, and Roger Mortimore (2003). 'Market segmentation and product differentiation in political campaigns: a technical feature perspective'. *Journal of Marketing Management*, 19(1/2): 225–49.

Bannon, Declan P. (2005). 'Internal marketing and political marketing'. PSA Annual Conference, University of Leeds, 4–7 April 2005.

Barber, Stephen (2005). *Political Strategy: Modern Oolitics in Contemporary Britain*. Liverpool: Liverpool Academic Press.

Booms, B.H. and M.J. Bitner (1981). 'Marketing strategies and organization structures for service firms'. In J.H. Donnelly and W.R. George (eds), *Marketing of Services*. Chicago, IL: American Marketing Association, pp. 47–51.

Bowler, Shaun and David M. Farrell (eds) (1992). *Electoral Strategies and Political Marketing*. Hampshire: Macmillan.

Butler, Patrick and Neil Collins (1996). 'Strategic analysis in political markets'. *European Journal of Marketing*, 30(10/11): 25–36.

—— and —— (1999). 'A conceptual framework for political marketing'. In Bruce I. Newman (ed.), *Handbook of Political Marketing*. Thousand Oaks, CA: Sage Publications.

——, —— and Martin R. Fellenz (2007). 'Theory-building in political marketing: parallels in public management'. *Journal of Political Marketing*, 6(2/3): 91–107.

Cosgrove, K.M. (2007). 'Midterm marketing: an examination of marketing strategies in the 2006, 2002, 1998, and 1994 elections'. Paper presented at the annual meeting of the American Political Science Association. Available online at www.allacademic.com/meta/p209749_index.html (accessed 19 March 2008).

Dann, Stephen, Phil Harris, Gillian Sullivan Mort, Marie-Louise Fry and Wayne Binney (2007). 'Reigniting the fire: a contemporary research agenda for social, political and nonprofit marketing'. *Journal of Public Affairs*, 7: 291–304.

Franklin, Bob (1994). *Packaging Politics: Political Communications in Britain's Media Democracy*. London: Edward Arnold.

Granik, S. (2005). 'Membership benefits, membership action: why incentives for activism are what members want'. In W. Wymer and J. Lees-Marshment (eds), *Current Issues in Political Marketing*. Binghamton, NY: Haworth Press.

Henneberg, Stephan (2002). 'Understanding political marketing'. In Nicholas O'Shaughnessy and Stephan Henneberg (eds), *The Idea of Political Marketing*. London: Praeger.

—— (2004). 'The views of an advocatus dei: political marketing and its critics'. *Journal of Public Affairs*, 4(3): 225–43.

—— and Nicholas O'Shaughnessy (2007). 'Theory and concept development in political marketing: issues and an agenda'. *Journal of Political Marketing*, (2/3): 5–31.

Hughes, A. and S. Dann (2004a). 'Political marketing 2006: direct benefit, value and managing the voter relationship'. Australian and New Zealand Marketing Academy Conference, Queensland University of Technology, 4–6 December.

—— and —— (2004b). 'Political marketing and stakeholders'. Australian and New Zealand Marketing Academy Conference, Queensland University of Technology, 4–6 December.

Jackson, Nigel (2005). 'Vote winner or a nuisance: email and elected politicians' relationship with their constituents'. In W. Wymer and J. Lees-Marshment (eds), *Current Issues in Political Marketing*. Binghamton, NY: Haworth Press.

Jones, Bill and Michael Moran (1994). 'Introduction: explaining politics'. In Bill Jones (ed.), *Politics UK*. London: Harvester Wheatsheaf.

Kavanagh, Dennis (1995). *Election Campaigning: The New Marketing of Politics*. Oxford: Blackwell.

Kotler, Philip (1972). 'A generic concept of marketing'. *Journal of Marketing*, 36: 46–54.

—— (1979). 'Strategies for introducing marketing into non-profit organisations'. *Journal of Marketing*, 43: 37–44.

—— and Sidney J. Levy (1969). 'Broadening the concept of marketing'. *Journal of Marketing*, 33(1): 10–15.

—— and A. Andreasen (1991). *Strategic Marketing for Non-Profit Organisations*. London: Prentice-Hall.

Lees-Marshment, Jennifer (2001a). *Political marketing and British Political Parties: The Party's Just Begun*. Manchester: Manchester University Press.

—— (2001b). 'The marriage of politics and marketing'. *Political Studies*, 49(4): 692–713.

—— (2003). 'Political marketing: how to reach that pot of gold'. *Journal of Political Marketing*, 2(1): 1–32.

—— (2004). *The Political Marketing Revolution: Transforming the Government of the UK*. Manchester: Manchester University Press.

—— (2008). *Political Marketing and British Political Parties* (2nd edn). Manchester: Manchester University Press.

Levitt, Theodore (1960). 'Marketing myopia'. *Harvard Business Review*, (July–August): 45–56.

Lilleker, Darren (2007). 'What is political marketing: a conceptual discussion'. UK PSA Conference. Available online at www.psa.ac.uk/journals/pdf/5/2007/Lilleker.pdf.

—— and N. Negrine (2003). 'Not big brand names but corner shops: marketing politics to a disengaged electorate.' *The Journal of Political Marketing*, 2(1): 55–76.

Lloyd, Jenny (2005). 'Square peg, round hole? Can marketing-based concepts such as the "product" and the "marketing mix" have a useful role in the political arena?'. In W. Wymer and J. Lees-Marshment (eds), *Current Issues in Political Marketing*. Binghamton, NY: Haworth Press.

Lock, Andrew and Phil Harris (1996). 'Political marketing – Vive la difference!'. *European Journal of Marketing*, 30: 10–11, 21–31.

Luck, D. (1969). 'Broadening the concept of marketing – too far'. *Journal of Marketing*, 33: 53–5.

McCarthy, E.J. (1964). *Basic Marketing*. Homewood, IL: Richard D. Irwin.

Mindak, William A. and H. Malcolm Bybee (1971). 'Marketing's application to fund raising'. *Journal of Marketing*, 35(3): 13–18.

Moloney, Kevin (2004). 'Is political marketing new words or new practice?'. UK PSA Conference. Available online at www.psa.ac.uk/journals/pdf/5/2004/Moloney.pdf.

Mullins, N.C. (1973). *Theories and Theory Groups in Contemporary American Sociology*. New York: Harper & Row.

Newman, Bruce I. (1994). *The Marketing of the President: Political Marketing as Campaign Strategy*. Thousand Oaks, CA: Sage.

—— (1999). *The Mass Marketing of Politics*. Thousand Oaks, CA: Sage.

Niffenegger, P.B. (1989). 'Strategies for success from the political marketers'. *Journal of Consumer Marketing*, 6(1): 45–61.

O'Cass, Aron (1996a). 'Political marketing and the marketing concept'. *European Journal of Marketing*, 30(10/11): 45–61.

—— (1996b). 'Political marketing: marketing, politics and ethical issues'. In C. Riquier and B. Sharp (eds), *Southern Marketing: Theory and Applications*. Proceedings of the 1996 Australian Marketing Educators Conference, Adelaide, II, pp. 24–31.

Ormrod, Robert P. (2005). 'A conceptual model of political market orientation'. *Journal of Non-Profit and Public Sector Marketing*, 14(1/2): 47–64.

O'Shaughnessy, Nicholas J. (1990). *The Phenomenon of Political Marketing*. Hampshire: Macmillan.

Robinson, Jim (2004). 'Repackaging our politicians' (Cover story). *NZ Marketing Magazine*, 23(5): 12–19.

Rothschild, Michael (1979). 'Marketing communications in non-business situations – or, Why it's so hard to sell brotherhood like soap'. *Journal of Marketing*, 43: 11–20.

Scammell, Margaret (1995). *Designer Politics: How Elections are Won*. New York: St Martin's.

—— (1999). 'Political marketing: lessons for political science'. *Political Studies*, 47(4): 718–39.

Shama, Avraham (1976). 'The marketing of political candidates'. *Journal of the Academy of Marketing Science*, 4(4): 764–77.

Shapiro, Benson (1973). 'Marketing for non-profit organisations'. *Harvard Business Review*, 51: 123–32.

Tucker, W.T. (1974). 'Future directions in marketing theory'. *Journal of Marketing*, 38(2): 30–5.

Webster Jr, F.E. (1988). 'The rediscovery of the marketing concept'. *Business Horizons,* 31: 3, 29–39.

Wring, Dominic (1994–5). 'Political marketing and organisational development: the case of the Labour Party in Britain'. Research paper, in *Management Studies*, 12. Judge Institute of Management Studies, University of Cambridge.

—— (1996). 'Political marketing and party development in Britain: a 'secret' history'. *European Journal of Marketing*, 30(10–11): 100–11.

—— (2002). 'Conceptualising political marketing: a framework for election-campaign analysis'. In N.J. O'Shaughnessy and S. Henneberg (eds), *The Idea of Political Marketing*. New York: Praeger.

—— (2005). *The Politics of Marketing of the Labour Party*. Hampshire: Palgrave Macmillan.

Zaltman, Gerald and Ilan Vertinsky (1971). 'Health service marketing: a suggested model'. *Journal of Marketing*, 35(3): 19–27.

3   Political marketing strategy

Practitioner perspective 3.1

Strategy development in politics is never easy, never comfortable. It is always challenging, often frustrating, as the sheer complexity of the strategic task has to be first made comprehensible, then manageable, and finally simple, uncomplicated and decisive. Effective political strategy is the result of bruising months of argument, counter-argument, testing, verification, endless meetings, constant setbacks and much frustration, attempting to tie together policy, politics, ideology and public opinion.

(Phillip Gould, UK Labour strategist, 2002)

Political marketing involves a number of activities, but one of the first things to learn is that it is also about strategy: how parties, candidates and governments think and plan in order to achieve their goals. As Barber (2005: 212) argued, strategy is about 'the forming of objectives and implementing the tasks necessary to achieve those objectives with a pattern of consistency over time given the limitations of available resources'. Strategy is not easily discernible, either in business or politics. It also is rarely fixed and needs to be flexible to changing circumstances; see Practitioner perspective 3.1.

Political marketing literature in this area is mostly concerned with how parties or candidates might become market-oriented or exhibit behaviour in line with market- or marketing-orientation. Applying the concept of market-orientation to politics has helped demonstrate that political marketing is not just about selling, but is also concerned with *what* politicians and governments try to sell, by examining the relationship between the political product and market demands. In politics, market-orientation has become concerned with how political elites become and remain responsive to market demand, helping them to stay in touch and deliver what voters need and want. As this could be a crucial aspect of how politicians win and get re-elected, which is one of the most debated areas of political science – and of course practice – market-oriented politics has attracted significant attention and focus from literature. It is also controversial and often criticised on ethical and normative grounds, because it elevates the position of the voter in the political decision-making process, a concern, given the potential limits of the voter noted in Chapter 1.

Therefore, while marketing students and academics might not see aspects of strategy in this chapter that they would usually see in a marketing textbook, this reflects the nature of both political marketing literature and politics itself. There nevertheless remain many issues to be discussed within the area of political marketing strategy. The chapter will explain the different academic theories and approaches in political marketing, along with different case studies, and outline issues to debate that arise from a market-oriented, strategic approach to politics.

A market-orientation in politics

A market-orientation in politics can be defined in numerous ways and is the subject of significant debate, reflecting the vast literature on this subject within business marketing (see Ormrod 2007). A number of scholars have dealt with this area, using different terms (customer-centric, consumer-led, market-oriented, marketing-oriented and voter-responsive) and different models. The main works that discuss market-orientation in how political elites behave are:

- Newman (1994): model of political marketing based in the USA.
- Lees-Marshment (2001): market-oriented party framework based in the UK.
- Ormrod (2005a,b): political market-orientation model.

All are rooted in classic work in the two disciplines: in political science, the Downsian (1957) model of rational choice; and in marketing, Kotler and Levy's (1969) initial statement that marketing can be broadened beyond commerce to all organisations. What the three models share is the principle inherent from the business marketing literature and rational-choice political science literature that, in order to gain power, political leaders need to be market-oriented. They also all draw on the basic principle that a market-orientation involves the politician or party being:

- in touch with ordinary voter concerns;
- interested in public views;
- responsive to what the public are concerned about; and
- demonstrating this in the way they *behave* – or in the political product they design, offer and implement, in order to ensure the product satisfies market demands in order to achieve the desired goals.

There are a few important points to remember about a market-orientation in politics:

1 This kind of behaviour is distinct from seeing marketing as being about selling; it is more concerned with the product.
2 A market-orientation is not just about doing what everyone (as the market can be segmented) wants (as it involves needs as well).
3 Each section of the market evaluates the product differently.
4 As the product is broad, the overall image, or brand, of the party can affect whether the public perceives the political leader to be in touch.

In order to understand a market-orientation in further detail, the different academic models will now be discussed.

Discussion point 3.1

How does the idea of a market-orientation in politics change previous conceptions of how politics works, and is this a good or bad thing? Reflect on personal political experience if appropriate.

Newman's (1994) model of political marketing

Newman (1994) portrays how candidates can use a range of marketing tools: see Box 3.1. This model suits the US system of primaries, as well as a final general election, but also shows the complexity of different factors that strategy needs to consider in any country.

Box 3.1 Newman's model of political marketing

Candidate focus

(a) Party concept
(b) Product concept
(c) Selling concept
(d) Marketing concept.

The marketing campaign

Market (voter) segmentation – to:

(a) assess voter needs;
(b) profile voters;
(c) identify voter segments.

Candidate positioning:

(a) assess candidate strengths and weaknesses;
(b) assess competition;
(c) target segments;
(d) establish image.

Strategy formulation and implementation:

(a) The 4Ps (product (campaign platform); push marketing (grass roots efforts); pull marketing (mass media); polling (research)).
(b) Organisation development and control.

Environmental forces

(a) Technology (the computer, television, direct mail).
(b) Structural shifts (primary convention and rules; financial regulations; debates).
(c) Power broker shifts in influence (candidate; consultant; pollster; media; political party; political action committees/interest groups; voters).

The political campaign

- Pre-primary stage
- Primary stage
- Convention stage
- General election stage.

Source: Newman (1994)

Newman (1999: 77–85) applied this model to the election campaign of President Bill Clinton in 1992 and argued that, by building a market-oriented campaign, 'built around voters' concerns and desires rather than his own', Clinton maximised message effectiveness. Clinton's campaign was informed by regular market intelligence to help frame political communication. Newman (1999: 85) argues that intelligence must be collected throughout an election. However, he also argued that candidates need to have 'a vision that is not subject to the vacillations of the public's reactions to the candidate's ideas or to his or her standings in the polls'. The points that these extracts raise will be discussed throughout the book: the extent to which political elites should follow or lead public opinion. Just conducting research and responding to it can increase support, but, equally, displaying too little leadership or conviction can also damage overall credibility.

Discussion point 3.2

Discuss the extent to which modern presidential campaigning makes use of the different components of Newman's model in countries such as the US. To what extent can politicians both respond to the market and maintain their vision, as Newman encourages them to?

Lees-Marshment's (2001) market/sales/product-oriented party framework

Lees-Marshment (2001) developed a more party-oriented framework of how parties might behave if they adopted a product-, sales- or market-orientation. Working from a political science perspective, this model argued that marketing concepts as well as techniques could be applied to the overall behaviour, suggesting a stage-by-stage process to show what a party might do from the beginning of an electoral term through to election and delivery in government. In particular, it distinguished between two very different approaches: the market and the sales-oriented form of political marketing. Market-oriented party (MOP) and sales-oriented party (SOP) concepts suggest very different relationships between parties and voters. The SOP's main aim is to persuade and change their minds, while, in contrast, the MOP aims to respond to voter views. Not only might the orientation a party chooses impact on its electoral support, but each concept has different potential positive and negative consequences for democracy.

The market-oriented party

A MOP designs its behaviour to provide voter satisfaction to reach its goal. It uses market intelligence to identify voter demands, then designs its product that meets their needs and wants, is supported and implemented by the internal organisation, and is deliverable in government. It does not attempt to change what people think, but to deliver what they need and want. This concept is very different from more traditional views of political parties as organisations that seek to pursue their ideological vision. It also differs from the narrow view that marketing, if used, would be used in political communication. Instead, the MOP concept places emphasis on the development of a product, and market intelligence, rather than communication and campaigning. Understanding that political parties are different to businesses, have complex products, markets as well as goals, and in particular have members,

“
”

Discussion point 3.3

What are the main differences between Lees-Marshment's notion of a market-oriented party and *either*:

(a) *for political science students*, other traditional models of behaviour, such as Duverger's Mass Party, Kircheimer's Catch-all Party and Panebianco's Electoral-professional Party in political science; *or*

(b) *for marketing students*, business models of market-orientation?

more informed politicians and ideological history, a MOP does not simply offer voters what they want, or simply follow opinion polls, because it needs to ensure that it can deliver the product on offer. A MOP needs to ensure that its product will be accepted within the party and so needs to adjust it carefully to take account of this, using party views and political judgement to inform how it responds to public concerns. Parties may use their ideology as a means to create effective solutions to public demands, but without trying to shape opinion. Therefore MOPs will not all become the same, nor assume the characteristics of catch-all parties, nor simply move to the Downsian centre-ground. The MOP political marketing process shows the different activities parties would carry out to achieve a market-orientation: see Box 3.2.

MOPs can be seen as more democratic as they encourage politicians to listen and respond to the public through market intelligence. However, as will be explored, they also challenge the conventional view that elites are elected to decide what is right for the country on the public's behalf.

Box 3.2 The political marketing process for a MOP

Stage one: market intelligence

The party aims to understand and ascertain market demands. Informally, it 'keeps an ear to the ground', talks to party members, creates policy groups, meets with the public. Formally, it uses methods such as polls, focus groups and segmentation to understand the views and behaviour of its market, including the general public, key opinion-influencers, MPs and members. It uses market intelligence continually and considers short- and long-term demands.

Stage two: product design

The party then designs its 'product', according to the findings from its market intelligence, before adjusting it to suit several factors explored in Stage 3.

Stage three: product adjustment

The party then develops the product to consider:

Achievability: ensures promises can be delivered in government. In an era of pledges, annual reports and timetables for action, delivery capability is a big issue. The factors that go into this include the overall leadership team, economic management, capability, party unity and voters perception of party's ability to deliver their desired outcome.

Internal reaction: ensures changes will attract adequate support from MPs and members to ensure implementation, taking into account a party's ideology and history, retaining certain policies to suit the traditional supporter market where necessary. Changes in policy thus need to be placed within, or with reference to, the party's traditional ideological framework, wherever possible. This will be a sometimes delicate, yet essential, balancing act between the demands of external (voters) and internal (members) supporters. This is, in effect, about internal marketing – and applying the same concepts for the wider public to those within the party organisation.

Competition: identifies the opposition's weaknesses and highlights own corresponding strengths, ensuring a degree of distinctiveness.

Support: segments the market to identify untapped voters necessary to achieve goals, and then develop targeted aspects of the product to suit them. The party does not adopt the 'catch-all' approach of trying to get everyone on board. It is more 'traditional market plus'.

Stage four: implementation
Changes are implemented throughout the party, needing careful party management and leadership over an appropriate timeframe to obtain adequate acceptance, to create party unity and enthusiasm for the new party design.

Stage five: communication
Communication is carefully organised to convey the new product, so that voters are clear before the campaign begins. Not just the leader, but all MPs and members send a message to the electorate. It involves media management, but is not just about spin-doctoring; it should be informative rather than manipulative, and built on a clear, internal communication structure.

Stage six: campaign
The party repeats its communication in the official campaign, reminding voters of the key aspects and advantages of its product.

Stage seven: election
The party should not just win votes but attract positive perception from voters on all aspects of behaviour, including policies, leaders, party unity and capability, as well as increased quality of its membership.

↓

Stage eight: delivery
The party then needs to deliver its product in government.

Source: Lees-Marshment (2001a)

The product-oriented party and sales-oriented party

In contrast, a product-oriented party (POP) is much more traditional: it argues for what it stands for, believing its product is of such value that people will vote for it because it is right. It doesn't use marketing to change its product or even its communication, even if it fails to gain support. A SOP is also more reluctant to change its product. However, what it does do is use marketing to identify persuadable voters and design more effective communication to sell the party to them. A SOP does not change its behaviour to suit what people want, but tries to make people want what it offers. Using market intelligence to understand voters' response to its behaviour, the party employs the latest advertising and communication techniques to persuade voters that it is right. Market intelligence is used, not to inform the product design, but to help the party devise the most effective presentation to persuade voters it is right: see Box 3.3.

Box 3.3 The political marketing process for a SOP

Stage one: product design
The party designs its behaviour according to what it thinks best.

Stage two: market intelligence
Market intelligence is used to ascertain voters' response to its behaviour and to identify voter segments that offer support, those that do not, and those that might be persuaded, and how best to communicate with target markets.

Stage three: communication
Communication is devised to suit each segment, focusing presentation on the most popular aspects of the product, while downplaying any weaknesses. Communication is highly professional and organised, using modern marketing communication techniques to persuade voters to agree with the party.

Stage four: campaign
The party continues to communicate effectively, as in Stage three.

Stage five: election
The general election.

Stage six: delivery
The party will deliver its promised product in government.

Source: Lees-Marshment (2001a)

SOPs therefore use a range of communication techniques noted in political communication literature, but which ones they use, together with how they use them, is informed by market intelligence to maximise the effectiveness of communication, as it is designed to suit the potential target.

A SOP also has both negative and positive democratic consequences. Marketing used in this way can help politicians to advocate their position more effectively and gain support for policies they believe in, sometimes aiding new government approaches to move up the agenda. However, it can also give elites manipulative power to gain support for initiatives that others might argue are not the right thing for the country or the world.

In trying to understand the different orientations, it helps to compare the stages they go through: see Box 3.4.

The SOP–MOP distinction conveys a common understanding: that, while marketing can just be used to help a party communicate more effectively, it can also be applied more broadly and strategically. The differences can most easily be seen in how the UK Labour Party's use of political marketing developed between 1983 and 1997: see Case study 3.1.

Box 3.4 The marketing process for product-, sales- and market-oriented parties

PRODUCT-ORIENTED PARTY	SALES-ORIENTED PARTY	MARKET-ORIENTED PARTY
STAGE 1 PRODUCT DESIGN	STAGE 1 PRODUCT DESIGN	STAGE 1 MARKET INTELLIGENCE
	STAGE 2 MARKET INTELLIGENCE	STAGE 2 PRODUCT DESIGN
		STAGE 3 PRODUCT ADJUSTMENT
		STAGE 4 IMPLEMENTATION
STAGE 2 COMMUNICATION	STAGE 3 COMMUNICATION	STAGE 5 COMMUNICATION
STAGE 3 CAMPAIGN	STAGE 4 CAMPAIGN	STAGE 6 CAMPAIGN
STAGE 4 ELECTION	STAGE 5 ELECTION	STAGE 7 ELECTION
STAGE 5 DELIVERY	STAGE 6 DELIVERY	STAGE 8 DELIVERY

Source: Lees-Marshment (2001a)

Discussion point 3.4

Discuss the main differences between Lees-Marshment's model of product-, sales- and market-oriented parties, and debate which approach is more likely to win an election.

Discussion point 3.5

Which category (product-, sales- or market-oriented party) do current parties/candidates/leaders best fit into?

Critiques of the Lees-Marshment market-oriented model

Lees-Marshment's model attracted significant attention, as, despite being based in the UK, examples of similar MOP behaviour could be seen in other countries, as shown in a comparative study edited by Lilleker and Lees-Marshment (2005). It also exemplified the difference between marketing as selling and marketing as product development, helping to open the way for a wider variety of political marketing research. It has been subject to a range of criticisms (see Coleman 2007, for example, and also Ormrod 2006). Some of the criticisms raise important issues, while others show misconceptions similar to those faced by Kotler and Levy's (1969) early article on broadening the concept of marketing. Many concerns are about the democratic consequences of political marketing: see Box 3.5.

Incomplete market-oriented parties: New Labour, new danger

Political marketing is often criticised because of its association with Tony Blair's UK New Labour design in 1997. Lees-Marshment argued that New Labour was not a perfect example of a MOP. Blair followed some, but not all, aspects of the MOP model. The main weaknesses were:

- *Internal reaction analysis*: changes Blair made to the party's product to increase its external support created significant dissatisfaction within the party; the change of Clause IV, a constitutional clause that was of ideological, emotive importance, embodying what members had been fighting for during all their years of involvement in the party.
- *Competition analysis*: Blair accepted the achievements of Thatcherism without saying how Labour would be that different; policy positions were extremely close to the Conservatives' and failed to differentiate the New Labour product.

New Labour in 1997 was market-*driven* rather than market-oriented. Market-*driven* means it was single-minded, determined and motivated by public opinion; the market drove the Party. Market-*oriented,* however, would be where there was more balance; where a Party is slanted or tilted towards to the public – not wholly driven by it. Blair was extremely lucky to face an ineffective Conservative Party during his time as leader, so he was never really to be assessed on his lack of delivery or lack of adjustment.

Box 3.5 Criticisms of the Lees-Marshment (2001a) model

1 The use of focus groups by New Labour did not necessarily mean Labour listened to voters' views; the moderator, Phillip Gould, set the agenda and influenced what voters said by taking an interventionist approach, which would encourage some opinions while inhibiting others.

2 No one party ever follows the MOP 100 per cent; parties do not always fit 100 per cent into a sales- or market-orientation; behaviour is always evolving, and internally a party may engage in a divisive debate about whether to take one or the other approach to electioneering.

3 'Surely an even more effective (and equally dangerous) way of permanently reflecting public opinion would be to introduce plebiscitary direct democracy' (Coleman 2007: 181).

4 Parties often adopt a hybrid approach, implementing either sales- or market-orientation, depending on the individual policy area.

5 'She seems to be suggesting that voters' views and preferences are sufficiently consistent to be suited to strategic reasoning. Most of the empirical evidence suggests that voters are promiscuous and rationally irresponsible in the range of inconsistent views they hold at any one time, and rarely think about long-term policy consequences in ways that politicians and their advisors are required to do' (Coleman 2007: 181).

6 'Lees-Marshment seems to believe that such ideological leadership is redundant in the age of MOPs' (Coleman 2007: 184).

7 The MOP model doesn't take account of the media.

8 'As good MOPs, parties should regard [voters'] inconsistencies as great opportunities to sell the public a credible version of its own wrong-headedness' (Coleman 2007: 182).

9 If parties simply repeat to voters what they say they want, this will not help develop a culture of mutual trust between parties and citizens.

10 Even if all major parties had exhibited behaviour that follows a market-orientation, we have been unable to prove that such parties consciously do this, or that this, rather than other political science theories, is what wins the election.

Discussion point 3.6

'The first thing that you need to identify about the process of formulating strategy is that there is no one model and no one process' (Murray McCully, New Zealand National strategist interviewed by Jennifer Lees-Marshment, August 2007). To what extent are the concerns about the MOP in Box 3.5 valid? Could any one model ever 100 per cent capture how parties utilise a market-orientation?

Discussion point 3.7

What can other leaders/parties learn from the way Tony Blair utilised the MOP concept?

Ormrod's (2005) model of political market-orientation

Ormrod (2005a,b) provides another political market-orientation model, drawing on further commercial marketing literature, and capturing additional dynamics, such as the overall environment, a greater range of actors and stakeholders, and the possibility of co-operating with competing parties are acknowledged, as is the importance of all stakeholder groups in society. He argues that a political market-orientation exists 'when all members of a party are sensitive to internal and external stakeholders' attitudes, needs and wants, and synthesize these within a framework of constraints imposed by all stakeholders to develop policies and programmes with which to reach the party's objectives'.

There are two main aspects to Ormrod's model: see Box 3.6.

Box 3.6 Ormrod's model of political marketing orientation

The behavioural chain: four consecutive stages of behaviour

Information generation (the party-wide generation of formal and informal information regarding all internal and external stakeholders)

↓

Information dissemination (the party-wide communication and reception of information through formal and informal channels)

↓

Member participation (the member participation construct as the process of including all members in creating a coherent party strategy; this facilitates consistent responses that are agreed upon by all party members)

↓

Consistent external communication (the process of communicating a consistent, agreed-upon strategy to external stakeholder groups)

The four stakeholder orientations

Voter orientation: an emphasis is placed upon social exchanges between individual actors, complementing the utilisation of traditional marketing management tools.

Internal orientation: includes all party members to foster party-wide awareness and acceptance of the value of other members' opinions, irrespective of position in the party.

Competitor orientation: the party-wide awareness of other parties' attitudes and behaviours, and an acknowledgement that co-operation with other parties may be necessary to attain the party's long-term objectives.

External orientation: reflects the importance of stakeholder groups in society that are external to the party and not voters or competing parties.

Source: Ormrod (2005a,b)

The four stakeholder orientations are applied to the four areas of behaviour in the behavioural chain. The model is designed to capture behaviour and be used by any party in any system and, in an important distinction from Newman (1994) and Lees-Marshment (2001a), 'to be used independently of the position in the electoral cycle'. It can be used by a party to measure its level of political market-orientation with different stakeholder groups in society, so that it can focus resources on those that need more attention.

Discussion point 3.8

Compare the Newman, Lees-Marshment and Ormrod models and make a list of the key differences. To what extent do the differences influence how effective they are at helping us understand current party behaviour?

Linking a market-orientation to election results

It is difficult to prove that, if a party adopts a market-orientation, as either Newman, Lees-Marshment or Ormrod portrays it, it will win an election, because it involves such a broad range of activities that are difficult to measure. Lees-Marshment argued that marketing sales techniques cannot make up for the lack of a comprehensive, unified political product that offers a positive, achievable alternative to an existing government and responds effectively to the concerns and demands of the public. Political marketing is more effective for major parties if it is used to inform how the product on offer is designed. However, the Lilleker *et al.* (2006: 252–4) edited study of the UK 2005 election concluded that:

- The parties did not really engage directly with voters in designing the product.
- Marketing was used more to design communication.
- Political products were not designed according to understanding from market intelligence to any significant extent.
- Parties exhibited both leading and following, with Labour showing more following than any other party.

Clearly, it is not the case that all parties, even major parties, try to be market-oriented. Smaller parties are able to gain support from a smaller niche market, with more ideologically driven policies that will help them achieve their goals of agenda-setting, rather than office-gaining. The George W. Bush/Karl Rove strategy in the US, from 2000 to 2008, could be viewed as a more sales-oriented approach, which won and maintained control of the presidency. However, given that public satisfaction with the Bush government declined alongside growing criticism, it could still be concluded that a more responsive, market-oriented strategy may have generated greater voter satisfaction and a more positive appraisal of the Bush presidency. Additionally, parties may adopt different orientations at different times, moving back and forth. Market-oriented strategies are not just used by parties in established democracies: see Case studies 3.2 and 3.3 at the end of this chapter on how the APRA party in Peru and the LDP in Japan adapted elements of the MOP to achieve their goals.

Market-oriented candidate theory

More recently, scholars have attempted to think about how the MOP concept applies to candidates, rather than party-based systems. Kotzaivazoglou, working on Greek politics, developed a theory of market-oriented candidates: see Box 3.7.

Box 3.7 The market-oriented candidate   *Iordanis Kotzaivazoglou*

The principles of the market-oriented party model (Lees-Marshment 2001a) can be extended to candidates for political office, e.g. MPs and municipal or prefectural councillors.

Stage one: market intelligence

The market-oriented candidate uses market intelligence to discover the voters' needs and wants. Individual candidates, however, do not usually have the financial means to gather formal market intelligence nor, like the parties, to hire professionals. They are therefore obliged to rely to a certain extent on desk research (secondary data) and informal market intelligence. In addition, candidates need market intelligence that focuses on the specific groups of voters that they are targeting. They need to study, first of all, the demands and wishes of their chosen constituencies and, second, the impact that the candidate makes on them.

Stage two: product design

A candidate designs a product on the basis of the needs and wishes of the voters, as determined in Stage one, but, instead of addressing a mass electorate, as the party has to, the candidate can concentrate on one or two target groups to make the most efficient use of resources and to maximise the potential to satisfy the needs of specific groups. Target groups, such as the inhabitants of a particular region, people working in a particular sector, young people, women and even the non-politicised, can be identified by segmentation. Each group has its own specific needs and desires, different from those of other groups, and the candidate has to identify these and satisfy them. This niche marketing strategy will, if successful, give the candidate a strong, competitive advantage over other candidates with regard to these target groups.

Stage three: product adjustment

The candidate's product has to be adjusted according to:

(a) *Achievability*

The candidate, like the party, should not promise what he/she cannot deliver. He/she must ensure that the promised product will be achievable when he/she is elected.

(b) *Reaction analysis*

The product must be designed to fit in with the general context of the party or political body he/she belongs to. A candidate cannot adopt positions that run counter to those of the party. At the same time, the product offered is always constrained by the candidate's personality, ideology and history.

(c) *Competition analysis*

A candidate's competitors are his/her fellow candidates from the same party or organisation who are standing in the same electoral district and appear on the same list. The candidate product has to be designed on the basis of a strengths, weaknesses, opportunities and threats (SWOT) analysis, permitting differentiation from the competition.

(d) *Existing/needed support analysis*

The candidate has to design his/her product in such a way as to win the support of a sufficient number of voters to ensure the possibility of success. A product design focusing on a small number of voters who will actually vote for the candidate is preferable to one that will ensure greater publicity but will not win votes.

Stage four: implementation

In this stage, the candidate will implement the findings from the three preceding stages, managing potential problems such as: the party leadership rejecting his/her positions, for example, and sidelining or even dropping him/her; or he/she being simply unable to deliver, in practice, a market-oriented product.

Stage five: communication

The candidate's product must be communicated to voters using the most appropriate and effective communication techniques. This can be done with a variety of means, such as press releases, advertising, public appearances and speeches, and media appearances, but it has to be done systematically and continually, not just during the campaign. Personal contact with the voters also plays an important role. The candidate will be limited by his or her own budget, however, which can make communication significantly more difficult. Even the best-designed product has to be presented to the public.

Stage six: campaign

The election campaign is the candidate's last chance to promote the electoral product. The candidate essentially represents only himself, and the campaign is simpler and more controlled than for a whole party. On the other hand, the candidate may not have the financial resources to conduct his/her campaign and present his/her positions in the way he/she would like to, or to hire professionals. Much of his/her campaign work is likely to be done by volunteer supporters.

Stage seven: election

The candidate's marketing strategy is judged on election day. The criterion of success is whether the voters 'buy the product' by voting for the candidate in sufficient numbers to ensure his/her election.

Stage eight: delivery

What and how the candidate delivers to the electorate after election plays a determinant role in voter satisfaction and therefore in his/her subsequent electoral career. His/her personal delivery is, however, usually influenced by that of his/her party. Poor party performance can have a negative effect on his/her own actions and image and lead to voter dissatisfaction.

Discussion point 3.9

Apply Kotzaivazoglou's theoretical framework to candidate campaigns. To what extent do local politicians appear to follow its principles?

US presidential political marketing strategy model

Gorbounova and Lees-Marshment produced a revised model for candidates to suit presidential elections in the US by incorporating added factors from the Newman 1994 model and the Butler and Collins market positioning model: see Figure 3.1 for a diagram and Box 3.8 for the explanation. Gorbounova and Lees-Marshment applied this model to Hillary Clinton's bid for the Democratic presidential nomination, and a case study on this appears in Chapter 5.

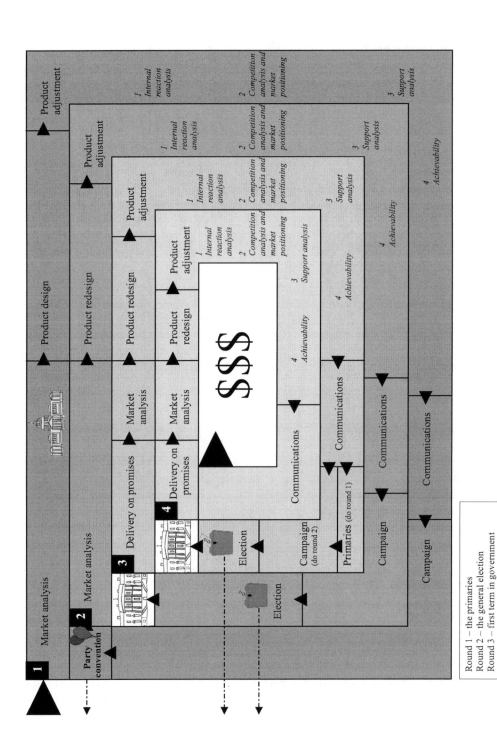

Figure 3.1 Diagram of US presidential political marketing strategy model

Model and diagram devised by Jennifer Lees-Marshment and Daria Gorbounova. Graphic design by Emma Mcfarlane

Box 3.8 US presidential political marketing strategy model
Daria Gorbounova and Jennifer Lees-Marshment

This model was devised by adapting the Lees-Marshment (2001a) model for market-oriented parties and taking into account both the distinctive features of the US political marketplace – what Newman (1994) calls 'environmental forces'; its systemic candidate-focus; and the market-positioning elements from Butler and Collins (1996). It is intended for a market-oriented presidential candidate in the US – one that forms his/her product on the basis of market intelligence about voter preferences, with the ultimate goal of delivering this product and thereby satisfying the electorate, but also considers the four different rounds that US presidential elections and government involve. The model also departs from the original Lees-Marshment model where appropriate: the implementation stage is omitted, because implementing the product throughout the party is not essential owing to the US system's candidate-focus.

Round 1: primaries
Market analysis

Market intelligence
Research about voter preferences will focus heavily on the internal market, because the candidate is seeking the support from members of his/her own party in this round. The fact that primaries are not held simultaneously, but in succession, allows candidates to use exit polls and official results from earlier primaries as market intelligence for upcoming primaries.

The marketplace
Candidates should also consider the implications of the political context in which they operate for their marketing strategy and product, such as the influence of high levels of Internet use on communications strategy. The marketplace is influential throughout the model.

Product design
The candidate should avoid making too many concrete promises in Round 1, because unexpected developments may force them to change and risk being criticised for inconsistency.

Product adjustment

Internal reaction analysis
Winning the approval of his/her party faithful is a hurdle the candidate must overcome to progress onto Round 2. The candidate must attract the party's core support base, while retaining room to broaden the product's appeal in later rounds. Electability credentials are important, because the internal market may choose the candidate most likely to defeat the rival party's nominee, even if this candidate is not its first choice internally.

Competition analysis
Candidates' products are likely to be similar, since they come from the same party and ideological tradition, and therefore require differentiation. However, criticism of fellow candidates is problematic: it can alienate potential primary party voters who might otherwise be persuaded to switch support; intra-party animosity could undermine the prospects of the eventual nominee by weakening them in the run-up to Round 2; and the candidate may want to keep the option to become a presidential running mate open should they not win. Market share will affect how candidates position themselves (as leaders, challengers, followers or nichers) and react to

opponents. Candidates often encroach on other's market share more easily and have greater trouble safeguarding their own. Primaries are unpredictable races, and often a candidate who starts out as leader can find him/herself subject to significant attack by challengers and see their positions reverse.

Support analysis

This involves the usual segmentation and targeting, but in this round it is applied to the party vote, not yet the wider electorate at this stage. Candidates need to consider whom they are most likely to attract support from, whom is not worth paying attention to, and who may be persuaded.

Achievability

While the product is not yet finalised, candidates are open to attack for promises being too vague or unrealistic, or for lacking experience necessary to deliver in government. It is hard to balance the need to be realistic with the aim of remaining open to a change in strategy, should the market conditions require it in later rounds.

Communications

Candidates must communicate their product, which at this stage may be more about themselves than the party, to the internal market in a way that suits different targets and increases support.

Campaign

The primary campaign can be short or drawn out until the party convention in the summer if no clear front-runner emerges. Hence, resource rationing is important.

Party convention

This is Round 1's election, and at this point the party chooses its nominee.

Round 2: presidential election

Market analysis

Now the candidate is selected, he or she can begin to plan a more thorough election campaign. This stage emphasises segmenting and targeting groups within the entire electorate so that resources and strategy can identify those voters the candidates most need to gain support from to win. It also involves continual monitoring of opinion to enable responses to changing demands and to inform more defined product development, and also candidate and opposition research to inform competition analysis.

Product design

With the election nearing, the product will be finalised. The party can now help support the candidate.

Product adjustment

Internal reaction analysis

The nominee must reconcile the internal market's preferences with those of the wider electorate, with more emphasis on the broader electorate now that they are open to the whole market.

Competition analysis

This becomes more important as the focus is now on the candidates, and not on the parties. The candidate must focus on the other party's nominee as both compete for the leader position. Differentiation and superior product performance, such as governing ability, become more important, as does avoiding showing any weaknesses.

Support analysis

The candidate tries to increase support from target segments, particularly in swing states and among groups he/she is targeting. However, campaigns also focus on getting traditional supporters out to vote.

Achievability

This becomes more important as candidates seek to demonstrate superior ability to deliver on promises.

Communications and campaign

Candidates must broaden the means used in Round 1 to reach a wider audience and different target segments.

Election

If the candidate wins, he/she then moves into the White House.

Round 3: first term

Once in government, the president now has to both govern and remain market-oriented.

Delivery

The candidate has to deliver on market intelligence-based product promises so as to provide voter satisfaction – this is the essence of the market-oriented model.

Market analysis

This should be continuously conducted and will include appraisals of presidential performance and delivery in power, analysis of support among key target groups and stakeholders who may affect legislation and delivery, as well as consideration of changes in the marketplace.

Product (re)design and adjustment

To seek re-election, the presidential product has to be refined in response to fresh, post-election market intelligence to prevent voters from feeling cheated because the product is altered post-purchase. This will also be adjusted to consider internal reaction analysis and party supporters; non-party supporters in the wider electorate identified by support analysis; achievability, especially in light of success in delivery and governing realities such as the economy; and finally competition, both internally, if the party holds primaries (and thus a repeat of Round 1), and externally, from the other party's nominee.

Communications and campaign

The president benefits from state resources and incumbency effect, and can now focus on positive achievements and delivery. However, he/she also has to manage any weaknesses in government and is subject to far greater scrutiny than as a candidate.

Election

If the candidate wins re-election, he or she then moves onto Round 4 and their second term in office.

Round 4: second term

A second-term president is under the least pressure at any time, given he/she cannot seek any more than two terms, and so no longer faces another election. However, he/she may choose to remain market-oriented for various reasons, such as concerns about his/her legacy. Without the possibility of being sanctioned at the ballot box, some presidents may become product-oriented.

Delivery remains important, however, as presidents still receive continual market intelligence that monitors public support, and many wish to use their second term to enact more effective, possibly controversial legislation to achieve their personal vision. Adjustment may be used to understand potential support for delivery of certain promises and to help achieve goals, but generally presidents are freer at this stage. Communications stress delivery and may be used to gain support for new or bold initiatives.

Conclusion

This four-round framework shows how the US political system and political marketplace create significant complexities, and that marketing therefore has to be adjusted to suit each round. The considerations going into a particular stage in Round 3 (first term) differ, sometimes drastically, from those going into that same stage in Round 4 (second term). A candidate's political marketing strategy has to be updated according to many different variable factors as he/she progresses through the rounds. US presidential political marketing strategy is more complex than may at first be thought.

Discussion point 3.10

Compare the 2008 US presidential primary campaigns and/or other presidential campaigns with the principles of Gorbounova and Lees-Marshment's US presidential political marketing strategy model. What does this reveal with regard to how effectively such campaigns and candidates have utilised political marketing?

Broader strategy frameworks

Strategy also involves consideration of other factors and approaches. Baines and Lynch (2005: 2) argue that strategy needs to consider many different factors, such as the context, content and process: the nature of the market, history, culture and governance, economic and political principles that inform wealth distribution, and the media. Barber (2005) argues that other factors affect the success of a strategy, including existing market support, resources such as staff, organisation and finances and party culture.

Despite the apparent simplicity of market-oriented strategies, the reality is more complex. Barber (2005) argues that often strategies fail owing to internal party conditions. When Tony Blair took over as leader of the UK Labour Party in 1995, he faced a very different set of circumstances and found it much easier to impose a voter-responsive strategy because the party was power-seeking after losing so many successive elections from 1979 to 1992. Unclear objectives and an inappropriate strategy are also problems, as are controversial, dominant issues that block emergent approaches. Lindholm and Prehn (2007) studied strategy in Denmark and concluded that strategy is harder to develop when support is high, as there seems less need to innovate and reorientate. Additionally, parties are freerer in opposition to adopt new strategies by bringing in new people and getting the support of politicians. Strategy formation should involve and consult the grass roots to help test new initiatives and ensure members feel ownership of the new strategy. They also suggest twelve pieces of good advice for strategists: see Box 3.9. To gain greater insight into strategy in practice, read Case study 3.4, which applies strategy to the case of the UK's third biggest party, the Liberal Democrats.

Box 3.9 Lindholm and Prehn's advice for budding political strategists

1 Put your heart into it.
2 Have the facts at your fingertips and know what you are talking about.
3 Create a simply policy you can explain.
4 Make a plan and write it down.
5 Define your target group and go after this group, not the entire electorate.
6 Work to improve your communication skills.
7 Absorb knowledge, learning from what you see.
8 Be pragmatic.
9 Be courageous and strong.
10 Reinforce your analytical skills and learn to read the interests of others.
11 Define where you see yourself in five to ten years and work to get there.
12 Be very patient.

Source: Lindholm and Prehn (2007: 59–69)

Discussion point 3.11

Consider Practitioner perspectives 3.1 and 3.2 and the case studies at the end of this chapter. What factors provide the greatest blockage to using strategy effectively? Draw on personal experience of trying to achieve change in direction in politics or any other organisation if appropriate. Can you suggest additional solutions to those in Box 3.9?

Military strategy in politics

Military concepts of strategy can also be applied to politics. Marland (2003) lays out political examples of different military strategies: see Table 3.1.

Smith (2006: 9–10) also outlines a number of other competitive tactics from military and political illustrations:

1 **Set a goal and stick to it, concentrating forces.**
New Labour followed this in 1997 with their sound bite *Education Education Education* (as did Bill Clinton in 1992 with *It's the Economy Stupid*).

2 **Act aggressively.**
George W. Bush did this successfully against his opponent John Kerry in the 2004 US presidential election, labelling him as a flip-flopper.

Table 3.1 Offensive military strategy applied to political marketing

Military strategy	Political marketing description	Political example
Bypass attack	Attacking using new rules such as previously ignored market segments	A mainstream party promoting environmental policies to attract green voters
Counter-offensive defence	Use of head-on counter-attack by market leader to equal or exceed opponent's action	A centrist party targeting centre-right and centre-left voters
Diplomacy	Collaboration with opponent	Party enters coalition
Encirclement attack	Marketing directed at all areas using superior resources	Governing party invests in expensive tactics to lure a range of electors
Flank attack	Marketing directed at elector or geographical segments where an opponent is most vulnerable	Left-leaning party targets competitors' female supporters as they are more likely to value social programmes
Flanking defence	Defending previously undefended segments	Marketing targets core supporters (also internal marketing)
Frontal attack	A direct attack on an opponent, and the one with the greatest resources wins	Heavily funded campaign overwhelms an opponent
Guerrilla attack	Weakening and demoralising an opponent through a series of small, unpredictable efforts to secure permanent elector support	Use of testimonials, case studies and special events to suggest grass-roots frustration with an incumbent
Mobile defence	Diversification by attracting targeted new voters when party traditionalists have been attacked	Targets at recent immigrants, youth (and, for example, emerging pensioner segments and homosexual double-income vote)
Position defence	Reinforcement of weakest supporters to prevent loss of core supporters	Targeted at own soft supporters supporters
Pre-emptive defence	Attacking opponents before being attacked	Use of public relations and attack advertising to suggest flaws of opponents
Strategic withdrawal	Focusing on core supporters and giving up attracting new, but weaker supporters	Appeasement and reassurance of the party faithful (also UK Conservatives under William Hague abandoning market-oriented strategy in 2003–4 and focusing on core supporters)

Source: Marland (2003: 111–12)

3 Maintain morale and unity of command.

Factions destroy parties, as has been seen in the UK Conservative Party during the leaderships of John Major, William Hague and Iain Duncan-Smith; Labour sought to manage any potential disunity through positive election communication about the relationship between Gordon Brown and Tony Blair in the 2005 election.

Discussion point 3.12

Try to identify examples of such tactics used in politics and discuss the extent to which military strategies can be useful for the practice and study of politics.

Measuring strategic behaviour

One of the difficulties with studying market-oriented behaviour and strategy is that, because it is a subtle, complex and evolving process, it is difficult to measure scientifically for research purposes. Quantitative analysis does not always produce better understanding, but it is often popular in academic spheres because it can appear to offer a greater degree of scientific analysis or 'proof'. It isn't always easy to judge whether a party or leader is being market-oriented or not, or what strategy they are pursuing, and whether it is effective.

One example of this dilemma is UK Prime Minister Tony Blair's second term of government, when he took more of a leadership line on the Iraq war and lost public support, the question was: was this in line with, or against, the MOP? It is not as straightforward to answer as might first appear. Indeed, critiques have conflicted on this point. Coleman (2007: 182) notes how

> in the light of the Iraq war . . . it could be argued that, rather than pursuing a MOP-like desire to win elections at any cost, New Labour has in fact adopted a complex strategy aimed at balancing (for the first time in its history) core social-democratic values with the stubborn realities of the capitalist market and unpredictable global arena.

However, Corner (2005) disagreed with the suggestion that the Iraq war could be an example of why leadership was needed, arguing that 'a bit less "leadership" and a bit more marketing sensitivity might have led to better political judgements here'.

So was the war decision market-oriented or not? The answer is no. Why? It is not just a case of failing to respond adequately to public opinion, which could be argued to be changeable over time on an issue such as war. It is not just that commentators do or do not agree with the policy decision. The crucial *political marketing* point is that he did not adjust his policy in response to internal reaction analysis. The MOP model takes the *party* into account. Blair did not. The war did not fit traditional Labour ideology, promises, beliefs, members' desire and parliamentarians' views. Furthermore, there seemed very little desire to even *consult* the parliamentary and membership sections of the party on the war, let alone respond to their concerns. Responding can include explaining and justifying a position, not just changing it, but there was no sense of this until the 2005 campaign, when more effective communication put Blair in the public eye to explain his position. The *party* is what makes the difference with a full market-orientation; but analysis of this involves analysis of what leaders do, what the public think, and how the internal market reacts – and arguably a whole range of other factors in conjunction with each other, all of which is hard to model and test quantitatively.

However, more recently scholars have tried to develop more quantitative measurements. Ormrod and Henneberg (2006) analysed UK party manifestos in the 2005 election, operationalising Ormrod's concepts through QSR NVivo, a qualitative research tool, to test number of occurrences and relationship of occurrence; and assess whether they were not developed, somewhat developed or highly developed, with the following results: see Tables 3.2 and 3.3.

O'Cass (1996) developed quantitative measurements of market-orientation, conducting interviews and a survey in Australia: see Box 3.10.

Strömbäck (2009) created a survey to explore the extent to which parties in different countries both used political marketing techniques and adopted the orientations within the Lees-Marshment model and what affect the system might have on this: see Box 3.11.

The big question – *should* parties be market-oriented?

While there remain academic debates about which models capture market-oriented behaviour more effectively and how it can be measured, a more fundamental question is, *should* parties be market-oriented?

Box 3.10 O'Cass's 1996 survey measurement of market-oriented attitudes

The questions O'Cass used in the survey explored respondents' responses (strongly agree, agree, disagree, strongly disagree or neither agree nor disagree) to the following statements:

1   Business organisations' activities should be devoted to determining customers' wants and needs and then satisfying them, while making a profit over the long run.
2   Political parties' activities should be devoted to determining voters' needs and wants and then satisfying them, to obtain government and stay in government in the long run.
3   Political party decisions should be voter oriented to determine voter needs and wants and attempt to satisfy them, within ideological bounds and parliamentary numbers, rather than percentage of vote be the standard for evaluating marketing performance.
4   The notion of being oriented towards satisfying voter needs and wants is too vague and general to be really useful in making decisions within the . . . Party.
5   In reality, there are basic conflicts between attempting to satisfy voters' needs and wants and political party objectives.
6   In the event of conflict between voter needs and wants and political objectives, political ones would be the overriding consideration within the . . . Party.
7   The concept of determining needs and wants of voters in order to satisfy them to obtain office is a philosophy used by the . . . Party.
8   The Party has given considerable lip service to the marketing concept, but in general it has had little influence on the management campaigns of the . . . Party.
9   The concept of determining voters' needs and wants and attempting to satisfy them to obtain and maintain political office would increase the attention and effort devoted to planning and controlling political and campaign activities.
10   The concept of determining voter needs and wants and then attempting to satisfy them would work within the business world but not the . . . Party.

Table 3.2 Ormrod and Henneberg's results of testing Ormrod's political market orientation against UK 2005 party manifestos

	Labour	*Conservative*	*Liberal Democrats*
Voter orientation Importance of current voters Importance of future voters Awareness of voter opinions	High	High	High
Competitor orientation Long-term co-operation with competitors Short-term co-operation with competitors Awareness of positions	Medium	Medium	High
Internal orientation Inclusiveness of the party Importance of members Existence of members	Low	Low	Low
External orientation Media Interest and lobby groups Public sector employees Community-level organisations	High	High	High

Source: Ormrod and Henneberg (2006: 46)

Table 3.3 Ormrod and Henneberg's results of testing strategic political postures against UK 2005 party manifestos

	Labour	*Conservative*	*Liberal Democrats*
Ideology orientation Needs and wants analysis Ideology centrality Policy justification/integration Rationale for conflict resolution	Medium	High	Medium
Dialogue orientation Communication channels Empathy Feedback Multiple/reversing agenda	High	Low	High
Stakeholder orientation Electoral actor coverage Governmental actor coverage Low politics actor coverage Intermediary actor coverage	Medium	Low	High
Temporal orientation Future projection Future extrapolation Periodical focus	High	Medium	Low

Source: Ormrod and Henneberg (2006: 50)

❝❞

Discussion point 3.13

What do these results show about UK parties' use of marketing in the 2005 election?

Box 3.11 Strömbäck's survey of political marketing

Section A asked respondents to rate the extent to which they agreed or disagreed with the statements:

1   It is important for a party to know the kinds of individual and group that are most likely to vote for the party, and target them accordingly.
2   When party policies are being formulated, a trade-off may have to be made between the opinions of voters in general and the core values of the party.
3   Opinion polls are indispensable for a party to determine the views of individuals and groups likely to support the party.
4   If a party fails to do as well in an election as it expected, the most likely reason for this is that it did not have the appropriate policies to address important social problems.
5   If a party fails to do as well in an election as it expected, the most likely reason for this is that it did not communicate its policies effectively enough.
6   If a party fails to do as well in an election as it expected, the most likely reason for this is that it did not adequately respond to the wants and needs of its target groups.
7   If a party does well at an election, the most likely reason for this is that its campaign was very effective.
8   If a party does well at an election, the most likely reason for this is that it was able to identify the wants and needs of voters and adapted it policies accordingly.
9   It would be unacceptable to change core policy positions because opinion polls suggest that it would convince more people to vote for the party.
10 A party that decides to revise its policies and programmes should first and foremost listen to, and discuss with, its own members and activists.
11 As a Member of Parliament it is my duty to follow my own ideas and opinions when voting in Parliament.
12 As a Member of Parliament it is my duty to follow the official party line when voting in Parliament.
13 As a Member of Parliament it is my duty to follow my voters' opinions when voting in Parliament.
14 The most important thing during an election campaign is to persuade people to want what the party has to offer.
15 The most important thing during an election campaign is to show people that the party offers what people want.

Section B asked respondents to rate the extent to which they thought the following aspects were important when people decided which party to vote for:

1   the trustworthiness of the party leader;
2   party identification;
3   the party's core values;
4   the party's performance since the last election;
5   the party's promises for the future;
6   the issues and policy positions that the party emphasizes;
7   the candidates;
8   the party's image;
9   the party's ability to fulfil its promises.

Section C asked respondents to rate the extent to which they thought the following aspects were important in determining whether a party does well in an election:

1 effective identification of target groups;
2 the use of opinion polls;
3 the use of focus groups;
4 the news media coverage;
5 posters and ads;
6 direct and addressed mail;
7 telemarketing;
8 knock-on-the-door activities;
9 the party leader;
10 the individual candidates;
11 the party's issue positions;
12 the party's ideologies;
13 how long ahead of election day a party starts its campaign;
14 the organisation of the campaign headquarters;
15 the party's website;
16 access to, and use of, voter databases;
17 the use of campaign consultants;
18 the use of attack strategies to undermine opponents;
19 effective defence strategies against opponents' attacks.

Source: Strömbäck (2009)

Discussion point 3.14

Discuss how strategy or market-orientation can best be measured.

The most frequently cited benefit of political marketing is that it encourages politicians to listen to voter demands and helps them understand the market more effectively. If both major parties become market-oriented, the level of political debate and policy solutions could be significantly raised. A market-orientation that places voter satisfaction at its heart elevates the citizens' position in the political process.

Nevertheless, there are a number of potential losses. The Blair/UK New Labour case suggests political marketing results in a loss of ideology and hinders the development of fresh new thinking on policy. There were concerns that the Clinton presidency in the 1990s left the US Democrats with a vacuum of policies, lacking a clear vision or ideology. Another dilemma involves more complex, inter-governmental, international issues, such as war. Blair's market-driven approach made it difficult for him when he began to take a leadership position on the Iraq war. Market-oriented politics may undermine leadership, preventing politicians from listening and then making the best decision for the country. Creating pledges on credit cards creates the perception politics can be delivered or changed in a short period.

Even though a market-orientation in business, let alone politics, is not just about following what public opinion polls say, nor is it about ditching all ideology, this is clearly a contentious area for debate. Full discussion about the democratic implications of every aspect of political marketing will be presented in the last chapter of the book, but, for now, as well as learning what strategy and market-oriented politics are about, an understanding that they raise important normative questions is important.

Debate 3.1

Proposition: market-oriented parties are good for democracy.

Summary

An important part of political marketing is the way parties and candidates think and behave in relation to the electorate. This informs every other aspect of marketing, which will be explored in subsequent chapters. Strategic marketing can also be used in government, as Chapter 8 will show; and the market-oriented party framework, consultants and other aspects of political marketing strategy have also been used comparatively, as Chapter 9 will explore. However, before parties, candidates and governments can respond to what the market demands and how it behaves, they need to know what that is. The next chapter will look at how political elites seek to understand the market.

ASSESSED WORK

Essays
1   Consider the previous elections in your country. To what extent did the parties that won power follow the market-oriented party model?
2   Discuss the effectiveness and limitations of the Lees-Marshment model of market-, sales- and product-oriented parties as a means of explaining modern party behaviour.
3   Is the current . . . Party product-, sales- or market-oriented?
4   Critically evaluate whether the . . . Party lost the . . . election because of their advertising strategy or their product.
5   Critically explore the effectiveness of the sales-oriented approach to political marketing, utilising case studies to support your answer.
6   Explore and evaluate the lessons that today's political leaders might learn from how Tony Blair and Bill Clinton used political marketing strategy.
7   In what ways might the political marketing strategy used by smaller parties differ from that of major parties?
8   To what extent did the Republican and/or Democrat presidential candidates for the 2008 US presidential election follow the US market-oriented president model?
9   To what extent have recent US presidential candidates followed Newman's model of political marketing?

Practical/applied
1   Apply the Lees-Marshment MOP or Ormrod model to a current political party.
2   Apply the Newman, Kotzaivazoglou, or Gorbounova and Lees-Marshment models to a candidate.
3   Use the O'Cass survey questions or Strömbäck's survey and do your own research on party members, politicians or party staff.

4   Interview party strategists and see if their views coincide with the literature on strategy.
5   Political marketing plan: write an original, present-day political marketing plan that assesses how well a party uses marketing strategy, and recommendations for how it can improve its use of marketing, to achieve its goals or objectives. Write as if you were a marketing consultant, planning how it can use marketing over the years leading up to the next election. The plan is not a traditional essay and can therefore be written in report style, although it should include references to academic literature, where relevant, and primary sources as usual, even if it is an Internet site or your own interview.

Case study 3.1 The Lees-Marshment POP–SOP–MOP model applied to UK Labour, 1983–97   *Jennifer Lees-Marshment*

This case illustrates how Labour moved from product- to sales- to market-oriented between 1983 and 1997, by noting key behaviour for each stage suitable to each orientation.

Labour in 1983: a product-oriented party

In 1983, Labour was largely product-oriented. Its product was created within the Labour Party, and debates about how to behave focused internally. The leader, Michael Foot, was chosen to encourage party unity, rather than reflect voter opinion. Constitutional changes promoted dominance of the left. Policy was changed to suit left-wing, not majority voters', views, and the manifesto was full of unpopular promises. Communication was traditional, with Labour arguing its point of view, and the Labour Party telling its advertisers to put their argument in the campaign. Labour lost and therefore did not get a chance to deliver.

Labour in 1987: a sales-oriented party

The Labour leader, Neil Kinnock, was elected in 1987 to unite the Party and appease its left wing, but lacked wider electoral appeal. A number of other product weaknesses were apparent, such as the Labour membership (or sections of it, such as the militant and the trade unions) being unpopular, and the Party conference/hard left continued to argue against changing policy to suit voters' views. There were unpopular policies in the manifesto, e.g. unilateralist policy on defence, expansion of state ownership and intervention in the economy; the Party had a poor image on economic management, and unions remained in the manifesto.

However, staff with professional expertise, such as Peter Mandelson, were recruited to run communications; an advertising agency was appointed; and a new symbol was adopted: a red rose. The Party began to focus on communication, and market intelligence was conducted to inform this. Labour appointed MORI early on to conduct surveys, polling and a panel study, especially of target groups and marginal seats, to inform campaign design. Focus-group research was conducted by Philip Gould. This revealed weaknesses in product; and the results fed into the design of communication and campaigning.

Labour conducted an audit of the existing communication operation. The whole system was consequently reorganised; more power was given to the Director of Campaigns and Communication; a Shadow Communications Agency was created; and more use was made of mass media. The new Party symbol helped to downplay the Party's reputation for only representing the working class. The Party conference was more stage-managed, and several mini-campaigns were run in years running up to the election. The campaign was well planned in advance and effectively organised; good use was made of photo opportunities; the timing of events was determined to suit television news deadlines; and an effective election broadcast focused on the leader. However, Labour still lost, with polls indicating public dissatisfaction with the product, so they did not get a chance to deliver.

Labour in 1997: a market-oriented party

In the run up to the 1997 election, Labour conducted extensive market intelligence that informed the development of the product. Post-election analysis was conducted, focusing on traditional Labour supporters who had voted Tory. Internal discussion occurred through policy groups, NOP conducted surveys and polls, and focus groups were run. Proposed policies were even pre-tested.

In terms of product design, the new leader, Tony Blair, had fewer links to the traditional Labour movement, was pro-change, a strong leader and popular with voters. MPs and candidates were under strict leadership. Individual members' rights were increased, and the Party distanced itself from trade unions, which were unpopular with the public. Increased use was made of staff with professional expertise, especially those closest to the leader, such as Alastair Campbell. Clause IV of the constitution was altered to remove unpopular commitment to state ownership, and the slogan *New Labour, New Britain* was adopted. Specific pledges were made in issue-areas most important to voters, e.g. education, health service, general commitment to fiscal prudence, low government spending and income tax. A mini-manifesto was launched a year before election to pre-test policies; the final manifesto was popular.

Product adjustment was also carried out. Specific pledges for delivery were short and limited and included details on how they would be achieved, e.g. cutting waiting lists in the NHS by reducing money spent on bureaucracy. Internal members were consulted on changes to Clause IV and balloted on the manifesto. Past weaknesses were removed, e.g. the link with trade unions was reduced, and reassurances were made on income tax and economic management; Conservative weaknesses were exploited. 'Middle England' voters were targeted, especially in communications. A strong leadership style ensured high party unity; the public accepted the Party had changed, and so implementation was largely successful.

Communications were tightly run from a new centre in Millbank Tower. A strategy to gain a positive relationship with the press was pursued, and the product was well communicated to voters before the campaign even started. The campaign was tightly run and well planned; there was good communication within the party organisation; and the message that Labour had changed was repeated. Campaigning on the ground focused on target seats needed to win. Posters reinforced the Party's pledges.

Labour won the 1997 election with 419 seats and 43 per cent of the popular vote; membership also rose. Once in government, the Party focused on delivery, issued annual reports on its performance, and delivered on constitutional reform, although there was voter dissatisfaction with the quality of public services.

Case study 3.2 The re-launch of the APRA Party in a new political era in Peru *Pedro Patrón Galindo*

This case study explores how the Peruvian central leftist party APRA (People's Revolutionary American Alliance) utilised political marketing to reorganise and relaunch after losing popularity in the late 1980s during its term in office and while support for independent candidates rose during an 'anti-politics' decade in Peru. Peru lacks a solid political system, and the Peruvian democracy is weak: appreciation of democracy in Peru is dependent upon governmental performance and the 'consumerist' nature of citizens (Tanaka and Zárate 2002). Nevertheless, the APRA has successfully utilised many aspects of the Lees-Marshment MOP model, adapting it to suit the Peruvian political context and taking advantage of the collapse of the Fujimori regime in 2000, which left an open market free of partisanship and the usual constrictions more established democracies face.

APRA's market-oriented practices

The APRA performance utilised various means of data collection among different voter segments, separated by geography, gender, age etc. The leader, Alan García, boasted about the APRA's use of marketing research methods, considering it as a positive development that the party gathered data on people's expectations. In terms of the product, APRA adapted the Haya de la Torre doctrine, which had an impact on the 'conservatives' in the party who recognised that little of the core discourse had changed, and the 'liberals', who wished to see a more up-to-date programme.

Regarding competition analysis, APRA responded to the position of other parties on the left who had failed to represent the poorest in Peruvian society. APRA filled this gap in the marketplace, ideologically positioning itself on the centre-left, as a reflection of the specific circumstances of the political situation. They did so carefully, without being too radical or extremist, because they were also seeking support from key sectors, such as the private sector and international organisations and corporations.

In terms of implementation, the whole organisation of the party was changed to adapt it to the new state structure. The *Comité Ejecutivo Nacional – CEN* (National Executive Committee) of the party was divided into several national secretariats, specialising in key subjects such as education, public health, labour, agriculture, international relations, etc. There was also a new School of Training in Municipal Issues. These branches were in charge of producing updated documentation for policy-making and preparing party members for lobbying, negotiation and governing.

The communication aspect of the construction of the political spectacle was carried out using a sophisticated marketing strategy. Alan García's new image as a 'mature' and 'centred' politician was promoted to voters and party members. This responded to public concerns about García and the APRA: there was a degree of anti-APRA sentiment among a significant proportion of the population, combined with negative perceptions of when García was president of the government between 1985 and 1990. The approach was successful: the Party and García won power in 2006.

Lessons for political marketing

Marketing can clearly be used in new democracies, despite unstable political conditions and culture. APRA displayed significant adaptability and responsiveness overall to changed conditions in Peru. The interpretation of Marxism is based on Hegelian dialectics that allows constant negation, and adaptation to different realities. This is key to understanding the way in which the APRA evolved ideologically and strategically in order to achieve power. The transition from 'state-centric' politics to 'market-centric' politics in Peru, through the changes introduced in the 1990s, also reconfigured the organisation of labour, unions, social movements and political participation. There was a debate between the different social segments in which the role of the mass media was crucial, and this opened up new forms of participation and interaction with power (Tanaka and Zárate 1998: 245). Alan García took advantage of this by linking APRA with new and current organisations in the Peruvian society of the twenty-first century. A market-oriented organisation has as its goal the satisfaction of the user. It tries to understand those whom it intends to serve and to deliver a product that reflects their needs and wishes. It is willing to change its behaviour in order to obtain more support: the APRA followed this model.

Another key issue is what Johansen (2002) discusses regarding the voters' expectations and needs. Customers do not always know what their real needs are, cannot verbalise their needs, can articulate their needs only in terms of the familiar, and cannot predict how their needs will be changed by interaction with society (Johansen 2002: 19). This is the fundamental role of political parties. APRA fulfilled this role by reconnecting with social, political and economic institutions in Peru and conducting market research, but also by adjusting its product design according to long-standing ideological constraints, such as the lack of legitimacy of leftist parties in Peru.

Finally, the use of political marketing might enhance democracy in Peru, through political participation. However, economically speaking, in a country where people's attitude toward democracy depends upon their life standards, the use of political marketing might easily become a further cause of division and exclusion, as not all the parties and political movements would be able to use political marketing techniques. In the end, the usefulness of such a model will depend upon the practicability of applying them to the specific characteristics of the country. Alternatively, we may see Peruvian political parties take advantage of new means for political participation and economic development. It is a great challenge, at the heart of which is political marketing.

Sources and further reading

Barnechea, Alfredo (2001). *La república embrujada*. Lima: Editorial Nuevo Siglo.

Johansen, Helene P.M. (2002). 'Political marketing: more than persuasive techniques. An organisational perspective. Paper for the 2002 Political Marketing Conference. University of Aberdeen, 19–21 September 2002.

Meléndez Guerrero, Carlos. (2003). '¿Adiós a los outsiders?' *Revista Quehacer*. 140. Fundación Desco, Lima. March–April, available online at www.desco.org.pe/qh/qh140cm.htm (accessed November 2007).

Partido Aprista Peruano (APRA Party's Official Web Page). www.apra.org.pe (accessed November 2007).

Tanaka Gondo, Martín and Patricia Zárate Ardela (1998). *Los espejismos de la democracia. El colapso del sistema de partidos en el Perú*. Lima: Instituto de Estudios Peruanos.

——— and ——— (2002) *Valores democráticos y participación ciudadana en el Perú 1998 – 2001*, Lima: Instituto de Estudios Peruanos.

Case study 3.3 Principle versus patronage: the Lees-Marshment method and political marketing in Japan

Bryce Wakefield

Japan is often overlooked in surveys of political behaviour in liberal democracies. To some, Japanese democracy appears 'unique' or 'remote' from the western experience and thus provides little basis for comparison with Northern American and European nations, which are more frequently the subjects of comparative analysis. This is unfortunate, as Japan can provide a 'testing ground' for theories that should apply to all liberal democracies. The Lees-Marshment model of political marketing is one theory that does hold its validity when transferred to a Japanese context. Indeed, the model – with a Japanese twist – almost perfectly reflects Japan's democratic experience throughout most of the post-war period. During this time, moderates within the Liberal Democratic Party (LDP) adopted market-oriented strategies to secure victory after victory, while product-oriented parties on the left languished in the polls.

The post-war system

Two issues dominated dialogue between left-wing parties and the public during the post-war period: (1) opposition to a security treaty negotiated with the United States that saw American forces based on Japanese soil; and (2) support for the post-war constitution that banned the use of force as an instrument of foreign policy.

The Socialist Party of Japan (SPJ) sought to persuade voters to support their policy using a top-down communication strategy, claiming 'the authority *as professional politicians* to control and direct the organization and ideological content of the movement against' the security treaty (Sasaki-Uemura 2002), through associated elites in the media, unions and academia. The party focused on principle, but at the expense of popular support. They did, however, succeed in winning enough votes to deny the LDP the two-thirds majority necessary for constitutional revision. SPJ members held the 'product' to be more important than winning elections and continued with a product-oriented approach, but this lost them a considerable share of the vote, and they collapsed altogether in the early 1990s.

In contrast, however, the LDP understood the importance of conducting market intelligence, designing and adjusting its policies accordingly before implementation, and communicating its policy messages to potential voters. In response to strict election regulations, LDP candidates developed and nurtured *kōenkai* – private support organisations affiliated with individual candidates rather than the party. *Kōenkai* engaged in campaign activities, such as door-knocking and distributing leaflets, that were illegal for volunteers acting on behalf of the party. *Kōenkai* also helped provide market intelligence, their broad membership constantly providing candidates with a source of information about voter preferences. Communication between the candidates and the public was a continuous process rather than the differentiated step in the MOP model, but the way candidates and the public interacted within the *kōenkai* reflected all elements contained in the market-oriented model.

Because contributions to *kōenkai* were not included in official political fund totals, they provided an important, unofficial revenue source for candidates' campaigns. As LDP representatives came to rely on these funds, they became beholden to private interests at the local level. This resulted in a system where LDP candidates would use their influence in Tokyo to secure lucrative public construction projects. As concrete flowed to LDP districts, loyal voters were rewarded with jobs, and local businesses that had contributed to the LDP were rewarded with contracts. Public works projects were often superfluous, but the employment that they provided ensured voter satisfaction. Post-war development thus continued apace, and the system ensured that LDP policy was highly region-specific. At a national level, meanwhile, the party emphasised the economic gains felt by the voter. General elections almost became a matter of course as the voters responded positively to the economic inducements offered by LDP candidates. In effect, this made the LDP market-oriented at local levels.

Problems in government

This Japanese-style use of the MOP concept was not without its problem. The system was contingent on delivery of promises at the local level. During the economically leaner times of the 1990s, the corruption that arose from close working relationships between the government and business interests eroded public faith in the LDP at the very time that the central government in Tokyo was unable to 'buy' the public's favour with more public works projects. In 1993, the LDP fell from power, to be replaced by an unwieldy coalition of opposition parties, including the SPJ.

The coalition government made sweeping changes to the electoral law, including legal restrictions on private contributions made to *kōenkai*. However, it also contained too many competing interests and collapsed only eight months after gaining power, leading the SPJ to negotiate another coalition deal with its old rival, the LDP, even dropping long-standing policies, including opposition to the security treaty with the US. Nevertheless, this responsiveness came too late, and instead the SPJ's change now lost it support from its core voters and captured only 2.2 per cent of the vote in 1996.

Meanwhile, the LDP hung onto power throughout the 1990s, forming coalitions of convenience in order to stay in power. Its responsiveness declined as traditional LDP conservatives proved unable to develop a response to voters' demands for economic reform. However, new leaders appeared within the LDP, advocating market reforms. As prime minister from 2001 to 2006, Jun'ichiro Koizumi's willingness to challenge entrenched elites catered to a public desperate for leadership after a decade of economic stagnation and sclerotic political management. To prove that he was a man of the people, Koizumi selected popular candidates and had a public relations firm set up town meetings to consult with the public on government policy. It was later revealed that these meetings were stacked with government supporters, but they at least provided the image of an administration attempting to communicate with its voters. Finally, Koizumi swept much of the remaining old guard from the party in the 2005 election by withdrawing LDP support for candidates who refused to endorse his agenda. Because Koizumi claimed to be adopting a market-oriented party approach that involved listening and responding directly to the public, he was returned in 2005 with one of the largest political lower house majorities in Japan's post-war history.

Koizumi's term showed that the Japanese public respond to the market-oriented approach. The LDP now faces competition to be market-oriented: a relatively new opposition party, the Democratic Party of Japan (DPJ), began to win votes by proposing policies aimed at solving the everyday problems of the Japanese populace and now has a fair chance of replacing the LDP as the governing party. Japan now resembles a 'traditional' two-party system, and it is possible that in the future we will see power alternate between the LDP and the DPJ, as both parties adapt their respective, market-oriented strategies.

Sources and further reading

Sasaki-Uemura, Wesley (2002).'Competing publics: citizens' groups, mass media, and the state in the 1960s'. *Positions*, 10:1 (Spring).

Case study 3.4 The strategy of the British Liberal Democrats

Stephen Barber

First-past-the-post electoral systems tend to encourage dominance by just two major parties. However, the strategic decisions taken by British Liberal Democrats made them serious contenders, despite difficult market conditions when the electoral system produced landslide victories for the Labour party under Tony Blair. Strategy involves setting realistic objectives, given available resources, and putting in place a plan to achieve those aims. Parties are more sophisticated than existing simply to win and hold office in the Downsian, rational, sense. In the Liberal Democrats' case, their goal has been to pursue policies derived from the ideology of liberalism, rooted in the old Liberal party, the nineteenth-century liberalism of Gladstone and the twentieth-century liberalism of Lloyd George.

The current form of the party was formed in 1988 from different party factions. With support falling to 2 per cent in opinion polls at one point, new leader Paddy Ashdown recognised the need for a new and bold electoral strategy. The strategy used in the next election, 1992, was just to survive. The Liberal Democrats fought the campaign from an almost fictitious strategic position of 'equidistance' between the other two parties. However, after the election and a fourth Conservative victory, Ashdown challenged his party to accept co-operation with Labour to defeat the Conservatives. It was not until May 1995, when, significantly, the fresh-faced Tony Blair had been installed as Labour leader, that equidistance was formally abandoned, and Blair and Ashdown secretly created a plan to cement their two parties' strategies into forming a formidable, anti-Conservative force. The strategy was both office-seeking and policy-pursuing. A shared agenda – most notably in respect of constitutional reforms – was part of discussions. The strategy was a success. Perhaps too much of a success. Without substantially increasing their share of the vote, the Lib Dems doubled their seats in the House of Commons in 1997, while Labour was returned with a landslide so large that it precluded formal coalition. A new strategy was required for the new parliament.

Having brought 'the project' to electoral fruition, the party needed to adapt to the new situation of a powerful new Labour government, with which, initially at least, it shared an agenda, and a demoralised and defeated Tory party, in opposition for the first time in eighteen years. The strategic answer was only ever going to be short lived. With coalition ruled out and Blair reneging on his commitment to electoral reform, the Liberal Democrats joined a governmental cabinet committee, policy pursuing in its influence on the government. The party's strategic position was given a name: *constructive opposition*.

This strategy was again shifted as the inevitable happened: policy differences began to emerge between Labour in government and the Lib Dems in opposition. The joint cabinet committee was suspended indefinitely under a new party leader, Charles Kennedy. Given that the Tories remained in disarray, the new strategy became known as *effective opposition*. Events, which could not have been foreseen, showed the strategy to have been sound. Had the Liberal Democrats not existed in British politics, it would have been necessary to invent them. With consensus between Labour and the Tories, Prime Minister Blair took Britain into an unpopular war in Iraq. The Lib Dems alone among the leading national parties opposed the government. It was a policy-pursuing strategy built on the bedrock of principle, and they gained more support in the 2001 election.

However, since 2005, the partial rejuvenation of the Conservatives under David Cameron and the challenges of a new Labour prime minister in Gordon Brown summoned a return to traditional, three-party politics. The strategic question that now needed answering by Kennedy's successors Ming Campbell and then Nick Clegg was 'what are the Liberal Democrats for?'.

The answer seemed to lie in the substance of its philosophy and the electoral possibilities of a hung parliament. For while parties coalesced around the linear centre of left–right British politics, there remained a need for a libertarian voice to counter what had become an authoritarian consensus, bidding war even, between Labour and the Conservatives, seen as a threat to civil liberties. Meanwhile, the removal of Iraq as an issue meant that a major obstacle was removed in terms of renewed relations with Labour.

Lessons for political marketing

Strategy always needs to be changing to suit different circumstances. The key difference between the strategies of a party and that of, say, a pressure group is that its objectives are not simply met. It is a journey rather than a destination.

FURTHER READING

Baines, Paul and Richard Lynch (2005). 'Guest editorial: the context, content and process of political marketing strategy'. *Journal of Political Marketing*, 4(2/3): 1–18.

Barber, Stephen (2005). *Political Strategy: Modern Politics in Contemporary Britain*. Liverpool: Liverpool Academic Press.

Butler, Patrick and Neil Collins (1996). 'Strategic analysis in political markets'. *European Journal of Marketing*, 30(10–11): 32–44.

—— and —— (1999). 'A conceptual framework for political marketing'. In Bruce I. Newman (ed.), *Handbook of Political Marketing*. Thousand Oaks, CA: Sage Publications.

Coleman, Stephen (2007). 'Review'. *Parliamentary Affairs*, 60(1): 180–6.

Collins, Neil and Patrick Butler (2002). 'Considerations on market analysis for political parties'. In Nicholas O'Shaughnessy and Stephan Hennenberg (eds), *The Idea of Political Marketing*. London: Praeger.

Corner, John (2005). 'Review of the political marketing revolution'. *Parliamentary Affairs*, 58(2): 443–91.

Downs, Anthony (1957). *An Economic Theory of Democracy*. New York: Harper.

Gould, Philip (2002). 'Labour strategy'. In J. Bartle, S. Atkinson and R. Mortimore (eds), *Political Communications: The General Election Campaign of 2001*. London: Frank Cass.

Kotler, Philip and Sidney J. Levy (1969). 'Broadening the concept of marketing'. *Journal of Marketing*, 33(1): 10–15.

Lees-Marshment, Jennifer (2001a, 2008). *Political Marketing and British Political Parties: The Party's Just Begun* (1st and 2nd edns). Manchester and New York: Manchester University Press.

—— (2001b). 'The marriage of politics and marketing'. *Political Studies*, 49(4): 692–713.

—— (2001c). 'The product, sales and market-oriented party: how Labour learnt to market the product, not just the presentation'. *European Journal of Marketing*, 35(9/10): 1074–84.

—— (2005). 'The marketing campaign: the British General Election of 2005'. *Journal of Marketing Management*, 21(9/10): 1151–60.

Lilleker, Darren and Jennifer Lees-Marshment (eds) (2005). *Political Marketing: A Comparative Perspective*. Manchester: Manchester University Press.

——, Nigel A. Jackson and Richard Scullion (2006). *The Marketing of Political Parties: Political Marketing at the British 2005 General Election*. Manchester: Manchester University Press.

Lindholm, Mikael R. and Anette Prehn (2007). 'Strategy and politics: the example of Denmark'. In Thomes Fischer, Gregor Peter Scmitz and Michael Seberich (eds), *The Strategy of Politics: Results of a Comparative Study*. Butersloh: Verlag Bertelsmann Stiftung.

Marland, Alex (2003). 'Marketing political soap: a political marketing view of selling candidates like soap, of electioneering as a ritual, and of electoral military analogies'. *Journal of Public Affairs*, 3(2): 103.

Mochrie, Robbie (2003). 'Niche marketing as an entry strategy: formation and growth of the Scottish Socialist Party'. Paper presented at the PSA Annual Conference, University of Leicester, 15–17 April 2003.

Newman, Bruce I. (1994). *The Marketing of the President: Political Marketing as Campaign Strategy.* Thousand Oaks, CA: Sage.

—— (1999). *The Mass Marketing of Politics: Democracy in an Age of Manufactured Images.* Beverley Hills, CA: Sage Publications.

O'Cass, Aron (1996). 'Political marketing and the marketing concept'. *European Journal of Marketing,* 30(10/11): 45–61.

—— (2001). 'The internal-external marketing orientation of a political party: social implications of political party marketing orientation'. *Journal of Public Affairs*, 1(2): 136–52.

Ormrod, Robert P. (2005a). 'A conceptual model of political market orientation'. *Journal of Non-Profit and Public Sector Marketing,* 14(1/2): 47–64.

—— (2005b). 'A conceptual model of political market orientation'. In Walter Wymer and Jennifer Lees-Marshment (eds), *Current Issues in Political Marketing.* Binghamton, NY: Haworth Press.

—— (2006). 'A critique of the Lees-Marshment market-oriented party model'. *Politics*, 26(2) (May): 110–18.

—— (2007). 'Political market orientation and its commercial cousin: close family or distant relatives?'. *Journal of Political Marketing*, 6(2/3): 69–90.

—— and Stephan C. Henneberg (2006). 'Different facets of market orientation: a comparative exploratory analysis of party manifestos in Britain and Germany'. 3rd International Conference on Political Marketing, 5 April 2006.

Robinson, Claire E. (2006). 'Advertising and the market orientation of political parties contesting the 1999 and 2002 New Zealand General Election campaigns'. Ph.D. thesis, Massey University, Palmerston North, New Zealand.

—— (2007). 'Images of the 2005 campaign'. In Stephen Levin and Nigel S. Roberts (eds), *The Baubles of Office: The New Zealand General Election of 2005.* Wellington, New Zealand: Victoria University Press.

Savigny, Heather (2007). 'Focus groups and political marketing: science and democracy as axiomatic?'. *British Journal of Politics and International Relations*, 9: 122–37.

Smith, Gareth (2006). 'Competitive analysis, structure and strategy in politics: a critical approach'. *Journal of Public Affairs*, 6(1): 4–14.

Strömbäck, Jesper (2009). 'A framework for comparing political market-orientation'. In Jennifer Lees-Marshment, Jesper Strömbäck and Chris Rudd (eds), *Global Political Marketing.* London: Routledge.

Worcester, Robert and Roger Mortimore (2005). 'Political triangulation: measuring and reporting the key aspects of party and leader standing before and during elections'. *Journal of Political Marketing*, 4(2/3): 45–72.

Wring, Dominic (1997). 'Reconciling marketing with political science: theories of political marketing'. *Proceedings of the 1997 Academy of Marketing Conference.* Manchester: Manchester Metropolitan University.

—— (2002). 'Conceptualising political marketing: a framework for election-campaign analysis'. In N.J. O'Shaughnessy and S. Henneberg (eds), *The Idea of Political Marketing.* New York: Praeger.

4 Understanding the market

Market intelligence, consultation and participation

Market intelligence is the key to political marketing. Without knowing what the market is, how it behaves and what it wants, politicians cannot make informed decisions about how to respond to it. This chapter will examine how candidates, political parties and governments use market intelligence, including how the market is identified, segmented and profiled; understanding market demands; policy and opposition research; and intelligence as a form of consultation. It will also discuss practical and democratic issues with conducting market intelligence.

Identifying, segmenting and targeting the market

In politics, segmentation is used to break up the heterogeneous mass electoral market into smaller sections that have something in common; this helps ensure resources are allocated where they can have most effect. Strategists can use segmentation to identify a number of groups to which a candidate or party can appeal to win power (Baines 1999: 405, Smith and Hirst 2001). Newman (1999: 263) argued that Bill Clinton's presidential re-election bid in 1996 succeeded by creating a message that appealed to the desire for an American dream across four segments of voters:

1   rational voters, driven by their American dream expectations;
2   emotional voters, driven by the feelings aroused by their desire to achieve the American dream;
3   social voters, driven by the association of different groups of people and their ability to achieve the American dream;
4   situational voters, driven by situations that might influence their decision to switch to another candidate.

In the UK 1997 election, Labour targeted Middle England, with policies and communications designed to gain their support. Even as far back as the late 1970s saw Margaret Thatcher, the UK's first female prime minister, gain support from a new segment – the skilled working class – through a policy enabling tenants to buy their council/state house. Segmentation is also used to try to make sure a candidate's own supporters actually turn out to vote. Get out the vote (GOTV) activities are extremely important when elections are close. They can help with fundraising and identify grass-roots supporters, and members, candidates and parties can build a long-term relationship.

Segmentation methods

How such voter groups are identified depends on the segmentation method used. Segmentation tries to identify common characteristics: see Table 4.1.

The importance and value of different methods of segmentation vary over time and between countries. In the new democracy of Ghana in Africa, for example, ethnicity and religion are important segmentation methods to use; Alabi and Alabi (2007) discussed how this was reflected in parties' choice of leadership and images.

Furthermore, within each segmentation group, further division can occur. An increasingly important group within democracy is age; within this is the elderly or pensioner group; and then within this, as Davidson (2005: 1181) noted, 'someone in their 70s could be working full time and be fit and healthy, another person in their early 50s could be living with a long term chronic condition and forced out of the labour market.' Further division is needed; in the 2005 election, UK Labour identified different groups such as 'low income elderly', 'childfree serenity' and 'small town seniors'. Categorisation is therefore increasingly complex. Marketing consultants, such as Mark Penn of PSB associates in the US, who advised Bill Clinton in office and Hillary Clinton in her primary campaign in 2007–8, segment the market into micro-targets. Penn (2007) suggests various new market segments under different categories: see Box 4.1.

Data gathering on voters is necessary to enable such groups to be identified and can involve a complicated statistical process. Software such as Voter Vault and Mosaic offers tailor-made programmes to parties: for example, the Republican National Party in the US has its own, password-only system at https://votervault.com/vv/, while the Democrats use Data Mart, called Demzilla. The Conservative Party of Canada uses the Constituent Information Management System (CIMS).

Targeting

Once data have been gathered and processed, and different groups have been identified, parties or candidates then choose which ones to focus on, or *target*. To spend often-restricted

Table 4.1 Segmentation options

Geographic	• where people live, with differences between countries and regions within that country;
	• this can affect their choices and opinions;
	• analysis suggest that in some cases people choose to live in a particular area because they hold similar socio-economic, cultural and lifestyle characteristics;
	• is easy to measure and provides easy information.
Behavourial	• segments based on actions of individual, e.g. loyalty to the party or candidate, or what benefit they seek from the product.
Demographic	• age, family nature, social class, income, etc.
Psychographic	• considers lifestyle characteristics, e.g. leisure choices, tastes, readership of newspapers/magazines;
	• identifies common values and segments customers according to their beliefs, attitudes, activities, interests and opinions;
	• more valuable because considers individual's actual behaviour and lifestyle rather than inferring that from other characteristics.

Source: adapted from Bannon (2004) and Smith and Saunders (1990)

Box 4.1 Examples of Mark Penn's micro targets

1   **Work life**: working retired, extreme commuters, stay-at-home workers, wordy women, ardent amazons.
2   **Race and religion**: stained glass-ceiling breakers, pro-semites, interracial families, protestant Hispanics, moderate Muslims.
3   **Family life**: old new dads, pet parents, pampering parents, late-breaking gays, dutiful sons.
4   **Politics**: impressionable elites, swing is still king, militant illegals, Christian Zionists, newly released ex-cons.
5   **Food, drink and diet**: vegan children, a disproportionate burden, starving for life, caffeine crazies.
6   **Lifestyle**: long attention spanners, neglected dads, native language speakers, unisexuals.
7   **Money and class**: second-home buyers, modern Mary Poppinses, shy millionaires, bourgeois and bankrupt, non-profiteers.
8   **Education**: smart child left behind, America's home schooled, college dropouts, numbers junkies.

Source: Penn (2007)

campaign funds communicating with every voter is less effective than focusing on particular segments. Some people will never support a candidate; some always will. The former can be ignored, while focus can be targeted on those who don't yet, but might with targeted products or communication.

Who to target?

There are a number of ways in which politicians decide who to target. The most basic is to identify:

*   traditional supporters who, if they vote, will support the candidate/party but need to be persuaded to get out and actually vote; and
*   floating voters, defined by Baines (1999: 404) as: 'a voter who is unsure for which candidate or party to vote', as they can have greater effect on the election outcome.

A more complex method is that suggested by Bannon (2004), who argues that different levels of suitability can be taken into account:

1   Primary targets: attractive segment(s) that are responsive to stimuli.
2   Secondary targets: less attractive segment(s) that are responsive to stimuli.
3   Relationship building: attractive segment(s) that are less responsive to stimuli.
4   Wasteland segments: unattractive segment(s) that are unresponsive to stimuli.

Additional factors are potential for growth include how the competition appeals to the potential target; whether the product can be differentiated to suit the segments' demands; whether the candidate is well known or not; and ease, cost and effectiveness of access to the segment (Bannon 2004). For example, distribution of political literature is easier in urban rather than rural areas, and it is also easier and less expensive if there is an active local branch to deliver material.

In the 2005 UK election, the UK Conservatives placed voters into distinctive Voter Vault cells, indicating different potential behaviour and support for the party. Seawright (2005) noted how the party issued a training video to constituencies and advised them to contact those in six and eight cells, which were Conservative voters who were fairly likely to vote, and undecided voters who were most likely to vote because they could make more difference to the election outcome. Indeed, all of the three main parties in the UK identified key target groups: see Table 4.2.

Such groups were then targeted with direct mail and telemarketing (see Savigny 2005).

What strategy to use with the target?

Segmentation also informs what is done with each target group to maximise effectiveness. Different strategies can be used for each target group, as noted by Newman and Sheth (1987), depending on the nature of support or opposition:

- *Reinforcement strategy*: voters who already support the candidate for the right reasons, so focus a campaign on reinforcing their choice by arguing it is the right one.
- *Rationalisation strategy*: voters who already support the candidate but for the wrong reasons, so the campaign tries to connect with them in a different way.
- *Inducement strategy*: voters who support the opposition for the right reasons, so the strategy is to show them that the candidate offers them what voters want as well as something extra; rather than trying to change what voters want, the campaign explains why the candidate or party offers a superior product to the competition.
- *Confrontation strategy*: where voters support the opposition for the wrong reasons, such as they're the best option out of what is available, or are voting tactically.

Targeting is arguably even more important for smaller parties, as it helps conserve precious resources and deploy them more effectively. The UK Liberal Democrats increased their power in parliament by focusing on target areas, so that campaign efforts were placed in areas that had a chance of winning, instead of being spread evenly through the country, with less overall effect. They also sought to build up geographical clusters, with seats next to each other, which, as Russell and Fieldhouse (2005: 210) noted, enabled grass-roots supporters to work across seats if needed and helped to build up 'shared credibility from having a historical and realistic chance of winning seats in the region'.

Volunteers can be identified using segmentation according to potential levels of participation and contribution: see Table 4.3.

Segmentation informs GOTV activities and is concerned with giving loyal supporters a reason to get out and vote. For example, in the 2005 election in New Zealand, the Labour Party, realising the election result was going to be close, sent direct mail shots to voters who lived in South Auckland in state/council homes. The mail suggested that a victory for the opposition, the National Party, would result in state homes being sold and the tenants having to find an alternative home, so it was designed in the form of an eviction notice. Turnout went up among this segment. They naturally supported Labour anyway, but the direct mail helped ensure they actually voted, helping secure an election victory. In this example, key segmentation options were about where they lived and home tenancy, but there are many variations.

Another example of how GOTV was used and how it helped secure victory in a close race is San Francisco's 2004 mayoral election in the US, where the candidate, Gavin Newsom, lost on election day but won on election night, because he received 20,000 more

Table 4.2 Target groups identified by UK parties in the 2005 election

Labour	Conservative	Liberal Democrats
Cultural leadership Educated people, many of whom work in the liberal professions, government or arts. They live mostly in areas such as Dulwich or Highgate. They like gourmet food and holiday in rural France. **Symbols of success** Professionals who work in the big city, such as lawyers, surgeons and professors. **Fledgling nurseries** Broadminded but not interested in social, environmental or political issues. **Upscaling new owners** Don't believe in consumption as means of expression. Busy people, so convenience is the watchword. **Affluent blue collar** Older manual workers living in decent-sized semi-detached homes with gardens and garages. Use retail loyalty cards. Politically once solid Labour, flirted with Tories under Thatcher but now New Labour. **Coronation St** Found in northern maritime and industrial regions. Represent good market for mass brands. Tins and packets preferred over fresh ingredients. **Rustbelt resilience** Found in traditional mining communities, gardens well tended, with newly painted house exteriors. Few read books ortravel to offbeat holiday locations. They eat fish and chips. Solidly Labour.	**Corporate chieftains** Senior business people living in large detached houses in outer metropolitan suburbia. Tend to have four-bedroom homes surrounded by trees and protected from view by laurels and rhododendrons. Little time for aesthetics; drive Lexus or BMW cars. **Burdened optimists** Modest qualifications; many have built up debts trying to emulate middle-class lifestyles. Made the Thatcher revolution. No belief in collective social responsibility. Place high value on personal freedom. Indulgence and immediate gratification sets the trend for everything, from eating the wrong food to impulse buying. **High technologists** Live along M3/M4 corridors in large modern detached homes. Plants are trimmed, not rambling. They help Conservative candidates. **Semi-rural seclusion** Live in environmentally attractive villages requiring long commutes from places such as Hampshire and Oxfordshire. Do not watch TV or videos often, but like nostalgia themes.	**Golden empty nesters** Wealthy older people living in provincial regions in 1930s houses. Lib Dems have strong challenge to Tories in this sort of neighbourhood. Support the National Trust. They are not concerned about the economy but rather with value for money. They like and admire well-known brands. **Provincial privilege** They tend to be aged in their 50s and 60s and hold jobs in institutions such as universities or hospitals. They like socially responsible brands and have switched to the Liberal Democrats. **University challengers** Mostly aged 18 to 24, in areas of provincial cities which contain halls of residence. Much less ideologically driven than previous generations, though they are respectful of the green agenda.

Source: Wintour (2005)

Table 4.3 Political marketing segmentation by social group behaviour

Segment	Behaviour	Desired outcome	Action plan
Politicians	Political representative	Competent/non-accident prone/re-electable	Strategic input and implementation
Hyper activist	Politically active	Evangelist	Involvement in decision-making process
Activist	Positive advocate	Loyalty	Maintain relationship
Supporter	Active	Vote/member/donor	Inform/nurture/develop relationship
Potential supporter/undecided	Passive	Vote	Persuade/communicate
Non-voter	Inactive	Active	Communicate importance of being an active voter
Non-supporter	Active negatively	Inactivity/inertia	Communicate/ignore/disillusion/squeeze
Opposition	Negative advocate	Neutralise	Dis-information, negative campaigning

Source: Bannon (2004)

postal votes than the opposition (see Ross 2008). This was partly owing to an advance programme to identify potential voters and target them to submit a postal vote if they weren't likely to vote on election day. Volunteers were used to ask voters to 'endorse' Gavin Newsom for mayor in a petition, which identified 24,000 supporters who were then input into a database, and those who were not registered to vote had an application delivered by a Newsom volunteer, thereby registering 5,000 new voters most likely to support the candidate.

Other registered voters who had not endorsed Gavin Newsom were called, and, without using negative communication, this produced another 25,000 identified as potential Newsom supporters, even though many of them lived in neighbourhoods that would not have previously been considered supportive of the candidate. Half of these voters were not certain to vote, and so a GOTV campaign went into gear to try to get them to vote by mail, with several phone or in-person contacts made until they registered for a postal vote. By the time of the election, the Newsom campaign had already got 8,000 votes through the post. This and other GOTV activities became even more important when there was a repeat or run-off election a month later. Ross argues that the campaign taught them several lessons:

1   You can start voter identification early, and those voters that endorse early, if you communicate with them, will stick with you.
2   Reach out to areas or communities that may not universally support you; a campaign can find pockets of support in even the most hostile areas.
3   If possible, use vote-by-mail or absentee voting and early voting to extend your GOTV efforts.
4   Use volunteers to reach the voters you can't reach through other means.

One important point to note is that, even if all candidates/parties use segmentation, obviously they can't all win, so segmentation is not a sure way to achieve victory.

Furthermore, there are democratic implications of segmentation and targeting, because parties and candidates now chase certain voters during a campaign rather than all of them, and marketing tools enable a very precise selection to take place. This means that not all voters are equal; some become more important than others, which works against the democratic principle of one man one vote, as noted by Savigny (2008), which will be discussed further in Chapter 10. Electoral commissions in different countries also try to increase turnout, but for all parties, because, as noted in Task 1.1 in Chapter 1, the failure of any individual to vote is arguably seen as a loss to democracy.

Discussion point 4.1

Discuss the effectiveness and democratic implications of segmentation. If an election were held tomorrow in your electorate/country, consider what segments might be most important and why.

Understanding market demands

Political elites also need to understand what the market wants from them. The use of market intelligence in politics has increased tremendously worldwide, in both size and the range of methods employed. A whole range of political-public organisations conduct intelligence, both formally, using outside professionals, and informally, in-house: see Task 4.1.

Formal market intelligence is divided into quantitative and qualitative research.

Task 4.1

The market intelligence industry: search for polling or research organisations you know of online and explore the work they do on websites, or use the examples below to begin with.

- PSB (Penn, Schoen and Berland associates) (US and worldwide): www.psbresearch.com/
- Gallup (global): www.gallup.com/
- Ipsos MORI (UK): www.ipsos-mori.com/
- Opinion leader (UK): www.opinionleader.co.uk/
- Opinion research (UK): www.opinionresearch.com/
- UMR: www.umr.co.nz (New Zealand) and www.umr.com.au/index.html (Australia)
- Gfk NOP: www.gfknop.com/customresearch-uk/
- ICM (UK): www.icmresearch.co.uk/
- Digi poll: www.digipoll.co.nz/main.html
- Colmar Brunton: www.colmarbrunton.co.nz/
- Neilsen (global): www.nielsen-netratings.com/
- IDC (global): www.idc.com/
- Survey USA: www.surveyusa.com/
- American research group: www.americanresearchgroup.com/
- Mason-Dixon (US): www.mason-dixon.com/public/index.cfm
- Roy Morgan research (Australia): www.roymorgan.com.au/

Quantitative research

Quantitative research produces numbers and has several characteristics:

1   It provides big numbers – surface level data – but can identify strength of opinion.
2   It uses closed questions and samples and *measures*, rather than *understands* behaviour.
3   Examples include polling; consumer panels; telephone surveys; personal interviews, both door-to-door and in the street; panel studies; and mail surveys.
4   Constraints include the potential for bias in question design, which is a big issue, and the financial cost of the research.
5   Advantages are that it provides accuracy just before an election and trends over time; it is also easy to administer, deliver data and compare results.

Quantitative research has to be designed carefully to produce accurate results. It is impossible to ask everybody in the market, because the market is too big. Instead, a sample is taken. Whereas the *population* includes all elements, units or individuals that are of interest to researchers for a specific study, a *sample* is a smaller-size population: a segment of people that will reflect or represent characteristics of an entire population (for further explanation on the methodology of polling see Moon 1999).

There are different options for the types of question asked:

1   structured (multiple choice);
2   opinion scales: very happy – happy – neutral – unhappy – very unhappy;
3   rank order: 'in your opinion rank the following . . .';
4   alternatives or paired comparisons: 'is x candidate lively or dull?'.

Quantitative polling is used in different ways at different stages during a campaign. Rademacher and Tuchfarber (1999: 203–5) argue there are three different aspects:

1   **Benchmark polls**: the earliest poll, with thorough sampling to provide a standard or baseline of voting intentions to help measure the effectiveness of the rest of the campaign. This measures aspects such as candidate recognition, standing relative to other candidates, market segments, current perceptions of the candidate and key issues that voters want addressed.
2   **Follow-up polls**: shorter polls, focusing on specific issues in a more in-depth fashion, which test reaction to the campaign.
3   **Tracking polls**: polls conducted regularly throughout the campaign, which are very short and focused on a particular aspect, such as on important issues.

Examples of political polls can be found online. The simplest polls simply ask for voting preferences, but more detailed questions give an idea of how voters perceive particular characteristics and track ongoing levels of support. For an example see Ipsos Mori's Political Monitor: see Box 4.2.

Like segmentation, market intelligence is used in many different ways. In the 2007 presidential election, the candidate Nicholas Sarkozy used a number of tools during the campaign from January to April, such as online panels to identify why voters might leave/join a particular candidate and then test their reactions to the candidate's main TV or radio appearances during the campaign. Teinturier (2008: 150–1) explains that such intelligence was used in several ways in the campaign:

Box 4.2 Ipsos Mori Political Monitor

Q1 How would you vote if there were a general election tomorrow?

Q2 Which party are you most inclined to support?

Q3 Are you satisfied or dissatisfied with the way the government is running the country?

Q4 Are you satisfied or dissatisfied with the way Mr Brown is doing his job as Prime Minister?

Q5 Are you satisfied or dissatisfied with the way Mr Cameron is doing his job as leader of the Conservative Party?

Q6 Are you satisfied or dissatisfied with the way Nick Clegg is doing his job as leader of the Liberal Democrats?

Q7 What would you say is the most important issue facing Britain today? (Spontaneous)

Q8 What do you see as other important issues facing Britain today? (Spontaneous)

Q9 Do you think that the general economic condition of the country will improve, stay the same, or get worse over the next 12 months?

In another poll they asked more specific questions of leaders such as:

- In choosing between Prime Minister Gordon Brown, Conservative leader David Cameron or Liberal Democrat leader Nick Clegg, which leader do you think:
  - best understands the problems facing Britain?
  - would be best in a crisis?
  - leads the most united team?
  - is best able to deal with the challenges of the twenty-first century?

Source: www.ipsos-mori.com/polls/2008/s080110.shtml (accessed 4 March 2008)

Task 4.2 Evaluating polls

Identify different polls used in your country. Consider aspects such as any weaknesses in their methodology and how useful they would be to politicians and their advisors.

1   to support the foundations of strategy using public opinion results;
2   to select candidates;
3   to help improve the language and create the effect of reality in political communication;
4   to identify strong public support, which would then reduce criticisms from commentators.

Another example is Vicente Fox's campaign in the 2000 Mexican election. Rottinghaus and Alberro (2005) explored how polls were used to inform the selling of the candidate at key chronological points, such as:

1   to establish whether a candidate who was not from the PRI could ever win;
2   to establish which candidate traits were the most desirable;
3   to decide on using a message of change that Fox could win support for;
4   to test the effectiveness of the ongoing campaign, including whether voters remembered the key messages;

5   to determine what was most important to voters, which was honesty, followed by reliability and good proposals. Fox connected all three in his speeches, talking of honest new faces to form a new government, declaring he was strong enough to do the job.

Polling is not confined to establishing democracies – it is also used in developing democracies (see the Abad and Ramirez (2008) study of the Philippines, for example). Nor is it confined to campaigns – polls can also be used in government and used to develop the product. Rothmayr and Hardmeier (2002: 130–1) analysed how the Swiss Federal government used polls to inform government communication. Market intelligence provided a basis for arguments in decision-making, supported existing decisions, criticised alternative proposals, informed social marketing and monitored public satisfaction with government services. More examples of using polls in product development will be explored in Chapter 5.

Qualitative research

The characteristics of qualitative research are:

*   It probes deeper: it reaches values, beliefs, attitudes and influences behind opinion formation.
*   It explores whether opinion can be changed.
*   It is used to *understand* rather than measure.
*   It is open-ended and produces narrative data.
*   Examples include focus groups; semi- or unstructured indepth interviews; projective techniques; word associations; and consumer drawings.

Focus groups are small samples of typical consumers under the direction of a group leader, who elicits their reaction to a stimulus, such as a political party. Participants have to be selected carefully and rewarded for their time, and analysis is conducted, not just of what is said, but of body language. Focus groups can be used to understand why a party has lost support, as well as to develop new strategy to regain votes in the future. Johnson (2007: 104) argues that they add 'a human dimension that cannot be matched by traditional survey research methods . . . participants are free to express themselves, to complain, and to vent their anger'.

Newman (1999: 40) notes how, in the 1988 US presidential election, George Bush's pollster, Bob Teeter, ran a focus group with voters loyal to the Democratic candidate, Michael Dukakis, and found they were critical of his position on crime, thinking he was too soft. The campaign devised a hard-hitting 'Willie Horton' advertisement that suggested Dukakis would let criminals out of jail. This also repositioned Dukakis as weak on crime and defence, so that Bush himself appeared a much safer leader (Smith 2005: 1136). After the UK Conservatives lost the 1997 election, a Channel 4 television programme 'Portillo's progress' filmed one ousted MP, Michael Portillo, travelling the country to find out why. Part of this involved a focus group run by MORI that asked participants, all former Conservative supporters, to answer the question: 'How would you describe the conservatives if you thought of them as a car?'. The answers were not particularly flattering! They included 'an old banger needing a new engine and major overhaul' and 'an old Morris minor on bricks with no wheels!'.

Focus groups can work well, but only if run appropriately. Box 4.3 has a guide as to the dos and don'ts of focus groups.

Box 4.3 Dos and don'ts of focus groups

1   **Determine your goals and objectives**. This helps the facilitator stop the group wandering off the topic. Discussion questions and follow-up points should be open-ended to encourage a response.

2   **Select participants carefully**. Make sure it doesn't just become a moaning session, and select the group carefully, using professional screeners who can ensure the sample is representative or reflects the target group. Refreshments help welcome the group and facilitate conversation.

3   **Get a professional facilitator**. Experienced focus-group moderators know how to ask questions and run the discussion, ensure all participate, and draw out comments: 'the biggest mistake clients can make is to be their own facilitator.'

4   **Listen to everyone, including the most dominant**. Most focus groups have a dominant participant who may influence other participants, but this reflects the marketplace, and trained facilitators will ensure other participants get a chance: 'you gain helpful insights by observing what the "influencers" in the room do or say.'

5   **Remain flexible**. The group may come up with comments you had not anticipated but would like explored further, and this can be arranged by calling the facilitator out of the room temporarily to ask him or her to do this.

Source: excerpts and adaptations from Krotz (no date)

Focus groups prompt significant discussion in political marketing, as will be noted in Chapter 10, in part because Phillip Gould, advisor to former UK Prime Minister Tony Blair and the successful New Labour design that won three elections from 1997, wrote a book about his work, providing unusual material about their potential influence. Indeed, there are more examples of qualitative work from the UK than any other country, because other practitioners have also discussed their work there. For example, qualitative methodology was also used by the company Promise for Labour, once in power, to help reconnect (see Promise 2005, Scammell 2008), as will be explored in the chapter on marketing in government. Promise conducted unusual market intelligence, involving expressive techniques using role-play and feelings and action, which enabled people to express deeply held feelings from which to then reconstruct solutions for Labour. They asked participants to write letters to Blair: see Table 4.4.

Obviously, parties and candidates often commission both quantitative and qualitative research and use them for different purposes. Sparrow and Turner (2001: 999–1001) provide an example of how a party uses both qualitative and quantitative research, reporting the results of research they did for the UK Conservative Party, 1997–2001: see Table 4.5.

Discussion point 4.2

What are the pros and cons of qualitative and quantitative research?

Table 4.4 Fictional letters to Blair in expressive market intelligence by Promise

Key phrases from letter	Underlying emotional	Desires/wishes/direction tone/experience
Theme 1: You left me! • E.g. you should have come home (tsunami) • You should put our people first • All the promises you made that never came to fruition	Abandoned and unimportant	Put us first Get back in touch Get more involved with us/be more hands on
Theme 2: Too big for your boots/celebrity • E.g. a president with Cherie • Globe-trotting holiday-makers • Apply more suntan lotion • Celebrity hero worship (Bush) • Leadership not image • Thought you were a people's person, not a movie star	His self importance and global lifestyle leaves me feeling inferior, undervalued	Reorder priorities Get back to basics Get real
Theme 3: Reflect and change • E.g. take the time to think • How foolish you have been • You have lost sight of reality, how the person in the street lives	Not held in mind Uncontained Out of control	Think, reflect – are you still the bloke we elected or have you moved on to bigger things?

Source: Promise (2005)

Discussion point 4.3

What can be concluded from the results of market intelligence about the UK Conservative Party in Table 4.5? In what way could the Party have responded in how they developed their strategy, the product and/or communication?

Opposition, candidate and policy research

Opposition research is conducted to identify potential weaknesses, controversies and also comparable strengths of the party/candidate and the opposition. There are companies specialising in this work, and, while it is notorious for digging up personal scandals, analysis of public documents can be as valuable as the more clandestine, private investigator type of research. Sources include:

1   elected official's records;
2   campaign contribution records;
3   records of the politician's voting;
4   court files;
5   personal and business records, including property records and property tax payment histories;
6   media, including newspaper, magazine and journal articles and the Internet;
7   other behavioural records, such as club membership and military service;

Table 4.5 UK Conservative market intelligence, 1997–2001

1 Where are we now?

	Conservative Party	Conservative leadership	Labour government
Quantitative research	Poor poll findings: stuck on 30% for five years. 1997 defeat part of wider premeditated rejection. Forfeited reputation for economic competence.	Leader's standing in polls worse than party's. Low 51% think he's doing a good job.	Expectations of electorate about 'change', 'things can only get better'. Labour should 'be given a chance'. Economy, health and education the main benchmark issues to be targeted.
Qualitative research	Perceptions of party as selfish, sleazy, out of touch, arrogant. Before 1997, divided, loss of direction. After 1997, invisible, stagnant.	Perceived personally as a hedgehog. Projection of flaws ascribed to party. Lack of knowledge of Hague. Seen as a public school boy. Respondents surprised when shown video clips of PMQT with good performance.	Blair a lion. Sense of anti-climax; not much has happened. More should be spent on NHS, schools. Going back on their promises.

2 Where do we want to go?

	Conservative Party	Conservative leadership	Labour government
Quantitative research	Polls indicate that people do not perceive that the party knows why it lost and has subsequently changed. Policy renewal through policy testing.	Develop issues that polls indicate are favourable to the projection of leader's image. Tracking of support on saliency of leadership issues.	Tracking of changes in Labour support. Labour issue tracking.
Qualitative research	To ascertain what people really care about. Party messages to reflect what people really think. Policies to reflect what people feel most matters. Listening to Britain: understand people's real concerns, policy vulnerabilities and develop a new narrative.	Regular focus groups on issues and party image. Research to inform leadership about what people really care about, how they express it and what they expect. Research to clarify Labour weaknesses.	Perception of Blair as ordinary bloke, strong and a family man, but also all things to all men. Research on Labour's vulnerabilities: belief in everything and nothing and non-delivery of policies. Research on expectations not fulfilled. Focus group recollections of attacks, cronyism, Ecclestone funding affair, Lord Irvine's wallpaper.

Source: Sparrow and Turner (2001)

8   comments from previous associates, whether work colleagues, family, friends or former partners; and

9   more recently, with the advent of YouTube, audio-visual footage.

Candidate research informs strategy and communication and can be used positively as well as negatively: as Johnson (2007: 57–8) observed, 'it builds the case that the incumbent has established a solid record of achievement . . . and it devises strategies to protect that record.' Candidates' accomplishments, if they are already in office, include legislation assisted or blocked, grants obtained, votes cast, favourable ratings, supporting or criticising the government, and constituency work. Research investigates what would attract support from different groups of people or constituents, as not all behaviour is interesting to all voters (see also Varoga and Rice 1999: 255).

Self-reflective candidate research helps prepare candidates for attacks and helps them prepare rebuttal, so their campaign is less likely to be sent off course. In the 2004 US presidential election, John Kerry, the Democrat candidate, made his military service in Vietnam a key part of his campaign, assuming it to be a win–win characteristic. When he was attacked by a Swift Boat Veterans ad, there was no response from Kerry's team, and the media were able to continue criticism. O'Shaughnessy and Henneberg (2007: 261) noted this shows 'the need for candidates to fully think out strategically their areas of vulnerability well before the beginning of the campaign'. Kerry could have anticipated the attack, as there was an 'inherent contradiction in his Vietnam-era role and his post-service militant peace activism'.

Opposition and candidate research can be used in any race and was on show during the 2008 Democratic primaries, when the extended competition between Hillary Clinton and Barack Obama encouraged each side to uncover potential weaknesess in their opponent. In May 2008, Obama resigned from the Trinity United Church of Christ in Chicago, which he had been a member of for twenty years, because of controversial comments made by the pastor, the Reverend Jeremiah Wright, and other ministers, which were relayed on different media for everyone to see for themselves.

Candidates can expect their entire professional career to be scrutinised, even if it wasn't in politics, and whether or not they were responsible for everything that happened. Even their education or training will be considered. Personal family issues, such as choice of school for their children (rather than the more obvious skeletons such as affairs) can be included in the campaign (Johnson 2007: 70–1), particularly if private behaviour contradicts public political positions. As the candidate is such a key part of the product, such details become important in a way that would not happen in the commercial world, where the life of the chief executive is rarely examined.

Changes in policy position also need to be explained: as Johnson (2007: 66) observes, while a change in position can indicate 'growth and maturity', in politics it is criticised as weakness or populism. If changes can be justified and explained, this can be defended, but the candidate risks being accused of flip-flopping, lacking certainty and conviction, or only changing their position for electoral expediency.

Discussion point 4.4

Is opposition research a problem for democracy or just a necessary part of tactical marketing?

Research of this nature can exhibit lower standards than academic or government research as it is conducted with explicit aims of helping a candidate or damaging their opponent. Nevertheless, facts need to be correct, or claims and defence lack credibility, which can damage the overall campaign. False accusations can backfire.

Party, candidate and government consultation

Another way parties and governments carry out market intelligence is by conducting consultation exercises. Parties often do this after losing power, but candidates seeking office also conduct listening exercises or conversations with the public. Hillary Clinton engaged in consultation called 'Let the conversation begin' in her bid to gain a seat in the US Senate, and then again in her bid to secure the presidential nomination for the US Democrats. Clinton encouraged voters to submit their ideas and questions to her, and she responded to them, calling for a two-way dialogue.

Governments also engage in consultation, either generally to get back in touch with the public, or specifically on certain policy areas. When the UK Blair government was beginning to seem out of touch, mainly because of the Iraq war, the 'Big Conversation' was launched in November 2003. This was an extensive range of events that facilitated positive, reflective and constructive discussion – a different mode of market intelligence from focus groups and polls – as a way of engaging the public beyond the party. It attracted over 40,000 direct submissions. The format encouraged fewer confrontations and more mature discussion: a minister commented that, 'it was amazing – two hours with sixty people and no one had a go at me'. It identified key public priorities: see Box 4.4.

Such party- or candidate-run initiatives can be less scientific and more prone to bias. The approach is not, however, without merit. Not only can it enable politicians to hear new ideas and gain a greater understanding of the concerns of specific sections of the electorate, it generates an image of responsiveness

A two-way dialogue of consultation rather than just listening, where different views are exposed and realities are incorporated, can be more effective. Consultation can be run in

---

Box 4.4 Labour Big Conversation priorities

Top concerns

1   Education (especially student finance)
2   Immigration/asylum (national and local)
3   Health (especially public health)
4   Council tax
5   Crime and ASB

Emerging priorities

1   Opportunity: early years
2   Health: prevention and public health
3   Anti-social behaviour: youth provision – neighbourhood governance
4   Work: skills, work–life balance
5   Prosperity: housing supply, tomorrow's pensioners (30–40-year-olds now)

Source: internal Labour Party document, quoted in Lees-Marshment (2008)

different ways. One possibility is to consult citizen experts – voters with experience of a particular issue, either professionally or personally, so they will offer more informed views. The UK Conservatives engaged in an extensive policy consultation process under the leadership of David Cameron in 2005–7. The policy groups were chaired by Conservatives, but operated somewhat independently from the party and drew on varied groups of people with different expertise. Different methods of consultation can improve debate and integrate information, as will be explored in later chapters on marketing in government (Chapter 8) and political marketing and democracy (Chapter 10).

Using market intelligence in positioning

Both market intelligence and segmentation can also be used in terms of deciding on the position to take within the market, taking into account the competition. Collins and Butler's (1996 and 2002) theory of market positioning, adapting marketing theories of competitive advantage, reflects this: see Table 4.6. They argue that candidates need to be realistic and take this into account, for example nichers are unlikely to move to being a leader in a single electoral period. Each position has different marketing options.

Case studies 4.1–4.3, at the end of this chapter, explore market positioning using the Butler and Collins framework in the countries of Belgium, Finland and Poland.

Table 4.6 Constraints and options for each market position

	Constraints	*Options*
Market leader	Has to appeal to a broad range of voters, and their interests conflict. For example, may want to support farmers who want higher food prices, whereas consumers want lower. Subject to continuous attack.	Defensive strategies. Expansion or increase of market share.
Challenger	At first, championing new issues early on can make challenger appear to be out of step with public opinion. Similar product to leader; has to show differentiation or superiority.	Characterise leader negatively, e.g. as corrupt or incompetent. Back door strategy: identify new emerging issue and brand it early, gaining support once the issue becomes more salient.
Follower	Market intelligence is expensive, as is product development and beyond most follower resources. Subject to attack from other competitors especially challengers. Must avoid alienating large segments of the market to protect existing support.	Cloning: copy the leader, but in interest of existing customers. Imitating: similar to leader but with some differentiation. Adapting: adapting leader's product, perhaps to suit different market or segment. Protecting: protect generally stable market share, rather than challenge. Avoid radical change or attacking opponents.
Nicher	Specialises in serving the needs of a niche better than other competitors, so has to protect this niche and its competitive advantage.	Can transform through radical strategic change. Highly focused product positioning. Communication used before change in direction.

Source: Collins and Butler (2002: 7–13)

“
”

Discussion point 4.5

Discuss Case studies 4.1–4.3. What do these three cases demonstrate about marketing positioning, in terms of its effectiveness for winning voter support and its utility to explain party behaviour and election outcomes?

Different factors impact on the success or failure of positioning. Bannon (2004) argues there are five key factors for successful positioning (see also Baines 1999):

1   Clarity of the position: know what the competitive advantage is and what voters think of this.
2   Consistency of position: a voter needs to know where they are; the organisation needs to offer a consistent and sustained approach.
3   Credibility of positioning: the voters' judgement of the quality of political proposals will always prevail.
4   Competitiveness: offer value that competing products do not.
5   Communicable: position must be easily communicated to targets. In the Scottish parliamentary elections in 2003, the Greens adopted the slogan '2nd vote green'. This was a reference to the PR regional vote that was widely regarded (wrongly) as a second preference vote. The message was successful, and the Greens won eight MSP places.

There are also a number of barriers to consider (see Baines and Worcester 2004 and Smith 2005). It is difficult for incumbents to reposition, because they are bound by their previous behaviour and record. In the UK 2005 election, this was illustrated in several respects. As Smith (2005: 1137–9) observed, if Labour moved to the left, it would open up the market for the Conservatives; if it moved to the right, it would open up other sections of the market to the Liberal Democrats. The Conservatives found it hard to show differentiation from Labour, because Labour copied their positions on choice and efficiency in the public sector. Nevertheless, Labour enjoyed positive points of difference over both competitors, being perceived to hold better policies on the two most important issues, health services and taxation/public services.

Triangulation and positioning

Baines and Worcester (2004) outline two triangulation theories. The first, by Dick Morris, who advised Bill Clinton in the presidency, argued for creating a third position between and above the traditional stances of the two parties, Republican and Democrat. In this way, Clinton could respond to the demands, and attract the support of, supporters from both parties, appealing to the maximum number of voters. One example of this is how Clinton implemented previously promised tax cuts for the middle classes, but, instead of generic change, focused them on those who took personal responsibility, such as college students and those saving for their pension.

The second theory, the Worcester concept of triangulation, considers voters' attitudes to the parties, their leaders and their policies. By measuring the importance of the different aspects of the triangle, this helped create a weighted data model to inform party campaigning.

Barriers to market intelligence being used in politics

Historically, there have been many barriers to politicians and parties commissioning, let alone responding to, market intelligence, although it has become much more acceptable since the end of the twentieth century. Wring (2005a) explains how the UK Labour Party's traditional culture, mission and ethos involved education and persuasion, which made it difficult for professionals and party figures to gain acceptance for the use of marketing in presentation, let alone product design. Not every politician or party wants to just win an election – they also want to change the world. Individual politicians often think they know best and that their gut instinct is the right one – and their agenda and goals can be to advance a particular cause, not subject their behaviour to the dictates of the market, let alone the median or target voter.

Kavanagh (1996: 105–10) noted how there are a number of factors that enhance or constrain the attention politicians pay to market intelligence results, such as:

1   In power or opposition: politicians get complacent in power, and ministers are more interested in justifying existing programmes than considering where new proposals would attract market support, whereas, when a new party leader takes over after an election date, they are more open to information to aid them in a change in direction.
2   Politicians' own views: individual politicians and different party groups prefer one policy to another and look for results that support a particular position: 'Mrs Thatcher was deaf to the message of the polls about the unpopularity of many of her privatisation measures, health service changes and the poll tax. When the Harris agency reported on the unpopularity of the poll tax, the party chairman Kenneth Baker dismissed the findings as "unhelpful".'
3   Internal confusion over the role of market intelligence: some party figures want polling to help primarily with targeting communications, making policy decisions, or getting positive evaluations about existing behaviour to boost morale.
4   Resentment towards negative results: 'In 1991 and 1992, even tentative suggestions from the Labour Party's communications advisers about the electoral dangers of the party's proposals for tax increases were dismissed by politicians as out of order.'
5   Time constraints: often polling is commissioned at the last minute or conducted during a campaign, which limits its usefulness.

The trend currently is for pollsters to be part of the strategy campaign planning, as advertisers, public relations experts, and a variety of professionals are engaged in formulating, adjusting and implementing strategy, but this varies from one campaign to another.

Limitations of market intelligence in politics

There are many practical, as well as democratic, issues with market intelligence in politics.

There are problems of accuracy with polling. Polls can be wrong, such as in the UK 1992 election and US 2000 presidential election. In the latter, media networks called the election result using exit polls in only a small number of precincts, saying Gore was ahead by 6.5 per cent, but they then had to backtrack as more results came in to suggest a Bush win. There is a margin of error in every poll or survey and biases against young and 'not at homes' (see Rademacher and Tuchfarber 1999: 205–15 for further detail). In developing democracies, security risks and political culture can make it difficult to collect effective and accurate intelligence. Abad and Ramirez (2008: 273–4) note that, in the Philippines where rebels operate, interviewers have been robbed, and the lack of reliable public transport makes it hard to get to the place to conduct polling. Nevertheless, they conclude that 'with appropriate quality-control measures, polling can be a reliable tool even in a developing democracy like the Philippines with its challenging geography, poor infrastructure and widespread corruption' (Abad and Ramirez 2008: 280).

Segmentation and vote profiling packages such as Voter Vault are only as good as the data the party collects to feed into the system. Canvassing by party supporters or members on the ground to ascertain their opinions and political behaviour is one of the sources for political data, and this can be problematic. Furthermore, assumptions about their political opinions, judgements and response to party/candidate communication and behaviour are only that: an assumption. Candidates and parties may be spending a lot of money communicating inappropriate messages to people.

Researcher bias can creep into data collection. Sparrow and Turner (2001: 993) note how 'focus groups must avoid what Dunscbome has called the interview effect, according to which the social characteristics of the moderator may have a disproportionate influence on respondents and the information they are prepared to divulge.' Savigny (2007: 130) argued that, in the case of UK Labour in the 1990s, 'Gould also used focus groups as a site to test his own ideas [r]ather than listening and collecting the opinions of the selected public . . . Gould's interventionist approach, to argue and challenge participants.' The way focus groups are run can inhibit rather than facilitate the expression of what the market wants.

The interpretation of results is another area of debate. Wring (2007: 87) argues that the problems with focus groups used by Labour between 1992 and 1997 also included that they were used to push a political agenda, leaked to the media selectively to generate support, and reported without full complexity and acknowledgement of the limitations of the focus group method.

Consultation exercises attract educated, middle-class people – so whole groups in society are ignored. Party-run exercises tend to disproportionately attract party members, producing biased results. UK Labour's 'Big Conversation' existed only for a limited time, and it was criticised for not reporting back to the public, and just being a PR exercise (see Wring 2005b: 60 for example). Similar comments have been applied to Brown's citizen juries: see Box 4.5 below.

Segmentation, as already noted, can have democratic implications because, while a small section of voters is targeted, others are ignored (Savigny 2008). Public opinion can be very volatile and hard to measure. Any method captures a snap judgement only, and it could be different to the actual decision or final vote. People may hold views on both sides that conflict and change. Asher (1995) noted an example of polling, conducted by the Harris organisation during the 1980 presidential primaries, that asked respondents about their preference for the candidates and then asked more questions about current government issues; when the respondents were asked at the end to reaffirm their voting preferences, support for former US President Carter declined. The explanation was that, on being reminded of Carter's record, voters became more negative. Yet it would be difficult to know if this

Box 4.5 'Sham' citizens' juries face controls: overhaul for Brown's 'big idea' to engage voters, as critics say they are just glorified focus groups

Citizens' juries and other forms of research into public attitudes are to be more tightly controlled amid growing concerns that they are a 'sham' listening exercise used for political purposes, rather than a genuine way of canvassing opinion.

The Observer has learned that the bill for citizens' juries is likely to reach more than £3m this year. Ministers are increasingly commissioning research which involves recruiting a panel of members of the public who meet for a day to consider new policy ideas. Researchers can gauge the level of popularity before the ideas are officially adopted or rejected ... Yesterday, a panel was meeting to discuss the future of children's services. In a few weeks, a 'citizens' summit' will be convened to decide on a new motto for Britain to encourage patriotism.

Amid growing worries about the juries' power and unaccountability, the National Consumer Council (NCC) and a new pro-democracy group called Involve are drawing up a code of practice which will set out how such panels should be controlled.

Ed Mayo, the NCC's Chief Executive, said: 'There has been a genuine surge of enthusiasm for citizens' juries and summits over the past year. However, they are only worth doing if they give people a genuine say. Otherwise they are, at best, glorified focus groups and, at worst, no more than a pale sham of democratic dialogue.' He said that people now identify 'fake listening' as one of their top gripes. In July, Gordon Brown described citizens' juries as Labour's 'big idea', arguing that it was important to engage people, particularly those from more deprived areas, to revitalise interest in government and politics. But there are concerns that many of the debates could be used to steer the public in particular ways.

Citizens' juries are like focus groups, but with the key difference that they are controlled by a facilitator who introduces particular ideas and directs the conversations around the table. The juries – panels of twenty or more people who can meet for one day or over several days – can call witnesses to hear evidence before deciding how they feel about policies. Some participants are paid nothing, while others get more than £100 a day ... many juries are run by Opinion Leader Research (OLR), whose chief executive, Deborah Mattinson, is one of the Prime Minister's most trusted advisers and his personal pollster. It runs juries, forums and polls for an array of public and private sector clients ... The Department of Health told MPs recently that it is paying OLR £70,500 in the current financial year to consult on the future of the health service. Earlier this year, a one-day 'participatory summit' was held by the Department for Work and Pensions to talk about pensions policies. It cost the taxpayer £153,000.

Dr Tom Wakeford, an expert in public engagement research at Newcastle University, said: 'There is a lot of worry about whether these are genuine consultations and deliberations. If used in the wrong way, they can actually close down debate rather than open it up.'

Source: excerpts from Revill (2007)

would happen in their actual voting decision, as they may not think at such length about the governing record.

Push polling is criticised for several reasons. This is where, instead of trying to measure opinion, the questions asked frame issues to try to influence the recipients' beliefs. The results are not analysed, as the aim is to change opinion, not respond to it. The influence can range from just reminding voters of a candidate's position to downright manipulation of factors to damage the reputation of the opposition: see Box 4.6.

It was alleged that, in the US Republican primaries in 2000, George W. Bush's campaign asked voters in South Carolina: 'Would you be more likely or less likely to vote for John McCain for president if you knew he had fathered an illegitimate black child?', even though McCain and his wife had in fact adopted a Bangladeshi girl. A blogger during the 2008 US Democrat primaries recalled receiving a push poll (www.bakelblog.com/nobodys_business/2008/02/when-push-comes.html, accessed 4 March 2008). At first, questions were normal and asked about views on the candidates. Then the caller read a series of statements and asked whether, if true, they would raise doubts about the candidate. The statements were problematic and fitted the push poll definition, for example:

> The non-partisan *National Journal* has called Obama the country's most liberal candidate. He's for gay adoptions and driver's licenses for illegal immigrants. He voted against allowing people to have guns to protect themselves in their own homes. He is weak on terrorism and has said he would personally negotiate with terrorist nations like Syria and Iran. Would this cause me to have: very serious; serious; minor; or no doubts about Barack Obama?

The American Association of Political Consultants has condemned push polling. Market intelligence is also only as good as the response made to it. Results are not always listened to. Furthermore, market intelligence can't tell you everything. It often presents leaders with a dilemma. Newman (1999: 41) notes how Bill Clinton wanted to push for a bill to protect gays in the military at the start of his presidency, but many interest groups were against it, so he had to pull back from this, even though he had promised to do it during his campaign. Indeed, the Bush White House shied away from admitting poll usage, fearing it would be accused of lacking leadership. There is also a need for politicians to be authentic and genuine and not, as Newman (1999: 42) notes, running campaigns with images 'that, in many cases, have no resemblance to either them or their ideas'.

Box 4.6 Definition of push polling

The National Council on Public Polls:

A 'push poll' is a telemarketing technique in which telephone calls are used to canvass vast numbers of potential voters, feeding them false and damaging 'information' about a candidate under the guise of taking a poll to see how this 'information' effects voter preferences. In fact, the intent is to 'push' the voters away from one candidate and toward the opposing candidate. This is clearly political telemarketing, using innuendo and, in many cases, clearly false information to influence voters; there is no intent to conduct research. These telemarketing techniques damage the electoral process in two ways. They injure candidates, often without revealing the source of the information. Also, the results of a 'push poll', if released, give a seriously flawed and biased picture of the political situation.

Source: NCPP (1995)

Potential of market intelligence in politics

There remains debate about the value of market intelligence, but it is unlikely any modern candidate or party would not gather any, given the choice. Bannon (2004) outlines how market segmentation encourages the development of products and services that match the success criteria of a segment and allows the tailoring of communications and channels of distribution to customer needs, providing higher customer satisfaction and leading to loyalty. Segmentation can ensure a high return on resources and development of more individualised plans for each segment. It also reduces the amount of resources wasted. Furthermore, as Sparrow and Turner (2001: 992) argue, market intelligence has 'a role to play in helping politicians understand how voters think', and focus group research is now 'up-turning many assumptions made by elite politicians about the political world as experienced by ordinary people' (p. 995). As Gould's quote in Practitioner perspective 4.1 suggests, it helps politicians to understand voters more effectively. Market intelligence isn't a perfect conversation between government and the public, but it does go some way to bringing the two closer together. Without understanding the market, all other marketing activities would have to rely on gut instinct and guess work. But it does remain an area ripe for discussion: see Debate 4.1.

Practitioner perspective 4.1

If people think you've stopped listening, you're sunk.

> (Bill Clinton, in his memoirs, about losing re-election as Arkansas governor in 1980)

On focus groups:

With the exception of 'spin-doctors' no campaign phrase has ever been imbued with a greater air of nonsensical mystique than 'focus groups'. Their importance is they enable politicians to hear directly the voters' voices.

> (Phillip Gould, advertising executive UK Labour, in his book on New Labour, 1998)

Debate 4.1

Proposition: Market intelligence, far from being an instrument that gives the public a voice in a democracy, is a method by which politicians and economic elites manipulate people to buy their products and/or give them their votes.

Summary

Market intelligence provides politicians and their staff with information that they can then use to make decisions about all other aspects of marketing, including product development and communication. Options such as segmentation, targeting and opposition research provide different ways of looking at the market, but they also have limitations and are not quick fixes to secure success. Without using such methods to understand an increasingly diverse public, however, politicians would be relying on gut instinct and guess work, which would be more prone to bias and inaccuracy and unable to provide the detailed breakdown of the electorate now offered by computerised segmentation models. While there are democratic issues with the use of market intelligence, most of these develop because of the way elites choose to use it. The process of market intelligence is not always straightforward. Parties and politicians need to listen, interpret and respond carefully before using it to develop their product, which is the focus of the next chapter.

ASSESSED WORK

Essays
1   Explore the different ways political parties and candidates use market intelligence.
2   Discuss the potential and limitations of market intelligence in politics.
3   Outline and evaluate normative or ethical issues with market intelligence in politics.

Applied work
1   Conduct a literature review of focus group methodology, then design and hold your own focus group on a particular candidate, party, government or political issue. Observe how people make judgements and reflect on the reliability of the method and your particular results.
2   Interview local politicians and ask what they think about market intelligence and what methods they use to ascertain the views and demands of their constituents.
3   Survey students in your year, drawing up an appropriate sample group and devising survey questions, and analyse the results as well as reflecting on the overall research design.
4   Design and carry out a citizen jury or other deliberative democracy method on a particular issue and evaluate the experience.
5   Design, execute and evaluate any form of market intelligence – see www.usability.gov or www.marketingpower.com for a guide.

Case study 4.1 Bye bye Belgium? Reputation and competitive positioning in the historic 2007 federal election and formation period   *Dave Gelders*

This case will examine the reputation and competitive positioning of the political parties and their leaders in Belgium in 2007.

Belgium is a very complicated federal state, composed of a federal parliament, a federal government and a federal civil service. The federal parliament consists of Dutch-speaking and French-speaking MPs. Belgium has federated entities: Flanders (Dutch-speaking), Wallonia (French-speaking) and the Brussels-Capital Region (bilingual), each with its own parliament, government and civil service. The main parties are:

*   the Liberals (Flemish party Open VLD and Francophone party MR);
*   the Socialists (Flemish party Sp.a and its Francophone counterpart PS);
*   the Christian-Democrats (CD&V and cdH);
*   Green parties (Groen! and Ecolo);
*   and a Flemish, extreme-right party (Vlaams Belang).

Classifying Belgian parties
According to Collins and Butler (1996), the federal prime minister, Guy Verhofstadt, and his Flemish party, Open VLD, were the 'market leader' of the moment, even though the polls

predicted electoral defeat for the party. Yves Leterme and his Flemish CD&V and N-VA cartel acted as the 'challenger', stating that the purple (minus Green) coalitions led by Guy Verhofstadt (1999–2003; 2003–07) lacked 'good governance' (demonstrating this by the reform problems of the federal finance and justice). Leterme promoted his own government as the prototype of good governance (his government's 'brand'), although the same purple parties were in his government (in addition to his own Christian-Democrat party). The Liberal and Socialist parties (Open VLD and SP.a) tried to counter this charge with similar examples in the Flemish government of the practices of which CD&V accused them.

Besides using its brand of 'good governance', during the campaign, the CD&V and N-VA cartel stressed the need for a fundamental state reform, with the transfer of competences to the communities and regions and the split of a contentious Belgian electoral arrondissement (Brussels-Halle-Vilvoorde) due to language and power. The cartel announced it was not willing to participate in a federal government if these issues were not part of the new federal coalition agreement.

Federal Prime Minister Verhofstadt tried to organise a television debate with the popular Christian-Democrat federal candidate Yves Leterme, but the latter refused. This action by Verhofstadt illustrates not only that the prime minister had become a challenger, despite his position as prime minister, but also that Leterme (without having a position at the federal level) was perceived as a winner and market leader and as the future federal prime minister (given the positive opinion polls for him and his cartel and given his popularity at the Flemish level). Yves Leterme tried to save the image of 'good governance' and his reputation of being 'down-to-earth' by participating at the end of the federal election campaign and by focusing on his policy announcements and promises.

In the Francophone part of the country, the Socialist Party (PS) was leading before the elections, but it was challenged by the Liberal Party (MR), which urged for an alternative to the long-dominant PS, as PS was charged with corruption in a major Francophone city.

In addition to these leaders and challengers, there were 'followers' that imitated rather than innovated. The Flemish Socialists, for example, were not setting the tone and tried to be 'the third dog running away with the bone' in the battle between the Flemish Liberals (Verhofstadt) and Christian-Democrats (Leterme), but they did it late in the game.

Finally, there were 'nichers' in the market, such as the Green parties, Groen! and Ecolo, and the nationalist party N-VA (in cartel with CD&V), focusing on communal issues. The latter party played an important role in the aftermath of the elections.

The 2007 results

On the Flemish side, the alliance of CD&V and N-VA received an increased share of the votes compared with the 2003 results and became the largest political formation in Belgium, leading the coalition talks for a new federal government. Prime Minister Verhofstadt's purple coalition was punished; Sp.a chose immediately to be in the opposition, as they lost more than Verhofstadt's Open VLD. The Francophone situation did not mirror its Flemish counterpart. While Open VLD struggled, its Francophone sister party MR managed to defeat the long-dominant Francophone Socialist party, PS. The Christian-Democratic cdH gained somewhat more representation.

The period in which a government was formed lasted 196 days, with several leaders involved in the negotiations; Yves Leterme was twice appointed by the King as *formateur* (i.e. the next prime minister). There came a realisation that Belgium could not afford such indecision. After the elections, the Flemish and Francophone groups worked together to formulate a programme and a government. Negotiations were mainly held between the Christian-Democrats and Liberals.

The situation ended temporarily in an 'interim coalition' led by Prime Minister Verhofstadt (prime minister for eight years and known for a more moderate position), in order to tackle the most urgent political problems, and aimed to set up an actual government led by Leterme by the end of March 2008. This interim government, led by Verhofstadt, included Verhofstadt's rival, Leterme, as deputy prime minister. This created an impression of a lack of competence and credibility of the popular Leterme, who received a high personal score of 800,000 preferential votes in the election. Besides the Flemish and Francophone Liberal and Christian-Democrat parties, surprisingly, the Francophone Socialist party PS was included in the government (PS was preferred by the so-called Christian-Democratic 'buddy' (cdH), but not by its long-standing rival MR).

Lessons for political marketing

The historic formation crisis demonstrated the importance of competitive positioning and reputation, linked with the perception of results and expectations and the importance of perceptions of competence and credibility to deliver what is promised. The crisis also illustrates that positioning and reputation are not only influenced by personal blunders, but by more system-related issues, such as the party and electoral system of a federal country *sui generis*. Belgium has a politically fragmented system, without federal political parties and with different electoral platforms working in different parts of the country, but under the same umbrella of so-called 'federal' elections, which lead to a federal government in which the pronounced statements of small but influential (cartel) parties play an important role. The case study indicates that more prudent competitive positioning is necessary when one takes the potential negotiations and long-term reputation into account. One may be seen as efficient and credible through promises, but the delivery of these promises can be difficult owing to, among other factors, less attention to federal logic and the sensitivities of political actors and public opinion in the other part of the country, while risking destroying a reputation at the considerable cost of rebuilding it.

Sources and further reading

More detailed information about the Belgian 2007 federal election campaign and the formation period in English is available online at http://en.wikipedia.org/wiki/Belgian_general_election%2C_2007 and http://en.wikipedia.org/wiki/2007_Belgian_government_formation

---

Case study 4.2 The Finnish case – strategic positioning of a niche party: the Swedish People's Party

Susanne Jungerstam-Mulders

The Finnish party system today can generally be described as a consensus-oriented, fragmented, multi-party system, with three dominant parties. The party system structure originates, in terms of Lipset and Rokkan's theory of cleavage structures (1967), primarily from the division between class-based and urban and rural interests. Herein, the small Swedish People's Party (SPP) has been in a unique position compared with parties of similar size in other moderate and polarised multi-party systems in Europe: having gained less than 5 per cent of the vote in the past decade, and less than 8 per cent throughout the whole post-war period, the party has taken part in almost all governments in Finland during the country's independence.

The SPP describes itself as a broad-minded, liberal party that works for two living national languages in Finland, Finnish and Swedish (see http://sfp.fi/files/program/Steget%20fore.pdf, accessed 1 December 2007). Therein, the party is inclusive for a range of political ideals, sharing an interest in defending minority language matters, and being more of a pragmatic party than an ideological one. The party endures primarily because of its specialist appeal to a small, but stable segment of the voters and its long-term, strong relationships with that segment, i.e. the Swedish-speaking minority (approximately 5.5 per cent of the population today). In addition, the SPP has clearly chosen to be part of the executive rather than being a challenger party, even if executive powers and responsibilities have not gained the party's purposes or ideals at all times. However, considering the rather constant share of votes that the party receives in national elections, it appears that the electorate does not judge the party so much by the government's performance, as according to its defence of special interests. Following Butler and Collins' theory, the SPP may be considered a rather typical niche party – and a party that is likely to face similar strategic challenges and options as other niche parties in general.

As pointed out by Butler and Collins, the major difficulty for any niche party is that of the niche disappearing. In the time period of the next few decades, this also seems to be the dilemma facing the SPP: the Swedish-speaking population is slowly, but gradually, reducing in proportion to the total population, whereas young Swedish-speaking Finns generally have excellent skills in the majority language of the country, and the number of bilingual Finns is increasing. For many of these, the immediate need to defend their linguistic rights is not imperative at all times. At the same time, there are a more general trend towards the erosion of party loyalties and a decrease in voter participation, which will eventually affect a niche party as well as any other party.

According to Butler and Collins, a niche party can opt for basically three strategies to endure on the political scene: to create, expand or defend its niche. Herein, the SPP has made no serious efforts to create a new niche. Instead, the SPP has chosen to act more decisively at defending its niche – and expanding its niche. However, it seems that the strategy of expansion may prove counter-productive in respect of defending its traditional niche.

The SPP's expanding strategy has mainly included addressing and including bilingual policies in the party's political agenda. In doing so, the party has shifted its focus from defending the position of Swedish in Finland as a condition for equal rights of an acknowledged minority group, to understanding language as a culture- and identity-carrying feature to be stimulated in a bilingual environment. However, this shift has not been appreciated by all segments of the party's supporters. The traditional party electorate, especially those living in more or less unilingual, Swedish-speaking rural areas, have felt betrayed by the shift in rhetoric. At the same time, it is also questionable whether the tactic of expanding towards bilingual voters can actually be a successful one: genuinely bilingual voters tend to be less attached to the linguistic agenda than unilingual voters, and they have a range of parties representing different ideologies and agendas to choose from. In addition, voters with an ideological conviction other than the (social-) liberal stance of the SPP will find Swedish-speaking branches in some of the major, established parties.

Moreover, structural conditions influence the strategic choices made by any party, as well as by a small, niche party. Party behaviour is conditioned by the electoral system, in particular, the position of the leader, a country's political culture and the availability of resources. Of these, the electoral system is perhaps the most important determinant of strategic behaviour in Finnish politics, affecting both the position of the leader and the need for resources during – and between – elections. Closely related to the election system, especially in the Finnish context, is 'issue ownership' as a strategic device to attract voters.

The Finnish electoral system is a PR system, with open party lists that require preference voting. Under this system, the allocation of seats to parties (including electoral alliances) is proportional to the votes obtained, following d'Hondt's formula. The allocation of seats to candidates is, in turn, entirely based on the number of individual votes of a candidate in his/her district. As a consequence, Finnish politics have become rather personalised.

On the party level, the personalised character of Finnish elections has resulted in it not being uncommon to enter established politicians representing different sexes, ages, backgrounds, interests and competences on the party election lists, in order to attract as broad a range of voters as possible. In addition, it is fairly common to enter candidates with a high profile and a popular appeal, including sportsmen, well-known writers, politicians with a colourful past etc. as well. The reason for this is two-fold: first, parties hope to gain attention and media coverage by entering 'interesting' people on their list, and, second, they hope to attract new voters and voters from other parties because of the candidate's appeal. This strategy is applied by the SPP as well as by any other party; however, being a small party, the loss of one most well-known and appreciated candidate has occasionally had grave consequences for the party's successes.

Lessons for political marketing

Niche theory is a useful one to understand party behaviour. However, it is not without its difficulties in terms of practice. Voters are likely to vote for the party that generates the most attention for its own issue, while a party that 'owns' an issue that does not gain any visibility does not generate electoral support. In the case of the SPP, the language issue is undisputedly owned by the party – whereas the bilingual issue is yet unestablished and may be much harder to possess, and gain attention for, because of the reasons discussed above. In addition, bilingualism appears to be a much easier issue for other parties to challenge the SPP on than the SPP's original language issue: entering (popular) bilingual politicians on their lists, these can easily address both the SPP's traditional electorate and a predominantly (Finnish-speaking) class-based or ideologically-based electorate. Therefore, the SPP's shift from stressing language politics in its own right towards stressing bilingual value-carrying structures may, again, be hazardous for the party. Yet, defending its traditional niche without attempting to extend its niche is equally hazardous, considering the erosion of party loyalties and decreasing numbers in the party's core electorate. This leaves the SPP in quite an awkward position, where neither of the niche party strategies that the party attempts to utilise seems ideal.

Source and further reading

Lipset, Seymour Martin and Stein Rokkan (eds) (1967). *Party Systems and Voter Alignments: Cross-National Perspectives*. New York: The Free Press.

Case study 4.3 Market positions of Polish political parties in 2007

Wojciech Opioła and Arleta Opioła

The Polish political scene has changed rapidly since 1989, the year in which capitalist democracy was introduced. In the 2005–07 parliamentary term, there were eight parties comprising the Sejm (Lower House) including:

1   Law and Justice (Prawo i Sprawiedliwość, PiS) – 26.99 per cent support; 155 seats.
2   Civic Platform (Platforma Obywatelska, PO) – 24.14 per cent support; 133 seats.
3   Democratic Left Alliance (Sojusz Lewicy Demokratycznej, SLD) – 11.31 per cent support; fifty-five seats.
4   League of Polish Families (Liga Polskich Rodzin, LPR) – 7.97 per cent support; thirty-four seats.
5   Self-Defence of the Republic of Poland (Samoobrona RP) – 11.41 per cent support; fifty-six seats.

6   Polish People's Party (Polskie Stronnictwo Ludowe, PSL) – 6.96 per cent support; twenty-five seats.

7   German Minority (Mniejszość Niemiecka, MN) – 0.29 per cent support; two seats.

8   PiS, which won the election, formed a coalition government with Samoobrona RP and LPR.

Early parliamentary elections were held in Poland in 2007, in which there were ten contesting parties. Each party applied its own strategy according to its market position.

Market leaders

PiS is a right-wing political party, and **PO** is a centre-right party. Since 2005, both parties have always gathered over 20 per cent of support in various polls and elections. In the polls carried out before the 2005 elections, PO gathered 29–41 per cent of support, and PiS gathered 24–38 per cent. Both parties have many members. Differences in choosing marketing strategies resulted from the different roles both parties played. PiS was a governing party during the campaign and thus aimed at defending its market position and increasing the number of representatives in the Sejm by means of marginalising Samoobrona RP and LPR and leading a negative campaign against PO and the Left and Democrats (Lewica i Demokraci, LiD). PiS accused PO and LiD of being parties of the 'system' – a vague term standing for the parties whose members, according to PiS, have connections with business leaders, the crime world and communist security services. According to the polls, PO was the only real alternative to PiS. PO was to expand the market by means of gaining PiS voters (who were not satisfied with the way their party governed) and leftist voters (who did not have an opportunity to oust the ruling party).

Challengers

LiD is a centre-left coalition formed by the SLD and three other leftist parties. After the 2005 election defeat, the Polish left wing found itself in a crisis. Therefore, before the 2007 elections, a coalition of four parties was formed – three social-democratic parties and a Liberal Democratic party (Partia Demokratyczna) – under the name LiD. Aleksander Kwaśniewski, a former president of Poland, led the 2007 election campaign. The aim of the coalition was to gain the third place in the Polish parliament (after PO and PiS).

Samoobrona RP was a member of the ruling coalition (2006–07) and its leader – Andrzej Lepper – became deputy prime minister of Poland and Minister of Agriculture. The effective PiS actions and political blunders of the Samoobrona leaders resulted in a fall in support. Members of the party, who in the 1990s put pressure on the government by means of roadblocks or protests, did not find their place in the parliament. The party started in the 2007 parliamentary elections in order to get a second chance from its voters.

Followers

Right of the Republic (Liga Prawicy Rzeczpospolitej) is a coalition formed by three parties: LPR, which was part of the former governing coalition, and two smaller parties. All the parties forming the LPR coalition are conservative-liberal. Since none of these parties had a chance to enter the parliament, conservative-liberal parties, just like the leftist parties, formed a coalition. The abbreviation of the name of the party did not change: it is still LPR, after the name of the leading party (Liga Polskich Rodzin) forming this coalition.

Patriotic Self-Defence (Samoobrona Patriotyczna) was formed by former members of Samoobrona RP, who, as a result of the argument with the leader of the party, Andrzej Lepper, formed their own political party. Owing to the fact that Samoobrona Patriotyczna managed to register its electoral committee in just one electoral district, the party had no chance to enter the parliament. The strategy of the party was based on the similarity to Samoobrona RP – similar name, similar logo and similar manifesto.

Nichers

PSL is one of the most stable players in the Polish political market. The name of the party has not changed since 1990, and it had representatives in each tenure of the Sejm. The chairman of the party is Waldemar Pawlak, who twice served as Polish prime minister. PSL is an agrarian political party. The party receives the greatest support in country boroughs. Stability and an unaggressive campaign were to be characteristic features of the electoral campaign of PSL. The party aimed to gain supporters among those who were not satisfied with the brutality of life and political discourse.

The **Women's Party (Partia Kobiet, PK)** was registered in January 2007. Among the members and supporters of the party, one can find many famous women, for instance Manuela Gretkowska (a well-known Polish author), Maryla Rodowicz (a famous Polish singer) and Beata Tyszkiewicz (a well-known Polish actress). The party aims to represent the interests and concerns of women. Opinion polls prove that the voters' segment of the party is very limited. Therefore, the character of the campaign was more informative than persuasive.

The **Polish Labour Party (Polska Partia Pracy, PPP)** is a social-democratic party. Owing to the strong competition from LiD, PPP puts an emphasis on such issues as socialism, ecology and alterglobalism.

MN is a political party of the German minority in Poland, which is the most numerous national minority in the country (ca. 0.4 per cent of the population). As a party of a national minority, it is not required to pass the election threshold of 5 per cent, as standard political parties in Poland are. The German minority lives mainly in Opole Voivodship (70 per cent of the whole population of Germans in Poland), where the party creates its electoral registers. There are fewer and fewer representatives of MN in the Polish parliament each year.

21 October 2007 Polish National Assembly election results

Leaders

PO:	42 per cent of the vote; 209 seats
PiS:	32 per cent; 166 seats

Challengers

LiD:	13 per cent; fifty-three seats
PSL:	9 per cent; thirty-one seats

Followers

Samoobrona RP:	2 per cent; no seats
LPR:	1 per cent; no seats

Nichers

PPP:	0.99 per cent; no seats
PK:	0.28 per cent; no seats
MN:	0.20 per cent; one seat
Patriotic Self-Defence:	0.02 per cent; no seats

Lessons for political marketing

Where there is a multi-party system, market positioning theory is effective in helping us understand party behaviour and election results; leaders clearly won most support, with challengers coming second.

FURTHER READING

Abad, Mercedes and Ophelia Ramirez (2008). 'Polling in developing democracies – the case of the Philippines'. In Marita Carbello and Ulf Hjelmar (eds), *Public Opinion Polling*. Berlin: Springer-Verlag.

Alabi, Joshua and Goski Alabi (2007). 'Analysis of the effects of ethnicity on political marketing in Ghana'. *International Business and Economics Research Journal*, 6(4): 39–52.

Althaus, S. (1996). 'Opinion polls, information effects, and political equality: exploring ideological biases in collective opinion'. *Political Communication*, 13: 3–21.

Asher, H. (1995). 'Polling and the public: what every citizen should know'. Washington DC: Congressional Quarterly Press.

Baines, Paul R. (1999). 'Voter segmentation and candidate positioning'. In Bruce Newman (ed.), *Handbook of Political Marketing*. Thousand Oaks, CA: Sage.

―― and Robert M. Worcester (2004). 'Two triangulation models in political marketing: the market positioning analogy'. Elections on the Horizon Conference, London, 15 March 2004.

――, ――, David Jarrett and Roger Mortimore (2003). 'Market segmentation and product differentiation in political campaigns: a technical feature perspective'. *Journal of Marketing Management*, 19(1/2): 225–49.

――, ――, ―― and ―― (2005). 'Product attribute-based voter segmentation and resource advantage theory'. *Journal of Marketing Management*, 21(9/10): 1079–1115.

Bannon, Declan (2004). 'Marketing segmentation and political marketing'. Paper presented to the UK Political Studies Association, University of Lincoln, 4–8 April.

―― (2005). 'Electoral participation and non-voter segmentation'. In W. Wymer and J. Lees-Marshment (eds), *Current Issues in Political Marketing*. Binghamton, NY: Haworth Press.

Broughton, D. (1995). *Public Opinion Polling and Politics in Britain*. London: Prentice Hall.

Burton, Michael John (2008). 'Political marketing matters: identifying the effect of candidate positioning in congressional elections'. *Journal of Political Marketing*, 6(4): 33–50.

Coleman, Stephen (2007). 'Review of Lilleker and Lees-Marshment (2005) *Political Marketing: A Comparative Perspective*'. *Parliamentary Affairs*, 60(1): 180–6.

Collins, N. and P. Butler (1996). 'Positioning political parties: a market analysis'. *Harvard International Journal of Press/Politics*, 1(2): 63–77.

―― and ―― (2002). 'Considerations on market analysis for political parties'. In Nicholas O'Shaughnessy and Stephan Henneberg (eds), *The Idea of Political Marketing*. London: Praeger.

Daves, Robert-P. and Frank Newport (2005). 'Pollsters under attack'. *Public Opinion Quarterly*, 69(5): 670–81.

Davidson, Scott (2005). 'Grey power, school gate mums and the youth vote: age as a key factor in voter segmentation and engagement in the 2005 UK General Election'. *Journal of Marketing Management*, 21(9/10): 1179–92.

Gould, Philip (1998). *The Unfinished Revolution: How the Modernisers Saved the Labour Party*. London: Little Brown.

Heith, Diane (2004). *Polling to Govern: Public Opinion and Presidential Leadership*. Palo Alto, CA: Stanford University Press.

Herbst, S. (1993). *Numbered Voices*. Chicago, IL: University of Chicago Press.

Howard, Peter and Shoon Kathleen Murray (2002). 'Variation in White House polling operations'. *Public Opinion Quarterly*, 66(4): 527–58.

Johnson, Dennis (2007). *No Place for Amateurs* (2nd edn.). London: Routledge.

Kavanagh, D. (1996). 'Speaking truth to power? Pollsters as campaign advisers?'. *European Journal of Marketing*, 30(10/11): 104–13.

Krotz, J.L. (no date). 'Dos and don'ts of focus groups'. Microsoft business center. Available online at www.microsoft.com/smallbusiness/resources/marketing/market-research/dos-and-donts-for-using-marketing-focus-groups.aspx (accessed 5 March 2008).

Lees-Marshment, J. (2008). *Political Marketing and British Political Parties* (2nd edn). Manchester: Manchester University Press.

Lipari, L. (1999). 'Polling as ritual'. *Journal of Communication* (Winter edn): 83–101.

Macedo, Stephen, Yvette Alex-Assensoh, Jeffrey M. Berry, Michael Brinthall, David E. Campbell, *et al.* (2005). *Democracy at Risk: How Political Choices Undermine Citizen Participation and What We Can Do About It*. Washington, DC: Brookings Institution Press.

Moon, Nick (1999). *Opinion Polls: History, Theory and Practice*. Manchester: Manchester University Press.

Moore, D.W. (1992). *Superpollsters: How They Measure and Manipulate Public Opinion in America*. New York: Four Walls Eight Windows.

Myers, Greg (2004). *Matters of Opinion: Talking About Public Issues*. New York: Cambridge University Press.

National Council on Public Polls (1995). 'Push Polls'. Press release, 22 May. Available online at www.ncpp.org/?q=node/41 (accessed 4 March 2008).

Newman, B. (1999). 'A predictive model of voter behaviour: the repositioning of Bill Clinton'. In B. Newman (ed.), *Handbook of Political Marketing*. Thousand Oaks, CA: Sage.

—— and J. Sheth (1987). *A Theory of Political Choice Behaviour*. New York: Praeger.

O'Shaughnessy, Nicholas J. and Stephan C. Henneberg (2007). 'The selling of the president 2004: a marketing perspective'. *Journal of Public Affairs*, 7(3): 249–68.

Penn, Mark with E. Kinney Zalesne (2007). *Micro-Trends: The Small Forces Behind Tomorrow's Big Changes*. New York: Twelve, Hachette Book Group.

Promise (2005). 'Reconnecting the Prime Minister'. Company paper, Promise UK. Available online at www.promisecorp.com.

Rademacher, Eric W. and Alfred J. Tuchfarber (1999). 'Pre-election polling and political campaigns'. In B. Newman (ed.), *Handbook of Political Marketing*. Thousand Oaks, CA: Sage.

Revill, J. (2007). '"Sham" citizens' juries faces controls: overhaul for Brown's "big idea" to engage voters as critics say they are just glorified focus groups'. *The Observer*, 30 September. Available online at www.guardian.co.uk/politics/2007/sep/30/immigrationpolicy.observerpolitics (accessed 5 March 2008).

Ross, Jim (http://jimrossconsulting.com/) (2008). Excerpts from www.completecampaigns.com/article.asp?articleid=27 (accessed 4 March 2008).

Rothmayr, Christine and Sibylle Hardmeier (2002). 'Government and polling: use and impact of polls in the policy-making process in Switzerland'. *International Journal of Public Opinion Research*, 14(2): 123–40.

Rottinghaus, Brandon and Irina Alberro (2005). 'Rivaling the PRI: the image management of Vicente Fox and the use of public opinion polling in the 2000 Mexican Election'. *Latin American Politics and Society*, 47(2): 143–58.

Russell, Andrew T. and Ed Fieldhouse (2005). *Neither Left nor Right? The Liberal Democrats and the Electorate*. Manchester: Manchester University Press.

Salmon, C.T. and T.L. Glasser (1995). 'The politics of polling and the limits of consent'. In T.L. Glasser and C.T. Salmon (eds), *Public Opinion and the Communication of Consent*. New York: Guilford Press.

Savigny, Heather (2005). 'Labour, political marketing and the 2005 election: a campaign of two halves'. *Journal of Marketing Management*, 21(9/10): 925–41.

—— (2007). 'Focus groups and political marketing: science and democracy as axiomatic?'. *The British Journal of Politics and International Relations*, 9(1): 122–37.

—— (2008). *The Problem of Political Marketing*. London: Continuum.

Scammell, Margaret (2008). 'Brand Blair: marketing politics in the consumer age'. In D. Lilleker and R. Scullion (eds), *Voters or Consumers: Imagining the Contemporary Electorate*. Newcastle: Cambridge Scholars Publishing.

Seawright, David (2005). 'On a low road: the 2005 Conservative campaign'. *Journal of Marketing Management*, 21(9/10): 943–57.

Sherman, Elaine and Leon Schiffman (2002a). 'Trends and issues in political marketing technologies'. *Journal of Political Marketing*, 1(1): 231–3.

—— (2002b). 'Political marketing research in the 2000 US election'. *Journal of Political Marketing*, 1(2/3): 53–68.

Smith, Gareth (2005). 'Positioning political parties: the 2005 UK General Election'. *Journal of Marketing Management*, 21(9/10): 1135–49.

—— and Andy Hirst (2001). 'Strategic political segmentation: a new approach for a new era of political marketing'. *European Journal of Marketing*, 35(9/10): 1058–73.

—— and John Saunders (1990). 'The application of marketing to British politics'. *Journal of Marketing Management*, 5(3): 295–306.

Sparrow, N. and J. Turner (2001). 'The integrating of market research techniques in developing strategies in a more uncertain political climate'. *European Journal of Marketing*, 35(9/10): 984–1002.

Teinturier, Brice (2008). 'The presidential elections in France 2007 – the role of opinion polls'. In Marita Carballo and Ulf Hjelmar (eds), *Public Opinion Polling in a Globalized World*. Berlin: Springer-Verlag.

Varoga, Craig and Mike Rice (1999). 'Only the facts: professional research and message development'. In B. Newman (ed.), *Handbook of Political Marketing*. Thousand Oaks, CA: Sage.

Weissberg, Robert (2002). *Polling, Policy and Public Opinion: The Case Against Heeding the Voice of the People*. New York: Palgrave.

Wintour, Patrick (2005). 'Postcode data could decide next election'. Available online at www.spinwatch.org/content/view/613/9/ (accessed 8 May 2008).

Wring, Dominic (2005a). *The Politics of Marketing the Labour Party*. Hampshire: Palgrave Macmillan.

—— (2005b). 'The Labour campaign'. In Pippa Norris and Christopher Wlezien (eds), *Britain Votes 2005*. Oxford: Oxford University Press.

—— (2007). 'Focus group follies? Qualitative research and British Labour Party strategy'. *Journal of Political Marketing*, 5(4): 71–97.

Yorke, D. and S.A. Meehan (1996). 'ACORN in the political marketplace'. *European Journal of Marketing*, 20(8): 73–86.

5 Product development and branding

This chapter will explore ways in which parties and candidates develop their products and overall brand, and how they utilise marketing orientation, strategy and market intelligence in doing so. It will discuss examples of how parties develop their product in different countries, and then the branding of leaders and parties. The next section will explore the practical difficulties and limitations of product design by public opinion and problems in branding. Finally, the last section will explore democratic implications of product development and branding.

Product development

Market intelligence provides a deeper understanding of the mass electorate, enabling political elites to consider public demands before making political decisions. Academic analysis increasingly explores ways in which marketing can influence the political product, such as Newman's (1999) analysis of US presidential campaigns. Newman (1999: 72–77) notes how a number of US presidents changed their product in response to market intelligence. In 1984, Reagan emphasised his delivery record on the economy and peace to win re-election, and in 1988 Bush responded to the market desire for no tax rises, occupying a clear position in the marketplace. In 1992, Clinton focused on a message of change and economy. Table 5.1 summarises a number of examples where products have been developed in response to market demands, while Case study 5.1 provides a more detailed example of how the Moderate Party in Sweden changed its product in response to falling electoral fortunes.

Product development does not necessarily mean everything has to be changed; politicians may only need – or choose – to adapt a few aspects of their product. They can also respond to particular segments of the market only. Case study 5.2 shows how the Hungarian Socialist Party sought to win votes from young people using transactional marketing by changing certain aspects of the product.

Political marketing product development is, in practice, often complex and constantly evolving. Case study 5.3, about Hillary Clinton's bid to secure the Democratic presidential nomination in 2008, shows the complexities involved.

❝❞

Discussion point 5.1

Discuss the examples of product design in this chapter and try to identify other examples of current parties or candidates responding to the market in product formulation.

Table 5.1 Comparative political marketing product development

Case and author	Product developments in response to market intelligence
US Democrats/ Bill Clinton in 1992 Ingram and Lees-Marshment (2002)	• Distancing himself from traditional Democrat large government programmes. • Differentiation: he differentiated himself from the Republican President Bush by attacking his economic record and encouraging voters to view the election as a referendum on Bush's economic management. • Targeting: policy focus was on issues of concern to both target middle-class voters and traditional Democrat supporters, such as the economy and health care. • Delivery: a detailed economic plan was created that scaled back a number of Clinton's spending pledges and other promises, including his plans for infrastructure spending and deficit reduction, in order to make them more believable.
New Zealand Labour 1999 Rudd (2005)	• Adopted pledge cards to make the product more tangible. • Responded to market intelligence in policy development, especially in key areas. • Identified as of particular importance to voters, such as health, pensions, jobs, and law and order, as well as the general desire for positive vision and achievable proposals.
US Republicans/ George W. Bush in 2000 Knuckey and Lees-Marshment (2005)	• Leader: George W. Bush appealed both to swing voters and the Republican base; Bush portrayed himself as a different type of Republican – a compassionate conservative – and as a different type of politician – a uniter not a divider. • Policy: evolved to focus on issues that opinion polls showed to be of paramount concern, as well as where Democrats were traditionally strong, such as education, social security and health care. • Included traditional Republican themes such as tax-cuts, smaller government and a stronger military as well to appeal to internal markets. • Competition: criticised Al Gore as an 'Old Democrat' whose 'Big Government' programmes and tax plan showed that he did not trust the people. Contest became one between a 'New Republican' and an 'Old Democrat'. • Targeted: new market segments, including blacks and especially the growing Hispanic vote. Positive ads also targeted three other markets among the white electorate: women, moderates and independents.
German SPD's 1998 Bundestag election campaign Lees (2005)	• Developed policy themes based upon four 'positives' associated with the SPD that had become apparent in the party's private research. These were: (i) the idea of 'political change'; (ii) 'leadership'; (iii) 'innovation'; and (iv) 'justice'. • Concentrated upon policy areas where SPD was strong, such as labour market regulation, social and health provision, family life and youth. • Regained a reputation for economic competence. • Adjusted product to make it achievable and superior to competition. • Leadership: La Fontaine appealed to internal supporters, while Gerhard Schröder offered more modern approach, associated with the Third Way or *Neue Mitte* (New Centre).
Brazil, PT and Lula de Silva in 2002 Cotrim Maciera (2005)	• Leader: Lula became more moderate in policy speeches and positioning to suit the market. • PT moved to the centre ideologically and policy-wise. • Became more pragmatic in response to coalition-making. • Created a more mature, realistic set of promises. • Changes to attract female voters previously alienated. • Avoided complete criticism of competition.
Peru, APRA party and Alan Garcia Patrón-Galindo (2004)	• More modern, realistic and responsive policies with the New Minimum Programme. • Offered policies where opposition was weak. • Positioning on the centre-left to fill gap in marketplace left by more radical left parties.
Australia, Kevin Rudd Labour Party, 2007 Keenan (2007)	• Research found people wanted vision and hope for the future, but with Labour, they wanted reassurance there would be continued competent economic management. • Rudd proclaimed to be an economic conservative, and reassured there would be no change from the existing Howard-Liberal government. • Labour also downplayed or ignored its founding principles related to the working class. • Rudd adopted some socially conservative policies. • Focus was on education and other public service issues. • But also provided differentiation on issues such as the environment, ratifying Kyoto and withdrawing from the Iraq war.

Discussion point 5.2

Think of other examples where parties or candidates develop specific aspects of their product to respond to particular market segments, and discuss their effectiveness.

Not just in the US primaries, but in all elections, there is arguably always a need for continued development/redevelopment over time and particularly in power. Newman (1999: 47) argues that candidates maximise their potential to maintain support if 'they reposition their policies and images in response to the changing needs and wants of voters following the same marketing formula that works for companies'. Another way to examine this is to consider the product life cycle. In business, it is argued that all products have a certain shelf life: they only dominate the market until new or better products are created, and are subject to changes in market demands. The stages a new product goes through are: introduction, growth, maturity and decline. In business the basic notions are:

1   Introduction stage:
    * cost high;
    * sales volume low;
    * no/little competition – competitive manufacturers watch for acceptance/segment growth losses;
    * demand has to be created;
    * customers have to be prompted to try the product.

2   Growth stage:
    * costs reduced owing to economies of scale;
    * sales volume increases significantly;
    * profitability;
    * public awareness;
    * competition begins to increase with a few new players in establishing market;
    * prices to maximise market share.

3   Maturity stage:
    * costs are very low as you are well established in market and no need for publicity;
    * sales volume peaks;
    * increase in competitive offerings;
    * prices tend to drop owing to the proliferation of competing products;
    * brand differentiation, feature diversification, as each player seeks to differentiate from competition with 'how much product' is offered;
    * very profitable.

Discussion point 5.3

Why did Hillary Clinton's market-oriented bid fail to win the Democrat nomination in 2008?

How easy is it for candidates or political leaders to formulate a marketing strategy and product and stick to it? What are the advantages and limitations of changing a position half way through a campaign?

4   Decline or stability stage:
  * costs become counter-optimal;
  * sales volume decline or stabilise;
  * prices, profitability diminishes;
  * profit becomes more a challenge of production/distribution efficiency than increased sales.

This is obviously written for business, with considerations such as price and sales. However, it could be applied to politics. Different options to avoid such a decline can be considered: see Box 5.1.

The other important aspect of product design is branding.

Branding

Branding is about how a political organisation or individual is perceived overall. It is broader than the product; whereas a product has a functional purpose, a brand offers something additional, which is more psychological and less tangible. It is concerned with impressions,

---

Box 5.1 Options to avoid product decline

1   Product diversification – creating different product variants.
2   New product uses – applying the core product to different uses.
3   Changing product layers – altering the product features and creating different product families.
4   Repositioning – changing the perceived values and intent a product has in the mind of the consumer.
5   Co-branding – enhancing (or diluting) the product's brand equity by association with another strong brand.
6   Repackaging – literally placing the product in a new package so as to revive its appeal.
7   Rebranding – a drastic and costly measure used to disassociate the brand from the previous values associated with it.
8   Increasing frequency of use – encouraging consumers to break away from traditional models of product usage.
9   New markets and segments – this strategy is an attempt to penetrate non-traditional markets or consumer segments.
10 Pricing and special offers – pricing is a positioning tool and a way to influence sales through the use of various price and payment schemes and models.

Source: Steinhardt (2007)

Discussion point 5.4

To what extent does the new product life cycle help to explain the changing fortunes of politicians in power? Could any of the suggestions in Box 5.1 (as well as other marketing literature) offer solutions for candidates, parties and government?

images, attitudes and recognition. Branding helps the party or candidate to help change or maintain reputation and support (see Smith 2001, Schneider 2004, Needham 2005, 2006, Lloyd 2006 and Scammell 2008). Brands:

1   create a feeling of identity with the party or its candidates;
2   can be used to reinforce partisanship, despite declining forces in the market;
3   help consumers process information and feel more secure about their decision;
4   help voters understand what a party is about;
5   help distinguish a candidate or party from the competition;
6   are made up of many different aspects, which makes them hard to measure, and also to change;
7   can emerge from customer experience;
8   involve market intelligence, product/brand (re-)design and product/brand delivery, with all three aspects merging into one another.

Lloyd (2006) examined the uses of branding in the 2005 UK General Election. Her research showed that the different colours of the three main parties, Labour, Conservative and Liberal Democrat, worked well to differentiate the parties and create enduring brand associations. Voters' associations with brands were predicated on previous party behaviour at past elections, not just what the parties offered in 2005 – showing the longevity of brand image. The leaders' behaviour had affected perceptions of the brand – e.g. perceptions that Blair had misled the electorate over the war coloured perceptions of the New Labour brand; and the Lib Dem leader Charles Kennedy's appearances on television comedy shows encouraged participants to dismiss the brand as not being serious enough. While the leader was therefore an important part of branding in politics, it was also problematic if the leader's popularity declined. Needham (2005) details what makes a successful political brand: see Box 5.2.

These elements, when achieved, help to create a trusting relationship between producer and consumer. Case study 5.4 illustrates the differing fortunes of branding in recent presidential elections in the US (see also Gould 2003).

Practitioner perspective 5.1

In terms of content alone, politics is different to buying a car. However, we can learn from brand advertising, how certain instruments, concepts and images can be used to depict political content.

(Matthew Machnig, Bundestag Chief of the SPD, interviewed and quoted by Schneider 2004: 50)

Box 5.2 Needham's criteria for successful brands

1   Brands act as simplifiers, so voters do not need such detailed product information.
2   Brands are unique and clearly differentiated from the competition.
3   Brands are reassuring and make voting for them seem less risky.
4   Brands are aspirational and evoke a positive vision of a better way of life.
5   Brands symbolise better internal values of the product or organisation compared with the competitors.
6   Brands are perceived as credible, delivering on their promises.

Source: Needham (2005: 347–8)

Branding is also an issue for leaders once elected. Needham (2005) also assessed US Democrat President Bill Clinton and UK Prime Minister Tony Blair in power: see Table 5.3.

Branding can be carried out in any country: see Case study 5.5 on Ghana. Redevelopment of the brand can be used to help the party or candidate reach new markets. However, it can be more difficult to rebrand an old political product than a new one, and it is harder to rebrand when in office than in opposition. Rebranding is even more complex within the US system, where parties are officially separated from nominees until one victor emerges from the primary process. Nevertheless, the overall brand image of the party in the eyes of the voter can affect election results.

Nevertheless, Scammell (2008) notes how Blair was rebranded in his second term, leading up to the 2005 election. The market environment was not positive, as his popularity had declined significantly. Scammell reported how Labour enlisted the company Promise to work with strategists and develop ways to reconnect Blair to the electorate: see Box 5.3.

Branding can also be used to sell policies. Barberio (2006) explores how branding can be used by US presidents trying to sell policies to various stakeholders – Congress, interest groups, the media and the public. Branding, distinct from traditional leadership communication tools such as demagoguery, can be seen in a form of branded rhetoric that 'provides clues to the specific segments of the public about the true intent of policies or positions in a way that either resonates positively with the rest of the public or falls harmlessly outside their knowledge or interests'. He outlines principles of presidential branding:

1   Appeal to universally desired values such as strength, reliability and fairness.
2   Make claims and offer a comparison about how their product, service or plan more fully provides these values, or, in extreme cases, how the competition's offering is completely devoid of these values.
3   Encourage the consumer to see a benefit beyond the one immediately evident in the product, service or plan offered. This encouragement may come directly, by means of code words, or indirectly, by the use of symbols.

Barberio (2006) notes examples such as 'The Square Deal', 'The New Deal', 'The Great Society' and, more recently, 'No Child Left Behind', arguing that presidents use branding strategies to gain public support before engaging in traditional political combat with organisations and institutions. They try to do so using value-based words, phrases and symbols that resonate with voters and their values, aided by staff and organisational developments in office such as the White House Offices of Communications, Public Liaison and Media Liaison. The George W. Bush administration used careful language to suit the new target markets – e.g. 'softer, female-friendly language,' such as 'employers' instead of 'business', 'moms and dads' in place of 'parents', and 'tax relief' rather than 'tax cuts' (Fritz *et al.* 2004: 19).

Practical issues with product design and branding

There are many examples and theories of branding and product development, but there are a number of issues and difficulties that can arise in practice.

Product development

There are a number of factors that need to be remembered when considering how to develop a product, particularly in relation to marketing demands.

Table 5.2 Blair and Clinton's brand performance

Successful brand criteria	Bill Clinton, 1992–2000	Tony Blair, 1997–2005
Simple	• Clear communication and organisation of communication staff. • Conveyed Clinton story in first few months of office: 'government failed us, betrayed our people and our values'. However: • Lack of clarity due to media attention on sub issues rather than main focus on economic plan and health care.	• Clear communication and organisation of communication staff, e.g. 'opportunity for all' and 'investment and reform'. However: • Also subject to criticism of too much spin.
Unique	• Differentiated himself as a New Democrat, using personal credentials; rising above both opposition and his own party. • Not just no tax cuts, or yes to tax cuts, but certain tax cuts. • Third way.	• Effective differentiation, highlighting positives, e.g. social justice against opposition weaknesses, e.g. backward looking. • Third way.
Reassuring	• Continued policy to suit new middle-class voters, e.g. middle-class bill of rights, including tax cuts and help with college fees. However: • Failure to provide reassurance as aborted social conservative campaign stance for social liberal, losing votes in 1994 mid-term elections. But: • Regained popularity when focused on public sector delivery.	• Implemented middle class-friendly policies, e.g. anti-crime and cutting government waste. • Avoided returning to old Labour era of strikes and high taxes. However: • Failed to meet high expectations associated with New Labour design and landslide Victory.
Aspirational	• Emphasised appeal to aspirant hard working families. However: • Once in power, began to lose touch.	
Value-based	• Developed values agenda in later years; opportunity, responsibility and community. • Fitted policies around values. However: • Damaged by Lewinsky scandal.	• Used language of values e.g. equal worth, opportunity for all, responsibility and community. But: • External communication criticised as shadowing lack of policy depth, principles and ideology. • Blair seen as willing to consider any value; so contaminated the brand.
Credible by delivering on promises	• Targeted promises. However: • Constrained in implementation by political system – e.g. failure of health care plan. • Voters did not believe claims of smaller deficit and more jobs. So: • Focused on advocating action at state level, not federal. • Achieved more positive perception of delivery over time.	• Targeted pledges. • Annual reports on delivery. However: • Still perceived to have failed to deliver by voters.

Source: Needham (2005: 349–55)

Box 5.3 Rebranding of Blair in power

Roy Langmaid, co-founder at consultancy Promise
(see www.promisecorp.com/people/index.htm)

We have experience of developing leadership attributes and brand strategy through working with the New Labour strategy team in the run-up to the British General Election of 2005. The work encompassed brand analysis and qualitative research on behalf of the government, and looked at the incumbent New Labour brand, the reputation of Prime Minister Tony Blair and how these compared with the opposition Conservative Party and its then leader Michael Howard. Brand management can often be an operation that sits apart from daily corporate life. But managing political identities is a live exercise, charged with emotion and changing second by second. Consumer relationships must be nurtured and appreciated, both instantly and over time.

The research
We organised four groups of people to obtain feedback on the New Labour brand. There were two groups of women and two of men, who were:

- Labour loyals (voted Labour last time and would do again);
- undecideds (voted Labour last time but undecided in 2005).

As we talked to these groups, we started to put the issue into a branding context. We saw that people's needs were very different from when New Labour was originally elected in 1997. We believed there was a new climate of insecurity, fostered by events such as the terrorist attack on the World Trade Centre and domestic issues of lawlessness and disrespect.

We hypothesised that the New Labour brand, personified by Tony Blair, had lost its attraction for the British public. Some of the disillusionment stemmed from developments in respondents' relationships with Blair on a personal level, and this was a crucial element. We needed to look at Blair's brand as a leader and how he could reconnect with the electorate. Blair was [at] the lowest point on the undecided voters' chart. Brands such as Mercedes and Tesco exceeded the political sphere in terms of reputation, while even public transport was see as delivering better than Blair and New Labour.

The worrying result for New Labour was that consumers saw the Conservatives as outperforming them on all the attributes that might drive their voting in 2005. It appeared that there was a groundswell of hostility towards Blair and Labour, particularly among women.

The brand model
It was not just Blair who needed work as a brand. It appeared to us that New Labour also needed analysis. It was built on an existing brand – Labour – that had, broadly speaking, become irrelevant to the public. The history of the brand revealed that it had moved from a product-oriented party to a sales-oriented party and then a market-oriented party. But, in 2005, the New Labour brand – personified to voters by Tony Blair – had stopped listening. It had become too reliant on its figurehead – despite his failings. New Labour seemed lightweight without Blair. The New Labour brand was hollow, described by many as the triumph of spin over substance.

The research respondents revealed, not only the brand issue for New Labour, but also the potential threat of the Conservatives. They claimed that more substantial brand equity lay with the Conservatives, who appeared to stand for something real, if dated. Attributes such as competence, integrity and teamwork came through as three of the most important elements for any brand. These three issues had been undermined for voters by the perceived inability of the prime minister to listen (principally over Iraq), the divisiveness of the media and the infighting within the party.

We developed a model that we believed contained the 'essence' of New Labour. While the brand in 1997 had been built on promises, New Labour in 2005 was being judged on delivery. We described New Labour as 'progressive realists'. We advised the Government to embark on four key strategies for bringing the brand to life:

- Show strength in depth: illustrate party unity; bring others to the fore; create advocates at a local level; and allow party spokespeople to show a degree of autonomy, while keeping them on message.
- Be seen to deliver: reiterate a domestic focus; accentuate positives such as the economy; keep promises manageable and accountable and even create a set of pledges. Talk about 'we', not 'me', and spending on public services.
- Communications: make sure everything is 'on-brand'. Messages must be not only engaging but credible. Assess current communications through the new brand lens. Make sure you are consistent with your identity, using 'New Labour', not just 'Labour'.
- Leadership: reconnect through this. Make sure behaviour, communication and image personify the brand.

People have love affairs with brands; these can fade or go abruptly wrong, and consumers often need to be nurtured and courted to regain their positive feelings. You must treat all your customers with care and respect. When Tony Blair was confronted by a pensioner who had been forced to pull out her own teeth as she could not find an NHS dentist, he had to treat her with sympathy and interest. This was a very extreme act, but he had to treat her complaint with full attention and compassion.

The New Labour case study also shows the importance of being 'on message' across the entire organisation. The chief executive must be saying the same things as the head of HR and the director of marketing. Mass-market brands must be careful, like Blair, not to appear patronising or out of touch.

The political case study also has a message about brand partnerships. You need to choose a partner that has the same aims and objectives as you. While the US may have had the same objectives as the UK in going to war in Iraq, it is not clear that the countries share the same values. British people are proud to be different from Americans – failing to understand this is a mistake.

It is important to understand that sometimes you may need to overhaul your strategy. Labour was not elected in its old incarnation as a left-wing party. It found success as New Labour. In the same way, Apple has moved from the IT sector, where it struggled, to the creative and entertainment areas, where it has found new relevance. Make sure your brand has the skills to adapt too.

Source: *Brand Strategy* (2006)

Discussion point 5.5

Try to describe the brand of current political leaders of parties. How might following the principles of successful branding outlined in Box 5.2 and lessons from Case studies 5.4, 5.5 and Box 5.3 help increase their standing?

Factor 1: Product development must be realistic

Case study 5.6 illustrates how products must be achievable, showing how unrealistic promises were made that, despite the best marketing, limited their success.

Factor 2: There are a number of reasons why new political products will not gain support

The market determines the success of products as much as the value of that product. One example is environmentalism. Environmental issues have been adopted by mainstream major parties, aided by former Vice President Al Gore's work around his documentary *An Inconvenient Truth*, but this is decades after the first environmental protests. It is frustrating for political activists and politicians who may believe, or even know, that a policy needs to be implemented, but without the public will or market demand it is difficult to succeed.

Factor 3: Not all parties everywhere use marketing to inform the product

Product development also depends on internal party demands, the goals of an individual politician or party, belief, ideology and changing fortunes in the market place. Certain trends, such as increased professionalisation of parties, may encourage more market-oriented behaviour, but it is not yet clear. Lilleker and Lees-Marshment's (2005) comparative collection showed that, while there were a number of market-oriented parties around the world, parties also adopted more sales-oriented approaches, determining their product to suit elite decisions and using marketing only to sell it to voters. This was particularly true of small parties. Often politicians, once they get into power and have access to the government bureaucracy and further policy advice, change their perspective on policy and downgrade the value of the market as a potential contributor to political decisions, as will be explored in Chapter 8.

In addition to designing the specific product to be offered to voters at election time and implementing it, parties and candidates can consider their overall brand, which is more complex but remains potentially influential on long-term success.

Discussion point 5.6

What does Case study 5.6 show about the importance of product adjustment and offering realistic promises? Are there any other cases where politicians have made unrealistic promises?

"
"

Discussion point 5.7

Discuss the nature of the products offered by political parties in your country. How have they have been developed (e.g. in response to market intelligence, competition, governing realities, belief, a particular leader or ideology)? Does this relate to how well the party is doing in terms of attracting support (i.e. votes, members, stakeholders, funding, poll standing and winning or losing elections)?

Branding

There are a number of practical factors that make branding difficult in some cases.

Factor 1: Branding activities need to be authentic

It is no good conducting research and asking politicians to change to suit it in a way that does not suit them and will not be convincing. Needham (2006: 179) explains that there must be 'congruence between the internal values of the product . . . and its external message'. Case study 5.7 illustrates this.

Factor 2: Branding has to deliver

White and de Chernatony (2002: 50) argue that the UK New Labour brand 'came to be devalued when some of the important promises made were not delivered'. The brand promise in 1997 had been vague: 'aimed to reassure, to allay fears and to convince the electorate that Labour would provide a new kind of government'. Despite effective communication, the difference between government talk and public perception of reality created negative feelings towards the whole brand.

Factor 3: Even the best marketing research and advisors cannot ensure rebranding of a party will be successful

Because a brand involves long-term identity and psychological perception, it is harder to change. A party's failure in government can haunt it for a long time in opposition. After losing power in 1997, the new leader of the UK Conservatives, William Hague, tried to change the overall brand of his party, utilising significant research and changing its organisational structure as well as communications style. Hague and the party were pictured in counter-intuitive situations to convey the message that the party had changed: Hague visited the multicultural Notting Hill Carnival, and his team were pictured in baseball caps with the 'fresh start' logo at an adventure park, trying to suggest a party that was pro race, women and youth and that accepted non-traditional lifestyles. However, the public was reluctant to believe this new approach, it failed to attract public support, and the rebranding strategy was abandoned mid-term (Lees-Marshment 2008: 216).

Case study 5.8 on ACT, a minor party in New Zealand, illustrates this further. Like most marketing techniques and concepts, as Scammell (2008: 109–10) observed, 'branding is not the elusive magic bullet to political success. There is no magic formula.' Barberio (2006) observed that branding did not work for President George W. Bush when he tried to implement new social security reforms, despite 'the trappings of branding including high value content and phrasemaking featuring "personal" rather than "private" accounts.'

Branding has to change over time to be successful

When parties or presidents win power, they have to continue to respond and rebrand. Cosgrove (2007) argued that the Republican loss of seats in the 2006 mid-term elections was because of problems in delivery, but also because the Republicans:

> added nothing to their brand since 2002 that was relevant to the voters' concerns. In such a circumstance, consumers will always start to look for something different and it is for this reason that old products must go away while new ones must be added.

UK Labour recognised the need to change over elections, as Scammell (2008: 108–9) observed:

- 1997 branding was about reassurance, to convince voters that New Labour really was *new*.
- 2001 branding was about refreshing the brand and showing leadership.
- 2005 branding was about re-establishing Tony Blair as a responsive, in touch leader voters had supported in 1997.

Differentiation is needed, especially from one leader to the next. Needham (2006) also observes how Bush Senior and John Major failed to win a second election because they failed to offer an alternative brand offering to their predecessors. The same was true of Al Gore and is, potentially, of Gordon Brown. Gore tried to distance himself from the problems of Bill Clinton but, in doing so, could not then take credit for the achievements of the government. Rebranding presents difficulties for successors of strong brand leaders.

Discussion point 5.8

Consider Case studies 5.7 and 5.8 and/or other attempts by parties or politicians to rebrand themselves. How successful have they been and why?

Democratic issues with product development and branding in politics

There are a number of democratic issues to consider with branding and designing the product to suit the market (Needham 2005, Barberio 2006, Scammell 2008): see Table 5.4.

Overall, marketing political products raises questions about the ability of the public to make the right decision. However, even in consumer commercial profit marketing there are concerns about ethics and principles and also need for professional input. This is a rich area for debate.

Debate 5.1

Proposition: Politicians and parties should change their behaviour to suit public opinion instead of following their own principles.

Table 5.3 Potential democratic consequences of product development and branding

	Positive consequences	Negative consequences
Product development	• Makes elites more responsive to market. • Those in power are aware of public reaction when making decisions. • Does not have to mean wholescale change. • Does involve elite decisions; it is a balance of leadership and listening.	• Changes traditional notions of democracy. • Undermines ideology. • Potentially threatens the notion of representative democracy where the public elects politicians to make decisions in their interest.
Branding	• Helps differentiation, thus enhancing choice. • Can generate unity and help pass legislation.	• Simplifies discourse, so public relies on the brand without detailed scrutiny of elite behaviour. • Plays on emotion, reducing debate. • Can also prevent effective variation and appropriate freedom at local level. • Can encourage confrontation instead of compromise needed to make government work.

Summary

Marketing can influence how politicians behave and be used to inform how the product is developed as well as the overall brand. Both candidates and parties, in opposition and government, can utilise marketing to attempt to improve their performance, although it is not without its issues, both practical and democratic. Furthermore, elites also need to consider the divergent views of internal supporters and how to motivate such volunteers to help the campaign. Political marketing involves a complex balancing act of responding to traditional supporters, new markets, internal members and the opposition, while all the time conveying the sense of a vision that means something and will achieve deliverable change to people's lives. The next chapter will discuss internal marketing.

ASSESSED WORK

Essays

1   'The election campaign is the least important part of political marketing.' Explain and critique the validity of this statement, illustrating your argument with examples and theory.
2   Discuss the potential and limitations of developing the political product according to public opinion.
3   Apply the new product life cycle to politics. Does it help to explain changing fortunes of politicians in power?
4   Consider the suggestions in Box 5.1 (as well as other marketing literature if you want) about how to beat the product life cycle, and consider if any of these offer solutions for candidates, parties and government.
5   How successful is political branding? Explore both theory and examples to develop your answer.

Applied

1   Develop a product development plan for a party or candidate in your country, according to recent, publicly available market intelligence results.

2   Conduct a market intelligence assessment on a candidate or party, and then develop a rebranding strategy to counteract any negatives in time for the next election.

Case study 5.1 From the 'old' to the 'new' moderates: a Swedish case study   *Jesper Strömbäck*

Sweden is a parliamentary and party-centred democracy, with a proportional electoral system. Since 1994, the party system has consisted of seven significant parties. From left to right, these are the Left Party, the Social Democrats, the Green Party, the Centre Party, the Liberal Party, the Christian Democrats and the Moderate Party.

The left–right ideological continuum is of the utmost importance in Swedish politics. This has not changed, although electoral volatility has increased, and party identification has decreased during recent decades (Holmberg and Oscarsson 2004). Generally speaking, people tend to vote for the party they perceive to be closest to themselves on the left–right continuum, both ideologically and with respect to the most salient issues in an election.

Such an electoral environment does not create strong incentives for the parties to become market-oriented (Strömbäck 2007). Rather, it encourages a product- or sales-orientation. Research has also shown that most Swedish parties should be classified as sales-oriented, with some leaning towards a product-orientation (Nord and Strömbäck 2003, Petersson *et al.* 2006). Changes might be under way, however, most clearly exemplified by the Moderate Party.

The Moderate Party is the party most to the right of all Swedish parties. Since the late 1970s, it has been the largest of the parties to the right and the leading opposition party to the Social Democrats. Its policies could be described as displaying a mixture of conservative and neo-liberal values, and it has been a strong proponent of policies aimed at decreasing the size of the welfare state, privatisation, lower taxes and deregulation. Such policies have been controversial in a society strongly influenced by decades of Social Democratic rule and a strong welfare state. In fact, the only periods since the 1930s when the Social Democrats have not formed part of the government have been between 1976 and 1982, and 1991 and 1994. This has caused a lot of frustration among people and parties that do not form part of the left bloc.

Table 5.4 The Swedish elections and governments, 1994–2006

	1994 (%)	1998 (%)	2002 (%)	2006 (%)
The Left Party (V)	6.2	12.0	8.3	5.8
The Social Democrats (S)	45.3	36.4	39.8	35.0
The Green Party (MP)	5.0	4.5	4.6	5.2
The Centre Party (C)	7.7	5.1	6.0	7.9
The Liberal Party (FP)	7.2	4.7	13.3	7.5
The Christian Democrats (KD)	4.1	11.8	9.1	6.6
The Moderate Party (M)	22.4	22.9	15.2	26.2
Turnout	88.1	81.4	80.1	82.0
Parties in government	(S)	(S)	(S)	(M)+(FP)+ (C)+(KD)

Source: www.val.se; www.scb.se

In 2002, the Moderate Party faced its worst election result since 1973. This happened after it ran a rather traditional campaign, with a strong emphasis on the need for lower taxes, despite polls showing that this issue was not high on the voters' agenda. After that election, the former leadership was heavily criticised, and then-party leader Bo Lundgren had to resign.

In October 2004, the Moderate Party elected Fredrik Reinfeldt as its new party leader. From the beginning, it was clear that he intended to initiate some changes to the party. This was the first starting point for the changes that subsequently came about.

The second starting point came on 4 April 2004, when Reinfeldt and two associates published an article with the headline 'We are changing our economic policies'. In the article, the authors explained that the party's former economic policies were unfair, in the sense that they would mostly benefit people with higher incomes, and that, in addition, they would result in weaker state finances. Therefore, the party had decided to change economic policies, in essence moving the party towards the centre of the Swedish political spectrum.

Never before had a party criticised itself so hard and so publicly, and never before had a party announced such a dramatic policy shift. Yet this was just the first policy shift, and, in the following years, the party changed its policies with respect to many other policy areas. As soon as July 2004, journalists wrote about the changes as 'a total renovation' of the party. This was also when the party started to talk about 'the new Moderates', a clear parallel to the British Labour Party under Tony Blair's leadership. Later on, Reinfeldt even started to talk about the Moderates as the new 'labour' party.

The motive for these changes was the conclusion that the Moderate Party, in order to increase its share of voters and oust the Social Democrats from power, simply had to change and be perceived as less right-wing. The catastrophic election result in 2002 was interpreted as a clear signal that the 'old' Moderates could not continue as if nothing had really happened, and it also gave the new leadership a mandate for change. Further contributing to this mandate was that the Moderate Party has a strongly hierarchical political culture (Barrling Hermansson 2004).

The change from the 'old' to the 'new' Moderates also made possible a formal 'Alliance for Sweden', made up of the centre and right-wing parties and launched in August 2004. This alliance subsequently won the 2006 Swedish election, and, for the first time in history, these parties formed a majority coalition government. Reinfeldt became the new prime minister.

Underlying many of the policy changes is that the 'new Moderates' seek to take the voters, and their understandings of everyday reality and what constitutes problems, as the starting point. As expressed by Per Schlingmann, the party secretary: 'it is the voters' everyday experiences that guide the policy formation and how we express ourselves'. This suggests that the change from the 'old' to the 'new' Moderates should be interpreted as a sign of the party having become more market-oriented.

At the same time, Schlingmann and other representatives of the Moderates denounce the notion that the party has become market-oriented. According to Schlingmann, there is a crucial difference between taking the voters' experiences and perceptions as a starting point, to seek to redress the problems that ordinary voters experience in their everyday lives, and to simply follow the results from various polls and focus groups. Thus, according to him, it is less important to use or to follow these results, and more important to do a thorough analysis of how people experience and perceive everyday life and the problems connected to that, and then design the policy solutions. He also states that it is important to challenge people, and that the branding of the party as the 'new labour party' was not the result of polls or focus groups. Instead, the party uses focus groups mainly to test the reactions to messages already decided upon.

Thus, according to the Moderate Party itself, it is not market-oriented. At the same time, it is clear that the party continuously attempts to calibrate its policies and messages so that they are in accordance with the wants and needs of selected target groups. Hence, if political market-orientation is characterised by a needs assessment approach, where a party attempts to identify and then design a political offering to meet and satisfy expressed, as well as latent, wants and needs of selected target groups, then the Moderates should be characterised as market-oriented. In this context, the means used are less important than the overriding philosophy that a party should take the experiences and perceptions of ordinary people as the starting point for both policy formation and communication.

However, there are reasons to be cautious when drawing conclusions, as it is yet unclear how deep-rooted and lasting the changes are. Becoming more market-oriented is one thing; maintaining a market-orientation is another, and the latter can be just as difficult as the former (Lilleker and Lees-Marshment 2005). Perhaps one general rule of thumb in this context, therefore, should be not to characterise a party – as opposed to a particular leadership – as market-oriented before it has faced the voters as market-oriented in at least two successive elections.

Sources and further reading

Barrling Hermansson, K. (2004). *Partikulturer*. Uppsala: Statsvetenskapliga institutionen, Uppsala universitet.

Holmberg, S. and H. Oscarsson (2004). *Väljare. Svenskt väljarbeteende under 50 år*. Stockholm: Norstedts Juridik.

Lilleker, D.G. and J. Lees-Marshment (2005). 'Conclusion: towards a comparative model of party marketing'. In D.G. Lilleker and J. Lees-Marshment (eds), *Political Marketing: A Comparative Perspective*. Manchester: Manchester University Press, pp. 205–28.

Nord, L.W. and J. Strömbäck (2003). Valfeber och nyhetsfrossa. Politisk kommunikation i valrörelsen 2002. Stockholm: Sellin & Partner.

Petersson, O., M. Djerf-Pierre, S. Holmberg, J. Strömbäck and L. Weibull (2006). *Media and Elections in Sweden*. Stockholm: SNS Förlag.

Strömbäck, Jesper (2007). 'Antecedents of political market orientation in Britain and Sweden: analysis and future research propositions'. *Journal of Public Affairs*, 7: 1–11.

Case study 5.2 The Hungarian Socialist Party winning young people
Balázs Kiss

The background

In the period of 2002–06, the government side, with the Hungarian Socialist Party (HSP) in leading position, had a majority of ten mandates only in the parliament of 386 seats. The small majority forced the party to make a decision well before the next elections in 2006: which new segment to win in order to widen its electorate and retain its position. The HSP chose young people, particularly first voters and university and college students. In August of 2004, Ferenc Gyurcsány was elected prime minister, and in two weeks the Hungarian Socialist Party also got a new president, István Hiller; both persons appeared suitable to win support from the Hungarian youth.

Transactional marketing in use

For the analysis of the HSP marketing strategy, the most traditional approach will be used, the mix of four marketing activities: product, price, placement and promotion. The segment of the young was entirely new for the party; therefore the party and the prime minister had to be constructed as consumable for young people; from the young, they had to ask for efforts that it was ready to exert; they had to make themselves available for the youth in a specific way; and, finally, they had to communicate the new image in the way that is attractive for the segment.

Product

In political marketing, product covers the leader image and party image first of all, and, to a certain extent, specific policy issues.

Leader image

Through the media, or directly by Internet, posters, direct mail etc., the image-makers of the prime minister offered components with the help of which young people were expected to build the image of a young politician. Ferenc Gyurcsány was suitable for the following reasons:

1   He was a young-looking man. He was forty-four years old, definitely younger than the previous leaders of the party.
2   He looked rather young with tall, slim figure, light hair and white teeth and moved like a young man.
3   He had young wife, who looked even younger than her age; he had a mother to be publicised – old people do not have mothers, publicly at least; and he had small children.
4   In his youth he had exhibited a passion for sport, namely jogging, for dance and for youthful pastimes such as partying.
5   His willingness to appear very often in funny situations in the tabloid papers qualified Ferenc Gyurcsány as young, because he was definitely different from the rest of the politicians.

There were components in the image of Ferenc Gyurcsány that did not have too much in common with the actual social positions of the young, but with their dreams and endeavours:

1   He was extremely rich: one of the wealthiest people in Hungary.
2   He became rich very quickly, during the first decade after 1990.
3   He was obviously a powerful man, who got to the position of prime minister almost by chance, definitely not after a long campaign period at least.
4   He had a passionately lovable partner, which may be the dream for many young people.
5   He had a good, loving mother.

Party image

The party image was also refreshed: the new leaders wanted to suggest that the HSP had become a modern, dynamic, proudly leftist party, not an old one, still unable to get rid of the past when it used to be the only party, before 1990.

Policy offer

The government was very active in abolishing compulsory military service and the communication of the abolishment afterwards; a programme called Nest Building was prepared in order to help young people with their housing problems, and another programme called Baby Bond was introduced for newborns. A government programme for the support of Hungarian pop music was also launched in 2005.

Price

In a political context, price means vote, activity expected from the supporters and the psychological prices: the fears and the hopes the party expects the supporters should feel as a reaction to the party messages. For the first time in the post 1990 history of the party, a huge rally was organised in the centre of Budapest some days before the election day: the Socialists wanted to attract the youth, which is supposedly fond of big demonstrations.

Amoeba, a special Internet-based organisation and game, openly aimed at drawing young people into politics, required the most effort. The participants were expected to read the news provided by the website and then to recommend solutions to political problems. The website said that a participant should be prepared to devote half an hour a day to the game.

Placement

The prime minister made himself available for the young in several places:

1 During the spring of 2005, he paid visits to all the university towns of Hungary, gave speeches and held forums.
2 After the forums, he went to a pub frequented by students and young intellectuals to talk to the youth.
3 The pub visits also served the promotion of the Internet portal and game Amoeba, which became the most important direct communication channel.
4 He met the participants of Amoeba regularly in real life too.
5 From January 2006, his weblog could be reached through the website of Amoeba, and he took part in the Internet talks launched on his web diary entries.
6 Ferenc Gyurcsány visited several festivals and rock concerts in the summer of 2005, where young people could meet him.

Promotion

The media were the channel of promotion in most of the cases.

1 The youth of the new leaders was mentioned several times, but mostly in political and not in physical terms: Gyurcsány and Hiller were born after 1956 and therefore they are innocent of the sins their predecessors may have committed then.
2 Gyurcsány was frequently photographed while jogging. On his first day as prime minister, he actually went running into the parliament.
3 He had four children; actually, two teenagers and two younger ones; but mostly the latter were focused on.
4 He became notorious for his love for dancing. In one of the leaked videos, Ferenc Gyurcsány was imitating Hugh Grant's dance from the film *Love Actually*.
5 Occasionally, he mentioned and visited pubs and clubs that were very fashionable among the young in Budapest. His youth was also suggested by his attendance at the festivals and rock concerts organised for young people.

The promotion of the party image

1 The campaign of autumn 2005 used new colours, new slogans and a new iconography.
2 The organisers of the rallies emphasised the youth of the party by seating young people, particularly girls, on the stage behind the speakers.
3 The party published a CD of pop hits in the Hungarian issue of Cosmopolitan.
4 Another time, the party advertised its new (Coca-Cola) colour in *Playboy,* with a fairly erotic picture of a young woman with paprika chillis in her mouth.
5 On the Internet site of the youth organisation of the party, one could see a picture of a condom, with the new socialist red ('the colour of safety').

Conclusion

The strategy was successful: the HSP managed to remain in government and, moreover, the left reached a larger majority than previously. According to opinion polls, the HSP raised its support among young people from 18 to 23 per cent during the first months of 2006.

Case study 5.3 Political marketing strategy of Hillary Clinton in the 2008 Iowa and New Hampshire primaries

Daria Gorbounova and Jennifer Lees-Marshment

This case study analyses Clinton's market-oriented political marketing strategy in the first two Democratic Party primaries that took place: Iowa and New Hampshire on 3 and 8 January 2008, respectively, using the Gorbounova and Lees-Marshment US presidential political marketing strategy model outlined in Chapter 2.

Market analysis

Market intelligence

Clinton hired political consultants The Glover Park Group and polling firm Penn, Schoen, Berland & Associates and could consult official results and exit polls obtained in Iowa for New Hampshire. Research was internally focused on Democratic Party supporters, as they would be the ones participating in the primaries. Additionally, as she launched her presidential bid, Clinton declared, 'Let the conversation begin'. Voters were given ample opportunity to submit their views and questions to Clinton, who listened and responded. Such research lacked scientific measures, but the image of responsiveness cultivated through this exercise was an asset in itself.

Political marketplace

Clinton was the first major female presidential candidate and pervasively well known, because of being a former First Lady, and this clearly impacted on her campaign. At the same time, new information technologies were changing the political landscape in the US, with greater emphasis on building grass-roots campaigns.

Product design

The Clinton product was largely informed by market intelligence. It promoted the theme of responsiveness discussed earlier. It had a heavy policy focus, emphasising Clinton's proposals on issues that worried voters most: ending the Iraq war, universal health care and reviving the economy. In terms of Clinton herself, they focused on characteristics such as:

- experience, having been tested and vetted already;
- gender (stressing the historical significance a female president would have, using misogynist attacks to evoke the glass ceiling Clinton was running to break);
- bipartisanship;
- compassion;
- intelligence and hardworking nature.

Bill Clinton also played a prominent role, although given he was a former president with certain associations, this could have been both positive and negative.

After Iowa, the Clinton product evolved to portray Clinton as friendlier, more approachable and less politically calculating. It also tried to reconcile Clinton's experience and ability to make change, stating the former is a prerequisite for the latter.

Product adjustment

Internal reaction analysis

Clinton was in line with the Democratic Party's traditional values, such as collective responsibility; a strand of its ideology, progressivism; and policy positions, such as affordable, universal health care. She also appealed to its core supporters, such as low-income voters. The sole exception was Clinton's somewhat hawkish stance on foreign policy, security and defence.

Competition analysis

Clinton was the market leader (Butler and Collins 1996). She defended the existing market share, such as the women's vote, and attempted to expand it to incorporate younger voters in New Hampshire, but made few gains. Clinton was initially seen as the inevitable nominee, while Obama was the challenger, the underdog. Yet the proportional allocation of delegates made Clinton's market share more vulnerable to encroachments by other candidates – for instance, Obama took most of the female vote in Iowa. This may have underpinned the role reversal that occurred as the primaries progressed, with Obama emerging as the new market leader.

Clinton sought to differentiate herself from fellow Democratic candidates, but since policy differences were subtle, the experience–naivety dichotomy between her and Obama was drawn instead, especially after Iowa. Clinton argued that he was unelectable, inconsistent, hypocritical and, above all, untested and inexperienced, capable only of inspiring oratory, not governing or delivering. Obama also condemned Clinton, for example, painting her as a stale Washington insider. Clinton's ability to withstand the Republican attack machine, if nominated, and her experience in doing so were also accentuated.

Support analysis

Based on market analysis, Clinton chose to target women, lower-income and middle-class Democratic voters in Iowa and New Hampshire, also pursuing the youth vote in the latter. Republicans or Independents rated Clinton very unfavourably; moreover, shifting her product to appeal to them could alienate core Democratic supporters.

Achievability

Clinton made her product achievable and credible by making the product realistic, demonstrating she knew how tough it is being president, reminding voters the president isn't all powerful – there are checks and balances – and persuading voters she will deliver, based on her track record of doing so.

Communications

Clinton's communication was both negative and positive, persuasive and (re-)informative, dispelling false perceptions. It was based on market intelligence and targeted, for instance, using online media to appeal to youth. A myriad of means, from mailers to social networking sites, from television advertising to door-to-door canvassing were also used in different combinations. Clinton invested heavily in emotional outsourcing: people who knew Clinton featured in clips on TheHillaryIKnow.com website, while people who did not know her, but were impressed by seeing her in person, were staples in Clinton campaign videos. By getting third parties to vouch for her, Clinton sought to compensate for her low likeability and trustworthiness ratings. Clinton's aforementioned conversation with voters also played an integral part, making communications a two-way process.

Campaign

The Clinton campaign was consistent and professional, with a high level of message discipline (perhaps too much – the campaign's inner circle, 'Hillaryland', was notorious for its insularity). Voter engagement was stressed, with ample, often creative, options for voters to contribute to the campaign. Turnout was encouraged by stressing the elections' historical importance and explaining how to participate – take Clinton's 'Caucusing is easy' advertisement broadcast in Iowa. In terms of state targeting strategy, Clinton invested many resources in the Iowa campaign, despite the unequivocal recommendation made in 2007 by Mike Henry, then deputy campaign manager, to skip Iowa, given the likelihood of defeat there.

Official results

Candidate	Iowa (%)	New Hampshire (%)
Obama	37.6	36.5
Edwards	29.7	16.9
Clinton	29.5	39.1

Lessons for political marketing

Clinton was indeed intent on being a market-oriented candidate, using market analysis to inform her product design, adjustment, communications and campaign, and deliberately engaging in a wholesale conversation with voters. However, the changing fortunes in Clinton's support and ultimate inability to win the nomination raise questions about whether we can guarantee a market-oriented strategy will always win. In large part, it depends on the nature of the competition, and Barack Obama was a strong opposer. There are other interesting lessons we can draw from Clinton's campaign:

1   In candidate-driven elections, personal qualities are weighted heavily. Clinton had great trouble convincing voters that her experience and policy detail were important, and she too could make change.
2   What works in one market at one time may not work in another at a later stage, and every trait can have both positive and negative ramifications. Although Clinton made great efforts to play to her strengths and defuse problems arising from her weakness, she could not control how she was perceived.
3   Remaining a market-oriented candidate in the US requires thorough attentiveness to the market, because market demands and competition are constantly changing in unexpected ways, and the product and strategy need to be flexible enough to cope with this.

Websites to visit

www.hillaryclinton.com
www.thehillaryiknow.com
www.hillaryhub.com
www.hillblazers.com
www.gloverparkgroup.com
www.pbs.research.com
http://pewresearch.org/
www.election.tv
http://politics.nytimes.com/election-guide/2008/results/votes/index.html (official results and breakdowns of each candidate's support, state by state)

Case study 5.4 Branded American politics   *Kenneth M. Cosgrove*

This case study examines the way in which branding has been used in American politics, first by Conservatives and now by some Democrats, to market themselves. It outlines the way in which Conservatives distributed their brand through the Republican Party. The work will look at three specific cases: Ronald Reagan, George W. Bush and the branded presidency, and the Democratic adaptation of the strategy during the 2006 Congressional elections and 2008 Obama campaign.

A brand is the overall summation of a product or company that includes the logo, a narrative, a consistent set of visual images and three to five specific selling points about the products that it is supporting. Examples of successful brands include Volvo, Ryanair and the Boston Red Sox baseball team (Red Sox Nation). A brand is a unique marketing tool that builds lasting value, makes specific promises and is constructed to build durable relationships between the consumer and producer. The brand puts a picture in the consumer's mind and feelings in their heart about a product or company. In each case, the brand name evokes a specific set of feelings and images associated with the product. Through the creation of line extensions, a variety of products can be marketed using the same brand, or specific offshoots can be marketed to specific audiences via sub-branding, and through co-branding unique products can be paired together to reach a target audience. The brand works best when it is supported by positioning and differentiation marketing to clarify its space and the space of its opponents in the mind of the prospect, and it can be very effective when aimed at niche audiences or if used as a conduit through which micro-targeted messages can be passed.

Figure 5.1 shows how branding and positioning work together to shape their popular perceptions. It rates candidates on two traits: (1) ideology and (2) the extent to which their presentation is seen as being closer to the average American, in the specific way that Ronald Reagan, George W. Bush and Bill Clinton were, versus closer to the effete elite, in the way that John Kerry and Al Gore were during their campaigns. The arrows show how these candidates

Branding – Positioning Political Candidates

'Average American'

Ideal Position

McCain Post-Primary

McCain Primary

Conservative — Liberal

H. Clinton Late Primary

Obama Late Primary

Obama Early Primary

H. Clinton Early Primary

'Effete Elite'

Figure 5.1 Branding: positioning political candidates

have moved on the rating scales. McCain has shifted towards a more conservative position in order to align with the Conservative brand; Clinton made a big push to be more like average Americans as the primaries unfolded, and Obama has moved slightly in the same direction.

The brand allows candidates to change their areas of emphasis without seeming to be inconsistent while doing so, and we will examine three cases in which branding was successfully used by American political candidates.

Case 1: Reagan

The brand's political career began in the service of the Conservative movement, partly because of the consumer-oriented business backgrounds many Conservative leaders had. Branding allowed Conservatives to build a populist grass-roots movement over time. Conservatives built a brand that stressed traditional cultural values, reduced regulatory and tax regimes, and limited government. It took one of the original movement leaders to bring the movement to national prominence through the use of the brand: Ronald Reagan. Reagan possessed a unique skill set in that he was an actor, but he had also been a corporate spokesperson for General Electric, the upshot of which was that Reagan and the people around him made a concerted effort to brand him in a way that was consistent with the work done by other Conservative activists. The Reagan brand (1) featured a colour scheme of red, white and blue; (2) focused on the themes of (a) American renewal and (b) a strong America; (3) usually contained either a flag, some symbol of state or both; and (4) presented a limited number of policy proposals that were applied to multiple situations. Reagan made Conservatism popular, became its face and is now its heritage brand. This explains why all subsequent Republican candidates have presented themselves as a line extension of Reagan.

Case 2: George W. Bush

George W. Bush shows the way in which Republicans use branding and the Reagan heritage. Brand W built fellowship with Reagan in terms of residence, governing style and policy interests. It used (1) fonts and colour schemes similar to the ones used by Reagan; (2) the same visual cowboy image upon which Reagan's team relied; and (3) policies that were presented as being similar in nature to those of Reagan. The administration branded its response to the events of September 11th in a way that mirrored Reagan's messaging on the Soviet Union. The Bush administration packaged everything from enhanced airline security to a war in Iraq into a brand called the War on Terror. Unlike for Reagan, Bush's use of branding ended badly because of: (1) its unfounded rationale for war in Iraq; (2) its failure to find Osama bin Laden; (3) its botched response to Hurricane Katrina; (4) its promotion of, and ultimate failure to pass, social security reform; and (5) its ethical problems. This combination led the public to feel that promises made were not promises kept in the case of Bush and the Conservatives. The Bush case shows the upsides and downsides of branding. The upside is that it is easier to sell a series of products and to produce a series of positive feelings about the executive than it otherwise might be, while the downside is that the brand promises must be kept, or else disaster can ensue.

Case 3: Post-Bush branding

Arguably, the Bush brand failure created the conditions under which Democrats built a winning brand around Republicans in 2006 and created the conditions under which the Obama and McCain campaigns built winning brands in 2008. The 2006 mid-term Congressional elections saw the Democrats run a branded campaign against the 'Culture of Corruption' that allegedly developed in the Congress under Republican rule. It worked because the Republicans didn't respond quickly and with unity, and because it showed that the majority that had been created out of the 1994 Contract with America was no longer keeping its promises. In 2008, the Obama campaign built on the sense that Bush and the Republicans had not kept their promises. The Obama campaign sold itself more like the Conservatives have sold themselves than in the Democratic tradition. The campaign has a specific logo, uses the red, white and blue colour scheme and only changes in appearance to include the name of the state in which the campaign is being contested at the time. The main selling point to the Obama campaign is the notion of providing 'hope' for America, and, in keeping with the brand, the message is micro-targeted to fit specific audiences. The problem that campaign had is that, while it is long on visuals, narrative and emotions, it is short on policy specifics. The Clinton campaign shows the opposite side of the problem: because it has relied on specific proposals and micro-targeting, it has not built an overarching brand and is therefore much more of a traditional Democratic campaign than is the Obama effort. Obama has prospered, Clinton has struggled, and the brand has shown that it can work for both parties. In the end, the problem is that the American political system has not changed, and offering people hope and change will be a daunting promise for any branded candidate to deliver in the real world.

Sources and further reading

Cosgrove, Kenneth M. (2007) *Branded Conservatives: How the Brand Brought the American Right from the Periphery to the Center of American Politics*. New York: Peter Lang.

—— (2007) 'Brand failure'. Paper presented at the Annual Meeting of the American Political Science Association. Chicago, Illinois, September.

Case study 5.5 Segmentation and brand development: an African perspective *Kobby Mensah*

Introduction

Ghana's 2000 election is a success landmark in the country's chequered political history. Part of this success is the professionalisation of the political campaigning offered by the political parties. The opposition party, the New Patriotic Party (NPP), offered the incumbent, the National Democratic Party (NDC), a new kind of political competition, leading to the NDC's loss of political power after being in government for almost twenty years (including its military regime).

The electoral situation

The 2000 general presidential and parliamentary elections kicked off with an active mood of generic discontent among the people of Ghana in all areas that a government professes to represent – governance, education, economic, social, cultural etc. People had grown weary and were unhappy with the economic performance of the nation; the mischievous attitudes of some government officials; the existence of infamous policies such as the criminal libel and sedition laws, which stifled free speech; and corruption allegations levelled against the government. Although these issues offered the NPP fertile grounds upon which to craft competitive campaign themes, they were insufficient and far from spelling the electoral doom of the NDC. Two previous electoral campaigns, in 1992 and 1996, since democracy had been restored, had – no less – been fought on these issues, yet the NPP lost in both. The party itself actually had image issues to contend with. The following paragraph highlights the problems NPP faced.

The NPP's foremost problem was the seemingly unprecedented popularity of the ruling party's founder and the former president, Jerry Rawlings (1997), who had swept almost 58 per cent of the presidential vote, against Kufour's 39 per cent, in the 1996 elections. Although he was not a candidate, his party, the NDC, was to receive that level of goodwill, for his name's sake. Furthermore, the politics of fear seemed to have played into the fortunes of the ruling party. Voters preferred keeping to the incumbent government, credited with the peace and stability that the nation enjoyed. Their minds were firmly fixed with the adage 'the devil you know is better than the angel you don't know'.

However, the most difficult problem was NPP's perceived image of being an elitist and historically divisive party, Christian dominated and mostly Ashanti – a tribe located in the middle belt of the country. In short, although the NPP seemed to have identified the right message for the people, they had been less successful in terms of the messenger. Neither the party nor the leader, John Kuffour – also an Ashanti – seemed the right kind of messenger to carry the 'good message' to the people. As a result, a strategic plan of segmentation, targeting and branding was the way forward for Jake Obetsebi Lamptey, the marketing and advertising guru appointed as the campaign manager. His experience as a former managing director of a giant advertising agency, AP Lintas, was to prove crucial to the fortunes of the party.

The political marketing strategy applied

The NPP began the campaign with the broadcast message 'Agenda for positive change', to reflect on the general mood of the people of Ghana. Those who expressed active discontent were to be assured of good economic performance and good governance; and those who entertained fears of electoral chaos were to be reassured of the party's commitment to the relative peace and stability the nation enjoyed. Furthermore, the party identified five clear narrowcast messages as policy initiatives, which bordered on the interest of five influential segments of the Ghanaian society – besides ordinary voters. These were: a proposed repeal of the criminal libel and sedition laws, which was targeted mainly at journalists; passing a dual citizenship bill to ensure the integration of the Ghanaian diaspora into the mainstream citizenry for development; forming an all-inclusive government; setting up a national reconciliation committee; and implementing zero tolerance for corruption were interest areas of smaller parties, NGOs and the international community.

However, with a stigmatised party image and a relatively less competitive flagbearer (Interview with Jake Obetsebi Lampley, July 2007), the party had to look for strategic means to penetrate into areas where it was weakly represented. For example, the Volta region, the 'electoral world bank', was a stronghold of the NDC party, where it swept all constituencies in previous elections. Against this background, the party embarked on initiatives that were akin to the brand endorsement strategy in commercial marketing. In brand endorsement, a company aims to add the higher values of an endorser to that of the host, in order to extend the host's competitive reach into areas where it previously lacked market access. The endorser brand possesses market assets in the form of credibility and reassurance to be passed on to the host. These qualities are to assure customers of the host brand's certainty to deliver the brand promise. The host brand, on the other hand, offers choice as value to the customer (Kapferer 2004).

Like the brand endorsement strategy, the NPP identified and created 'endorsers', who became the mouthpiece of the party in areas where it was weakly represented. First was the selection of a Northerner and a Muslim as deputy to the flagbearer, to bridge the perceived north–south/Christian–Muslim divide; then was created what was called the Nassara Club (Interview with Jake July, 2007), a youth wing of the party in the 'Zongo' area – Muslim-dominated communities in southern Ghana – to strengthen the Muslim presence in the party and to combat the elitist image. Other tribal communities and regions, such as the Volta region, saw the widespread use of top party officials who hailed from there as mouthpieces for the party; an example is Major General Quarshigah, a prominent former Army General of good repute in his region, the Volta. Again, the candidate's wife, who been to school and worked in the region earlier in her life and speaks the tribe's language, was occasionally brought in to interact with the locals, as a sign that the party was indeed for them as it was for every Ghanaian. Other mundane attributes of the presidential candidate, such as his build, about 6'3'', and tall and calm demeanour, were summed up into a composite political asset and he was promoted as a team leader who has the ability to rally around all minds to form a government of national character, devoid of antagonism. As a result, the well-popularised 'Gentle Giant' was couched (Interview with Jake Obetsebi Lampley, July 2007).

Furthermore, to demonstrate that the party had really changed and was up for the job, the NPP created a coalition of independent minds to trumpet the well-managed change. A number of press briefings ensued as a result. The strategy yielded sympathetic reporting for the NPP, to the extent that the media were overtly seen as pro-opposition.

Finally, the NPP set the whole country singing by skilfully developing a melodious song, with its issue positions and the name of the flagbearer in advertising commercials. This was aired on four television stations and thirty radio stations and was printed in a number of newspapers across the country. A tactical approach to generate recall among the electorates.

Conclusion

The NPP's case offers lessons on how to break into political hegemonies, aided by tribal, ethnic or any sectional predispositions, such as those found in Africa, where these sectional elements are part of the political process. As demonstrated, the use of segmentation, targeting and branding could prove crucial to these markets; however, a critical assessment of the prevailing electoral environment is imperative.

Case study 5.6 From database to relationship marketing – a case study of Fidesz   *Zsuzsanna Mihályffy*

Summary of the background

This case study concerns the Fidesz, one of the leading parties of Hungarian politics, who had been in power between 1998 and 2002 but then unexpectedly lost the 2002 election, despite citizens being satisfied with the government. Fidesz was a successful innovator, and the campaign utilised professional advice and the latest communications, strategy and positioning of the leader Viktor Orbán as a candidate for prime minister, which were extremely new in post-communist Hungary. The case study focuses on the party's efforts, between 2002 and 2006, to establish and make use of a supporters' database.

Case study

Building a database

After the 2002 defeat, reconstruction began in the party. The first step of this process was an extremely successful campaign tool, called the 'National Petition', in the run-up to the 2004 European parliamentary elections. The party expressed some popular demands, such as stopping privatisation in health care and limiting the increase of energy prices, and planned to pressurise the government by collecting a huge number of signatures supporting the petition. The Fidesz planned to collect one million signatures within three months that it could use to build support, and was successful.

The data collection appeared to be to start a referendum, which was legal under overcautious and unnecessarily strict laws concerning access to personal data, whereas creating a long-term database to contact voters was more problematic. The database was first used to send thank-you letters to those who had signed the petition and then was used for an actual 'Double referendum' campaign. Three million direct mails were delivered to voters with the help of activists. The addressed letters had two versions, one for those who had signed the national petition and one for first-time voters.

Using the database

The Fidesz communication strategy continued on this path in the following year, subordinated to the goal of broadening the database and refining the data it contained. The first attempt for this was the so-called 'Sympathy vote' in April, when the party asked citizens' opinion about the candidates for the president of the Republic. Viktor Orbán had already announced, in his annual 'State of the nation' address in February, that 2005 would be the year of consultation: 'We would not like to persuade people, we would like to listen to them' he said. The 'National consultation' was indeed an umbrella term for several events, lasting about eight months and employing a broad arsenal of communication tools. It included three series of events that targeted different groups of people:

1   'Village parliaments': through June and July, village parliament meetings were held in 700 villages. Villagers were given questionnaires concerning policy preferences, how they feel about the period since the system change, what their expectations are, needs and disappointments, etc. The questionnaires were sent out to several households as well. To motivate people, there was a prize draw among those who submitted the questionnaires by 30 July, with the top prize being a VW Polo.
2   'Budapest fora', from May to September, targeted the population of the capital. In about 150 venues, activists asked people about their views concerning the situation of the capital.
3   A 'Consultation on economy', from September to January 2006, was designed to listen to entrepreneurs with small or medium-sized businesses, and other important actors of the economy, to compile a programme to solve the problems of the Hungarian economy.

According to the party's official statement made in October, 1.6 million people took part in the different events of the national consultation. The information gathered was summarised and made public in three booklets, entitled *We have listened to Hungary*, *The new Budapest plan* and *The Consultation on economy*, respectively.

Goals

The Fidesz had two main aims with the national consultation. The first one, which was overtly communicated, had to do with the party's new image: instead of trying to persuade people, the party continuously stressed its commitment to listen to people and respond to their problems. The party promised to incorporate the results in its election manifesto, and strategists also claimed that the campaign was largely based on their experiences from the consultation. In other words, this was an attempt at customer partnering. The Fidesz sought to create a long-term relationship with its core supporters by involving them in product development.

The second, equally important, aim was a strategic goal. The party needed voter information, because it planned a large-scale polling day operation to mobilise its vote. The Fidesz needed to enlarge its base and wanted to reach those who sympathised with the party, but might not turn out to vote. Those identified as weak supporters were contacted several times during the last week of the campaign.

Lessons for political marketing

The Fidesz relied on several aspects of political marketing, from simple database marketing to advanced relationship marketing, product development and customer partnering. It matched its product to voters' needs.

However, little else was completed in marketing terms. Moreover, it incorporated a lot of unrealistic promises in its programme, because that was what people had wanted to hear. The strategy unfortunately did not bring success. Marketing techniques themselves do not guarantee success without careful thought.

The most important lesson from this case study, learned hopefully not only by the Fidesz, but by the other parties as well, is that there are constraints on product development and on the extent to which parties should try to meet voters' needs. There are challenges in matching voters' expectations with actual circumstances, but the product must be adjusted so that it can be delivered. The winner, MSZP, did the same, and its supporters became deeply disappointed upon realising that the party would not fulfil its programme after the 2006 election.

Case study 5.7 To thine own self be true: branding, authenticity and political leadership – the case of Don Brash
Jon Johansson

In September 2005, the leader of the centre-right National Party, Dr Don Brash, narrowly failed to win a tense election campaign against the then two-term Helen Clark-led Labour Party in the New Zealand General Election. Although Brash was elected National Party leader less than two years before the election, he nearly doubled his party's share of the crucial party vote from the previous election in 2002. This was achieved through the strong marketing of Brash as his party's primary brand agent, most especially through highly innovative and effective advertising. Yet he failed to secure a victory owing, in large part, to a fatal erosion of National's vote during the final week of the campaign (Johansson 2007: 64). His Labour opponents asked New Zealand voters to consider whether, by voting for Brash's party, they might 'put it all at risk' – that is, the economic successes and policy predictability of the preceding six years – by electing a leader who Labour claimed was likely to pursue a different set of policies from those he was pledged to during the election campaign. In a knife-edge election, this doubt, reinforced by a weak final two-week performance by Brash, arrested the previously surging National Party and denied them victory, despite evidence showing that, if the election had been decided solely on policy issues, National would have comfortably won it (Levine and Roberts 2007: 377).

This case discusses the interesting intersection between political leadership, the marketing concept of the primary brand agent (Vincent 2002) – that is, the party leader – and the idea of authenticity, because it was the voters' lack of trust in the authenticity of National's primary brand agent that allowed the 'don't put it all at risk' slogan to succeed against Brash. Brash became leader in October 2003. Long seen as a strong supporter of neo-liberal policies, Brash was largely marketed to the electorate as a man of deep principle and integrity, as well as an unconventional non-politician. However, at the deeper level of voter perception, Brash throughout his leadership was consistently viewed as less trustworthy than the prime minister.

The crux of the Brash/branding conundrum was that he had, during a public career spanning well over twenty years, left an incredibly in-depth and detailed record of his deeply felt convictions about the types of policy he believed were required to improve the performance of the New Zealand economy (Hager 2006: 71–8). These policies are accurately described as purely neo-liberal, including Brash's support for a flat tax of 25 cents, his strong preference for privatisation of state assets and responsibilities, and a preoccupation with generational welfare dependency. Thus, in developing their primary brand agent as part of the overall product design phase, Brash's advisors faced the problem of how to maintain his authenticity while publicly modifying his deeply held ideological convictions. The ideological right was therefore highly susceptible to accusations of pursuing 'secret agendas'.

The National Party benefited in the initial development of its branding of Brash by cleverly exploiting public frustration over indigenous rights issues in a speech Brash delivered at Orewa in January 2004 (Brash 2004). An overwhelming public backlash against the Labour-led government that followed Brash's speech saw National gain 17 per cent in opinion polls, virtually overnight, and reinforced National's preferred framing of Brash as the man of deep integrity who felt 'deeply saddened to have to make a speech on issues of race' (Brash 2004: 15). Throughout the remainder of 2004, National sought to inoculate against its perceived political negatives, so policies, such as opposing a government policy for an additional week's annual leave for workers, pursuing further privatisations of state-owned enterprises and abolishing the government's superannuation fund, were jettisoned to cement the more moderate, centrist positioning thought most likely to secure an election victory. Then, during the pre-campaign period, National unfurled a series of highly catchy and innovative advertising billboards, each providing a simple contrast between National's primary brand agent and the incumbent prime minister across a range of policy realms. Following on the heels of an unpopular budget, National again challenged, and then overtook, Labour as the most popular political party.

During the final two weeks of the election campaign, however, several incidents served to erode the integrity of National's primary brand agent. A covert third-party campaign conducted by a conservative religious sect against one of the government's support parties was revealed to have been undertaken with the foreknowledge of Dr Brash, but only after Brash had vehemently denied any involvement in public. Leaked internal emails also showed the awareness of Brash's initial backers, his ideological fellow travellers, none of whom was a member or supporter of the National Party, that he would need to camouflage his true beliefs to get elected (Hager 2006: 15). Brash also revealed real gaps in his knowledge of party policy and obfuscated whenever he was faced with a question that caused dissonance between his authentic beliefs and his newly constructed, more 'moderate' ones. Coinciding with these mishaps was Labour's release of its effective 'Don't put it all at risk' message. Polling revealed that Brash's negative perceptions matched his positive ones, while Prime Minister Clark remained a strong net positive for her party brand (Levine and Roberts 2007: 369). In a tight election, the leadership differential was a crucial one, especially among female voters (Johansson 2007: 63).

In terms of evaluating Dr Brash's effectiveness as the primary brand agent, doubts about his authenticity eroded the strength of both his and his party's brand. A perceptible gap emerged between his persona and his true self, consistent with Gardner's (1996: 293) thesis that one cannot fool all of the people all of the time. The failure of National's primary brand agent also revealed a party that proved ultimately more of a sales-oriented than a fully fledged market-oriented party. Advertising took the product close to having the largest market share in the

2005 election, but once the inauthenticity of its primary brand agent was revealed it created a ceiling that prevented it achieving its ultimate goal. Not enough effort and integrity was invested in the product design and product adjustment phases (Lees-Marshment 2001: 32–3, Hager 2006: 79–232), and so National was unable to move beyond its self-imposed product limitations to achieve electoral success. Brash's ultimate failure was nicely anticipated by Shakespeare in *Hamlet* (2008 edition: 176), when Polonius cries out to Laertes:

> This above all: to thine own self be true
> And it doth follow, as the night the day,
> Thou canst not then be false to any man.

By corrupting his personal authenticity, Don Brash reinforced an important point for the future development of the political marketing literature. Authenticity matters, which provides a fertile ground for future research linking this idea to the concept of primary brand agents and political leadership.

Sources and further reading

Brash, Don (2004). 'Nationhood'. Speech to Orewa Rotary Club, 27 January.

Gardner, Howard, with Emma Laskin (1996). *Leading Minds: An Anatomy of Leadership*. New York: Basic Books.

Hager, Nicky (2006). *The Hollow Men: A Study in the Politics of Deception*. Nelson: Craig Potton Publishing.

Johansson, Jon (2007). 'Brash, Orewa and the politics of race: "critic and conscience" in a desperate campaign'. In Stephen Levine and Nigel S. Roberts (2007). *The Baubles of Office: The New Zealand General Election of 2005*. Wellington: VUW Press.

Lees-Marshment, Jennifer (2001). *British Political Parties and Political Marketing*. Manchester: Manchester University Press.

Levine, Stephen and Nigel S. Roberts (2007). *The Baubles of Office: The New Zealand General Election of 2005*. Wellington: VUW Press.

Shakespeare, William (2008). *Hamlet*, G.R. Hibbard (ed.). Oxford: Oxford University Press.

Vincent, Laurence (2002). *Legendary Brands: Unleashing the Power of Storytelling to Create a Winning Marketing Strategy*. New York: Dearborn Trade Publishing.

Case study 5.8 ACT New Zealand and branding

Chris Rudd and Geoffrey Miller

Background

ACT was formed in 1994 out of a pressure group known as the Association of Consumers and Taxpayers. The party's first leader was Roger Douglas who, as a former Minister of Finance in the Labour government of 1984–90, had spearheaded a series of controversial neo-liberal reforms that collectively became known as 'Rogernomics'. Douglas relinquished leadership of the party in 1996 to another former Labour cabinet minister, Richard Prebble, who had also been an outspoken advocate of the neo-liberal reforms. The current party leader, Rodney Hide, took over from Prebble in 2004. Unlike Prebble, Hide began his political career only with the formation of ACT, but he quickly established a reputation as a scandal-monger and 'perkbuster', with aggressive parliamentary attacks on other MPs over alleged misuses of public monies.

ACT contested its first election in 1996, standing on a policy platform that was very much in line with the earlier neo-liberal programme, with key features being a flat tax, sale of state assets, and privatisation in the health and education sectors. The party won 6.1 per cent of the party vote in 1996 and gained eight seats. At the next two elections, in 1999 and 2002, the party won 7 per cent of the vote and nine seats.

In 2005, however, ACT barely survived, winning just 1.5 per cent of the vote and only two seats. Questions were asked as to why the party had failed to hold on to its modest share of support among New Zealand voters. In this case, we consider how a tainted brand image lost ACT support, drawing on Miller (2007).

Problems with the original brand

A key aim of brand management is to ensure that the perception of the brand will evoke positive associations in the consumer's memory – that is, the consumer will recall 'good things' about the product or service. ACT's initial image was as a party for the wealthy, materialistic, white and male; with unpopular leaders seen as lacking compassion, trustworthiness and the ability to appeal to women; and an overall far-right location interested in representing business only. The brand image that developed during the formative years of ACT's existence was perceived by many voters as synonymous with *un*desirable qualities. What is more, this brand image has persisted over time, despite efforts by the party leaders to rebrand.

Attempts to rebrand

ACT tried to change voters' perceptions. Douglas made overtures to both women and Maori, resulting in Muriel Newman and former activist Donna Awatere-Huata becoming founding MPs. At the 1996 election, ACT employed a public relations firm to try and shift its image away from radical reform. In 2001, when the negatively perceived Douglas resigned as party president, his successor, Catherine Judd, a public relations consultant, began 'the Liberal Project' to convey a more positive image and appeal particularly to young, urban liberals. However, the use of the liberal branding was still limited, with the word not used in the party manifesto or on ACT's election billboards and advertising.

Following the 2002 election, Judd sought to introduce 'phase II' of the Liberal Project and began to consult with members over more formal rebranding, providing members with twenty-one different options. These ranged from cosmetic changes to the party logo, to a fully fledged name change, or both. However, conference delegates at the 'Scenic South' conference in 2002 were reluctant to change ACT's branding. In hindsight, former party communications manager Gavin Middleton points out that 'ACT had brand familiarity, for better or for worse' (personal interview). In the end, in May 2003, ACT changed its logo to include the motto *The Liberal Party*, which replaced *New Zealand* in the logo's bottom strip. The colour of the logo's 'tick' device was also changed, from white to yellow, but blue and green colours remained. In retrospect, both Middleton and Hide conceded that 'liberal' was a confusing term to use, although Middleton says it 'was the best label we had' (personal interviews).

Nevertheless the liberal rebranding had little apparent effect on voters. In retrospect, Hide considers the Liberal Project to have been a 'total failure' (personal interview). Middleton was more optimistic. While conceding that the rebranding was low key because 'at the end of the day the party was still ACT', he believes that the Liberal Project helped to 'break . . . away from that Roger Douglas, 1984–1990 stuff' (personal interview).

While it was certainly something new, it is doubtful that the Liberal Project was what ACT really needed to improve its image. The compromise 'Liberal Party' appendage to the party logo was too cautious to be noticed, yet, even if voters had been aware of it, it is likely that they would have been confused. The continued negative perceptions of ACT severely limited the pool of voters open to voting for the party, restricting it to a small niche. Both the ideas and implementation behind attempts to soften its image were too ill conceived to have any real effect.

Lessons to be learned

The evidence from the surveys and focus groups, along with the media commentary, strongly emphasises how difficult it is to shake off a negative brand. It is possible, however, for an organisation to repackage itself and change a negative brand image to a much more positive one. Take, for example, the Skoda car: synonymous with unreliability and inferior workmanship until the 1980s, but now sold as a high-quality European vehicle in New Zealand. However, the desire to rebrand and the success with which this can be achieved may be more difficult in the political world than the manufacturing one. Parties are offering promises – and these cannot be experienced before purchase in the same way as one can test-drive a car. As a result, voters are being asked to place a great deal of faith and trust in what they are told by party leaders. And it may be very difficult for leaders, who are seen to epitomise that which the voters distrust and dislike, to convince voters that the party really is different. In the case of ACT New Zealand, the efforts to date have largely been unsuccessful.

Sources and further reading

Banducci, S. (2002). 'Gender and leadership'. In J. Vowles, P. Aimer, J. Karp, S. Banducci, R. Miller, and A. Sullivan (eds) *Proportional Representation on Trial: The 1999 New Zealand General Election and the Fate of MMP*. Auckland: Auckland UP, pp. 50–65.

Judd, C. (2001). *The Liberal Project*. Available online at www.act.org.nz/action/campaign/liberal/index.html, accessed 13 August 2003.

—— (2002). 'Liberal Project II: questionnaire on the name, logo and colours'. Wellington: ACT New Zealand.

Miller, Geoffrey (2007). 'From Douglas to dancing: explaining the lack of success of ACT New Zealand and evaluating its future prospects'. Available online at http://douglastodancing.blogspot.com.

FURTHER READING

Author unknown (2001). 'Branding political parties'. *Brand Strategy*, 152: 9.

Barberio, Richard P. (2006). 'Branding: presidential politics and crafted political communications'. Prepared for delivery at the 2006 Annual Meeting of the American Political Science Association, 30 August to 3 September 2006.

—— and Brian M. Lowe (2005). 'A "branded" nation? The social and cultural backdrop for "branded" legislation and policy initiatives'. Paper presented at the meeting of the Eastern Sociological Society, Washington, DC.

Brand Strategy (2006). 'Leading from the top'. 1 April. Available online at www.mad.co.uk/Main/News/Disciplines/Marketing/Articles/e57452e34386487ab7b4a93019da965c/Leading-from-the-top.html (accessed 19 March 2008).

Butler, Patrick and Neil Collins (1996). 'Strategic analysis in political markets'. *European Journal of Marketing*, 30(10/11): 25–36.

Cosgrove, K.M. (2007). 'Midterm marketing: an examination of marketing strategies in the 2006, 2002, 1998, and 1994 elections'. Paper presented at the annual meeting of the American Political Science Association. Available online at www.allacademic.com/meta/p209749_index.html (accessed 19 March 2008).

Cotrim Maciera, Josiane (2005). 'Change to win? The Brazilian Workers' Party's 2002 General Election marketing strategy'. In Darren G. Lilleker and Jennifer Lees-Marshment (eds), *Political Marketing: A Comparative Perspective*. Manchester: Manchester University Press.

Freedland, J. (1999). 'The trashing of Ken'. *The Guardian*, London, 17 November 1999.

Fritz, Ben, Bryan Keefer and Brendan Nyhan (2004). *All the President's Spin: George W. Bush, the Media, and the Truth*. New York: Touchstone.

Gorbounova, Daria and Jennifer Lees-Marshment (2008). 'The US Primaries 2007–8: a political marketing perspective'. Working paper produced by Auckland University Summer Scholar Scheme.

Gould, Jon B. (2003). 'It only feels like death: "rebranding" the Democrats for a post-2002 world'. *Journal of Political Marketing,* 2(2): 1–12.

Hughes, Andrew (2003). 'Can branding theory be applied to marketing political parties? A case study of the Australian Greens'. Paper presented at the Australian and New Zealand Marketing Academy Conference, University of South Australia, 1–3 December 2003.

Ingram, Peter and Jennifer Lees-Marshment (2002). 'The Anglicisation of political marketing: how Blair "out-marketed" Clinton'. *Journal of Public Affairs,* 2(2): 44.

Keenan, Elizabeth (2007). 'Kevin 07: Labor's winning brand'. *Time,* 3 December: 24–31.

Knuckey, Jonathan and Jennifer Lees-Marshment (2005). 'American political marketing: George W. Bush and the Republican Party'. In D.G. Lilleker and J. Lees-Marshment (eds), *Political Marketing in Comparative Perspective.* Manchester: Manchester University Press.

Langmaid Roy, Charles Trevail and B. Hayman (2006). 'Reconnecting the Prime Minister'. Paper presented at the Annual Conference of the Market Research Society, London.

Lees, Charles (2005). 'Political marketing in Germany: the case of the Social Democratic Party'. In Darren Lilleker and J. Lees-Marshment (eds), *Political Marketing in Comparative Perspective.* Manchester: Manchester University Press.

Lees-Marshment, Jennifer (2001). 'The marriage of politics and marketing'. *Political Studies,* 49(4): 692–713.

—— (2008). *Political Marketing and British Political Parties* (2nd edn.). Manchester: Manchester University Press.

Lilleker, Darren and J. Lees-Marshment (eds) (2005). *Political Marketing in Comparative Perspective.* Manchester: Manchester University Press.

Lloyd, Jenny (2005). 'Marketing politics . . . saving democracy'. In Adrian Sargeant and Walter Wymer (eds), *The Routledge Companion to Nonprofit Marketing.* London: Routledge.

—— (2006). 'The 2005 General Election and the emergence of the negative brand'. In Darren Lilleker, Nigel Jackson and Richard Scullion (eds), *The Marketing of Political Parties.* Manchester: Manchester University Press.

Needham, Catherine (2002). 'Branding public policy: marketed government under Clinton and Blair'. Paper presented at the Annual Meeting of the American Political Science Association, Boston, Massachusetts, 29 August to 1 September 2002.

—— (2005). 'Brand leaders: Clinton, Blair and the limitations of the permanent campaign'. *Political Studies,* 53(2): 343–61.

—— (2006). 'Brands and political loyalty'. *Journal of Brand Management,* 13(3): 178–87.

Newman, Bruce I. (1994). *The Marketing of the President: Political Marketing as Campaign Strategy.* Thousand Oaks, CA: Sage Publications.

—— (1999). *The Mass Marketing of Politics: Democracy in an Age of Manufactured Images.* Beverley Hills, CA: Sage Publications.

Patrón-Galindo, Pedro (2004). 'Symbolism and the construction of political products: analysis of the political marketing strategies of Peruvian President Alejandro Toledo'. *Journal of Public Affairs,* 4(2): 115–24.

Reeves, Peter, Leslie de Chernatony and Marylyn Carrigan (2006). 'Building a political brand: ideology or voter-driven strategy'. *Brand Management,* 13(6): 418–28.

Reid, David (1988). 'Marketing the political product'. *European Journal of Marketing,* 22(9): 34–47.

Rudd, Chris (2005). 'Marketing the message or the messenger?'. In Darren Lilleker and J. Lees-Marshment (eds), *Political Marketing in Comparative Perspective.* Manchester: Manchester University Press.

Scammell, Margaret (2008). 'Brand Blair: marketing politics in the consumer age'. In D. Lilleker and R. Scullion (eds), *Voters or Consumers: Imagining the Contemporary Electorate.* Newcastle: Cambridge Scholars Publishing.

Schneider, Helmut (2004). 'Branding in politics – manifestations, relevance and identity-oriented management'. *Journal of Political Marketing,* 3(3): 41–67.

Seligman, Paul (2006). 'Policies fail without buy-in'. *Marketing,* 26 April 2006.

Smith, Gareth (2001). 'The 2001 General Election: factors influencing the brand image of political parties and their leaders'. *Journal of Marketing Management,* 17(9/10): 989–1006.

Steinhardt, G. (2007). 'Extending product life cycle stages'. *Blackblot.* Available online at www.blackblot. com/files/articles/Blackblot_Extending_Product_Life_Cycle_Stages.pdf (accessed 18 March 2008).

White, Jon and Leslie de Chernatony (2002). 'New Labour: a study of the creation, development and demise of a political brand'. *Journal of Political Marketing,* 1(2–3): 45–52.

6 Internal marketing

Marketing to volunteers and the party

This chapter will explore how political marketing can be applied to the party or candidate organisation itself. There are two aspects to this: one is what marketers would call internal marketing, as it concerns marketing to those within the organisation. In politics, this means volunteers such as members. The aim is to apply marketing principles and techniques to ensure that volunteers become and remain effective activists for the party. The second is how to manage the implementation of a market-orientation. While this is not traditionally part of internal marketing in marketing textbooks, and of course not all parties adopt a market-orientation, political marketing research has shown that those that have tried to change the product to respond to electorate demands in some way often encounter barriers from party culture and stakeholders, even if such changes might help the party win the next election. Just the idea of a market-orientation and responding more to public demands over traditional party beliefs and ideals raises concern among volunteers and party figures, who have strong investments in, and attachment to, the party or candidate and strong views on how to change the world: that is why they got into politics in the first place. The implementation of a market-orientation therefore has to be managed as well as the volunteers.[1]

Internal marketing and marketing members

Members, but also grass-roots supporters, can affect electoral fortunes – the close outcome in the 2008 Democratic primaries in the US is testament to this. Members are important in a number of ways: as Lilleker (2005: 572) observed, they are the lifeblood of the party; together with Bannon (2005a) he noted that members carry out a number of functions:

1 they run local offices/branches;
2 they produce funds and donations;
3 they participate in internal debate;
4 they act as an electorate to validate internal party appointments and selections;
5 they provide local information;
6 they campaign locally;
7 they deliver campaign material;
8 they canvass votes;
9 they help with GOTV; and
10 they act as a socialisation mechanism.

Even in countries where there is not formal membership, mobilising grass-roots support is increasingly important.

What do members want?

Like voters, the attitude and behaviour of members have also changed over time. Membership has declined both in numbers and activity and commitment levels. Parties need to think more carefully about what their members want. Internal marketing can help increase motivation, commitment, co-operation and effort by supporters. There are different motivations for volunteering. Granik's (2005a,b) research into members of a UK party found that members scoring high on certain motivations are likely to experience higher levels of satisfaction with their role; the motivations were:

- social – political party membership is seen as a means of gaining approval;
- enhancement – political party membership boosts the self-esteem of individuals;
- understanding – membership of a political party is seen as a way of learning more about politics.

A well-organised local association or branch helped to maintain satisfaction among members, because it was enjoyable socially, likely to be more successful and so helped people feel part of a winning team. These are therefore some characteristics a party can consider implementing in their party organisation.

Marketing members

Another approach is to use internal marketing. It involves all marketing activities, not just communication. Bannon (2005a) suggests there are four key areas parties can address:

1 *Relationship development* – The values, attitudes and beliefs of members are germane and are usually overlooked, but parties or candidates need to hold closely related values.
2 *They say they listen, they even do listen sometimes, but they don't do anything about it* – Ongoing internal members surveys could serve as an opportunity for all members to feed back to the organisation their opinions, expectations, ideas and level of satisfaction. Segmentation of the internal market can also occur. However, such internal research also needs to generate appropriate product development so that action is actually taken.
3 *Communications strategy* – The nature and style of communications techniques selected should match the requirements of each of the identified segments so as to inform, persuade and encourage continued support and involvement. Joint ownership of policies is sought, and this requires the articulation of a shared vision starting from common ground. The communication needs to be responsive to the concerns and queries of members and eliminate any misconception.
4 *Cost/benefit analysis* – There is a cost involved in the internal marketing process, both to the organisation and the members. Non-financial costs include additional effort, removal from comfort zone, need to enhance skills and time, etc.

One example of this is how William Hague applied marketing to the UK Conservative membership between 1997 and 2001, introducing internal party democracy and creating other initiatives in response to market intelligence. Lees-Marshment and Quayle (2001) observed how several changes were introduced after a period of internal assessment and consultation:

1   A national membership base was created to ease communication with party members.
2   The party profiled existing members and then bought membership lists of names for wine clubs, garden centres, rugby/cricket clubs for a direct mail recruitment drive, sending out letters of invitation to become a member of the Conservative Party.
3   The *Conservative network* was launched, to offer a social and political programme to encourage young professionals to become involved in the party.
4   It provided training in skills needed for candidates, such as media management, presentation and speech writing.
5   The *Conservative policy forum* was established to give members more opportunity to discuss policy.
6   *Conservative future* was created for members thirty years old and under.

Effectively, the market-oriented principle was applied to the membership.

Marketing supporters or volunteers

Lebel suggested there are three aspects to managing volunteers (1999: 134–40):

1   **Planning**: plan their recruitment, roles and management, considering what motivates them.
2   **Recruitment**: consider those who fit most easily with campaign needs, including not just their attachment and commitment to a candidate but their skills; segmenting the message sent to volunteers where appropriate; taking into account what they expect to get from the investment of their time; making it easy for them to commit; contacting them within twenty-four hours of them offering to help, to capitalise on their enthusiasm.
3   **Management**: manage volunteers like money – considering the resources available and the needs of the campaign; matching capability with the nature of the task set; including training where needed; relating volunteer activities to the overall campaign; and promoting those who display particular skills.

In practical terms, making it as easy as possible to help is important. Bryant (2008) notes how Obama's presidential nomination bid in 2007–08 offered potential volunteers a specific goal and date (e.g. '1.5 million calls by Tuesday') and made them actionable and realistic through easy-to-use online tools (e.g. 'click on this button and make 20 calls from this list').

Most of all, volunteers need to feel wanted and valued. As Lebel (1999: 141) notes, 'volunteers often are at the low end of the campaign hierarchy, with the least access to the candidate and senior staff', so internal communication is extremely important to help them feel recognised and part of the overall campaign. In her bid to secure the nomination in 2008, the Hillary Clinton campaign tried to involve voters in the following ways, most of which were accessible through the 'Online Action Centre' on the campaign website:

•   join Team Hill;
•   make calls using the volunteer calling tool;
•   build our (Clinton campaign's) base;
•   attend/plan an event;
•   start a blog;
•   join/start a group;
•   send a message of support (to Clinton);
•   send a fundraising/recruiting email to a friend.

Online videos were also posted on the campaign website, showing Clinton supporters in action. One humorous video showed famous movie director Rob Reiner giving volunteers tips on how to be more optimistic and convince more people to support Clinton when door knocking and making phone calls. Marketing strategies that respect and engage supporters help to mobilise supporters, who in turn increase voter support and also convey a positive image of the overall campaign.

Segmenting the membership

Segmentation can be used on members as well as voters, as each group will have specific requirements, and internal marketing programmes can be developed for each one. Bannon (2005b) argues that political relationships generally can be divided into different types: see Table 6.1.

Christopher *et al.*'s (1991) relationship marketing loyalty ladder might also be applied to how people progress from voter, to member, to activist. This discusses the importance of customer relationship management (CRM) over time, where there is a move away from transactional marketing to relationship marketing: see Table 6.2.

Table 6.1 Typology of political relationships

Relationship	Characteristics
Hyperactivist	Party activist; *married* into the party for better or worse.
Blood brother	Blood ties, born into the party; treats the party as *the family*.
The idealist	Strongly held political views, developed usually in an individual's early life; this relationship is based on *true love*.
The mutualist	Seeks mutual outcomes, but with no contract; *kissing cousins*.
Loosely aligned	Relationship exists but not fully committed; the *open marriage*.
Multi-relational	A voter who has more than one preference; *tart syndrome*.
The transient	Floating voter; *one-night stands*.
The hostage	Cannot find anyone better to have a relationship with; *trapped lover*.
Nepotistic relationship	Seeks and gains favour from a party, the parasite; *married for money*.
The blackmailed	Coerced into supporting because the alternatives are worse, the voter is in some way locked into the relationship, barriers to exit maybe too high; the *forced partner*.

Source: Bannon (2005b: 85)

Table 6.2 Transaction vs a relationship marketing approach

Transaction marketing	Relationship marketing
Focus on single sale	Focus on customer retention
Orientation on product features	Orientation on product benefits
Short time-scale	Long time-scale
Little emphasis on customer service	High customer service emphasis
Limited customer commitment	High customer commitment
Moderate customer contact	High customer contact
Quality is primarily a concern of production	Quality is the concern of all

Source: Christopher *et al.* (1991)

Instead of focusing just on voters for the next election, parties could move to providing a high-quality service that will attract user commitment and retention over the long-term.

To date, research has not identified any significant segmentation of party membership, even though it has become common among charities (see Lees-Marshment 2004). Rogers (2005: 608) argued that parties could offer supporters different alternatives to formal membership. UK Labour did just this: in Spring 2006, Labour launched a 'Let's Talk' project and created a Labour supporters network in an attempt to restart the 'Big Conversation' and boost involvement in the party (Lees-Marshment 2008: 272). Relationship marketing could also offer further insight into marketing the membership.

Marketing membership communication

Marketing can also be applied to members and the grass roots in terms of communication. Bauer *et al.* (1996: 153) observed how German parties implemented special advertising to try to increase their membership, with the Greens holding an art competition to design a series of special posters. Obama used marketing communications to mobilise his grass roots during his bid for the Democratic presidential nomination. Bryant (2008) notes how the campaign, built on the themes of hope, action and change, was good at translating such values into simple slogans such as 'Change we can believe in' and 'Yes, we can'. They spoke 'positively to the subconscious in a way that would make NLP (neuro-linguistic programming) practitioners proud.' E-communication was also effective, and run by users themselves instead of the political elites. The *Yes We Can* viral video created by Will.i.am and cYclops achieved nearly six million hits on YouTube:

> Mark Jurkovac, CEO of cYclops and executive producer of the video, recalls that as soon as it went viral 'we got calls from all sorts of groups saying they wanted to do their version of the *Yes We Can* and so we decided to create an online community for this kind of content'. A Web site, hopeactchange.com, was created and has since become a social community for Obama user-generated content, a sort of pro-Obama YouTube.

Using marketing in fundraising

Members are also a source of funds. Candidates and parties need to understand who might give and why. Steen (1999: 161–4) observes that a number of factors can determine propensity to donate, such as affection for the candidate, agreement with the candidate's stance on issues or policy, and the candidate's power to influence legislation. Bannon (2005a) interviewed forty-seven individuals from various political organisations in the UK and found that parties ask for donations all the time, which can leave members feeling used and damage the relationship. Requests for donations should be related to outcomes or offer

Discussion point 6.1

Consider which party you support, either at the moment or at the last election, whether as a party member or voter. Discuss which of Bannon's (2005b) types applies: married, the family, true love, kissing cousins, open marriage, tart syndrome, one-night stands, a trapped lover, married for money or the forced partner.

benefits to the donor, such as greater access to the candidate. Fundraising events also need to be more social and enjoyable.

Various tools can be used in fundraising, including direct mail, telemarketing and events. More recently, the Internet is a source of fundraising. Howard Dean's bid to secure the US Democratic presidential nomination in 2004 was the first campaign to demonstrate the power of the Internet. Moreover, Dean didn't just fundraise but applied Joe Trippi's idea of virtual social networking, so the Internet was used not just to attract donors but to mobilise the grass roots, an approach taken further by presidential candidates in subsequent elections.

Marketing to the youth or a segment of the membership

Marketing can also be used to reach out to particular segments of society: see Case study 6.1.

There are therefore a number of ways in which marketing can be applied to volunteers, with varying effectiveness. The second area to consider is how to manage the whole party, particularly with regard to adopting a market-orientation.

Managing the implementation of a market-orientation

In political marketing, it is not just the volunteers, but the whole party, including politicians, candidates for office and party figures, that needs to be considered if party leaders or candidates want to change the product in any way. Changing the product is not as straight-forward for a party leader or chairperson, who has considerably less autonomy than most chief executives leading a business. As most party leaders are elected by a range of people from the party, their position is actually dependent on those below them.

A stage of implementation or management is therefore needed in the political marketing process, because political parties will not necessarily accept change, however important to win an election. Members may have different and conflicting demands, and parties have to try to reconcile these differences or to ensure that the membership is representative of the electorate, so that their goals and interests will be similar. Internal supporters tend to have a greater ideological or emotive attachment to the party, which makes it harder for them to accept new ways of operating. A market-orientation is particularly likely to attract opposition. As Lloyd (2005) noted, part of the product is investment; people who have been members of a party for years and have gone out and trod the streets to campaign on its behalf have an obvious investment. Lebel (1999: 133) also observed how volunteers in the US expect something in return such as 'access to the candidate'.

There are also other stakeholders parties need to consider, including elected politicians, office holders and candidates (see Dean and Croft 2001: 1206, and Hughes and Dann 2006a,b). Stakeholders can exert influence over different activities and decisions the party carries out; they also vary in how active or passive they are, and how much influence they

Discussion point 6.2

List all the ways in which marketing be applied to volunteers and decide which are most important and why, drawing on the examples here and any personal experience of volunteering.

have over political marketing. Overall, implementation and internal marketing is very much a necessary part of political marketing.

Barriers to overcome

Internal markets create a number of potential barriers or constraints on the marketing a party or candidate can engage in. There are a number of organisational and communication factors the leadership needs to consider. A party leadership intent on making the organisation market-oriented will inevitably encounter some hostility and resistance from stakeholders; they may also be hostile to marketing because they have misconceptions or a lack of knowledge about it (Lees-Marshment 2001: 37–8). The UK Labour Party provides a clear example of this, as internal debates about the purpose of the party directly challenged attempts to introduce a market-orientation. As Wring (2005), who analysed the emergence and development of marketing in the party in relation to internal debate and ideological considerations, noted over the course of the twentieth century, Labour held three approaches to electioneering up until Blair's victory in 1997:

1   **The 'educationalist' approach**: 'campaigning was primarily about converting people to their cause . . . dedicated to overcoming ignorance and emancipating the dispossessed' (Wring 2005: 16).
2   **The 'persuasional' school of thought**: 'favoured more persuasional forms of campaigning . . . designed to provoke more of a short-term emotional response and drew on Plato's contention that the Aristotelian ideal of democracy was an imperfection vulnerable to the tyranny of the suggestible mob' (Wring 2005: 17).
3   **Market research socialism**, introduced by Neil Kinnock, 1987–92, being more concerned with responding to, than reshaping, public opinions.

The third approach, more in line with a market-orientation, was obviously a direct challenge to the longer-standing beliefs. Wring (2005: 116) cited one example of a delegate who spoke out at the 1992 Annual Conference saying: 'we have allowed ourselves to be marketed by paid image-makers, but . . . we should beware of the paid image-maker. These are people, mainly middle-class graduates, who have learned their socialism from market research and opinion polls.' Tension in the party between doing what was believed to be right and winning elections continued through until Tony Blair's victory in 1997 and beyond. Leadership, party culture and party unity are important factors in the success or failure of implementation. Case studies 6.2 and 6.3 illustrate some of the problems that occur in practice when leaders try to change political parties.

Potential solutions

Marketing management literature suggests a number of guidelines for how to make the process easier: see Box 6.1.

Discussion point 6.3

What went wrong in Case studies 6.2 and 6.3? Are there any other examples where good marketing ideas have failed because of problems in implementation?

Box 6.1 Guidelines for implementing a market-orientation from marketing management literature

1 Create a feeling that everybody in the party can contribute to making it market-oriented and successful.
2 Acknowledge that the party may already be doing many things that would be classed as marketing activities.
3 Encourage all members of the organisation to suggest ideas as to how the party might respond more effectively to voters.
4 Create a system that enables all forms of market intelligence to be disseminated as widely as possible through the organisation.
5 Present market intelligence reports from professionals, especially in the form of statistics, in a way that everyone in the party can understand.
6 Appoint a marketing executive (or equivalent) to handle market intelligence from within the party and from professional research firms.
7 This executive should meet various groups within the party to learn what they think about the party and voters: first, explaining his or her job position and the nature of marketing and its uses, and then encouraging open discussion, inviting ideas for change within the party.
8 The importance of views other than those of the majority of the electorate and the party's history should be acknowledged.
9 Those within the party who support the idea of being market-oriented should be promoted to encourage market-oriented behaviour.
10 Emphasise that becoming market-oriented is the means to achieve the party's goal; it is not the goal in itself.

Source: collated in Lees-Marshment (2001)

Achieving a market-orientation arguably takes some time, especially if it necessitates major changes in values and beliefs. It is also unlikely that the leadership will achieve 100 per cent party unity or complete acceptance of a market-orientation, but it would aim for a majority of support for the new behaviour.

Another aid to easing implementation is to consider the internal market *before* completing plans for changing the product. The Lees-Marshment (2001) MOP model argues that parties should carry out internal reaction analysis, taking into account a party's ideology and history to ensure that some product aspects suit the traditional supporter market and MPs as well as new target markets; and Ormrod (2005) notes the need to consider stakeholders and members in an internal and external orientation.

Knuckey and Lees-Marshment (2005) analysed the US presidential campaign of George W. Bush, in 2000, who had reached out to new target markets, including middle-class and Hispanic voters, with policies on health care and childhood education, non-traditional Republican issues. During the primaries, he adjusted his behaviour to suit internal criticism, to ensure he would win the nomination. He tried to increase his own conservative credentials and temporarily replaced the 'Compassionate Conservative' slogan with 'A reformer with results' and stressed traditional conservative Republican themes, emphasising his belief in limited government. Once he had secured the party nomination, he moved back towards the centre and focused on issues that opinion polls showed to be of paramount concern for most Americans in the 2000 election: education, social security and health care, but alongside traditional Republican themes such as tax-cuts, smaller government and a stronger military. As Medvic (2006: 23) noted, Bush's emphasis on school choice, as well as local control and accountability, fitted Republican ideology but also appealed to swing voters.

However, meeting the needs of both internal and external markets is not always easy. The success of a market-oriented strategy, and getting it implemented, depends on timing, the nature of the competition and how long a party has been out of power: see Case study 6.4.

Balancing demands between the two markets is not easy. The National Party in New Zealand experienced the same problem after losing power in 1999. It tried to appeal to the centre ground and target middle-income New Zealanders, while being differentiated from Labour and the smaller, right-wing party ACT in time for the 2001 election. However, it also experienced internal opposition to widening its base to include Maori voters and trying to introduce new candidates. In the UK, upon becoming leader of the Conservatives, David Cameron attempted to appeal to both markets while seeking support: see Box 6.2.

Considering the internal market in product design is not just important to maintain party unity and enable change to be fully implemented; a balance between external and internal supporters may also be essential to the long-term success of political marketing in government. Internal marketing literature may also offer additional processes that can be adapted to politics.

Democratic issues

There is a democratic argument that political elites should consider the internal market. There is a problem with marketing political parties as businesses, if adjustment is not included in the process. As Lees-Marshment (2001: 190) argued, 'parties cannot simply shed their history. Because parties are different to businesses, they must adjust the product to suit internal demands which include party ideology and traditions.' Lilleker (2005) explored the positive and negative consequences of market-oriented political marketing at the party leadership level on internal party democracy and concluded that:

> In the era of managerial politics, ideas may still underpin political decisions, but only if gathered from the market and not from an abstract set of ideals. This attitude means that decisions cannot be open for ideological debate, a shift some find difficult to accept.
>
> (Lilleker 2005: 575)

However, marketing need not prevent debate. UK Labour responded in some way to discontent among its members: during 1997–2001, changes were made within the party, with the aim of making members more involved. Members-only sessions were introduced at the annual party conference, to ensure members had a chance to air their views without damaging the party externally. However, as Dean and Croft (2001: 1207) observed,

> the enigma for a political party is how to allow the diversity of party members, activists and elected members a say in the nature of the 'product offering', while still maintaining a degree of apparent unanimity for the consumption of less-controllable groups.

Box 6.2 Cameron attempts to appeal to internal and external markets, 2005 onwards

Appeal to external markets

- He created initial new policy positions on the environment.
- He talked about protecting and safeguarding the NHS.
- He conveyed a different persona via photo opportunities in Darfur and social action days with MPs.

Internal criticism

- Environmentally friendly policies suggested a less-friendly approach to business, with greater regulation: a potentially un-conservative position.
- Other policies, such as that on grammar schools for example, have been withdrawn after internal criticism.
- When backbench MP Quentin Davies resigned, he argued that the Conservative Party under Cameron's leadership has 'ceased collectively to believe in anything, or to stand for anything. It has no bedrock. It exists on shifting sands. A sense of mission has been replaced by a PR agenda.'
- Franz Luntz, a consultant, ran a focus group of floating voters on Cameron's first year as leader and noted that 'there is an underlying fear of "spin" that could undermine your long-term success . . . floating voters believe you are actively engaged in a sincere effort to bring about fundamental change, and they appreciate it . . . [but] they are afraid you'll turn into the Tony Blair of 2006' (the *Daily Telegraph,* 4 December 2006).

Appeal to internal markets

- Cameron talked of 'having an idea – social responsibility – that links all of the things we want to do' (interview with the *Daily Telegraph,* December 2006, available online at www. telegraph.co.uk/news/main.jhtml?xml=/news/2006/12/01/utranscript101.xml&page=3, accessed 26 April 2007). This sounds like a blend of traditional Conservatism, discussing responsibility, but also social, emphasising the concern about the nature of society.
- Cameron: 'What I say to traditional Conservatives is that we have lost three elections in a row, we have to modernise and change to reflect changes to British society . . . [but] . . . look at the centrality of what I am saying: social responsibility, parental responsibility –that the state doesn't have all the answers – . . . this is a profoundly *Conservative message* (from the *Daily Telegraph,* available online at www.telegraph.co.uk/news/main.jhtml?xml=/ news/2006/12/01/utranscript101.xml&page=3, accessed 26 April 2007).
- Continued focus on government supporting marriage.

Not just saying 'yes'

In the April 2007 party election broadcast, Cameron was seen meeting and talking to a variety of people, and not just listening, but sometimes saying no to what the participants wanted, suggesting a degree of leadership alongside responsiveness.

Source: adapted from Lees-Marshment and Pettitt (2009)

Discussion point 6.4

Consider the guidelines for introducing a market-orientation: are there any cases where a party or political leader has followed them through? Try to expand the list and make other suggestions for managing a market-orientation.

Discussion point 6.5

What advantages may come from conducting research and then redeveloping what is on offer to members or supporters?

Summary

Internal marketing is an important part of political marketing. It is often neglected, even though research indicates that, without it, good products can get blocked, and volunteers will do less or resign, and in the long-term it can undermine support for the party. Internal marketing is more subtle, behind the scene, and does not often yield quick results, but if it can be done well the product is more likely to be supported by committed and enthusiastic members and volunteers, and the next stage of communication and campaigning will be much easier.

ASSESSED WORK

Essays

1 'Implementation is the hidden, often-neglected but crucial key to successful political marketing.' Discuss the factors and complexities involved in implementing a market-oriented strategy within a political party, exploring examples of success and failure.
2 What barriers are there to implementing a market-orientation within a political party, and how might they be overcome?
3 How can marketing be applied to members, supporters or grass roots, and how effective is it?
4 To what extent might parties' previous marketing activities to increase their membership numbers and activity fit Christopher *et al.*'s (1991) relationship marketing principles and loyalty ladder, as opposed to transaction marketing principles?

Applied

1 Interview or survey party members about their views and satisfaction with their party. What does this indicate about how successfully the leadership has adjusted their product?
2 Analyse the extent to which candidates for presidential elections, whether in the US or another country, used marketing to mobilise their grass roots.
3 Conduct market intelligence among party members or supporters and produce from this a plan for improving internal marketing, including changes such as developing the product on offer to members and internal communication.
4 Assess the membership or supporter network (or a sample of it) from a local party organisation, branch, association or network, and identify how they fall into each of Bannon's (2005b) relationship typologies (married, the family, true love, kissing cousins, open marriage, tart syndrome, one-night stands, a trapped lover, married for money or the forced partner) and the implications for the party's strength of support.

Case study 6.1 Wasted on the young: marketing membership efforts by Plaid Cymru   *Sue Granik*

Picture this. In the boardroom, the director of marketing reports that, in the year ahead, vast resources will be put into attracting unprofitable customers. What would the reaction be? Anger, astonishment, tough questions asked, one potentially destructive plan ripped to shreds, and the Director's personal credibility in tatters.

Not so in UK political parties, where such propositions routinely meet with applause, approval and substantial budget and resource allocations. Why? Because recruiting young members to political parties is regarded as an important aspiration. It is commonly believed that, once young people are members, they'll stay members for life. They'll bring enthusiasm, exuberance and activity to the party. In short, they'll be the party's life-blood.

In reality, this belief is based on little more than myth. It's a myth that has consumed the resources necessary to run large student networks, various experiments at running youth wings (which often lead to political embarrassment) or expensive, parallel youth conferences and events. In practice, young people are only fickle friends of political parties and contribute little to the organisations so desperate to recruit them.

The percentage of young adults in each of the UK's major political parties is very small, accounting for less than 5 per cent of the total membership. True to stereotype, most political party members are over the age of forty-five. This tells us only that political parties are unattractive to young people, but doesn't tell us whether or not young people are really attractive members for political parties to have. Marketers would instinctively turn to research to try to find some answers. This case study looks at research (Granik 2003) carried out among members of Plaid Cymru, a Welsh nationalist party in the UK, the first to try to identify the key differences between young party members (up to the age of twenty-five) and their older counterparts. It discusses the results of analysis of data, the details of which can be found in the Sources and further reading section at the end of this Case study.

Analysis

The first key difference is that most young people in Plaid Cymru have parents who are – or were – also party members. Mass expenditure on youth recruitment raises the level of young people in the party by approximately 40 per cent. The second key difference is that a far greater percentage of young people (41.7 per cent) join political parties as a means to find out about politics than any other age group. An identical percentage joined the party without any expectations of membership. So, unlike their elder counterparts, young people are the least likely to report that they joined their party because of political beliefs. For them, party membership is an educational experience, or one that they drift into.

They also drift out of membership just as easily. Young people in Plaid Cymru are far less likely to keep their subscriptions up to date than their older counterparts. Incidentally, these findings are mirrored closely in earlier research carried out among English Liberal Democrat members some years previously (Granik 1997). The widely held belief that, once a young person joins a political party, they will stay in membership for life is not supported by reality. To compensate for this, while they remain in the party, young people are the group that is the least critical of party policies. No respondents under the age of twenty-five report any disagreement with current party policies.

Unfortunately, acceptance of policy does not convert into political action, despite the widely held myth that young people bring considerable benefit to their parties by contributing their enthusiastic and energetic participation. The Plaid Cymru survey indicated that young members are not the most likely group to be active in their party. It's those members aged between forty-five and sixty-four who are the most likely to participate in party activities, and those between forty-five and fifty-four, and sixty-five and seventy-four who spend the most hours per week on helping their party.

So, what explanation can be offered for this gap between political belief and political action? One likely reason is that young people have relatively low levels of political confidence, or efficacy, which we know has a direct relationship with participation (Granik 2005). They are the least likely to believe that they are good at political activity, or that the things that they do will have any noticeable effect. Young people score slightly below the average party score on this crucial factor. The highest scores on efficacy are those achieved by members in the forty-five to sixty-four age groups.

Finally, let's explore whether young members contribute to Plaid Cymru by donating to party funds. Again, despite their loyalty to party policy, younger members are the least likely to make a donation to the party, and when they do, they give the least.

Lessons for political marketing

In marketing terms, the proposition of spending a disproportionate amount of time and resources on gaining customers who don't benefit the organisation seems patently ridiculous. Yet, that is what most political parties are doing. In any other context, a marketer would use extensive customer information to decide which groups most benefit an organisation, and target the offerings of that organisation to the groups it chooses to serve. Resources would be used for product or service development that would meet the needs of targeted customer groups. Promotional effort would be focused at those groups, to the exclusion of others.

A shrewd marketer might ask which members could political parties recruit to their best advantage. These data indicate some uncomfortable answers. The most active party members are those aged forty-five to sixty-four. The members who are the most confident about being able to contribute through political activity are those aged forty-five to sixty-four. The members who are the most likely to make financial donations to their party are aged over thirty-five.

And there's one other advantage in recruiting people in their mid thirties and older. People in these age groups are likely to have children in or approaching their teens. The data from Plaid Cymru suggest that, if political parties want young members, asking their parents to network them into the party is the most cost-effective and reliable way of getting them. This frees up scarce resources to concentrate paid-for recruitment effort on the more productive – and more mature – members, who are the most likely to stay in and contribute to their party.

Let's be clear: it would be wrong to say that young people should be excluded from politics. That is most emphatically not the lesson to be learned from this research. The key marketing message is that, if a party is going to allocate resources towards recruitment, direct these resources to the groups of people most likely to benefit your party. Let young people join of their own volition. But don't throw money away on expensive and sophisticated attempts to lure them in. Heavy spending on attracting those in their late teens or early twenties into the party political fold is simply wasted on the young.

Sources and further reading, including data used for this analysis

Granik, S. (1997). 'Beyond belief: the consumer behaviour of political party members'. MA dissertation: University of Westminster (unpublished).

—— (2003). 'Managing memberships: participation and inclusion in a political party setting.' Ph.D. thesis: London School of Economics and Political Science (unpublished).

—— (2005). 'A reconceptualisation of the antecedents of party activism – a multidisciplinary approach'. *Political Studies*, 53: 423–5.

Case study 6.2 Examples of internal blockage to market-oriented strategy: the UK Conservatives, 1997–2001

Jennifer Lees-Marshment

After losing power in 1997, the UK Conservatives set about reforming the party and making it market-oriented again. William Hague, a former management consultant, reorganised the party, tried to recruit new members and a broader range of candidates, conducted market intelligence both formally and informally, and developed early policy priorities in response to public opinion. The party began to pursue a public services strategy in response to market intelligence, begun in major speeches made by Hague and deputy leader Peter Lilley in April 1999 and focusing on improving state provision of public services rather than looking to the market and simply reducing taxes. The plan was then to produce policy themes showing the more caring side of Conservatives. Guarantees launched in late 1999 responded to the results from market intelligence. They could have built the party's overall reputation for honesty and believability. They were also focused on areas of prime importance to voters. When it was first communicated, press coverage was potentially positive: it was seen as a new break with the past, a new way forward, even likened to Tony Blair's abandonment of Clause Four.

However, around mid-term in 1999–2000, Hague started to meet internal resistance to the changes proposed:

- Archie Norman, a successful businessman, became chief executive, opened up central office and reassigned staff, meeting internal opposition.
- Local associations with the power to select candidates were in some cases very unprofessional, sexist and homophobic, and this not only hindered the goal of broadening the candidates, it attracted poor media attention.
- Despite the changes made to the membership, the age overall remained high, and membership numbers dropped from 350,000 when Hague took over to 300,000 by the time of the election in 2001.
- Hague himself failed to win public support, and it was increasingly difficult for him then to impose authority on those who did not want to follow the market-oriented line.
- The party suffered from a number of defections or resignations.
- Speeches on the new policy direction away from Thatcherism were criticised internally; it was criticised as repudiating Thatcher's free-market legacy and stimulated a very negative reaction from the parliamentary party

Gradually, the early market-oriented policy announcements were withdrawn, and, a year or so before the election, strategy changed to focus on getting the core vote out, rather than new markets. The party focused more on its core vote and issues such as asylum. As Kenneth Clarke later commented, 'from about half-way through the parliament we stopped trying to broadening our appeal, we narrowed it' (BBC 1, *Question Time*, 5 July 2001). Overall, it abandoned the market-oriented strategy.

Implementation clearly failed in this case. The *idea* of a market-orientation was fully accepted by the central leadership, but was never fully accepted throughout the party. His entire approach attracted criticism right from the beginning. In September 1997, the then MP Alan Clark wrote a letter to *The Times* newspaper, criticising Hague for trying to tell the party to give:

> a blank cheque on a small coterie of management consultants to proceed as they think fit. Such a request, even if it were coming from a leader with a distinguished record of achievement, does not sit comfortably with our history.

The initial design to focus on public services was heavily criticised internally by staff and politicians. Hague's official reaction at first was to say he would not change this strategy: 'I will go thorough any number of arguments, take on anyone in debate, endure any criticisms, do whatever it takes to get across this position on health and education' (quoted in the *Daily Telegraph*, 29 April 1999). Over time, however, declarations focusing on improving public services were replaced by communications about popular positions on minority issues such as the asylum and the euro. The party had not sufficiently adopted a market-orientation that would ensure implementation and communication of a product and set of policies designed to suit voter demands.

This can also be seen in the amount of defections and disunity even at the top levels of the Tory Party, such as Shaun Woodward in December 1999 and Ivan Massow in August 2000. Ken Clarke reopened divisions over Europe, appearing on a shared platform with Labour (and Tony Blair) to launch the 'Britain in Europe' campaign and even stating 'I'm in favour of joining the single currency in principle. I don't agree with the party's policy' (*The Guardian*, 5 July 1999). This gave the impression that Hague was not in control and publicly demonstrated the disunity that damaged the product. Additionally, Hague's leadership was criticised by senior Tories, including John Major and Kenneth Clark from 1999 to 2001. Additionally, there was always talk of potential challengers to the leader, such as Ken Clarke and Michael Portillo, even extremely close to the general election. Overall, disunity, change of direction, defections and lack of cultural change at lower levels of the party prevented implementation, making communication very difficult.

Lessons for political marketing

This case shows that, just because leaders want to adopt and implement a market-orientation, it does not mean that it will be successful – they have to get support from the majority within the party. Factors such as internal culture, organisation and also previous state of market-orientation affect this. Hague suffered from bad timing – had he become leader one or two elections later he might have been more successful, not least in attracting public support to make his leadership more secure. This also demonstrates that parties will not always want to become market-oriented. Although it lost again in 2001, the party nevertheless failed to learn its lesson. Another new leader, Iain Duncan-Smith, also tried to reposition the party, focusing on responding to the less well off in society. He too failed to gain support from the public and internally from the party.

Sources and further reading

Lees-Marshment, Jennifer (2008). *Political Marketing and British Political Parties* (2nd edn). Manchester: Manchester University Press.

Case study 6.3 The problems of implementing medium-/long-term planning for political parties in Spain

Juan Ignacio Marcos Lekuona

It is difficult to discuss medium-/long-term planning with party leaders. Planning is seen as the domain of strategists, and any plans may not carry real commitment to a change in behaviour. This case explores an attempt to design and implement a mid-term development plan in three political parties in Spain.

In the years 2004–05, the author worked as a consultant with three parties:

- **Ezquerra Republicana de Catalunya** (ERC) – a party born in 1931 that gained the majority in Catalunya during the Second Republic, with the presidency of government and 100,000 members. It participated in the current government of the Catalan Generalitat.

- **Eusko Alkartasuna** (Basque Solidarity) – a party created in 1986 from a split of the preponderant Basque Nationalistic Party, which formed a coalition in the Basque Government. It has about 3,000 members.
- **The Bloc Nacionalista Valencia** – the result of fusions between Valencian nationalistic groups. It gained 5 per cent of the vote in a community that had four million inhabitants. The Bloc has about 5,000 members and it is present in about 100 municipalities.

The plan covered two elections, one in 2007, which elected the municipal governments and included '*forales*' in Euskadi where three powerful '*diputaciones*' were chosen. It also included elections to the autonomic parliament in the Valencian community, corresponding to the three historical territories into which the community is divided, where the Bloc gained two deputies. The second involved the preparation of the campaign for the state elections to the *Cortes Generales*. In the *Cortes Generales*, the ERC had its own parliamentary group with eight deputies but was predicted to lose them all, as was the EA expected to lose its one deputy, while the Bloc never had representation in the *Cortes Generales*.

Design of the development plan
With some small variations between the three parties, the plan used the following design (see Lynch *et al.* 2006):

Temporary horizon
The temporary horizon was 2007–11. In this period, municipal elections took place in 2007 (along with *forales* in Euskadi and the autonomic ones in the Valencian region); state elections took place in 2008; European elections in 2009; autonomic elections in Euskadi and Catalunya (2010); and in 2011 the same ones as in 2007. So, each one of these electoral landmarks served as a point for evaluation and replanning.

Strategic targets
The objectives were:

- targeting/gaining support from voters who declared themselves to be like nationalists and left of centre;
- getting party voters out;
- obtaining public institutional positions;
- increasing the number of affiliated and militant members;
- developing databases of voters, donors and volunteers;
- increasing budgets/income.

Situation and general strategy
Although the parties were safe and could gain a majority in a few municipalities, none of the three parties was first in its respective independent communities. The plan was therefore to move closer to the voter, i.e. the Lees-Marshment MOP concept, to gain support particularly from those who might otherwise not vote or be against the major parties.

The campaigns/the development projects
The heart of the plan was about developing the organisation and its direction that would ensure the party was able to manage electoral campaigns and build up the strategic resources to help achieve greater electoral success in 2011.

The campaign for each one of the elections takes a year of preparation, from the evaluation of the previous results by electoral section and its aggregates. Its execution is formed by the following stages:

- determination of objectives and priorities of electoral sections;
- advances in the identification of voters;
- mobilisation of militants and supporters;
- elaboration of manifestos from priorities of militants and voters;
- get out the vote.

The plan included a range of projects to be executed throughout 2007–11 to improve and to increase the strategic resources that would help the parties do well in the long term:

- The constitution and development of a centre of analysis for the identification of the segments of voters, as well as their motives for voting and evaluation of the 'political product'.
- The putting into practice of processes of collective elaboration of policies, with the participation of candidates and local leaders who obtain good electoral results, prior to the determination of the positioning in each election.
- The evolution of the organisation of the party, such as a tool of two-way communication with the voters, based on the empowerment of militants and medium managers of the party.
- The management of knowledge, such as the creation of processes that turn the tacit practical knowledge of the party members into a permanent school of political practice that guarantees the development of good political practices and suppresses bad practice.

During the 2007 election campaign, parties did follow some guidelines in a handbook of service to the voter, such as:

- Suppers with militants and supporters, where the directors of the party has gathered observations on the weak points of the party and proposals for policies. An immediate result has been an increase in the database of supporters.
- Electoral operations to identify voters in some municipalities and sections.
- An effort to surpass advertising by outlining a political position. In this sense, the Bloc's campaign, centred on the concept of bottom-to-top policy-making provided a great contrast to the top-to-bottom policy-making practiced by the major parties.

Results and conclusions

Despite the potential of such plans, and the adoption of some of the suggestions, the problem in practice was that it involved changing the behaviour of the executives and members of the party in the line of conscious political management, which led to internal opposition in the political parties. While the party asked for such plans to be drawn up and approved the plan, this does not mean it was committed to change its processes. Politicians even used the document as a source of ideas for speeches, but there still remained a big gap between what they said publicly and how they behaved. Despite the benefits of the plan, such internal barriers stop implementation of marketing, meaning that parties exhibit weaknesses such as:

- a disparity between the priorities of the government and the priorities of the voters;
- the party gives excessive attention to the internal management and lack of attention to voters.

In spite of these and some other improvements in political marketing and the direction of the party, the typical behaviour of the parties is far from following the strategy in the development plan.

Sources and further reading

Richard Lynch, Paul Baines and John Egan (2006). 'Long term performance of political parties: towards a competitive resource-based perspective'. *Journal of Political Marketing*, 5(3).

Case study 6.4 Resisting marketing: the case of the British Labour Party under Blair   *Robin T. Pettitt*

New Labour and market orientation

According to Lees-Marshment (2001: 181), the British Labour Party in its 'New Labour' incarnation is 'the most recent and easily identifiable case of political marketing. During 1992–97 the Labour Party became a classic Market-Oriented Party.' New Labour involved massive changes to almost every aspect of the party's life. However, Lees-Marshment (2001: 189–90) also criticises the Labour Party, arguing that Tony Blair failed to consult with the party before deciding on these changes, and that more consultation could have avoided some of the deep-rooted opposition in the party to 'New' Labour. This case study explores why these problems occurred and how the nature of the Labour Party made such consultation difficult.

Designing the product

Party behaviour, or its product, requires very different approaches when one is trying to 'design' it. Taking the Lees-Marshment definition of a product, leadership, Members of Parliament, membership and staff cannot be designed on a drawing board the way a symbol can. Rather, we are talking about the behaviour of individuals that has to be guided and controlled, although it is true that behaviour can be controlled according to voter demands. Obviously, this requires the co-operation of the individuals concerned, which they may not be willing to give. Symbols, constitution, activities and policies are much easier to design, as we are not dealing with people. However, it is still necessary for the party leaders to convince the rest of the party that changes in these areas are required, as party members may object to policies, etc. being designed according to voter demands rather than party ideology.

So, the extent to which party leaders can successfully make a party market-oriented depends on the willingness of party members to take orders and accept changes to the party's profile.

New Labour's challenges

As Kirchheimer (1966) points out, attracting new voters may mean jettisoning 'ideological baggage'. As we can see from Table 6.3, dumping party principles for electoral purposes is *not* popular in the Labour Party: 61.8 per cent of those asked in 1999 believed that the party should stick to its principles, even if it meant losing an election. This is almost identical to 1989–90, that is, before 'New' Labour. It seems that Labour members have a long-standing opposition to ditching party principles in the name of electoral expediency. Clearly, this will limit the manoeuverability of party leaders in adopting a new product.

Table 6.3 The Labour Party should always stand by its principles even if this should lose an election

	Agree/strongly agree (%)	Neither (%)	Disagree/strongly disagree (%)	Total
1989–90	60.8	11.9	27.3	4,936
1999	61.8	16.7	21.5	5,517

Source: Seyd and Whiteley (1999)

Further, a mainstay of New Labour's argument has been about capturing the middle ground of politics. However, as can be seen from Table 6.4, there has been considerable opposition to centre-seeking policies. It is true that, in 1999, 45 per cent of those asked supported the view that the Labour Party should move to the middle ground of politics. Nevertheless, over a third of the party opposed such a move. This explains both why the leadership was successful in moving the party to the centre, but also why it faced considerable opposition in doing so. The leadership could win a vote on centre-seeking policy proposals, but with a third of members opposed, it was never going to be done quietly. It is also worth noting that, even in 1989–90, four years before Blair came to power, there was considerable opposition to a centre-ground approach, with 32.8 per cent against. In other words, the opposition to moving to the centre ground is not a New Labour phenomenon.

Table 6.4 Labour should adjust policies to capture the middle ground of politics

	Agree/strongly agree (%)	Neither (%)	Disagree/strongly disagree (%)	Total
1989–90	57.3	9.9	32.8	4,911
1999	45.0	21.0	34.0	5,530

Source: Seyd and Whiteley (1999)

However, the opposition of members to certain policy initiatives is one thing. Quite another is their willingness to express their dissatisfaction: 'what is needed for membership dissent to occur is not just disagreement but also the willingness to dissent' (Pettitt 2006: 297). Even if members disagree with their leaders, they may still follow them. Table 6.5 shows that Labour has a somewhat sceptical view of leadership. A plurality of 42.1 per cent of members disagreed with the statement that the role of party members is to follow the leadership's decisions. There is, therefore, a significant group in the party who are willing to openly resist the leadership's decisions.

Table 6.5 The role of party members is to support decisions made by the leadership

	Agree/strongly agree (%)	Neither (%)	Disagree/strongly disagree (%)	Total
1999	39.6	18.2	42.1	5,568

Source: Seyd and Whiteley (2002)

Discussion

So, the New Labour leadership has had to deal with a significant section of the membership that was both worried about the New Labour project, and happy to express that worry. Further, it has not just been the 'New' Labour leadership that has come under attack from the members. Labour members have a long tradition of explaining to the leadership 'in great detail and at great length what it was doing wrong' (Pettitt 2006: 289). It was only with the New Labour leadership's so-called 'control freakery' that some of this dissent was brought under control. The solution to these problems was to quell dissent rather than consult. Based on the above, this may have been the only viable option. The price for quelling membership dissent has been, not only a sharp drop in membership, but also, as Lees-Marshment points out, a lack of acceptance of market-driven policies (Lees-Marshment 2001: 193).

The main lesson to be learned from New Labour is that, regardless of how the product is designed and adjusted, there will sometimes be considerable dissent, because the compromises necessary to avoid dissent would dilute the new product too much. Therefore, in some parties, the process can only be partially successful because the raw material – the party organisation – is simply not willing to become market-oriented. It may still be possible to use a market-oriented approach to achieve remarkable electoral success, as has been the case for the Labour Party since 1997. However, because of the nature of a party, there can be an unavoidable price for such success: in the case of the Labour Party, internal dissent and the loss of more than two-thirds of its members since the mid-1990s. Labour is therefore an example of what a market-oriented approach can do for a party, but also a warning of what the price can be.

Sources and further reading

Kirchheimer, Otto (1966). 'The transformation of the Western European party system'. In J. LaPalombara and M. Weiner (eds), *Political Parties and Political Development*. Princeton, NJ: Princeton University Press.

Lees-Marshment, Jennifer (2001). *Political Marketing and British Political Parties: The Party's Just Begun*. Manchester: Manchester University Press.

Pettitt, Robin T. (2006). 'Rebellion by the seaside: how single member plurality has affected membership dissent at the Labour Party conference'. *Representation*, 42(4): 289–301.

Seyd, P. and P. Whiteley (2002). Survey of Labour party members, 1997 and 1999. Colchester, Essex: UK Data Archive, October 2002, SN: 4466.

——, —— and D. Broughton (1992). *Study of the Labour Party Membership, December 1989– May 1990*. Colchester, Essex: UK Data Archive (distributor), July 1992. SN: 2920.

NOTE

1   Johnson, D.W. (2009) (ed.) *Routledge Handbook of Political Management,* which was in press at time of writing and therefore could not be included here, should be consulted for further literature about political management.

FURTHER READING

Bannon, Declan (2005a). 'Internal marketing and political marketing'. UK PSA conference paper. Leeds, 7 April.

—— (2005b). 'Relationship marketing and the political process'. *Journal of Political Marketing*, 4(2/3): 73–90.

Bauer, Hans H., Frank Huber and Andreas Herrman (1996). 'Political marketing: an information-economic analysis'. *European Journal of Marketing*, 30: 159–72.

Bryant, Illana (2008). 'An inside look at Obama's grassroots marketing'. *Adweek*, 12 March 2008. Available online at www.adweek.com/aw/content_display/community/columns/othercolumns/e3i714b5acb6525107fda1eb890ff94a48a (accessed 1 April 2008).

Christopher, Martin, Adrian Payne and David Ballantyne (1991). *Relationship Marketing.* Butterworth Heinemann (in association with the Chartered Institute of Marketing).

Dean, Dianne and Robin Croft (2001). 'Friends and relations: long-term approaches to political campaigning'. *European Journal of Marketing*, 35(11/12): 1197–1216.

Granik, S. (2005a). 'Internal consumers – what makes your party members join your election effort?'. Political Marketing Group Conference, London, 24–25 February 2005.

—— (2005b). 'Membership benefits, membership action: why incentives for activism are what members want'. In W. Wymer and J. Lees-Marshment (eds), *Current Issues in Political Marketing*. Binghamton, NY: Haworth Press.

Hughes, A. and S. Dann (2006a). 'Political marketing and stakeholders'. Australia and New Zealand Marketing Academy Conference, Queensland University of Technology, Brisbane, Queensland, 4–6 December 2006.

—— (2006b). 'Political marketing 2006: direct benefit, value, and managing the voter relationship'. Australia and New Zealand Marketing Academy Conference, Queensland University of Technology, Brisbane, Queensland, 30 December 2006.

Johnson, Dennis W. (ed.) (2008). *The Routledge Handbook of Political Management*. New York: Routledge.

Knuckey, Jonathan and Jennifer Lees-Marshment (2005). 'American political marketing: George W. Bush and the Republican Party'. In D.G. Lilleker and J. Lees-Marshment (eds), *Political Marketing in Comparative Perspective*. Manchester: Manchester University Press.

Kotler, Philip (1979). 'Strategies for introducing marketing into non-profit organisations'. *Journal of Marketing,* 43: 37–44.

—— and Alan R. Andreasen (1991). *Strategic Marketing for Nonprofit Organizations.* London: Prentice-Hall.

Lebel, Gregory G. (1999). 'Managing volunteers: time has changed – or have they?'. In Bruce Newman (ed.), *Handbook of Political Marketing*. Thousand Oaks, CA: Sage.

Lees-Marshment, Jennifer (2001). *Political Marketing and British Political Parties: The Party's Just Begun.* Manchester: Manchester University Press.

—— (2004). *The Political Marketing Revolution.* Manchester: Manchester University Press.

—— (2008). *Political Marketing and British Political Parties* (2nd edn). Manchester: Manchester University Press.

—— and Robin Pettitt (2009). 'UK political marketing: a question of leadership?'. In Jennifer Lees-Marshment, Jesper Strömbäck and Chris Rudd (eds), *Global Political Marketing.* London: Routledge.

—— and Stuart Quayle (2001). 'Empowering the members or marketing the party? The Conservative reforms of 1998'. *The Political Quarterly*, 72(2): 204–12.

Lilleker, Darren G. (2005). 'The impact of political marketing on internal party democracy'. *Parliamentary Affairs*, 58(3): 570–84.

Lloyd, Jenny (2005). 'Marketing politics . . . saving democracy'. In Adrian Sargeant and Walter Wymer (eds), *The Routledge Companion to Nonprofit Marketing.* New York: Routledge.

Medvic, Stephen K. (2006). 'Understanding campaign strategy "deliberate priming" and the role of professional political consultants'. *Journal of Political Marketing*, 5(1/2): 11–32.

Ormrod, Robert P. (2005). 'A conceptual model of political market orientation'. *Journal of Non-Profit and Public Sector Marketing*, 14(1/2): 47–64.

——, Stephan C. Henneberg, Nick Forward, James Miller and Leigh Tymms (2007). 'Political marketing in untraditional campaigns: the case of David Cameron's Conservative Party leadership victory'. *Journal of Public Affairs*, 7(3): 235–48.

Rogers, Ben (2005). 'From membership to management? The future of political parties as democratic organisations'. *Parliamentary Affairs*, 58(3): 600–10.

Skocpol, T. (2003). *Diminished Democracy: From Membership to Management in American Civic Life.* Norman, OK: University of Oklahoma Press.

Steen, Jennifer (1999). 'Money doesn't grow on trees: fund-raising in American political campaigns'. In Bruce Newman (ed.), *Handbook of Political Marketing*. Thousand Oaks, CA: Sage.

Ubertaccio, Peter (forthcoming). 'Network marketing and American political parties'. In Dennis W. Johnson (ed.), *The Routledge Handbook of Political Management*. New York: Routledge.

Wring, Dominic (2002). 'Images of Labour: the progression and politics of party campaigning in Britain'. *Journal of Political Marketing*, 1(1): 23–37.

—— (2005). *The Politics of Marketing of the Labour Party.* Hampshire: Palgrave Macmillan.

7 Marketing communication and campaigns

Communication and campaigning are the most obvious areas of political marketing, although there are many areas of marketing communications literature and theory that have not yet been applied to politics. This chapter will discuss direct marketing, e-marketing, local marketing, market-oriented communication and public relations within the political context, and will also explore democratic issues with marketing communications.

Why do politicians and parties want to use marketing communications?

Marketing communications are used for several reasons, not just to win an election, including to:

1   improve the candidate's or political leader's image;
2   represent what the party or politician is about;
3   persuade voters to a point of view;
4   make something clearer;
5   counter negative attacks from the opposition;
6   educate and inform voters;
7   gain or increase support for a particular piece of legislation;
8   place an issue on the agenda;
9   increase support for referendum proposition.

There are a number of people with whom politicians want to communicate, with voters being the obvious market and the focus of much of the literature, but segmenting the electorate and considering other stakeholders are also important. If politicians understand voters, they can create more effective communication; knowing who they are, what they want and how to reach them helps develop much more targeted and wanted communication.

When do politicians use marketing communications?

While much attention focuses on election campaigns – the official, shorter period just prior to voting day that begins after a government announces the election and dissolves the legislature or parliament – politicians and parties communicate all the time, as do governments. Where parties are strong, the leadership has to pay particular attention to what MPs and members of the party are doing, as they can convey complementary or divergent messages about the political product.

Communication can take place over several years if the aim is to change public opinion or put a previously ignored issue higher up the agenda. Parties may plan short or mini campaigns years away from the next election, to promote a new leader or to convey a new product or change in position. They may also engage in pre-campaign communication, sometimes called the near campaign, in the period before the election is called. In the US, presidential candidates have to communicate over a long period, first in the primary period, where they bid to become their party's nomination, and then finally, post-nomination, where they compete against the other candidate(s) to become president. Thus, the official election campaign immediately prior to the election is not necessarily the most important, unless elections are close, and the last chance to influence voting behaviour could make a difference to the overall outcome.

Using market intelligence to inform communication

Market intelligence informs the way politicians devise communication, choose which issues to focus on and present themselves. As Rademacher and Tuchfarber (1999: 202) argue, polling is used in different ways, depending on the stage of the campaign; in the early stages it identifies what messages to send to whom, and later it measures the effectiveness of different messages to inform any necessary changes. Intelligence can be used to inform the presentation of the leader or to inform the development of political advertising.

Leadership marketing communication

Communication about individual candidates for leadership positions, such as president or party leader, is especially important to get right. While communication can be used without marketing, intelligence ensures it is targeted and responds to market opinion in some way, and can help it be more effective in achieving its goals. Marketing communication about leaders needs to convey characteristics favourable to voters and includes nonverbal images (NVIs). Schweiger and Aadami (1999) noted how NVI marketing research can be used to understand what makes up a political image and measure responses from voters using a range of pictures representing different characteristics, both positive and negative. Table 7.1 shows examples of image attributes of a candidate.

Table 7.1 Image attributes of a political candidate

Dimension	Positive attribute	Negative attribute
Honesty	Honest Credible A man/woman of his/her word Transparent Reliable Honest reputation	Entangled in scandals Embezzlement Breach of contract
Quality	Knowledge Educational background Capable Mastermind Experienced	Does not know how to manage a government No business knowledge No international experience Not qualified
Strength	Strong Winner Carries his/her point Energetic Tough Successful	Weak Loser Without backbone

Source: Schweiger and Aadami (1999: 361)

As Ingram and Lees-Marshment (2002) note, market research in Bill Clinton's 1992 campaign suggested voters were more open to changing their view of Clinton if they heard him speak at length. Clinton therefore made frequent use of electronic town hall meetings, which allowed more direct and non-mediated access to voters, unavailable via traditional media. Case study 7.1 illustrates how a changed market can increase the importance of image as an influence on the vote, albeit it with limitations dependent on the particular country.

Marketers try to convey positive attributes within their communication to suit the individual market they work in. Although the product behind the presentation is important, it also needs to be conveyed. Schweiger and Aadami (1999: 348) argued that Helmut Kohl lost support in the German elections of 1998, despite delivery success in power,

> because his image was that of an old man, a political charger, and a bad-tempered man concerning the media. He was no slim, smiling, handsome political follower and did not fit in the political picture of a smooth 21st century.

Intelligence can identify potential weaknesses and enable communication to be devised to reduce them. Scammell (1995 and 1996) detailed how Margaret Thatcher, Britain's first female prime minister, who won three election victories in 1979, 1983 and 1987 for the Conservatives, utilised market intelligence in numerous ways. Thatcher was placed on non-political television shows to reach out to new audiences on the advice of Sir Gordon Reece, a television specialist (Scammell 1996: 117–18). She was also advised on strategies to 'create a more warm and womanly image for a leader generally perceived as aloof and rather superior', with Thatcher cuddling a newborn calf and executing housework to improve her image (Scammell 1996: 122). Similarly, Bill Clinton appeared on MTV and the *Arsenio Hall Show* to show his human side when campaigning for the US presidency in 1992 (Ingram and Lees-Marshment 2002).

Communication to alter public perception is not always effective, despite the best marketing. Thatcher's weaknesses, such as being out of touch and talking down to people, continued throughout her time in power (Scammell 1996: 122). Change needs to be authentic and is also limited by how well a leader is known before communication begins. Barack Obama benefited from portraying a youthful, change-driven image during his bid for the Democratic nomination in 2008. However, Hillary Clinton was hindered somewhat by already having an image, having been former President Bill Clinton's wife, as well as gender-stereotyping and criticisms.

Newman (2001: 210–14) drew the following political marketing guidelines from the 2000 US presidential election, which George W. Bush won and Al Gore lost:

1   Marketing is all about making an emotional connection with people:
    • Bush used his natural characteristics to connect, conveying positivity and likeability.
    • Gore showed more of a serious commitment to specific voters' concerns by talking about issues, but this lacked emotion.

2   Use one central vision that reflects the candidate's personality:
    • Bush's slogans were 'Compassionate Conservatism' and, later in the campaign, 'Real programs for real people', and this reflected how voters perceived him to be likable and caring.
    • Gore's slogans were less clear and not repeated enough to catch on; he also kept changing his look: 'from the *CEO* look (pinstriped suits) to the *Nightclub singer*

look (dark suit, dark shirt, loud tie) to the *Casual Al Gore* look (polo shirt and sport coat).' He kept trying to be 'all things to all people'.

3   Voters constantly want change:
   •   Bush offered an alternative, non-Washington DC approach, whereas Gore was too closely tied to the previous Clinton administration.

In the UK, when David Cameron took over leadership of the Conservative Party after the 2005 election, significant communication strategies were put in place to convey a new image of the party in response to market intelligence about what the public wanted from the party, as well as to decontaminate what had become a negative brand. This included photo opportunities of Cameron cycling to work, visiting Darfur in Africa, planting trees on a social action day, on a Friends of the Earth platform, visiting a Norwegian glacier and meeting Nelson Mandela, all of which helped to convey a new strategy of focusing on environmentalism, the poor and world affairs. The party also adopted a new party symbol, a green tree and blue sky, used the slogan 'vote blue, get green' in local elections and redeveloped the party website with fresh blue–green colours, using pictures that convey a more mainstream Britain.

Discussion point 7.1

Discuss the strengths and weaknesses of US President Barack Obama's image. To what extent has communication about Obama followed principles of political marketing and/or learned from former presidential contenders Clinton, Bush and Gore?

Using market intelligence to inform decisions about political advertising

Political marketing can also affect how adverts are devised. In Bill Clinton's 1992 presidential bid for the US White House, the campaign made several decisions about communication in response to market intelligence, both in the primaries and after nomination. Ingram and Lees-Marshment (2002) noted how, in response to public desire for Clinton to offer a New Democrat perspective that was different to Republicanism but without the old disadvantages of a 'tax and spend' liberal, television commercials showed Clinton and vice-presidential nominee Gore as a new generation of Democrats.

Using research in the whole campaign

Case study 7.2 illustrates how market intelligence and strategy informed campaigning in the 2006 Czech elections.

Discussion point 7.2

Discuss the range of ways in which market intelligence can inform communication. How important is it for parties and candidates to have access to intelligence in elections today?

Using segmentation and targeting in communication

Communication can be varied depending on who it is aimed at – trying to communicate the same thing to everyone can be less effective. Segmentation can help parties and candidates decide on which areas to target. In 1979, the UK Conservatives segmented the market – albeit more crudely than happens now – and focused communication efforts accordingly: see Table 7.2.

Targeting can be used by smaller, new parties, as well as older, more established ones. McGough (2005) illustrated how the Irish party Sinn Féin segmented the market into six different targets in 2002, understanding their different demands and adopting a different strategy for each one, where appropriate:

1   North – nationalist Catholics: fanatically faithful to the party; want a socialist, thirty-two-county Republic of Ireland. The party promoted a picture of their voters as barely free from the chains of conflict and still enduring sectarianism and intimidation from various quarters.
2   North – Catholic community: attracted by Sinn Féin policies on demilitarisation, policing, loyalist attacks, plastic bullets and Orange parades.
3   Alliance and soft Ulster Unionist supporters: the party tried to build bridges to this market.
4   Republic of Ireland voters: very different views from the party, so Sinn Féin focused on a socialist list of policies they wanted, rather than contemplating making any concessions to competitors. The party campaigned using an alternative language focused on change and responding to discontent among working class and for the second single transferable vote (STV) of the middle classes.
5   Ogra Sinn Féin – the all-Ireland youth wing: building long-term links with the youth.
6   Irish–American/international support: careful packaging to the international market.

The Brazilian left-wing party PT – Partido dos Trabalhadores (Workers Party) – led by Luiz Inácio Lula da Silva, changed its communication in the 2002 election to target female votes. Cotrim Macieira (2005) observed that Lula softened his image from a radical left-wing union leader to become more moderate, and Marisa da Silva, Lula's wife, accompanied her husband in the campaign rallies.

Baines *et al.* (2002) developed a strategic planning model for campaigning parties to improve their targeting and ensure they deploy resources most effectively to obtain maximum public support. They argue this should be done at local, not just national, level and develop a model using five factors associated with strategic marketing planning, the aim being to match organisational resources with market opportunities and threats: see Table 7.3.

Table 7.2 Targeted communication by the UK Conservatives, 1979

Target markets	Examples of communication geared to suit them
The skilled working class (C2)	Saatchi and Saatchi created posters with slogans that included the infamous 'Labour isn't working' and 'Britain's better off with the Conservatives'. One newspaper advert was entitled 'Why every trade unionist should consider voting Conservative' and appealed to traditional Labour supporters.
Women	Campaign adverts were placed in women's magazines.
First-time voters	Adverts were run in the cinema to attract support from first-time voters.
The party faithful	Thatcher's speeches appealed to traditional Conservative voters.

Table 7.3 Factors associated with political marketing planning process

Marketing planning function	Political marketing context
Market position analysis	Determine what voters think of the party, and where – opinions may vary geographically. This can include information gathering, such as identifying constituencies most likely to change; conducting market intelligence in various forms, using historical data, census statistics, constituency ranking, canvass records and constituency research. Constituency research should focus on: current level of support; types of people who support particular parties (indicating the major competition); types of people who have changed their support for a particular party since the previous general election; electorate's feelings regarding particular issues and policies; level of tactical and traditional voting; and whether or not the personal vote is significant.
Objective setting	Decide on issues and voter segments to focus on; take into account organisational resources.
Strategic alternative evaluation	Decide which segments to target communication at, and which messages to use, utilising market intelligence and also considering the stability, accessibility and substance of each segment.
Strategy implementation	Allocate resources accordingly, taking into account unpredictable finances and donations if appropriate, depending on regulations in country.
Monitoring and control	Monitor impact of strategy, as well as opposition; including after losing an election, to find out what went wrong.

Source: adapted from Baines *et al.* (2002)

Discussion point 7.3

Think of examples of political communication that are clearly geared to attract target markets. How effective are they?

Direct marketing

Direct marketing is a common part of marketing communications and includes direct mail, direct email, direct texts and any other form of communication that is sent directly to the individual, making the impact stronger. Direct marketing:

- takes the market directly to an individual consumer;
- is individual in some way;
- is interactive, providing the chance to respond;
- can take place anywhere;
- has a measurable response rate.

Direct marketing utilises data collected in market intelligence. Organisations send their direct marketing to three main types of list:

1   *Cold names*: targeted lists of people who have had no contact with the organisation, brought from list brokers; lists of people who have some identifiable characteristic or set of characteristics, such as those on a subscription list to a magazine.

2   *Warm names*: those who have already responded to the organisation or candidate campaign, a house list kept by the organisation's own database.
3   *Rented or swaps*: the house lists swapped with other organisations.

There are many different forms of direct marketing, all of which can be used in politics for several purposes, including: to increase support; recruit new volunteers or members; ask for donations; or get out the vote (see Sherman 1999 and Johnson 2007).

Direct mail

Direct mail is any form of communication posted directly to individuals, addressed with the individual's name. It consists of an outer envelope, letter, brochure, order form and reply card or envelope. It has several key characteristics:

1   It reflects each recipient's individual characteristics.
2   It gets the recipient's attention.
3   It explains why they should be interested.
4   It encourages them to act.

Often, the recruitment package includes some sort of 'free' benefit. It is a cheaper form of advertising than TV and other mechanisms. Organisations test their direct mail to see how effective it is. They establish a control or banker, which is the one that performs the best, and new designs are tested against this.

Direct mail has been used in politics for a long time. O'Shaughnessy and Peele (1985: 115) note how it was used by previous presidential candidates, including Barry Goldwater, George McGovern, Jimmy Carter, Edward Kennedy and Ronald Reagan. The UK Conservative Party used direct mail in 1997–2001 to try to boost and widen the membership using the agency Claydon Heeley International and Archibald Ingall Stretton. It profiled existing members and then bought membership lists of names for wine clubs, garden centres and rugby or cricket clubs for a direct mail recruitment drive (Lees-Marshment 2008: 208). Direct mail need not just be in paper form. In the 2005 UK election, Labour produced direct mail and DVDs for particular candidates in key seats.

Direct telemarketing

Telemarketing is often used by parties and candidates utilising call centres for a range of activities, including voter persuasion, voter identification, volunteer recruitment and GOTV efforts. O'Shaughnessy and Peele (1985: 116) note how telemarketing works well in conjunction with a mailing or to approach lapsed supporters or donors: '*Americans for Reagan* in conjunction with a mailing raised seven million dollars by telephone in 1980.' The 2005 UK Conservative campaign set up call centres in the West Midlands, Yorkshire, the West Country and Kent.

The weakness of direct marketing is that each new innovation is copied by competitors and so loses its competitiveness, and the public becomes immune to the methodology after a while. Response rates are often amazingly low, although, when they ask for donations, as long as the money received overall outweighs the cost, the exercise is often deemed worthwhile. Sherman (1999: 366) cites an example from the Bill Clinton presidency after his popularity dived:

In an effort to get increased support, the firm of Malchow, Adams and Hussey was selected to handle the Democrat's direct marketing fund-raising effort. In 1995 ... a closed-face envelope with a picture of the White House was sent to 600,000 individuals on Democratic National Committee lists. The message stressed that President Clinton said the recipient was a friend and that he or she was wanted as part of the steering committee. It was a soft call for money, with no explicit call for money until the PS at the end of the letter ... it pulled in $3.5 million.

Discussion point 7.4

How effective is direct marketing? How do you respond to to direct marketing yourself? What new forms of direct marketing might emerge in the future?

Insights marketing

Insights marketing, where communication is developed in response to understanding people's deepest values and fears, has been used in campaigning in recent elections, namely the Australian 2004, UK 2005 and New Zealand 2005 elections. The public relations firm Crosby-Textor first advised Australian Liberal Prime Minister John Howard to use insights or dog-whistle marketing – called dog-whistle because communication is devised only to be heard by the specific target market at which it is aimed. Such communication plays emotively on people's hopes and fears. Crosby-Textor advised the UK Conservatives and the New Zealand National Party, and in Australia communication focused on immigration; in the UK on crime. In the UK, their election posters adopted the slogan 'Are you thinking what we're thinking?', placed under simplified messages: 'It's not racist to impose limits on immigration', and with the use of handwriting, to connect with ordinary people (see Seawright 2005: 951; see also Gaber 2006).

Guerilla marketing

To maximise message impact, guerilla marketing can be used: i.e. communication that gets attention by being unexpected and novel and 'bypassing orthodox marketing channels and methodologies' (O'Shaughnessy and Henneberg 2007: 262). Careful presentation of the leader is not confined to the western world. Egherman (2005) discussed how Akbar Hashemi Rafsanjani (www.hashemirafsanjani.ir) utilised guerilla marketing to market his particular presidential brand:

> Jay Conrad Levinson is often called the father of guerilla marketing. He defines it this way: 'It is a body of unconventional ways of pursuing conventional goals ...' The methods that the campaign is using are, indeed, unconventional. They are particularly unconventional for post-revolutionary Iran. The Rafsanjani campaign has employed Iran's hip youth as its army of unpaid campaign workers. They wrap themselves in Hashemi stickers, tape his poster on their backs, celebrate soccer success in his name, attend performances at the candidate's Tehran headquarters and participate in skating events. They wear Rafsanjani campaign materials like fashion accessories.

This army of hip youth may be politically apathetic in large part, but that does not really matter. The Rafsanjani campaign has grabbed the image of youth and energy for itself. You might say that the Rafsanjani generation and the Pepsi generation are one. In other words, it may not matter to Pepsi whether the Pepsi generation drinks Pepsi, as long as Pepsi's sales are robust; similarly, as long as Rafsanjani wins the election, who cares who voted for him.

E-marketing

Online, or virtual, or e-marketing is one of the newest forms of marketing communications, as developments in communications technology have opened up new communications vehicles such as websites, email and text.

Direct e-marketing

E-marketing offers the potential to reach individuals directly, enabling the principles of direct marketing to be applied. Internet advertisements that pop up when the public is browsing are designed not just to reach them but be tailor-made to the recipient in terms of content and time. Additionally, recipients can choose to sign up to e-newsletters, which utilise some of the principles of direct marketing. In the US 2008 presidential nomination campaign, anyone who signed up as a supporter or interested party on the Obama site received emails regularly that asked for both support and donations. Often the attention-seeking element of direct marketing was utilised well, with recipients asked to donate by a certain time to allow Barack to stop fundraising for one day, or before some other deadline. Emotional appeals were also used, with some emails sent from his wife: see Box 7.1.

Relationship e-marketing

Cryus Krohn, a former Yahoo employee, worked for the Republican National Party in 2007 as E-campaign Director to apply the principles of Internet communication to politics, adding social networking and mobile alerts to the Republican National Committee (RNC) site (*Los Angeles Times*, 20 January 2008). As Jackson (2005: 159 and 2006) notes, websites can be used for long-term communication, offering a combination of direct marketing and relationship marketing, rather than just being used in short-term sales campaigning and one-off transactions. It holds the potential to reach new markets, particularly youth, who are often alienated by traditional forms of political behaviour and communication, but are the first users of Internet and digital tools. It may also enhance democracy, but that depends on how it is used. Geiselhart *et al.* (2003: 216) note that, just because there is Internet use within a democracy, does not guarantee e-democracy. Jackson (2005) has examined the way that UK MPs utilised email. He noted that email offers local representatives a cheap and easy means to contact their constituents in a target manner. It can be used (Jackson 2005: 95) to:

1   help them win votes;
2   put out unmediated communication over which they have greater control because they can speak directly to constituents;
3   as a source of market intelligence, to help MPs better represent their constituents and develop their political campaigns and policy stances;

Box 7.1 Emotional email appeals in Obama's presidential nomination campaign

From: Michelle Obama [mailto:info@barackobama.com]

Sent: Sat 05/04/2008 01:25

To: [recipient]

Subject: Yes, they can

[name of recipient]

Today is the 40th anniversary of the tragic assassination of Dr. Martin Luther King Jr., and I want to share a video that reveals how far we've come and how much this campaign owes to Dr. King's legacy.

Students at a high school in the Bronx, who had no real interest in their government, have found new hope. They were surprised by their own excitement and engagement, but to me, they embody so many reasons why Barack and I decided to get into this campaign.

It's truly moving to see young people inspired by a political leader – someone who gives them hope and reminds them that they can be anything they want to be if they work hard . . .

Much has changed in this country since Dr. King's death, and thanks to his life and work we have taken critical strides towards racial equality.

The simple fact that Barack is running a competitive campaign for President is a direct result of Dr. King's legacy – and this movement for change would be impossible without the support of people of all races, ages, and backgrounds.

I remember back in December of 2006, a group of us were discussing the possibility of Barack running for President. And as you might have read, I was hesitant about the idea.

But then Barack started talking about why he really wanted to do this – to bring people together and to change the tone of the way we talk to each other in this country. He talked about the need for people to be inspired by their leaders, and the importance of leadership to chart a different course. He talked about Dr. King and Bobby Kennedy, and their passion to challenge a new generation and provide them with role models . . . He shared his desire to reach out to our neglected inner cities, to strive to be a role model for young people, and to connect with people who are not involved in politics – those who feel their voices haven't been heard, those who have been left behind, and those who have been turned off by all the petty bickering in recent years.

We can change that, by standing on the shoulders of folks like Dr. King who came before us.

Watching these students who are excited about their own role in politics for the first time, and watching Barack as he strives to live up to the challenges Dr. King made possible, I am truly touched.

I hope you'll watch this video and share that feeling with your friends and family:

http://my.barackobama.com/yestheycan

Thank you,
Michelle Obama

4   build credibility and a delivery record, of particular use to incumbents seeking re-
     election;
5   offer the opportunity to engage in two-way communication.

Electronic communication provides the market with the chance to communicate with them on their own terms, to build up a long-term relationship with voters. Jackson (2005: 95) therefore assesses e-marketing by the following criteria for an effective relationship marketing approach:

1   It is regularly used outside an election campaign.
2   Communication is tailored to the requirements of the receiver.
3   Communication is two-way and not just one-way.
4   Builds 'networks' between an MP and the constituents.

Case study 7.3 examines MPs' websites from a marketing perspective.

Network e-marketing

Websites are an obvious campaign tool, not just to communicate with potential voters, but also to mobilise internal supporters. Online communication is rapidly developing to apply the concepts, not just the tools, of marketing. Facebook, YouTube and MySpace share the same principle of being positive and action-oriented. Such initiatives particularly suit younger voters, whose disengagement from politics is a big concern for political elites and political science. Developments in e-marketing or online activity are not just more means of communication, but hold the potential to reconnect people. Joe Trippi started this trend when he set up Howard Dean's website in his bid for the presidential nomination for the 2004 US presidential election. The thinking behind it is social networking – but applied in the virtual environment. If politicians/parties are clever, they will then use it to mobilise grass roots, bring supporters together and so stimulate actual social interaction through virtual interaction. This is beginning to happen in the US (see Shaw 2002), but it is still a process in development, and no one as yet knows for sure which way it will go. Obama also used the Internet to market volunteers in the primaries. Stirland (2008) observed how the Obama campaign ran a large grass-roots, GOTV effort that utilised technology effectively:

> At the center of it all [wa]s a hub of online networking tools enabling a wide spectrum of volunteers all over the country to get together in self-organized groups to help their candidate. From controlling the canvassing operations to corralling e-mail lists, organizing meetings and overseeing national phone drives, Obama's web network [wa]s the most ambitious, and apparently successful, Internet campaign effort in any presidential race in the web's short history ... Most prominent in Obama's suite of sites [wa]s the social networking tool. Since its launch [in 2007] a little more than 500,000 accounts [were] created and 30,000 supporter-created campaign events listed at the site. Facebook co-founder Chris Hughes work[ed] with grass-roots organizers on the system ... Many of the more active volunteers in Ohio and Texas note that the social networking technology enabled them, and the campaign, to quickly get up and running in the two states that few realized would be competitive at this stage of the 2008 Democratic presidential primary season ...' This technology encourages offline organizing, and it's a means for community members to network, and to do all of the old-fashioned organizing that we would never otherwise have had the time or resources

to manage,' sa[id] Ian Davis, another Obama supporter and community organizer in Austin. Davis recently organized a debate-watching party at a German pub in Austin after a year of organizing for the candidate independently. He advertised the event using the social networking tool, and an estimated 1,000 people showed up. He and his fellow volunteers used the event to sign the attendees up for get-out-the vote tasks, like door-knocking, block walking and waving campaign signs on street corners.

Limitations to e-marketing

Like all new tools, e-marketing cannot guarantee success. Such marketing methods are not without their limitations: see Case study 7.4.

The key to successful e-marketing lies in realising that developments in e-marketing are not just another means of communication, but hold the potential to reconnect people, because they are a virtual manifestation of good, old-fashioned, face-to-face social interaction and provision of high-quality service. The communication can also meet criteria similar to those for a market-orientation where user needs and satisfaction are considered. For example, Atkinson and Leigh (2003) set out the following principles for e-communication:

1 A focus on the needs of citizens/customers.
2 Information and transactions people want, rather than information government wants them to have.
3 Putting people in touch with solutions to their problems, not just giving them access to services.
4 Information organised around the citizen's needs.
5 Interaction with government more convenient, at a time and place to suit the consumer, e.g. tasks that previously required a visit to a government office during working hours can be performed by users whenever and wherever they please.

Most government websites may not achieve such principles. Atkinson and Leigh (2003: 167–9) argue that many factors block positive development, such as websites that promote government being linked to one service area only, being unfriendly to users and containing search engines that don't work. Similarly, campaign sites also fail to meet these principles. Virtual social networking needs to be two-way – one of the reasons it appeals to the youth is that it gives them the opportunity to be involved and be active, on their own terms, in a way that suits them. There has to be thinking behind the communication and interactive behaviour for this to work. The US have grasped the idea that it can be used to mobilise, engage and interact with voters, and even enable them to input into the process of developing political products – not just tell them what to think.

Local political marketing communication

Elected representatives and candidates for office also engage in marketing for their re-election. In some cases, local candidates need, and are encouraged, to develop their own marketing campaigns, divergent from the national plan, where the national party product has particularly disappointed local voters because of the particular needs and conditions in that electorate.

In the US, for example, Steger (1999: 663) notes how candidates employ their own staff and consultants and have more freedom from party control to tailor their positions and issues to suit their market. Incumbents get an informal feel for their market through 'direct

Task 7.1

Consider a national campaign and then study a local constituency, electorate or area. How could the national message be, or how was it, adapted to suit the local market?

interactive communication with their constituents to gain firsthand information about their concerns, complaints, and preferences' (Steger 1999: 667). Staff can also track communication from constituents to observe the most salient issues and record those most interested and likely to vote, which creates lists of warm names to send campaign material to. Segmentation is also used, and in campaigning they seek to advertise their achievements and delivery in office.

In countries such as the UK, with party-based systems, local MPs and candidates are traditionally more restricted, as campaigns are national and party-based. Nevertheless, research by Lilleker and Negrine (2002 and 2003) and Lilleker (2005 and 2006) suggests that candidates are increasingly running local marketing campaigns, realising the negative consequences of too much central control (see also Franklin and Richardson 2002). In some constituencies, local voters are particularly important and influential on the vote. Case studies 7.5 and 7.6 illustrate the potential and constraints of local political marketing.

Market-oriented forms of marketing communications

Marketing can also be used to devise communication that relates to the concept of a market-orientation. Robinson (2006) has formulated a theory of how political advertising can be devised to suit market-oriented principles: see Table 7.4. This framework could be applied to all forms of political communication.

This is further explained and outlined in Case study 7.7.

Public relations

Public relations involves different aspects of political behaviour: as Moloney and Colmer (2001: 958) argue, it 'follows the policy design, adjustment and implementation phases of policy development'. They provide an example from the 2005 UK campaign:

> On May 9th the Prime Minister talked to a Mr and Mrs Finnan in the tea room, the Royal Pump Rooms, Leamington Spa about their life over the last four years. The conversation looked natural on TV news but it took the media in its role as scrutineer to reveal how unnatural it was. The Finnans were hand-picked Labour members; the 60 other tea-takers included Labour councillors and Labour PR staff. To avoid distraction, nobody got tea or cake while the cameras rolled.

Planned events are created to be normal, whereas stunts are obviously so and can also go wrong easily, such as when a patient relative harangued Tony Blair about cancer care when he visited a hospital. Paven (2001) list a number of PR lessons from the 2000 US presidential election: see Box 7.2.

Jackson and Lilleker (2004: 512) explore how public relations can be used by local MPs in a symmetrical (two-way) or asymmetrical (one-way) manner. MPs often fall into the trap of only putting out asymmetrical communication and therefore failing to listen to and

Table 7.4 Robinson's (2006) criteria for identification of market-orientation in political advertisements

Market Orientation	Observable form
Voter orientation	
(i) Target voters identified	Images of target audience and environment featured
(ii) Sense, and respond to, voter needs	Images of party and/or leader interaction with target voters, including images of listening and words of togetherness
(iii) Maintenance of relationships with core voters	Evocation of party history and myth; acknowledgement of shared characters, themes and stories Images or words of care for core supporters The co-presence of other texts recognisable to core supporters Kept policy promises Consistent leadership offer from one campaign to another
(iv) Offer in exchange for party vote	Party vote requested, and what policy and leadership offered in exchange
Competitor orientation	
(i) Whether the party behaved as would be expected of a party occupying their strategic market position (e.g. market leader, challenger, follower, niche party)	Competition identified and targeted in messages Policy appropriated from smaller niche parties Concern to increase market share demonstrated Openness to coalition arrangements demonstrated Niche parties remain true to original *raison d'être*

engage the public; however, they can choose to respond to feedback and alter what they do accordingly. PR can help politicians build positive, long-term relationship to help 'weather the usual crisis and storms that all elected officials face' (Jackson and Lilleker 2004: 514).

Public relations can be used in any country, albeit adapted to the nature of the local system and market. Prasaad and Raghupathy (2005) studied elections in India in 2004 and how a candidate engaged in a number of PR tactics: see Box 7.3.

The aspects of marketing communications that have been discussed here are those that have been studied by political marketing research. Over time, other aspects of marketing communications, such as integrated marketing communications (see Chapman *et al.* 2003, for example), will doubtless be applied to politics and add to both the study and practice of marketing communications in politics.

Democratic issues

There are many democratic issues with political marketing communications. It can be argued that utilising market intelligence to make communication as effective as possible helps politicians sell the best, but unwanted messages. It can be seen as manipulative, as research enables political elites to get inside the head of voters. Dermody and Hamner-Lloyd (2006: 128) observe, from their conclusion that UK parties failed to utilise market-oriented concepts in their political advertising, that 'the way in which promotional marketing tools and concepts are being used in election campaigns, with the emphasis on creating distrust and suspicion of the competing parties, does not bode well for the future of democracy in Britain.' The emphasis on professionalism, which seems to accompany the use of marketing in

Box 7.2 PR lessons from the 2000 US presidential election

Get a message and stick to it
Bush repeated 'I trust people more than government' a million times. Gore said a million things. Bush won.

Involve PR at the top
Karen Hughes and Mark MacKinnon, Bush's communication director and media advisor, respectively, are role models for communications advisors. They put themselves in the middle of it all and directed from there.

Don't be afraid to make difficult decisions
Al Gore went with his gut in selecting Joe Lieberman as his running mate. It was one of the best moves of the entire race.

Let your message speak and not your body
Dick Cheney is a smart politician, but you wouldn't know it watching a TV interview with him. Dick, sit up straight, take your hands down from your face, look at the camera and use some intonation.

In a crisis, have the most up-to-date information
Bush told reporters Cheney didn't have a heart attack; hours later, doctors disagreed. We believed the doctors.

Be available to the media in good times and bad
John McCain kept the *Straight Talk Express* running when he was ahead, behind, in favour and out. That's why he is still one of the most powerful and popular politicians in the media, despite losing the race.

Know the perception and change it
Boston television reporter Andy Hiller nailed Bush with a foreign policy pop quiz. Bush took the hint and, in the second debate, polished up his knowledge and impressed everyone with the way he talked about US foreign policy, particularly specific actions he would take to curb civil disturbances in Africa.

Zip it unless you want them to print it
Always assume your microphone is on. Bush should have thought rather than spoken his opinion about a certain *New York Times* reporter. A major league what, Mr Bush?

Be the best you that you can be
All professionals need media and speech training, but don't let anyone coach you into being another person. Gore delivered his best messages when he directed and wrote most of his convention speech and defined his recount message. Finally, we heard Gore stick to his message 'A fair and accurate recount because every vote counts.'

Source: Paven (2001)

Box 7.3 Public relations by a candidate in India: Raghuveera Reddy, from the Indian National Congress Party (INC), seeking election to a seat in the southern India state of Andhra Pradesh in the 2004 Indian legislative elections

1 The campaign started with a pre-launch by a walkathon through the constituency's 336 villages, positioning the INC as a farmer-friendly political party by listening to grievances and noting their problems. This gained positive media coverage and positioned the INC 'as a party whose primary concern [wa]s people welfare, not party welfare'.

2 Reddy started a fasting programme to oppose the previous government's policies, which had damaged farmers' living; this obtained significant media coverage.

3 Reddy ran a series of Panchayat Raj (local self-government meetings – the grass-roots level of Indian democracy) in the five districts in his constituency and undertook village-focused campaigns; this also gained media coverage.

4 The candidate ran a caste-based campaign in every village, meeting the key figures in every caste and religion and noting their demands, gaining media coverage.

5 A youth congress activists meeting was held to discuss all the demands, leading to an agenda for the elections; and events such as a road show, street walk campaigns, music, songs including folk songs, a bike rally and street plays were run. Music fitted the normal medium for the localities. The candidate and his family took part in the rally, which gained newspaper coverage.

6 A popular film director, actor and comedian, Dasaro Narayan Rao, and an actress, Nagma, entertained the crown at rallies.

7 Reddy's family organised a free health camp for the aged and sick and gave free medicine.

8 Reddy's family performed a three-day festival, Sri Rama Navami Celebrations; and even performed 500 free mass marriages on the first day.

9 Reddy traveled 30 km on a bullock cart to file his nomination, gaining thousands of following carts from the constituency and gaining substantial media coverage as a result.

10 Reddy addressed organisational groups such as all-women meetings, teacher associations and sports clubs.

11 Reddy visited major South Indian temples, and, during one visit, flowers offered to the statue fell, which was considered to be a good omen.

12 Reddy won by a large margin – more than 100,000 votes.

Source: Prasaad and Raghupathy (2005)

communication, can also reduce the importance of internal members, while increasing that of unelected advisors (see Sackman 1996).

However, more interactive forms of communication, enabled by developing technology, may lift the citizen from passive consumer to active participant in the communication process. Market-designed initiatives, built over time, can improve relationships between politicians and the people. Recent developments in Web 2.0 and social networking offer more positive potential than has perhaps been the case in the past, where communication was merely a means for elites to sell a product to the public. Moreover, some would argue that it is better to use marketing communications to persuade people to support the right thing to do.

Debate 7.1

Proposition: Political marketing communications help politicians sell good politics that is right for the country but might otherwise be rejected by the political market.

Huge amounts of money are spent on political marketing communication, and this raises an issue as candidates focus more on raising and spending money in their campaign than actually doing a good job. Case study 7.8 on Arnold Schwarzenegger illustrates issues with campaign spending, celebrity and direct democracy.

Summary

Political marketing communication and campaigning are important areas. Marketing tools available in this vary in their nature, and their effectiveness depends on many factors. What works in one campaign may not work in another. They can be anti- and pro-democracy in their effects, depending on an individual's view, and can use concepts not just techniques. Once a politician has gone through the final campaign and won power, though, what happens then? The next chapter will examine marketing in government.

ASSESSED WORK

Essays

1 To what extent are political marketing communications just about persuading voters to support a particular party or candidate?
2 Analyse the potential and limitations of political marketing communication, using examples to illustrate your answer.
3 Discuss the potential and actual effectiveness of market-oriented advertising, utilising theory and empirical examples.
4 Discuss both the potential and current practice of e-marketing, utilising a range of examples.
5 Evaluate different forms of political communication, whether political advertising, websites, e-newsletters, direct mail or any other method, and discuss the extent to which they follow market-oriented principles such as those set out by Robinson (2006).
6 Explore how marketing communications can be used at a local, as opposed to national or federal, level in the political system.
7 Explore the potential of online communication to mobilise grass-roots supporters, with reference to the idea of social networking, evaluating the value of different parties' and candidates' usage of virtual networking.
8 In what ways, and with what success, have political leaders' image been improved by marketing?
9 To what extent do new methods of communication, such as e-marketing and online social networking, offer more effective and consultative means of involving the political consumer in politics?
10 What issues do campaign managers face when communicating a candidate?

Applied

1   Apply Jackson's relationship marketing email criteria to the use of email by elected representatives and discuss how effectively they are using email, making recommendations for improvement and further development.
2   Design your own direct mail for a forthcoming election, campaign or existing candidate or referendum, applying the principles of direct mail.
3   Design a local political marketing plan for an elected official.
4   Devise a public relations plan for a local politician, using guidelines and ideas from the other cases presented in this textbook.

Case study 7.1 Image supremacy? Lifting the veil in Belgium

Philippe De Vries, Christ'l De Landtsheer and Soetkin Kesteloot

Belgian politics takes pride in emphasising the supremacy of strong political parties and deeply rooted ideologies. Political marketing is described as a fringe phenomenon, at most belonging to the margins of Belgian political life. However, this case study will examine political image research within the Belgian context.

Belgium's political history

Belgium has a particular political system. In 1993, Belgium was reformed into a federal state, consisting of three regions and three communities: the Flemish, Walloon and Brussels regions, and Flemish, Francophone and German-speaking communities. Both the Flemish and the Walloon parts of the country have their own political parties. Consequently, the Belgian system is embedded in a seriously scattered political landscape. Belgian voting behaviour seemed clearly definable until the last quarter of the twentieth century, with the so-called *pillarisation* structure enabling an individual to spend his or her life in one of these *pillars* or institutionalised, societal dividers anchored within political ideologies. However, this started to change in the second half of the twentieth century, as the market was subject to the changes typical of all western liberal democracies.

Image emphasis

The diminishing power of political parties and the presumed fading of ideological dividing lines preceded the introduction of political marketing. As image is presumed to take centre stage, political images are created through the use of visual impressions, particularly communicated by the candidates' physical presentation (Schwartzenberg 1977). Consequently, political marketers invest in the shaping of these vitally important political images. Market segmentation and targeting are applied to identify voter needs (Baines *et al.* 1999), and political candidates are then positioned within the marketplace, a process in which image plays a central and prominent role.

Vote intentions

A post-electoral questionnaire in 2007 (17 July and 16 August) executed by TNS Media/Dimarso, with 2,902 respondents (response rate of 71 per cent) unveiled perceptions of Belgian voter motives. Some most interesting conclusions can be drawn. A significant majority of interviewees (84 per cent) claimed that party programme and issue positioning had a considerable influence in the voting process. The performance of the party was considered important as well (72 per cent). On top of that, more than half of the interviewees (52 per cent) indicated tradition and habit as a third important factor. When turning towards marketing-oriented aspects, image and presentation of the candidate or party played a considerable role for 57 per cent of the respondents. Communication of the party in the campaign was considered important for a mere 47 per cent of the questioned individuals.

Based on these data, the researchers concluded that especially rational and socio-psychological voting motives dominate Belgian voter behaviour nowadays, while aspects of image and communication seem to be relevant for a significantly smaller group of respondents. The reported moments of decision were in support of this assertion as well. No less than 58 per cent of interviewees claim they decided which party to vote for more than a month before the actual elections. When taking a closer look at party loyalty between elections, it can be noted that 73 per cent of the Flemish electorate remained loyal to their party (between the elections of 2004 and 2007). When taking perceived media exposure and influences into consideration, almost 80 per cent of the interviewees insisted that mass media had no significant influence on their voting decision. 10 per cent of the respondents stated that television played a decisive role in their political decision-making process. All other types of mass media information distribution had an even less significant impact. Moreover, respondents claimed that the Internet, polling results and posters had no decisive influence whatsoever. Clearly, the political market has changed in Belgium.

Image research in Belgian politics

These rather unexpected reflections on Belgian voters' own voter motives are in stark contrast to the results emanating from quantitative empirical research in political communication science, especially regarding the impact of visual political images in contrast with political content and ideology. Based on an established, overall politically suitable gestalt – retrieved for both male and female political candidates (De Landtsheer 2004) – the influence of the candidate image or appearance on voter attitudes could be tested within the Belgian political context. In order to do so, mock election campaigns were set out. Genuine Belgian politicians participated in these experiments. It was assumed that the power of the candidate's appearance would be significantly influenced by additional, politically relevant information. In short, the more information available, the less prominent the role played by candidate image.

These assumptions were not met. Although the provision of a party logo and slogan resulted in several significant and most interesting interactions, the multiple regression analyses confirmed that the image effect remained stable across the studies introducing different sets of incentive material. The image variable turned out to be a valid and significant predictor of voter preferences, apart from supplementary political information. Politicians presented with a politically preferable image or appearance were more likely to be chosen by the respondents (up to 38 per cent more chance to be chosen among the most politically suitable politicians), irrespective of the political message (De Landtsheer *et al.* 2005, De Vries 2007).

Concluding remarks

The findings retrieved from the post-electoral study might well be indicating how Belgian society and politics are still significantly segregated or *pillarised*: in other words, dominated by strong ideological beliefs and institutions. Nevertheless, a few pressing remarks are in order. Measuring voter motives is no sinecure. Socially desirable answers will automatically – even subconsciously – arise. Voting decisions should indeed be based on serious and rational considerations and argumentations, more so than on aspects of political image. It can be argued that individual voters genuinely believe they base their vote choice on rational arguments, even if they may be significantly steered – subliminally or not – by image aspects diffused through mass media. Therefore, the empirical image research briefly touched upon is significantly more reliable and measures the influences emanating from political images in a more consistent and reliable fashion.

The role played by candidate image, although eagerly minimised by voters themselves, must undoubtedly be considered a vital factor in voter decision-making processes. Belgian political marketing research is still in its infancy, which may under no pretext be interpreted as an indication for the minimal presence or application of marketing strategies.

Sources and further reading

Baines, P., F. Plasser and C. Scheucher (1999). 'Operationalising political marketing: a comparison of US and Western European consultants and managers'. *Discussion Paper Series*, London: Middlesex University Business School, 7.

De Landtsheer, C. (2004). *Politiek impressiemanagement in Vlaanderen en Nederland* [Political Impression Management in Flanders and the Netherlands]. Leuven: Acco.

——, P. De Vries and D. Vertessen (2005). 'Political impression management and perception politics in Belgium: the way of sound bites, personality profiles, and appearance effectiveness of politicians'. Paper presented at the International Political Marketing Conference, Kastoria, Greece.

De Ridder, H. (1999). *Vijftig jaar stemmenmakerij* [Five years of vote-producing]. Gent: Uitgeverij Scoop.

De Vries, P. (2007). 'Candidate image in Belgian politics'. Doctoral dissertation. Defended 7 December 2007.

Schwartzenberg, R. (1977). *Politieke superstars. Vedettencultus in de politiek* [Political Superstars. Celebrities in Politics]. Brussels: Standaard uitgeverij.

Case study 7.2 Czech Republic: Social Democrats strike back
Alexander Braun and Anna Matuskova

Which country is lucky? The Czech Republic: because they don't have to put up with a government.

This was a joke circulated in neighbouring Poland after the Czech parliamentary elections of 2006. The elections ended in a stalemate between the right-wing block led by Conservatives (ODS) and the left-wing block led by Social Democrats (CSSD) that ended in a hundred days of difficult government coalition building, during which a new government couldn't be formed. The party with most votes in the 2006 parliamentary elections was the conservative Civic Democratic Party (ODS) with 35.38 percent of the votes. ODS was followed by the Czech Social Democratic Party (CSSD) with a score of 32.32 per cent; the Communist Party of Bohemia and Moravia (KSCM) with 12.81 per cent; and the Christian and Democratic Union – Czechoslovak People's Party (KDU-CSL) with 7.22 per cent. The Green Party (SZ), which gained 6.29 per cent, surpassed the 5 per cent threshold and entered Parliament for the first time. The total electoral turnout was unusually high at 64.7 per cent.

How is it possible that the results between ODS and CSSD were so close when, just a year ago, CSSD trailed ODS in public opinion polls by more than 20 percentage points? Part of the answer lies in a new style of campaigning that the country hadn't experienced prior to the 2006 elections.

The Czech media described the campaign as 'negative, brutal, aggressive, confrontational, offensive and full of low blows' (Matušková 2006b: 5). However, the reality was that political parties carefully and systematically used methods of political marketing for the first time, analysed the electorate and went aggressively after all available voter groups.

The CSSD pioneered these new techniques in Czech, hiring the American political consulting firm Penn, Schoen and Berland Associates (PSB). PSB has worked on more than thirty elections worldwide, including US President Bill Clinton's campaign or the UK's PM Tony Blair's 2005 campaign. One of the authors of this case study was the on-the-ground PSB consultant and served as CSSD's pollster and chief strategist in the campaign. Traditionally, Czech campaigns were organised somewhat haphazardly and were conducted based on intuition and more or (often) less educated guesses. PSB suggested alternative approaches and first undertook a series of focus groups with swing voters throughout the country in the summer of 2005. Later, in the second half of September, the firm conducted an extensive quantitative benchmark poll, aimed at gauging the position and level of support of all the parties among different voter blocks, issue importance among voters and message and policy testing. Based on the results, PSB experts devised a campaign plan that first outlined overall goals, the situation in which the campaign was taking place and what the message was, and then the strategy to reach the goals and the tactics of what tools to use and how to use them to get there.

One of the things that was obvious to CSSD at the outset was that CSSD needed to capture and dictate the main theme of the campaign to succeed. Besides having only a third of the support that ODS had, the party was mired in corruption scandals, internal fighting and overall fatigue from leading the government for seven years. If the campaign became a referendum on CSSD, the party was doomed.

CSSD had a several advantages on its side, and a conscious effort was made to make the best use of them. The country was doing very well economically after seven years of CSSD government, and CSSD programme offerings for the new term consistently tested as being better than those of ODS. That's why CSSD started early on to aggressively pursue the strategy of contrasts between itself and its main rival ODS on social and economic issues. This accentuated its strengths and forced ODS to enter the campaign being defensive on its own main platform centrepiece of flat tax. Additionally, by constantly drawing a contrast between the two main parties of CSSD and ODS, other smaller parties were marginalised, which was crucial, given CSSD's traditionally fickle electorate, which was prone to deserting to these alternatives.

Additionally, CSSD knew from its polling that its leader, Jiri Paroubek, was more popular and was perceived as significantly more competent than his ODS counterpart, Mirek Topolanek. At the same time, it also knew that ODS as a party was perceived more favourably than CSSD as a party. CSSD's campaign therefore focused on framing the campaign as a referendum on who would be the best prime minister. Through heavy use of comparative campaigning and frequent calls on Topolanek to agree to more televised debates (including somewhat theatrical, but widely covered, stunts, such as sending a historical chariot to ODS' headquarters, where actors in medieval military costumes challenged Topolanek to a debate duel with Paroubek, or a laser light display above Prague one night asking Topolanek not to avoid TV debates – 'Don't hide Mr Topolanek!'), CSSD managed to double and eventually triple its support among voters. Also, one of the signs of success in both reducing the campaign to a question of the most qualified person to be the prime minister and marginalising smaller parties was that Czech TV channels eventually decided to hold televised debates before the elections, but only invited Topolanek and Paroubek to take part.

Furthermore, PSB kept on constantly polling throughout the campaign, to measure the mood swings in the public, test policies and strategy and refine the message. The use of public opinion research was unprecedented, and most experts agreed that it was one of the main reasons for CSSD's relative success. Other parties either didn't poll at all or had done one poll more than a year before the elections and therefore were not well informed about the changing perceptions among the Czech public.

Additionally, most of the other parties were taken aback by CSSD's forceful style of campaigning, which often focused on pointing out ODS weaknesses. ODS at first decided not to react and eventually was forced to answer the allegations, but was too slow to stop the momentum. It was only at the end of the campaign that ODS started to fire back and regained its footing (ODS eventually won the election, with 35 per cent compared with CSSD's 32 per cent – exactly the same support ODS had before the campaign, whereas CSSD started with 11 per cent support). The smaller parties on the Czech political scene failed to get much attention in the fight of the two dominant parties, with the exception of the Green Party. The party managed to cross the 5 per cent threshold in a February 2006 public opinion poll that attracted media attention, and the resulting momentum in the last three months really carried them into Parliament (with 6 per cent of the electorate voting for them).

Conclusion

The 2006 Czech parliamentary elections are a good example of the power of modern political marketing and its strengths when confronted with the older styles of campaigning. However, while modern political marketing allowed CSSD to triple its support in the electorate, it eventually still wasn't enough for the party to win, illustrating the limits of political marketing. It is only a tool of politics and not necessarily a saving grace for political parties and candidates. Ultimately, it is the voters who decide the elections and, while they can be influenced, they eventually make up their mind on their own. At the end, the voter is still the king.

Sources and further reading

CSSD (2006). *Jistoty a prosperita. Electoral Programme CSSD 2006.* Available online at www. socdem.cz/soubory/422010/vp%5F29%2E3%2E2006.pdf (accessed 10 June 2006).

Matušková, A. (2006a). 'Politický marketing a České politické strany'. In B. Dančák and V. Hloušek, *Parlamentní volby 2006 a česká politika*, Brno: Masarykova univerzita IIPS.

—— (2006b). 'Volební kampaň 2006: nástup politického marketingu do České republiky'. In T. Foltýn, D. Čaloud, V. Havlík and A. Matušková, *Volby do Poslanecké sněmovny v roce 2006*, Brno: CDK.

Centre for Public Opinion Research (CVVM): www.cvvm.cas.cz

Penn, Schoen and Berland Associates, Inc.: www.psbresearch.com/

Social Democrats: www.volbycr.cz/home.html

Czech Statistical Office – electoral server: www.volby.cz

Case study 7.3 UK MPs and the marketing of their websites

Nigel A. Jackson

The Internet has grown in importance in UK political campaigning; originally a novelty, the Internet is now a mainstream tool used by political parties (Jackson 2006, 2007). Individual politicians have followed suit, and most MPs now provide a website. The overall consensus is that MPs have not made best use of their websites, with most being static electronic brochures (Jackson 2006). However, approaches to e-marketing developed by businesses will inevitably influence how politicians use the Internet. Having a website has little value if it does not attract visitors. Academic study has identified a number of proven techniques for driving traffic to a website:

1   Ensure that all communications from an organisation promote the website address.
2   Combine offline and online promotional channels.
3   Regularly promote the site to the major search engines.
4   Encourage other websites to link to you.

Websites should also be evaluated: visitor evaluation should be a vital and regular part of website management, with software generating very useful data through the analysis of server files. For example, information can be gleaned on where visitors come from, and on which web pages they spend most time. To assess how MPs marketed and evaluated their website, a questionnaire was posted to the 327 MPs who had a website in 2003, and 134 responded, representing a 40.1 per cent response rate.

How MPs market their websites

Table 7.5 indicates that MPs are aware of some of the primary techniques for driving traffic to their websites, but the overall numbers using them are at best mediocre. Of the four main techniques outlined by the literature, MPs are most likely to rely on using all their communication to promote the website address. Therefore, 69 per cent of all stationery and 66 per cent of all promotional material include the website address, though this does suggest that a third of respondents do not promote their website address in other communication. MPs also use a number of offline communication channels, including their promotional material and press releases. However, of the online options such as the use of signature files and sending out emails, the response is much lower (at 18 and 9 per cent). Use of reciprocal links with other websites is the third most popular technique, but that only 45 per cent engage in this suggests that many MPs do not allocate resources for this promotional technique. Less than a third (30 per cent) of MPs had registered with search engines, and so most will not appear high on the major search engines. The data suggest that MPs rely on offline communication aimed at existing audiences, rather than new, online audiences.

Table 7.5 How MPs drive traffic to their website

1	All stationery includes my website address	69%
2	All promotional material includes my website address	66%
3	Reciprocal links with other websites	45%
4	Press release launch of the website	43%
5	Registered once on a search engine	30%
6	Use of signature files on all my emails	18%
7	Frequently re-register on a search engine	17%
8	Press releases of website updates	10%
9	Send out regular emails promoting the website	9%
10	Other	5%
11	Encourage visitors to recommend your site	4%

How MPs evaluate their websites

An unevaluated website is unlikely to be effective. Understanding what visitors think of a website can be achieved through a combination of quantitative and qualitative feedback. Table 7.6 suggests that those MPs who do evaluate concentrate on the former, with only 9 per cent asking their users for feedback. Moreover, only 13 per cent of respondents analyse server logs, the technique that is universally believed by experts to be the most effective. The most popular evaluation technique MPs use (40 per cent) is the number of emails they receive. This appears peculiar to MPs, presumably reflecting the nature of their representative work. Some MPs use number of hits and counters, yet these are generally seen by e-marketers as, at best, a useful backup and, at worst, misleading. Worryingly, over a third of respondents do not evaluate their website at all. On the whole, most MPs do not appear to have given much attention to evaluation and so to improving their website. Until this happens, a website is unlikely to be an effective promotional tool.

Table 7.6 How MPs evaluate their website

1	Number of emails you receive	40%
2	Number of hits	6%
3	I don't evaluate my website	36%
4	Visitor counters	19%
5	Analyse server logs	13%
6	Ask users for their feedback	9%
7	Monitoring your website availability	9%
8	Monitoring links to your website	8%
9	Number of click-throughs	7%
10	Check search engine ranking	7%
11	Number of press calls referring to website	7%
12	Other	6%
13	Communication audit	3%

Conclusion

To use their website effectively, MPs face the interrelated problems of attracting visitors and maximising the amount of time they spend on the site. Existing e-marketing expertise provides potential guidance on driving traffic to the site and how to utilise feedback.

This case study showed that MPs are reasonable at promoting their website, although they are too reliant on one or two methods. As a result, they should consider using a wider range of marketing techniques: some, such as communication audits and use of signature files on emails, are easy to achieve. Establishing reciprocal links with other websites and assessing search engine ratings, although they may involve considerable work, can make a significant difference. Therefore, MPs appear at least aware of commercial e-marketing advice, even if they only partially follow it.

MPs are much better at marketing their websites than they are at evaluating their value. MPs do not, on the whole, appear to focus much effort on how to improve their online presence. MPs are poor at evaluation, especially as a third do not evaluate their website all, which raises the question of why they actually have a website. Those MPs that do evaluate tend to ignore the most effective tool, analysing server logs. MPs appear to be ignoring the advice of e-marketers to view their website from the perspective of the visitor. However, the fact that the most popular form of evaluation is the number of emails they receive suggests that traditional e-marketing evaluation measures do not apply to politics, and, hence, separate political evaluation tools may be more appropriate.

Lessons for political marketing

Effective e-marketing requires a holistic approach, covering all aspects of website provision; MPs should not just dip in and out of those bits of e-marketing they like or understand.

Sources and further reading

Chaffey, D., F. Ellis-Chadwick, K. Johnston, R. Mayer (2006). *Internet Marketing: Strategy, Implementation and Practice.* Harlow: Prentice Hall.

Collin, S. (2000). *E-marketing: Work the Web.* Chichester: Wiley.

Jackson, N. (2006). 'Banking online: the use of the Internet by political parties to build relationships with voters'. In D. Lilleker, N. Jackson and R. Scullion, *The Marketing of British Politics: Political Marketing at the 2005 General Election.* Manchester: Manchester University Press.

—— (2007). 'Political parties, the Internet and the 2005 General Election: third time lucky?'. *Internet Research,* 17(3): 249–71.

Ward, S. and W. Lusoli (2005). 'From weird to wired: MPs, the Internet and representative politics in the UK'. *Journal of Legislative Studies,* 11(1): 57–81.

Case study 7.4 ACT New Zealand Party and the limits of technological marketing   *Gavin Middleton*

ACT New Zealand is a small, classical liberal party that is the only political party from outside parliament to win election since the country's shift to a 'mixed member proportional' representation system in 1996. Under this voting system, around half the MPs are directly elected from geographical constituencies, with the remainder of seats allocated to candidates from party lists, so that a party's total representation in parliament roughly reflects their support among a nationwide 'party vote'. ACT has successfully passed both thresholds required by a party to win representation in Parliament, holding the electoral seat of Wellington Central from 1996 to 1999 and the seat of Epsom from 2005 and receiving between 1.5 per cent and 7.1 per cent of the nationwide party vote.

ACT's key 'audience' consists largely of young, educated males of above-average socio-economic status. The significant overlap between this group and those who are early adopters of new technology has allowed ACT to seize on the Internet as a channel for delivering the party's message. Soon after its creation, ACT recruited a number of volunteers and staff who had the background and skills to implement emerging technologies to promote the party's messages.

Soon after being elected in 1996, ACT began issuing *The Goss*, a weekly newsletter available by email and fax that commented on current events in parliament. Later renamed *The Letter From Wellington* and available only by email, *The Letter* became the party's flagship publication and was used to influence the week's media agenda, being issued on a Monday afternoon before parliament began its business for the week. Key to *The Letter*'s success was its record in breaking a significant number of stories, making it widely read by journalists, business people and the wider public.

The Letter and the party's website were used between elections to run a 'permanent campaign' on a relatively low budget. Online petitions, website forms and subscribable, subject-based newslists allowed constituents to register their interest in particular issues, receive updates and let the party send out its perspective on current events, without needing to rely on coverage from journalists.

Recognising the opportunity to minimise communication costs through accurate targeting, ACT made a significant investment in a customer relationship management database and heavily customised it to approximately model the 'voter vault' system introduced by the USA's Republican Party. ACT's database eventually held electoral roll information on every registered voter – including residential and postal addresses, an occupation group and socio-economic code, age range (accurate to within four years), presumptive gender and residential meshblock (the smallest geographical area used by Statistics New Zealand).

Information for this database was acquired through publicly available sources and supplemented by the party's own campaigns. These campaigns usually began with a fax broadcast targeted at a list of businesses, or a direct mail letter sent to selected people from the database about whom the party wished to know more. Respondents continued receiving updates by email as the campaign progressed, with the database being used to track their interests (as well as any contact details they provided).

Over a number of years, these campaigns led to a significant amount of extra information being gathered, ranging from the general – policy areas of interest and a record of which surveys an individual had completed – to specific records about newsletter subscriptions, answers to survey questions, party membership details and any declared voting intentions.

All this information was compiled into a number of profiles, which could be extrapolated to cover every voter in the country at an individual level. Aggregating these data into averages at a meshblock level allowed each candidate to be given a map of which parts of their electorate were most likely to support the party.

As ACT maintained its level of parliamentary representation, the database was used to target voters in increasingly complex ways. Initially, people were targeted on the basis of policy issues they had expressly shown interest in – for example, by responding favourably to a survey on tax cuts – but, by 2005, the party had amassed enough information about lifestyle groups to identify those likely to support the National Party – a potential coalition partner for ACT – and target them with messages positioning ACT as offering National a stable and reliable support in government, even if the people targeted hadn't suggested to ACT that they were potential National Party supporters.

ACT had extremely high confidence that enough communication, targeted well enough, could help rescue it from a polling slump that occurred in early 2004, when a new National Party leader began making strong and successful appeals to ACT's traditional support base. In 2003 and 2004, more than a million postal communications – one for every four people in the country – were dispatched each year, with an estimated five million follow-up email communications a year.

While ACT was able to use technology to engage in such a large-scale, 'perpetual campaign' at low cost, the media were largely considered irrelevant. Compared with other, more established parties, ACT received a relatively small amount of media coverage, and the party saw benefits in having their messages communicated directly to voters, considering journalists as editorialising, confusing and misinterpreting their messages.

This heavy reliance on technologically targeted, direct communication met new challenges in the 2005 election campaign. Faced with the National Party's new leader and polling that had dropped to around 1 per cent, ACT's communication strategy of bypassing mainstream media and relying on technologically developed profiles of voters seemed unable to pull the party out of its political nosedive.

Although the party was able to identify the issues of concern to voters and could communicate policy positions that appealed to its target groups, the larger question of whether supporting the party would result in electing people to Parliament was unable to be answered satisfactorily.

Despite continuing the perpetual campaign strategy and launching 'Kiwis for ACT' – an attempt to highlight supporters across different lifestyle groups – the party was unable to shake the public perception that support for ACT had bled away, and that the party would fail to be re-elected in the 2005 election.

ACT were ultimately able to win an electorate seat and return two Members of Parliament, but this was ultimately owing to a return to traditional campaigning, which included knocking on doors, public appearances by the candidate and a campaign message that centred around electing the ACT candidate to guarantee a coalition partner for the then-incumbent MP's Conservative Party.

As campaigns in the USA – notably the presidential primary campaigns of Howard Dean and Ron Paul – have suggested, technology empowers large-scale and low-cost direct communication campaigns, but was not sufficient to sustainably direct voter behaviour.

Although ACT believed that actual levels of public support were higher than polling numbers suggested, media – and the public – ultimately considered polling a better measure of a party's strength than the number of newsletter subscribers, website views and database contacts maintained.

ACT's experience suggests that, although technology has a useful role to play in maintaining a group of warm supporters and generating profile without relying on mainstream media, credibility among political commentators remains more critical for a campaign than coverage in 'new media'.

Lessons for political marketing

While technology makes it possible to run large campaigns effectively to niche audiences at low cost, it is not a sufficient condition for electoral success.

Case study 7.5 Local political marketing: connecting UK politicians and voters   *Darren G. Lilleker*

A central tenet of good marketing communication is to make the message relevant to people's lives, connect to their fears and aspirations and offer something that they desire. However, the top-down and centralised model of party organisation that prevails in British politics can prevent effective communications, especially on the local level, where candidates increasingly see standardised messages as inappropriate and counter-intuitive (Lilleker and Negrine 2003). This case explores these issues by examining the campaign of Labour MP for Dorset South Jim Knight at the 2005 General Election, who faced a severe challenge after winning a narrow electoral margin in 2001 election, there being a swing in the polls away from the Labour government nationally.

Knight succeeded by selling himself as the product that his constituents wanted and promoted himself on his record of service locally. First, this involved permanent communication since his election in 2001. His presence in the local newspaper, the *Dorset Echo,* was unparalleled, and he gained further media coverage through supporting local campaigns, such as 'Keep the Purbeck safe', a campaign to reduce deaths on the roads in an area of the constituency popular with tourists and local youths. Supporting a family who had lost a child in a car accident, he managed to get the local police on board and was able, by 2005, to declare success in the reduction in the number of accidents. Knight also advertised the fact that, over the four years as MP, he had dealt personally with 5,953 individual pieces of casework – issues brought to him by constituents. This allowed him to argue that he was the best representative for the area.

Building upon this record, his campaign led with the promotion of Knight as *Just Jim*. While he defended the government's record, and explained why he supported the highly unpopular decision to commit troops to the invasion of Iraq in 2003, there was a degree of separation between him and the Labour party. His decision was to personalise the campaign, highlighting the marginality of the constituency, but also downplaying the effectiveness of a single vote on the national contest. The campaign was therefore able to focus on local delivery and the comparison between Knight as a proven product and his Conservative opponent, who was exposed as having doctored pictures on his election communication and leaked inaccurate rumours to the media.

At the heart of the campaign was a marketing philosophy developed, not from politics, but from Knight's previous career as a salesman for advertising space in *Yellow Pages*, the leading British directory of business telephone numbers. Knight argued that one of the key lessons he had learned in that career, and that he brought to politics, was that, if you sold a customer a product by promising delivery of key measurables, for any repurchase the customer must see that those promises had been delivered. Delivery of satisfaction, he argued, meant that customers awarded him permission to contact them. Knight argued that his record as a representative gave him the permission to contact voters within the Dorset South constituency; thus central to his representative style and his campaign was making contact with as many voters as possible.

Research showed that over 25 per cent of respondents to a survey had met their MP, some during doorstep visits, some on the streets, others by them making contact with Knight. Thus, the high-visibility campaign seemed to have worked.

High visibility on its own, however, did not secure election victory for Jim Knight. A range of factors relating to his performance as MP and the perceptions voters gained of him were the crucial factors. The research conducted showed that Knight was overwhelmingly seen as the 'best representative for me and my community' and the 'candidate who best addressed my concerns', and the score out of ten he was awarded for fulfilling his representative role by all respondents was 6.9 (standard deviation (SD): 3.01), but 8.8 (SD: 1.2) among those who voted for him. It seemed that this high score did indeed equate to permission to contact voters, with recall being 94.3 for receiving at least two pieces of communication from Knight, and there being a strong correlation between positive perceptions of Knight as MP and recalling being contacted by him. Importantly, however, all these factors amalgamated suggest that local factors prevailed over voter decision-making within the constituency (Lilleker 2005).

Why might this be the case? If we return to the key tenets of effective communication, we can see that it is at the local level that politics is experienced. While opinion polls may tell us that voters in general see the efficient running of the health service as important, all British parties also promise to do just that. It is the experience locally that voters are likely to measure against party promises. Knight was able to point to specific successes that related to his work as MP in tandem with Labour being in government. Thus, he translated politics into the life experiences of voters. Furthermore, he could offer a joint package: himself as an effective local representative, but with a hot line to central government; so he could argue that delivery on key public services was related to him being MP and a member of the governing party.

Knight also demonstrated his understanding of the people of Dorset South. He undertook extensive media monitoring to discover the issues of the area and held regular surgeries with constituents across the region. This gave him valuable insights into the concerns of the people. Key concerns that he could become involved with and deliver a solution to were converted into high-profile campaigns; progress was discussed within his newsletter, *The Rose,* and via the local newspaper and radio interviews. All achievements could then be fed back to reinforce the perception of Knight as a representative who was solving the problems of those whom he represented.

Finally, and most importantly, research indicated that Knight and MPs like him offer constituents the thing that, politically, they want most of all. That is representation within the democratic process. Those who attended focus groups held after the 2005 General Election often talked of politicians generally as self-serving, remote and untrustworthy. However, Knight offered a contrasting model of MP to the voters of Dorset South. He offered voters a positive reason to go to the ballot box and show their support for him. Therefore, it is perhaps true to argue that Knight showed a sound understanding of what political marketing should be, by actually giving voters what they wanted and delivering on his personal promises, as this is something many voters feel is absent from modern democracy. While it is true to say he was aided by a weak opponent, he won his seat against problematic national issues with his party, indicating the importance and influence of local political marketing.

Sources and further reading

Lilleker, D.G. (2005). 'Local campaign management: winning votes or wasting resources'. *Journal of Marketing Management*, 21(9/10): 979–1004.

—— (2006). 'Local political marketing: political marketing as public service'. In D.G. Lilleker, N.A. Jackson and R. Scullion, *The Marketing of Political Parties*, Manchester: Manchester University Press, pp. 206–30.

—— and R. Negrine (2003). 'Not big brand names but corner shops: marketing politics to a disengaged electorate'. *Journal of Political Marketing*, 2(1): 55–76.

MP Jim Knight's website: www.jimknightmp.com/

Case study 7.6 Canadian constituency campaigns　*Alex Marland*

In the commercial marketplace, major corporations staff a headquarters to guide the operations of local franchises. For example, the central employees of the USA division of McDonald's Corporation monitor American consumers' preferences and manage the brand nationally. Product distribution is left to individual restaurants across the country, whose operators have a limited ability to respond to local market conditions. Likewise, we can think about electoral politics as using a franchising organisational model, which involves an agency theory whereby work is delegated. The nucleus of a professional political party (the franchising company) is often based out of a capital city. This is where opinion research data, policy proposals and potential promotional activities converge in strategy sessions that increasingly include outside political consultants and preclude even top party candidates. Decisions are made on everything from responding to the latest opinion polls to determining what advertising wording should be tested in focus groups.

In Canada's parliamentary system, supporting such a marketing orientation necessitates ensuring that the party's candidates are 'on message' nationwide. Conveniently, this keeps power at the centre and helps to sustain party discipline. Federal election candidates in Canada are encouraged by the central headquarters to promote all things party – the leader, the label, the manifesto, the key messages, the overall brand – regardless of local electors' viewpoints. It can therefore be very difficult for the candidate flea to wag the party dog. For instance, in a 2002 by-election, a Liberal constituency campaign manager (correctly) expressed frustration with the party centre's research data, saying that '. . . the party's advice throughout the campaign was promote the leader, promote the leader. This is what our polls say, the leader's popular. It was in stark contradiction to what we were getting at the door.' At the risk of sanctions, a party candidate in such a situation may respond to local market conditions by downplaying but not disassociating from the party label in promotional activities, but they still have to support the national party overall.

This is similar to the constraints faced by a McDonald's franchisee. A key difference, however, is government regulation. Qualifying political parties now receive quarterly allowances from the state and they can issue tax receipts for donations. While there are regulations on campaign spending there are also pubic subsidies for marketing intelligence. Since 2003, Canada's federal candidates must file opinion survey research expense declarations, with a carrot being that some of them will qualify to have these costs refunded by up to 60 per cent.

Surely such public subsidies encourage candidates to purchase and respond to local opinion research? Or do they recognise that this could be a fruitless exercise in a strong party system? To examine this question, we can draw inferences from the extent to which constituency campaigns allocated their limited monies to collecting opinion data in the 2006 General Election.

Audited expenditure declarations suggest that most candidate campaigns indeed do not invest in gathering marketing intelligence during a general election period. The 2006 campaign saw Paul Martin's Liberal Party government replaced by Stephen Harper's Conservatives. Yet a majority of these parties' candidates did not declare monies in the 'election surveys or other surveys or research' category on their election expense return. Moreover, only a handful of candidates affiliated with the separatist Bloc Québécois and socialist New Democratic opposition parties did so, and none of the fringe Green party's candidates did. Apparently, these people don't read political marketing literature. But do they need to?

Research spending seems to have typically been on identifying supporters, rather than on scientific opinion survey data. Private firms such as First Contact, Voter ID Solutions and

Votertrack were hired, but, as these names suggest, the emphasis was on centralised party telemarketing to identify electors' voting intentions. As well, small amounts were often given to individuals, such as the Bloc Québécois team in Compton–Stanstead making eighty-nine payments (some as low as $30) totalling $7,428 to individuals, presumably for their canvassing to identify supporters. In many cases, money was transferred to the central office for research, such as with the $4,500 declared by the New Democratic Party in Esquimalt–Juan de Fuca, or in $20,000 payments from Conservatives to the 'Conservative Fund of Canada'. This too was likely used in part to fund centralised telemarketing.

Local survey research expenditures, 2006 Canadian federal election

Party	Total candidates (n)	Declared survey research (n)	Survey research spending (total)	Survey research spending (mean)
Bloc Québécois	75	8	$26,153	$3,269
Conservative	308	119	$1,220,722	$10,258
Green	308	0	$0	–
Liberal	308	94	$886,828	$9,434
New Democratic	308	10	$5,279	$528

Source: calculated from candidates' election returns submitted to Elections Canada

This indicates that candidates rely on other sources for data. They likely look to news media outlets' polling data, but also receive advice from central party officers who provide regional advice. Other expenditures, such as communications consulting, may include research not identified here. Moreover, anyone with a pure marketing orientation would have executed it well beforehand, thus rendering such spending unnecessary during the official campaign period. But this is largely marketing optimism. In 2002, a national Canadian pollster said the following about Canada's parties, let alone about their candidates: 'academia is very far from political marketing in terms of it being used by political parties themselves ... You'll rarely hear – even political consultants or polling firms – people referring to things that relate to either political or marketing theory.' The reality is that local party activists prefer to identify supporters in preparation for election day's GOTV activities. In fact, the party headquarters seem to encourage such behaviour.

Comparatively speaking, these franchisees are more concerned with getting hamburgers ready for a Saturday morning rush than they are with changing recipes. And so they should be. What good is a national marketing orientation without a strong distribution network? Or acting on a local marketing orientation if doing so would weaken the national brand?

Lessons for political marketers
Be mindful that what is seen to be critical at the party centre or in academia does not necessarily reflect the front lines. In practice, a marketing orientation may be the key to forming the government, but only if the local units of the party are principally involved in sales.

Sources and further reading
Bloc Québécois: www.blocquebecois.org

Canadian Election Study: www.ces-eec.umontreal.ca

Carty, R. Kenneth (2002). 'The politics of Tecumseh Corners: Canadian political parties as franchise organizations'. *Canadian Journal of Political Science,* 35: 723–45.

Conservative Party of Canada: www.conservative.ca

Elections Canada (2007). 'Election handbook for candidates, their official agents and auditors'. Available online at www.elections.ca/pol/can/EC20190_c2_e.pdf

Election Prediction Project: www.electionprediction.org

Liberal Party of Canada: www.liberal.ca

Marland, Alex (2005). 'Canadian political parties: market-oriented, or ideological slagbrains?'. In Jennifer Lees-Marshment and Darren Lilleker (eds) *Political Marketing: A Comparative Perspective*. Manchester: Manchester University Press, pp. 59–78.

New Democratic Party of Canada: www.ndp.ca

Pammett, Jon and Christopher Dornan (eds) (2006). *Canadian Federal Election of 2006*. Toronto: Dundurn Group.

Shane, Scott (1998). 'Making new franchise systems work'. *Strategic Management Journal*, 19(7): 697–707.

Case study 7.7 Market-oriented political advertising in the 2005 New Zealand election   *Claire Robinson*

Background

This case study applies an original political marketing framework for the examination of advertising content to the messages contained in the televised party opening addresses by the minor parties contesting the 2005 New Zealand General Election (a mixed member proportional (MMP) electoral system). In addition to the two major parties contesting the General Election (the incumbent Labour Party and the challenger National Party), there were six minor parties seriously competing for the party vote. In the first three MMP elections (1996, 1999 and 2002), the incumbent minor parties' combined party vote averaged 35.5 per cent. In 2005, however, this fell to 20 per cent. Can a study of market-orientation help explain this dramatic decline in support for the minor parties, and what lessons might minor parties learn from it?

Political advertising

Political advertisements are useful texts to examine for evidence of market-orientation. Because advertising affords parties control over timing, location, content and target audience, political advertisements tend to contain the messages parties absolutely want to convey directly to voters, before the messages get mediated by journalists and others (Kline 1997, Damore 2004). In addition, the structural features of advertisements enable parties to combine visual, verbal and aural signs that convey messages about so much more than policy alone. So, political advertisements may also carry messages about the people and places that are important to the party, the affinity parties feel they have with voters, the extent to which voters' needs have informed party priorities, myths and histories shared between party and voters, leadership offerings, and the threat parties sense from their competition. In other words, their market-orientation. By viewing advertisements as evidence of market-orientation, it is possible to analyse advertising content and uncover the political marketing factors that differentiate the 'winners' and 'losers' in a proportional election campaign (Robinson 2006).

The Robinson framework for analysis of advertising content used in this study is derived from the most commonly accepted definitions of customer and competitor orientation from the marketing literature, recontextualised into a political context. Although these are not the only factors that constitute market-orientation – many are internal to an organisation or political party – with an interest in the overt manifestation of market-orientation, the framework was developed around the orientations that actively intersect with the political marketplace. The criteria for analysis were developed from the literature on persuasion, rhetoric, visual language, political and commercial advertising. Underlying the framework is the assumption that voter and competitor orientation can be observable in an advertisement in a visual or verbal form.

To help explain the dramatic decrease in voter support for the minor parties in the 2005 General Election, the framework was applied to the content of the televised party opening addresses of the six minor parties. These addresses were funded by the New Zealand Electoral Commission and broadcast free by state broadcasters Television New Zealand and Radio New Zealand. They went to air four weeks out from election day and marked the commencement of the televised campaign period. There is obviously a risk in forming conclusions about election outcomes from the analysis of one set of campaign advertisements only. However, the risk is mitigated by the factors that turn these advertisements into substantial texts and evidence of party intent – the seriousness with which the parties regard them, and their length. In 2005, the larger parties had 12 minutes available to them for their addresses. Of the six minor parties, two had 4-minute slots, and four had 7-minute slots.

Lessons for political marketing

Although all minor parties in this study were returned or elected to parliament, only one of them (the Maori Party, a first-time, niche party) achieved its party vote goals. The remaining five failed to achieve the party vote goals they had set for themselves at the commencement of the campaign (which ranged from gaining sufficient party votes to bring one extra MP into Parliament, to becoming Parliament's third largest party). Applying the framework to the opening addresses of these parties, it was clear that three marketing errors were made.

First, there was little to no attempt at differentiating one minor party from another, in terms of policy offering and strategic position. Most were offering to be the balance between, or the insurance policy to cover, the major parties. Some even used slogans with similar words to convey this. Second, there was little of value offered in addition to leadership and policy messages from previous campaigns. Policy platforms that had been appropriated by the major parties over the years had not been replaced, making it hard for the minor parties to appear current. Third, despite starting out as niche parties opposed to government policies, most of the minor parties now desired to go into coalition with the 'winning' major party. They toned down their messages from previous campaigns and avoided attacking both major parties (something they had not done previously). In the effort to appear coalescent, moderate and sensible, their messages were devoid of new, interesting or challenging content. While some parties were successful in becoming part of the next coalition government, it does not appear that New Zealand voters were as willing to exchange their votes for minor parties offering 'more of the same' as they had been when the minor parties appeared more maverick. The lesson for minor parties wanting to achieve their party vote goals in future elections, then, is of the importance of consciously differentiating themselves from each other, of having the confidence to continue to attack the platforms and leadership of the major parties, and of continually refining and enhancing their policy offerings.

Sources and further reading

Damore, D.F. (2004). 'Using campaign advertisements to assess campaign processes'. *Journal of Political Marketing*, 3: 39–59.

Kline, S. (1997). 'Image politics: negative advertising strategies and the election audience'. In M. Nava, A. Blake, I. McRury and B. Richards (eds), *Buy this Book: Studies in Advertising and Consumption*. London: Routledge.

Robinson, C. (2006). *Advertising and the Market Orientation of Political Parties Contesting the 1999 and 2002 New Zealand General Election Campaigns*. Palmerston North: Massey University.

Case study 7.8 Terminating politics as we know it: the political marketing case of the 'Governator'   *David McCuan*

The 2003 California recall election, with the election of actor-turned-politician Arnold Schwarzenegger, was a seminal political event. This case study explores the nature of the 'Arnold phenomenon' by examining how his branding and personal style connect with our understanding of marketing in politics. It focuses on how professionalised campaigning merged with an expansive 'marketing model of politics', creating a hybrid model linking mobilisation, persuasion and market adaptation into a new political form.

Electoral institutions, spillovers and opportunity: the high-stakes marketing of direct democracy in California

Direct democracy campaigns in California are among the most expensive elections in the world. Between 1978, when the state's voters passed far-reaching property tax reform in the form of Proposition 13, and 1994, more than $800 million was spent throughout the process. In the subsequent decade, more than $1.2 billion was spent on ballot measures. While campaign contributions fuelled these campaigns, the marketing of ballot measures through the five stages of the process – from pre-qualification, qualification, into the campaign stage, onto typical legal challenges and, finally, an implementation stage – reflects costs associated with drafting ballot measures, signature gathering, media advertising, direct mail and consulting costs paid to 'political professionals'. Scholars and observers of California politics have noted the increasing frequency and gravity of popular ballot initiatives over this period, as the initiative process in California has become a 'parallel legislature' serving as the dominant vehicle of public policy formation in the state (Bowler and Cain 2004). The election of Arnold Schwarzenegger in the 2003 recall and his subsequent call for a 2005 special election presented further opportunities for political marketing professionals.

Creation of a political marketing infrastructure: the party known only as 'Arnold'

With the case of Arnold Schwarzenegger, constant elections became merged with policy made through initiatives, and the Governor's own style of politics has come to reflect this preference for rule by plebiscite. In 1999, Schwarzenegger had publicly expressed interest in running for governor and met with Karl Rove in 2001 to discuss the prospects of raising his role in politics. Subsequently, Schwarzenegger gained further visibility with sponsorship of an initiative, Proposition 49, to make state grants available for after-school programmes. This proposed ballot measure, known as the After School Education and Safety Program Act, appeared on the November 2002 General Election ballot, and voters approved this measure. This gradual, strategic move was designed to further establish Schwarzenegger's civic standing, and it also became evident to Schwarzenegger himself that his political instincts were best served through the arena of the 'parallel legislature' and direct democracy (Mathews 2006). Schwarzenegger's ability to leverage celebrity in the name of politics drove massive campaign spending in both the 2003 recall election and the 2005 special election. Moreover, this drive to the ballot box continued a trend where, between 2000 and 2006, California witnessed ten elections.

Campaign spending in the October 2003 statewide special election

According to compiled media reports and analysis of official campaign expenditure documentation, at least $89 million in total was spent on the 2003 special recall election. While difficult to gauge accurately, it seems that about $12 million was spent collectively on 'independent expenditures' – money spent supporting or opposing a candidate by an outside group. Political consultants alone received more than $4.5 million from the major gubernatorial candidates and interest groups in this election.

Campaign spending in the November 2005 statewide special election

In the 2005 special election, where voters rejected Governor Arnold Schwarzenegger's eight initiatives, the total campaign expenditures are estimated to have exceeded all previous ballot measure campaign spending. In fact, total campaign spending for the 2005 statewide special election was speculated by newspapers to have surpassed what John Kerry and President Bush spent in the 2004 national presidential election ($241 million and $306 million, respectively). In addition to the money that political actors and interest groups invested in this campaign, it is estimated that $55 million of public funds were spent to conduct the election, such as producing and distributing voter information ballots.

As far as campaign contributions are concerned, Governor Schwarzenegger outspent any individual special interest group by personally contributing $7.75 million in total to this campaign. Political consultants, pollsters and ad buyers received the bulk of the campaign expenditures. It is estimated that these three groups earned 10 per cent of total campaign spending, or about $30 million dollars. At least eight, and possibly nine, consulting firms were hired by both proponents and opponents of the initiatives during the election cycle, and more than $14.1 million was spent on consultants alone.

Spending fallout from spillovers: how was the money spent? The October 2003 statewide special election

Schwarzenegger brought on board top political consultants during this campaign, several of whom until recently have continued to advise him. Joel Fox, the former president of the Howard Jarvis Taxpayers Association, worked as senior policy consultant to Schwarzenegger during the 2003 recall. He also brought on the experienced consultant Mike Murphy as his chief campaign strategist, who has since stayed on as the senior political advisor in the Schwarzenegger administration. Schwarzenegger's media campaign was and is still co-ordinated by Don Sipple, another veteran operative who worked for former Governor Pete Wilson and many other Republican candidates.

The November 2005 statewide special election

Two campaign committees with close ties to Schwarzenegger, the governor's California Recovery Team (CRT) and Citizens To Save California (CSC), paid more than $4.9 million to consultants. That total included at least $194,000 to DC Navigators, whose founders include Mike Murphy, Schwarzenegger's chief campaign strategist. Other consultants receiving money for the special election who are close to Schwarzenegger included Marty Wilson, Schwarzenegger's chief campaign fundraiser, who received $120,000, Richard Costigan, the governor's legislative affairs secretary, who was paid $40,000, and Rob Stutzman, Schwarzenegger's communications director, who was paid $13,932 (Costigan and Stutzman took leaves of absence from Schwarzenegger's administration to work on the campaign). Likewise, National Petition Management, a company that gathers signatures to put initiatives and referendums on the ballot, received $1 million from CSC, a pro-Schwarzenegger committee. Similarly, Arno Political Consultants of Sacramento received $900,000 from the same committee.

Team Arnold: a new model for political marketing

The case of Arnold Schwarzenegger as politician is instructive for students of political marketing. The Governator has joined the politics of celebrity with the politics of direct democracy to create a new infrastructure of power. By recycling high-profile political professionals with skills gained through both the 'parallel legislature' and through candidate campaigns, Arnold Schwarzenegger the politician has further cemented the emphasis on electioneering over governing in politics. Furthermore, the exploitation of existing loopholes in campaign finance regulations has allowed

Schwarzenegger to use existing campaign finance regulations combined with his cadre of high-profile, experienced political professionals to raise money and create a solid infrastructure model of support that joins our previous understanding of how politics and marketing have altered politics.

Note

David McCuan would like to acknowledge research assistance from Stephanie Stone of The California Initiative Project, who assisted in the preparation of data associated with this case study. Data in this case were derived from various media and database sources.

Sources and further reading

Bowler, Shaun and Bruce Cain (2004). 'Introduction – recalling the recall: reflections on California's recent political adventure'. *PS*, XXXVII(1): 7–9.

California Secretary of State data: available online at www.ss.ca.gov/elections/sov/2004_general/contents.htm and www.ss.ca.gov/elections/sov/2005_special/contents.htm.

Institute of Governmental Studies Library. (2003). 'Hot topic: recall in California'. Available online at www.igs.berkeley.edu/library/htRecall2003.html (accessed October 2003).

—— (2004). 'California ballot propositions: November 2, 2004 general recommendations'. Available online at www.igs.berkeley.edu/library/htBallotRec2004NOV.html (accessed October 2004).

Mathews, Joe (2006). *The People's Machine: Arnold Schwarzenegger and the Rise of Blockbuster Democracy*. Los Angeles, CA: Public Affairs Press.

FURTHER READING

Atkinson, Robert D. and Andrew Leigh (2003). 'Serving the stakeholders. Customer-oriented e-government: can we ever get there?'. *Journal of Political Marketing*, 2(3/4): 59–81.

Baines, Paul R., Phil Harris and Barbara R. Lewis (2002). 'The political marketing planning process: improving image and message in strategic target areas'. *Market Intelligence and Planning*, 20(1): 6–14.

Bowler, Shaun and David M. Farrell (eds) (1992). *Electoral Strategies and Political Marketing*. Hampshire: Macmillan.

Chapman, Sherri, Edwina Luck and Charles H. Patti (2003). 'Building a brand relationship with voters: the need for IMC within political parties'. Paper presented at the Australian and New Zealand Marketing Academy Conference, University of South Australia, 1–3 December 2003.

Cotrim Maciera, J. (2005). 'Change to win? The 2002 General Election PT marketing strategy in Brazil'. In D. Lilleker and J. Lees-Marshment (eds), *Political Marketing: A Comparative Perspective*. Manchester: Manchester University Press.

Dermody, Janine and Stuart Hamner-Lloyd (2006). 'A marketing analysis of the 2005 General Election advertising campaigns'. In D. Lilleker, N. Jackson and R. Scullion (eds), *The Marketing of Political Parties*. Manchester: Manchester University Press.

Egherman, Tori (2005). 'The Hashemi brand in Iran's elections'. In *Marketing Profs*. Available online at www.marketingprofs.com/5/egherman1.asp?sp=1 (accessed 4 April 2008).

Farrell, David M. and Martin Wortmann (1987). 'Party strategies in the electoral market: political marketing in West Germany, Britain and Ireland'. *European Journal of Political Research*, 15: 297–318.

Franklin, Bob and John Richardson (2002). 'Priming the parish pump: political marketing and news management in local political communications networks'. *Journal of Political Marketing*, 1(1): 117–47.

Gaber, Ivor (2006). 'The autistic campaign: the parties, the media and the voters'. In D. Lilleker, N. Jackson and R. Scullion (eds), *The Marketing of Political Parties*. Manchester: Manchester University Press.

Geiselhart, Karin, Mary Griffiths and Bronwen FitzGerald (2003). 'What lies beyond service delivery-an Australian perspective'. *Journal of Political Marketing*, 2(3/4): 213–33.

Ingram, Peter and Jennifer Lees-Marshment (2002). 'The Anglicisation of political marketing: how Blair "out-marketed" Clinton'. *Journal of Public Affairs*, 2(2): 44–57.

Jackson, Nigel (2005). 'Vote winner or a nuisance: email and elected politicians' relationship with their constituents'. In W. Wymer and J. Lees-Marshment (eds), *Current Issues in Political Marketing*. Binghamton, NY: Haworth Press.

—— (2006). 'Banking online: the use of the Internet by political parties to build relationships with voters'. In D. Lilleker, N. Jackson and R. Scullion (eds), *The Marketing of Political Parties*. Manchester: Manchester University Press.

—— and Darren G. Lilleker (2004). 'Just public relations or an attempt at interaction? British MPs in the press, on the web and "in your face" '. *European Journal of Communication*, 19(4): 507–33.

Johnson, Dennis W. (2003). 'Anthrax and digital mail'. *Journal of Political Marketing*, 2(1): 113–15.

—— (2007). *No Place for Amateurs* (2nd edn). New York: Routledge.

Kavanagh, Dennis (1995). *Election Campaigning: The New Marketing of Politics*. Oxford: Blackwell.

Lancaster, Geoff and Lester Massingham (1993). *Essentials of Marketing*. London: McGraw-Hill.

Lees-Marshment, Jennifer (2008). *Political Marketing and British Political Parties* (2nd edn). Manchester: Manchester University Press.

Lilleker, Darren (2004). 'Micro-level political communication: is publicizing constituency service the vote winner that UK MPs perceive it to be?'. Paper presented to the UK PSA, University of Lincoln, 4–8 April.

—— (2005). 'Local campaign management: winning votes or wasting resources?'. *Journal of Marketing Management*, 21(9/10): 979–1003.

—— (2006). 'Local political marketing: political marketing as public service'. In D. Lilleker, N. Jackson and R. Scullion (eds), *The Marketing of Political Parties*. Manchester: Manchester University Press.

—— and Ralph Negrine (2002). 'Marketing techniques and political campaigns: the limitations for the marketing of British political parties'. Paper presented to the UK PSA, Manchester 7–9 April.

—— and —— (2003). 'Not big brand names but corner shops: marketing politics to a disengaged electorate'. *Journal of Political Marketing*, 2(1): 55–76.

Mauser, G. (1983). *Political Marketing: An Approach to Campaign Strategy*. New York: Praeger.

McGough, S. (2005). 'Political marketing in Irish politics: the case of Sinn Féin'. In D. Lilleker and J. Lees-Marshment (eds), *Political Marketing: A Comparative Perspective*. Manchester: Manchester University Press.

Medvic, Stephen (2006). 'Understanding campaign strategy "deliberate priming" and the role of professional political consultants'. *Journal of Political Marketing*, 5(1/2): 11–32.

Moloney, Kevin and Rob Colmer (2001). 'Does political PR enhance or trivialise democracy? The UK General Election 2001 as contest between presentation and substance'. *Journal of Marketing Management*, 17(9/10): 957–68.

Newman, Bruce (1994). *The Marketing of the President: Political Marketing as Campaign Strategy*. Beverley Hills, CA: Sage Publications.

—— (1999). *The Mass Marketing of Politics: Democracy in an Age of Manufactured Images*. Beverley Hills, CA: Sage Publications.

—— (2001). 'An assessment of the 2000 US Presidential Election: a set of political marketing guidelines'. *Journal of Public Affairs*, 1(3): 210.

O'Shaughnessy, Nicholas and Gillian Peele (1985). 'Money, mail and markets: reflections on direct mail in American politics'. *Electoral Studies*, 4(2): 115–24.

—— and Stephan C. Henneberg (2007). 'The selling of the president 2004: a marketing perspective'. *Journal of Public Affairs*, 7(3): 249–68.

Palmer, A. (1994). *Principles of Services Marketing*. London: McGraw-Hill.

Paven, Andy (2001). 'PR lessons from election 2000'. *Public Relations Tactics*, 8(2): 18.

Prasaad, K. Sai and Ramya Raghupathy (2005). 'A snapshot of a successful public relations strategy'. *American Behavioral Scientist*, 49(4): 629–33.

Prete, Maria Irene (2007). 'M-Politics: credibility and effectiveness of mobile political communications'. *Journal of Targeting, Measurement & Analysis for Marketing*, 16(1): 48–56.

Rademacher, Eric W. and Alfred J. Tuchfarber (1999). 'Pre-election polling and political campaigns'. In B. Newman (ed.), *Handbook of Political Marketing*. Thousand Oaks, CA: Sage.

Robinson, Claire E. (2006). 'Advertising and the market orientation of political parties contesting the 1999 and 2002 New Zealand General Election campaigns'. Ph.D. thesis, Massey University, Palmerston North, New Zealand.

—— (2007). 'Images of the 2005 campaign'. In Stephen Levin and Nigel S. Roberts (eds), *The Baubles of Office: The New Zealand General election of 2005*. Wellington: Victoria University Press.

Rottinghaus, Brandon and Irina Alberro (2005). 'Rivaling the PRI: the image management of Vicente Fox and the use of public opinion polling in the 2000 Mexican Election'. *Latin American Politics and Society*, 47(2): 143–58.

Sackman, Adrian I. (1996). 'The learning curve towards New Labour: Neil Kinnock's corporate party 1983–92'. *European Journal of Marketing*, 30(10/11): 147–58.

Savigny, Heather (2005). 'Labour, political marketing and the 2005 Election: a campaign of two halves'. *Journal of Marketing Management*, 21(9/10): 925–41.

Scammell, Margaret (1995). *Designer Politics: How Elections are Won*. New York: St Martin's Press.

—— (1996). 'The odd couple: marketing and Maggie'. *European Journal of Marketing*, 30(10/11): 114–26.

Schonker-Schreck, Daniella (2004). 'Political marketing and the media: women in the 1996 Israeli Elections – a case study'. *Israel Affairs*, 10(3): 159–77.

Schweiger, Gunter and Michaela Aadami (1999). 'The nonverbal image of politicians and political parties'. In Bruce Newman (ed.), *The Handbook of Political Marketing*. Thousand Oaks, CA: Sage.

Seawright, David (2005). '"On a low road": the 2005 Conservative campaign'. *Journal of Marketing Management*, 21(9/10): 943–57.

Shaw, Daron R. (2002). 'How the Bush and Gore campaigns conceptualized and used the Internet in 2000'. *Journal of Political Marketing*, 1(1): 39–65.

Sherman, Elaine (1999). 'Direct marketing: how does it work for political campaigns?'. In Bruce Newman (ed.), *The Handbook of Political Marketing*. Thousand Oaks, CA: Sage.

Steger, Wayne (1999). 'The permanent campaign: marketing from the hill'. In Bruce Newman (ed.), *The Handbook of Political Marketing*. Thousand Oaks, CA: Sage.

Stirland, Sarah Lai (2008) 'Inside Obama's surging net-roots campaign'. In *Wired GQ*. Excerpts available online at www.wired.com/politics/law/news/2008/03/obama_tools (accessed 1 April 2008).

Wring, Dominic (1997). 'Reconciling marketing with political science: theories of political marketing'. *Proceedings of the 1997 Academy of Marketing Conference*. Manchester: Manchester Metropolitan University.

—— (2001). 'Labouring the point: operation victory and the battle for a second term'. *Journal of Marketing Management*, 17(9/10): 913–27.

—— (2002). 'Conceptualising political marketing: a framework for election-campaign analysis'. In N.J. O'Shaughnessy and S. Henneberg (eds), *The Idea of Political Marketing*. New York: Praeger.

—— (2005). *The Politics of Marketing of the Labour Party*. Hampshire: Palgrave Macmillan.

8 Marketing in government
Delivering and staying in touch

Political marketing is most commonly associated with efforts to win an election – after all, once the hard bit of getting into government is completed, the politician then has power and access to state resources opposition campaigners never have. However, marketing in government presents its own series of challenges. In opposition, many promises are made, but once a candidate is voted in and the political consumer has 'bought' the product, it then needs to be delivered in power: see Practitioner perspective 8.1. Delivery is not easy in politics. It involves not just delivering policy goals through legislation and system changes but maintaining the overall brand and product communicated before the election. Even where they succeed, political consumers rarely give them credit for it – they either see weaknesses or gaps, or, where they accept something has been delivered, they then want more. Government presents new challenges, especially to staying in touch or market-oriented. Additionally, politicians have to think about re-election, and re-marketing a product from an existing position is more difficult. This chapter will therefore examine a number of issues involved with marketing in government, including the limitations, but also the potential.

The nature of government and the limitations it imposes

Government is different to opposition; as Newman (1999: 110) observes, a candidate must adapt 'from the campaign marketplace to the governing marketplace'. On one hand, there are more resources, with the state bureaucracy now employed to help the politician or party work in office. However, this also presents a new source of ideas, information and – sometimes conflicting – advice: see Practitioner perspective 8.2.

Government also throws up unpredictable issues, such as war and economic turbulence, that constrain the ability of politicians to carry out previous promises. Bill Clinton, elected

Practitioner perspective 8.2

Before you know it, you find that everyday problems have crept up on you and made their presence felt. Ministers are dragged into dealing with issues and media explosions. They have to attend events abroad, meet with pressure groups and participate in protracted meetings in parliament.

(Mogens Lykketoft, Minister of foreign affairs and minister of finance in the Danish Nyrup government and strategist, interviewed by Lindholm and Prehn 2007: 19)

in 1992 in the US as a New Democrat, tax-cutting, middle-class targeted president, found, once in office, that the actual deficit was far worse than they had previously been informed, and what they had promised to do was impossible. As Arterton (2007: 147) notes, in the US presidential structure, 'the government can neither dictate nor assume legislative action'. After 9/11, George W. Bush's 'Compassionate Conservatism' agenda was pushed to the background in favour of the 'war on terror' and more right-wing social agendas than was evident from his 2000 presidential campaign. Additionally, once parties and politicians are elected into power, they are more likely to be blamed for any problems that occur: once in government, parties can be subject to losing their support because of events beyond their control. Case study 8.1 illustrates this.

Pre-election government marketing and progress reports once in power

The first aspect to marketing in government is the consideration of delivery before the election and then reports on progress once in power. In the commercial market, consumers can be sceptical of goods that make unrealistic and apparently impossible promises with low prices, and the same is true of politics, given the cynicism of voters. Political marketing is not just about promising what voters want, but ensuring the product is achievable, even if parties are trying to be market-oriented (Lees-Marshment 2001). In recent years, this element of political marketing has become more important, as politicians and parties develop news ways of trying to convince the public they are capable of delivering in office.

Lederer *et al.* (2005) showed how part-marketing by the populist Freedom Party (FPÖ) in Austria, between 1986 and 2002, under the leadership of Jorg Haider, to get it into power in a coalition unravelled once in government. Although the FPÖ became the second strongest party in 1999, with 26.9 per cent of the votes and fifty-two seats, and entered government with the People's Party, in 2002 they lost almost 65 per cent of their former voters and were reduced to eighteen seats. Haider had promised unachievable products before election, such as the proposition of a flat tax in 1999, which they were unable to secure agreement for in the coalition. They lost votes in local elections and credibility and competence, as measured by opinion polls. Case study 8.2 raises other issues with failing to deliver.

Parties and candidates now try to make certain aspects of their product more prominent than others, by creating pledges or contracts or guarantees. One of the earliest examples of this was the 1994 mid-term 'Contract with America' put forward by the House Republicans in the US, gaining considerable votes but also a degree of a mandate to then dominate Congress for the rest of Bill Clinton's time as president: see Box 8.1.

Tony Blair's Labour Party in the UK issued both a contract and credit-card sized pledges, both to get into government and then when in power: see Box 8.2.

Box 8.1 Elements of the US House Republican Contract with America, 1994

1   The Fiscal Responsibility Act (balanced-budget amendment).
2   The Taking Back Our Streets Act (anti-crime package).
3   The Personal Responsibility Act (welfare reform).
4   The Family Reinforcement Act (enforcement of child support).
5   The American Dream Restoration Act (tax credit of $500 per child).
6   The National Security Restoration Act (strengthening of national defense).
7   The Senior Citizens Fairness Act (raising earnings limits for social security).
8   The Job Creation And Wage Enhancement Act (incentives for small business and capital-gains cut).
9   The Common Sense Legal Reform Act (reasonable limits on punitive damages and reform of product-liability laws).
10 The Citizen Legislature Act (term limits in congress).

Source: Arterton (2007: 163)

Box 8.2 Blair's New Labour Party credit card pledges

1997
1   We will cut class sizes to thirty or under for five-, six- and seven-year-olds by using money saved from the assisted places scheme.
2   We will introduce a fast-track punishment scheme for persistent young offenders by halving the time from arrest to sentencing.
3   We will cut NHS waiting lists by treating an extra 100,000 patients as a first step by releasing £100 million saved from NHS red tape.
4   We will get 250,000 under twenty-five-year-olds off benefit and into work by using money from a windfall levy on the privatised utilities.
5   We will set tough rules for government spending and borrowing and ensure low inflation and strengthen the economy so that interest rates are as low as possible to make all families better off.

2001
1   Mortgages as low as possible, low inflation and sound public finances.
2   Ten thousand extra teachers and higher standards in secondary schools.
3   Twenty thousand extra nurses and 10,000 extra doctors in a reformed NHS.
4   Six thousand extra recruits to raise police numbers to their highest-ever level.
5   Pensioners' winter fuel payment retained, minimum wage rising to £4.20.

2005
1   Your family better off.
2   Your child achieving more.
3   Your children with the best start.
4   Your family treated better and faster.
5   Your community safer.
6   Your country's borders protected.

Interestingly, the pledges changed over the three terms. They changed from outputs (what government would achieve) to inputs (what government would put into the system). Inputs are easier to control than outputs. Second, they changed from the second to third term to general rhetorical pledges. They were very vague on the front side, and on the back the measurements were flexible, e.g. 'mortgages as low as possible', which was easier for the party because it is harder to be measured exactly by general themes. The original spirit that encouraged the 1997 pledges seemed to disappear, the longer the party stayed in government.

Single pledges can also been used in politics. In the US, the think-tank campaign organisation Americans for Tax Reform has been successful in getting many candidates for Congress to take the 'no tax increase' pledge. The organisation gets candidates to sign a pledge not to raise taxes after the election. They hold politicians to account once elected, publicising any deviations from this policy. In 1988, Vice President George H.W. Bush was not doing well in the Republican presidential primaries, after losing badly to Bob Dole in the Iowa caucuses, and so asked his competitior, in a debate, to sign a pledge not to raise taxes; Dole refused, losing credibility with voters. Bush then went on to win the nomination and the presidency. However, he also reneged on his pledge in office and lost power in 1992. Americans for Tax Reform has signed up both congressional and presidential candidates and state legislators. Pledge cards can also focus on a particular issue area; the PES (Party of European Socialists) women launched a pledge card in 2005 focusing on women:

We are working for:

- more and better jobs for women;
- equal opportunities and equal pay;
- better childcare;
- an end to all forms of violence against women;
- women's rights and empowerment.

(www.pes.org/content/view/123, accessed 14 April 2008)

Discussion point 8.1

Discuss how effective pledge cards and contracts are at helping, not just win elections, but maintain support once in government.

Pledges and contracts have been copied around the world: Helen Clark adopted them for her Labour Party in New Zealand in 1999. Unlike Blair, she retained their more specific nature over time in government, and, in 2005, the pledges promised:

1   no interest on student loans;
2   final date for treaty claims 2008;
3   increase rates rebate;
4   Kiwi saver;
5   250 extra community police;
6   more cataract and major joint operations;
7   5,000 more modern apprenticeships.

Case study 8.3 highlights some of the broader issues surrounding the use of contracts, such as trust – an aspect governments care about deeply, because trust is essential to maintaining a positive relationship with voters in the long term.

Such measures do not always work to win, or maintain, support. The UK Conservative Party, in opposition in 1999, launched a number of guarantees as part of its Common Sense Revolution, responding to market intelligence and the need for achievable promises. However, if such commitments are to mean anything and have impact on the public, parties need to stick with them. Unfortunately the Tories did not, and as Lees-Marshment (2008b: 326, 331) notes, by the time of the election, the guarantees had all but disappeared following a period of statements from senior party figures that watered them down or abandoned them entirely. When pledges, contracts or guarantees are implemented effectively, they help to focus voters' and politicians' minds on what is most important. Politicians are saying 'at the very least we will get these few things done'. In government therefore, it is important that such proposals are closely followed, and attention is placed on them to ensure success in those areas at least.

Delivery

Actually delivering

Delivery is not easy to achieve in politics. Government involves a whole range of organisations, department and units, and within them staff who need to be on board to make it work – even when legislation is passed. Indeed, just the legislative process can thwart promises being converted into action. Once a party is elected, other stakeholders take more notice of their policies and how it might affect them and lobby to hinder or help policy being enacted through parliament or congress.

One of the most well-known cases of failed delivery was health care by Bill Clinton, whose package was blocked when it went through Congress, despite it being a visible part of the product he offered to voters and won election for. Newman (1999: 99–101) suggests one factor was that, whereas opposers of the plan articulated their argument very cleverly, utilising symbolic people called Harry and Louise, which gave a face to their campaign, the Clinton government never did. The government did respond by simplifying the message and reducing jargon to target those people who had most to benefit from gaining health care, as they were currently uninsured. New communication, with 'simple red, white and blue charts' and 'homespun humour', was test marketed and found to be more effective and was therefore used in a travelling sales seminar in 1994. However, the proposal 'was out of touch with market changes taking place as it was being developed, and was too complex' in contrast to effective opposition campaigning (Newman 1999: 101). The market was not convinced the end result would be an improvement.

The success of the Blair government in delivering on the 1997 pledges was closely analysed; for example, the television channel Channel 4 analysed the government's performance: see Box 8.3.

Failure in delivery undoubtedly causes concern for politicians and strategists, as it threatens the chances of re-election. However, it is impossible to ensure that 100 per cent success will be achieved. In business, this is known as the service delivery gap; as Newman (1999: 37–8) explored, there are gaps 'between quality specifications and service delivery', different constraints such as situational influences (e.g. the House of Representatives shifting from the president's party to the opposition mid-term) and the bureaucracy of government stop candidates from delivering even if they want to. Even where they understand market

Box 8.3 Assessment of Blair's success at delivering on 1997 election pledges

'We will cut class sizes to thirty or under for five-, six- and seven-year-olds by using money saved from the assisted places scheme.'

In 1997, 23.9 per cent of five- to seven-year-olds were in classes of thirty or more. The latest figures reported that 1.4 per cent of under sevens were being taught in classes of over thirty. Most of those were covered by various exemptions to the rules – only 0.2 per cent were in illegally large classes.

Source: Department for Education and Skills, www.dcsf.gov.uk/rsgateway/
DB/SFR/s000726/SFR16-2007a.pdf

Achievement score: 4

'We will introduce a fast-track punishment scheme for persistent young offenders by halving the time from arrest to sentencing.'

The government hit this target, and has more or less kept to it – a significant thing to do, as three months on remand is a long time for anyone, but particularly a child.

'But there were some unintended consequences', says Frances Crook, director of the Howard League for Penal Reform. 'Young people often go through a spell of offending, and under the old system this could all be taken into account in one sentence. Now the first sentence is sometimes rushed through, and some cases where you might have had one sentence, you now have two. And sometimes, that might be a jail term.'

Achievement score: 4

'We will cut NHS waiting lists by treating an extra 100,000 patients as a first step by releasing £100 million saved from NHS red tape.'

In 1997, 1.3 million were on waiting lists. By 2000, this target had been met – though, by focusing on waiting lists, the Government was accused of distorting priorities. Since then, the government has decided that it makes more sense to target waiting times, not waiting lists. In 1997, the guaranteed maximum wait was 18 months – Labour is now targeting a maximum wait of 18 weeks by 2008.

Achievement score: 5

'We will get 250,000 under twenty-five-year-olds off benefit and into work by using money from a windfall levy on the privatised utilities.'

More than 250,000 young people have passed through the New Deal and subsequently found jobs. But, in a growing economy with low unemployment, many would have found work anyway.

Professor John Van Reenen has estimated that the 'value added' by the New Deal programme amounts to around 17,000 extra young people in work per year – a success, at reasonable cost, but perhaps falling slightly below the levels promised by the pledge.

Achievement score: 4

'We will set tough rules for government spending and borrowing and ensure low inflation and strengthen the economy so that interest rates are as low as possible to make all families better off.'

Gordon Brown and Tony Blair have certainly presided over a long period of growth and economic stability (though some indicators, particularly inflation, have been heading upwards lately).

The 'tough rules' have been more controversial. The most controversial was the 'golden rule', which said that the government should balance the books over the economic cycle. The government has met this, but only by redefining exactly what constitutes a cycle.

The Government also pledged to keep government debt below 40 per cent of GDP, the 'sustainable investment rule'. This has been met, but public sector debt is rising, and the independent think tank, the Institute for Fiscal Studies, estimates that there's a 44 per cent chance it will be exceeded by 2010–11.

Other liabilities, notably public sector pensions and PFI borrowing, aren't included in that figure. If they were, it would be closer to 90 per cent. (For an exhaustive account, see www.ifs.org.uk/budgets/gb2007/07chap3.pdf)
Achievement score: 2

Source: www.channel4.com/news/articles/politics/domestic_politics/
factcheck+labours+election+pledge+cards/507807 (accessed 11 April 2008)

demand and accept the need for a problem to be solved, they may be incapable of doing anything about it: 'politicians are much more vulnerable to this gap than are other service industries as a result of the unexpected situations to which politicians always must respond' (Newman 1999: 38).

Others argue it is best to be honest about failures: see Practitioner perspective 8.3 on this. Patrón-Galindo (2004: 116) studied the first term of Peruvian President Alejandro Toledo after he won power in 2001. Although most election promises were achieved within a year or so of getting into power, people's expectations were not satisfied, and his popularity declined, owing also to problems such as a personal scandal and perception that rhetorical, vague statements led to complicated situations. Polls suggested the public thought he needed more time to solve the country's problems. One problem was that he took too long to acknowledge the problem he faced. Patrón-Galindo (2004: 122) observes that 'it was a mistake on his part to take so much time' to decide to be honest; he could have chosen instead to declare at 'a time chosen by him and not fixed by circumstances' and which was more favourable to him. This speaks to the need for a degree of honesty and admission of weakness or failings by leaders to maintain public support.

The UK Labour government issued annual reports in its first term from 1997 to 2001 and in these admitted to failing to deliver on some aspects – an approach that arguably helped to create more trust and a positive relationship with voters. In 2001, after winning his second term, Tony Blair declared that it was 'very clearly an instruction to deliver' (the *Independent*, 9 June 2001) and established the Downing Street Delivery Unit. Michael Barber, a former educational civil servant, was made director. Barber wrote about the experience of delivery in his own book (Barber 2007) and, in his *delivery manual,* outlined the need for delivery reports, setting targets, consideration of delivery chains, an assessment

Practitioner perspective 8.3

It's the willingness to say we didn't get that right. That's very hard in politics. Because politicians never, ever want to say we got anything wrong. And the reality of that is voters know that, they know you're going to screw some things up, so why are you pretending you got everything right? You'd be far better off saying yes; we missed that one so we're going to fix it.

(Ben Levin, former staff in the Canadian provincial governments of Ontario and Manitoba, interviewed by Jennifer Lees-Marshment 2008)

framework and sample presentations to the media. Barber's delivery unit has also been copied in other countries, such as the establishment of the cabinet implementation unit in federal government under John Howard and the premier's delivery unit in New South Wales State, Australia. As Peter Hamburger, Department of the Prime Minister and Cabinet, wrote, 'it is no longer enough for those advocating major policy to have a good idea ... the Government demands that we think through our ideas and how they are going to be implemented' (Hamburger 2006).

Political consumer perception of delivery

Once a party or candidate gets into power, voters start judging them on delivery – even delivery that the politician can't control. Suddenly the buck stops with them; they can no longer simply criticise the government, as they are the government. Political consumers may not always evaluate politicians' delivery objectively, fairly or clearly, and this makes political marketing harder. Barber (2007: 369–71) notes that, with delivery, 'citizens have to see and feel the difference and expectations need to be managed' and 'where progress is slow, it's even more important for people to understand the strategy.'

The definition of a market-oriented party is that a party should design its product to create voter satisfaction. It's a good idea, but more difficult to achieve in practice. It could be that parties do deliver, but voters are not aware of success or rarely credit the government with success. With UK Labour, a poll in October 2006 revealed that voters thought the service had got worse, not better, during Labour's decade in power, and that much of the government's huge extra investment in health care has been wasted. Yet, the public's personal experience of using NHS services is none the less overwhelmingly positive: 71 per cent of people say that their family and friends have had a good experience (Glover 2006).

Understanding what *would* satisfy voters, perhaps using consumer satisfaction literature within the management discipline, should also be built into the communication of delivery. A further layer of complexity is that, in all areas, not just politics, demand is insatiable. Even when voters do give credit for successful delivery, having been satisfied, they then want more. This is the problem with delivery – you succeed, but then people want more. It's how progress happens, but it presents continued challenges for government.

Individual politician delivery, e.g. Congressman/woman, MP, MEP

In the US, Steger (1999: 668–9) observed that, given the decentralised structure which means they act individually, elected officials in Congress are able to claim credit for a number of activities in their state, such as:

- fixing funding formulas to the benefit of their market;
- pressurising bureaucrats who decide who qualifies for funding;
- securing tax breaks for their constituents;
- opposing potentially damaging regulatory legislation;
- helping the public with problems with government and agencies and fighting for benefits and grants.

The resources of being in office also help congress men and women provide effective service for constituents, which both delivers and gains credit for delivery, although the incumbency effect can also hinder re-election if the governing party becomes unpopular in office and the local representative from the same party loses votes through no particular fault of their own.

In parliamentary and party-based systems such as the UK, it is harder to claim individual credit, and individual MPs are much more likely to be affected by national party fortunes. However, Lilleker (2006: 212–4) argues that, at a local level, an incumbent candidate's success in delivery in terms of the service they have provided for their constituents can affect the outcome of the election. MPs carry out case-work for their constituents, or campaign to attract industry or other funding, such as from the European Union, or create networks between associations; all of which can create a positive reputation for a politician when they face re-election. Butler and Collins (1999) also argue that, in Ireland, MPs try to improve their service delivery to provide a degree of immunity from electoral swings that may move against them. Local politicians focus on the implementation of politics on the ground, in a way that affects people's daily lives and may therefore gain their attention, even when they may appear to ignore national or federal politics. While MPs cannot enact substantial change in the public sector individually, they can help represent and support constituents in bringing complaints to government departments and fighting for benefit entitlements (1999: 1033; see also Butler and Collins 2001).

Delivery in coalition

Ensuring delivery in coalition is difficult for both major and minor partners. Major parties have to take care to compromise enough to keep their minor partner satisfied with the arrangement, but it can constrain their ability to deliver on everything they promised. Rudd (2005) notes how the New Zealand Labour Party tried to ensure it gave credit for delivery of certain policies to its junior coalition partner, the Alliance, during 1999–2002, such as the establishment of the 'People's Bank' as a subsidiary of New Zealand Post and the introduction of paid parental leave. It does not always work out an advantage to take part in a coalition for the junior partner. More protest-type minor parties can end up losing their original voter support. Lederer *et al.* (2005) note how the Austrian FPÖ, which entered coalition government in 2000, then found itself with a problem, as its scope to design its own product was considerably limited. Furthermore, it had attracted support by opposing the government; once part of the government, it lost this support. They found it impossible to gain delivery of their promises, as they were inexperienced in bargaining to get their policies accepted by their coalition partner. Credit for any popular policies was given to the Conservative People's Party (ÖVP) instead.

Communicating delivery

Delivery needs to be communicated as well as actioned. A blockage in this process is the media: they don't want to take positive success stories; they see their role as being to find the problems, not the solutions.

Practitioner perspective 8.4

'The media deliberately obstruct the link between government and hospitals/NHS' and when government has delivered 'they don't credit the government for it.'

(Alastair Campbell, Tony Blair's former Press Secretary, interviewed by Jennifer Lees-Marshment 2005)

“
”
Discussion point 8.2

Why is delivery so difficult? To what extent are current politicians in power succeeding in delivering on their promises? What tools have they used to communicate delivery, and how effective have they been?

Increasingly, governments seek to use a range of tools to communicate progress in delivery. These include annual or progress reports, newsletters within each electorate/constituency/branch or ward, talking about delivery in interviews and speeches, and online communication. This is also true at a local level. Local MPs in the UK also issued annual delivery reports, which were available on their websites and sent in hard-copy form to residents: a general search on google.co.uk will yield results such as: 'Edward Davey MP – Annual reports' and others (see Lilleker 2006).

Maintaining a market-orientation in government

Just as it is argued that parties and politicians need to be market-oriented in order to win an election, it can be argued the same is true of being in power: it helps maintain the support necessary to deliver and also enact the more problematic policies that government can necessitate. Market-oriented behaviour does not mean just following the public, and therefore there is room for leadership, as long as it remains within the broad confines of responsiveness. Responsiveness does not mean just saying yes all the time, nor does it exclude making the difficult but 'right' decisions. Nor does it mean succeeding at everything – it can include making mistakes the public might accept as inevitable. But it is about showing continued ability to listen and consider the market. This echoes the idea of the permanent campaign – it is about permanent marketing.

Forces against maintaining a market-orientation in government

There are many forces that work against the maintenance of a market-orientation in government. Government is a very different environment; it brings into play a whole new set of resources, information and advice, including the civil service or bureaucracy, but also think tanks who want to influence the detailed construction of legislation. While opposition parties may know this, trying to take this into account while developing the political marketing strategy and product, when other factors and stakeholders are more crucial to winning the election first, is not an easy process. Box 8.4, from Lees-Marshment (2008a), outlines the range of factors working against maintaining a market-orientation.

At the same time, the desire for the public to see tangible delivery and a difference grows. This is despite delivery being a slow process in government. The forces for the public perception of the leader's market-orientation to decline are also in place. Leaders in particular find it hard to remain in touch, as they enjoy power and also want to make a difference and impact during their time in office. A good example of this is Tony Blair: despite winning a landslide election in 1997 with market-oriented behaviour, in government Blair's popularity declined after decisions such as that to go to war in Iraq. Not only did his particular position prove unpopular, communication from him suggested he ignored the public's opposition, which made him seem dismissive and uncaring of public opinion,

Box 8.4 Factors hindering maintenance of a market-orientation in government

1   Loss of critical, objective advisors with that gut feel and ability to offer blunt criticism – such as Alastair Campbell in Tony Blair's case.
2   Realities and constraints of government, including unpredictability.
3   Increasing knowledge, experience and information among leaders, encouraging feeling of invincibility, arrogance and superiority.
4   Weak opposition, which encourages and facilitates complacency, as victory can be achieved without being overtly responsive.
5   Difficulty and slow pace of delivery in government.
6   Lack of time to think about future product development.

Source: Lees-Marshment (2008a)

making the situation worse. This and research by Promise show that leaders need to continue to conduct market intelligence and show awareness of the results, even if they don't always follow the opinions of the public in what they decide to do.

Another case of losing touch is that of Arnold Swarzenegger, governor of California in the US. In 2005, he called a special election to allow voters to decide on propositions regarding teacher tenure requirements (Proposition 74), the use of union dues for political campaign contributions (Proposition 75), state budgetary spending limits (Proposition 76) and redistricting (Proposition 77), which ended up losing him considerable support. California voters rejected all eight ballot propositions, despite the election costing hundreds of millions of dollars. The main reason, according to Mehlman (2006: 12) was that he broke a number of rules in public relations:

1   **Forgetting who elected you:**
    Swarzenegger won office in 2003 by gaining support across several markets, from moderate and conservative Republicans, Independents and even some Democrats, through an appeal to be a different kind of politician. At first, he governed in a bipartisan way, gaining increases in approval ratings. However, he then moved to the right, working against his allies instead of with them, and therefore abandoning his key supporter market.

2   **Picking too many fights:**
    In 2005, Swarzenegger began to look for fights and battles, fighting with public sector workers and being beaten back to withdraw a proposal to reform pensions; and fighting them all at once instead of one at a time. They worked together to fight back and were all over the state, criticising him no matter where he went.

3   **Not keeping it real:**
    He used various stunts that backfired and eroded his governing competence image; for example, he posed in front of a giant spigot from which poured red ink to try to highlight the budget deficit; he helped workers fix potholes in San Jose to show-case transport policies, but it later emerged the workers created the holes purely for the photo opportunity, at a cost of $25,000. He acted more like a celebrity than a politician.

Managing the loss of a market-orientation

Politicians may avoid losing a market-orientation, anticipating any problems in advance and acting on emergent issues as soon as they occurr. Conducting continual market intelligence is crucial to this – it can help ensure leaders remain aware of the impact their behaviour has on public support. Lilleker and Lees-Marshment (2005: 225–6) suggested strategies a government needs to ensure it finds space and time to think about product design/development for the next election. However, research on leaders who stay in power for more than one term suggests action only tends to be taken after there has been a loss in responsiveness in the eyes of the public. Studying empirical examples from Blair and Clark, Lees-Marshment (2008a) suggested a number of tools that can be used by governments: see Box 8.5.

Box 8.5 Tools helping to regain a market-orientation in government, with examples from UK Prime Minister Tony Blair and New Zealand Prime Minister Helen Clark, 2005–7

1   **Conduct listening or consultation exercises to get back in touch:**
    e.g. UK Labour's *The Big Conversation* in 2003 and *Let's Talk* in 2005.

2   **Refresh the overall team:**
    e.g. the UK Labour 2005 campaign conveyed Team Labour, showing a range of politicians within the government, not just Blair; and NZ Labour refreshed the cabinet in 2007 and encouraged older MPs to retire, leaving room to promote those more junior.

3   **Use public-friendly, non-political communication:**
    Blair appeared on non-political television, such as the popular daytime programme *Richard and Judy*, and *Ant and Dec*, a mainstream Saturday evening programme, before the 2005 election; and after winning a third term took part in a comedy sketch with comedienne Catherine Tate for the charity television fundraising show Comic Relief.

4   **Acknowledge public concern with leaders' difficult, unpopular decisions or issues:**
    e.g. UK Labour enacted a *masochism* strategy, where Blair met the public and listened to, and showed respect for, voters' disagreement with his war decision, explaining the pressures on a leader to take a decision whether it was popular or not.

5   **Develop new strategy for future terms; ensuring there is the space and time to think about product design/development for the next election:**
    e.g. in 2007, Clark implemented new policies such as Kiwi saver, free part-time child care and a new pension scheme; and acknowledged the need to reduce income tax in response to market demand and economic conditions; in the UK, a strategy unit established in the second term helped provide a means by which new ideas from academia, think tanks, private industry and non-governmental organisations were integrated into government.

Source: Lees-Marshment (2008a)

Discussion point 8.3

Think of governments that have won elections with significant public support, only to lose touch and, with it, lose votes over time. Identify and discuss any who have succeeded in regaining a market-orientation.

Strategy in government

Broader strategy, as explained in previous chapters, is a new area for political marketing and politics. However, Fischer *et al.*'s (2007) edited collection provides significant comparative understanding. This suggested that strategy was the key to long-term success and ensuring effective focus. Governments can form a strategy unit to help encourage new thinking and change the nature of the civil service to reward strategic thinking. The UK Labour government created a prime minister's strategy unit in 2003, its second term in office, which looked at spending reviews and five-year strategies for different departments: see Box 8.6.

The power of a government to implement its chosen strategy depends on a number of factors, such as:

1 its majority/seats in parliament;
2 the strategic qualities of the leaders;
3 the strategic ability of parliamentary groups;
4 political constellations;
5 market conditions such as the economy;
6 approaching elections.

Obstacles and aides to strategic thinking

One of the difficulties of strategising in government is the pressure of daily government business, which stops ministers having time to think. When the firm Promise presented to UK Prime Minister Tony Blair in 2004 about future strategy and rebranding, he asked his private secretary, Jonathan Powell, to make sure he had the time to think about it over the weekend (Promise 2005). Ministerial work is about *here and now* priorities. Government can end up being driven more by crisis – where it doesn't want to be – and less by strategy – where it wants to go.

In the US, Arterton (2007) found that strategy in government is underdeveloped, hindered by the machinery of the US government, which works against cross-unit or state co-operation

---

Box 8.6 UK Government's strategy unit

The strategy unit
The strategy unit has three main roles:

* to provide strategy and policy advice to the prime minister/No. 10;
* to support government departments in developing effective strategies and policies – including helping them to build their strategic capability;
* to identify and effectively disseminate emerging issues and policy challenges.

The strategy unit works closely, and often jointly, with other government departments and external stakeholders on a broad range of domestic policy issues. The unit puts strong emphasis on analytical rigour and an evidence-based approach to developing strategy, looking at issues from first principles. While some of its work is one-off, other work on issues such as education, health and home affairs tends to be ongoing.

Source: www.cabinetoffice.gov.uk/strategy/ (accessed 11 April 2008)

for long-term benefit. George W. Bush's attempt to push social security reform through in his second term of office is another example where, despite appealing to the public for support, the nature of government and special interests blocked the change (2007: 155–7). However, government also affords good resources. Both Glaab's (2007) and Lindholm and Prehn's (2007) analyses of Germany and Denmark suggested that strategy tended to become associated with, and carried out by, a small informal group – usually around the leader; indeed strategy worked only if they too were able to think strategically. Other obstacles to effective strategy include departmentalism, separation of policy and delivery, short-term distractions and politicians' lack of skill (Boaz and Solesbury 2007: 123).

Strategic thinking can come from outside or inside government. Strategies have to be realistic, flexible and pragmatic: politicians have to ensure they can get enough political support for any proposals, otherwise they have no chance of being implemented (Glaab 2007: 67, Lindholm and Prehn 2007: 23): see Box 8.7.

Positive influences that aid strategy (from Boaz and Solesbury 2007: 123, 132, and Glaab 2007: 100) include:

1 political stability;
2 stakeholder support and management;
3 leadership: support from politicians and senior bureaucrats to other staff engaged in strategy; and, in particular, actual leaders having time in the schedule to reflect about strategy;
4 seizing opportunities;
5 ability to learn;
6 maintenance of flexibility;
7 pursuing clear and coherent goals;
8 strategic spaces outside government apparatus to provide chance to think away from day-to-day political life;
9 organisational capability and links between strategic thinking and decision-making areas of government;
10 resistance of short-term problems.

The leader can play an important part in the success of a re-marketing. Fischer *et al.* (2007) conclude from their comparative study of strategy that leadership is important: the

---

Box 8.7 Core skills of a strategic thinker

1 Ability to shape and set the long-term vision and direction for the department, taking into account both wider government priorities and delivery systems.

2 Ability to identify tensions, set priorities and make trade-offs between different policy areas and over different time scales (short-, medium- and long-term).

3 Ability to present ministers and colleagues with key choices based on robust evidence and facilitate the strategic development process.

4 Ability to take a corporate perspective across government, proactively working as a team with Whitehall peers, influencing and shaping their strategic agendas and understanding key strategy and decision processes.

5 The ability to champion the role of strategic thinking in the organisation, working effectively with relevant internal and external experts.

Source: Boaz and Solesbury (2007: 121), quoting from
http://psg.civilservice.gov.uk/skill_list.asp

advantage with Tony Blair was a prime minister 'who thinks and acts in strategic terms ... encourages others to do the same', whereas the former German Chancellor Schröder was noted to have 'a situational and not entirely consistent leadership style that focused on immediate needs rather than the big picture', and this was 'detrimental to the development of a coherent strategy' (2007: 185).

Discussion point 8.4

Why is strategy both important and difficult in government? Discuss examples of good and bad strategy in government.

Redesigning and rebranding for future elections

One of the biggest challenges for a party or politician once in government is to redesign their product mid-term for the next election. Being in office presents new constraints: politicians can't rebrand, redesign, restrategise from new, as there is a recent history that the public, opposition and media will seize upon if they decide to change direction suddenly for no good reason. Yet freshness is important, otherwise people lose the need to vote for a politician again. It remains harder because of all the challenges previously discussed, particularly the attitude of the leader in power, who can become immune to, or ignore, bad poll results and not want to do anything to change them.

One recent case bucked this trend, however, providing an example of how to regain a market-orientation in power through a rebranding exercise. In 2004, the market relations company Promise (www.promisecorp.com) was asked to consider the problem of Labour's and Blair's declining public support, as well as potential threats from the Conservative opposition. Promise's analysis connected brand positioning and strength with the Lees-Marshment (2001) product-, sales- and market-oriented party, acknowledging the success of UK Labour in becoming a MOP with the launching of a new brand when Clause IV of the party constitution was reformed. However, given the brand had declined, they wanted to understand the negatives more effectively and create a way to wash them away, to enable a rebuilding of the brand (Promise 2005 and Scammell 2008). For a summary from Promise see Box 8.8.

This case shows the value of research and good advice, and the impact they can make on a party and leader's fortunes. The research utilised by Promise used various techniques to enable people to express deeply held feelings from which to then reconstruct solutions for Labour. They used 'two-chair work', where one of the people in a chair was a voter, and the other one played Mr Blair.

In the first role-play, the participants played Blair as voters currently saw him:

> I'm afraid you've only got part of the picture. From where I sit the war in Iraq was crucial to the cause of world peace. But I understand that it's difficult to see the whole thing for you. You put me in charge and I just do what I think to be the right thing. I am sure that history will prove us right in the end.

In the second, however, participants played Blair as they'd like him to be, where 'he' acknowledged their discontent and was more humble:

Box 8.8 Reconnecting New Labour and the public

With Promise's help, Tony Blair and New Labour set a political precedent by winning the General Election for a historic third time. In the months running up to the election, Promise helped turn a declining party into a winning force. A powerful reconnection strategy was launched which increased the female vote by 8 per cent and provided new insights into future election strategies. Having won the elections, Mr Blair said outside Number 10 'I have listened and I have learned. And I have a very clear idea of what the British people now expect from this government for a third term.' This opening sentence was inspired and drawn directly from the reconnection strategy devised by Promise.

The problem

Promise identified the disconnect between the public and the Labour Party as the underlying reason why they faced such animosity from voters . . . the public's idealisation of Mr Blair in 1997 turned into a negative view by 2005, with female voters characterising this broken relationship as a 'damaged love' affair. Also, Britain was faced with a new climate of insecurity . . . the New Labour brand, personified by Tony Blair, had lost its attraction for the British Public. The solution we proposed was the 'reconnection' strategy.

Our strategy

Having presented these ideas to the party, they were intrigued with the idea of how to reconnect Tony Blair with the electorate and saw this as the key challenge. The reconnection strategy included:

- reconnecting Tony Blair to the electorate;
- a strategy to deal with Tory competition;
- enhancing the New Labour brand.

Our solution

. . . The prime minister carried out the reconnection strategy by facing difficult discussions with live audiences on Channel 5 and, most notably, BBC's *Question Time*. Mr Blair was undoubtedly worried, perplexed and even shocked by these encounters, but he did not lose his temper, demolish or humiliate his critics. He endured the trials of reconnecting with people who had a tarnished opinion of him right up until polling day, using local radio phone-ins as a means of reconnecting with the regions.

Source: www.promisecorp.com/casestudies/pr_case_labour.pdf (accessed 19 March 2008)

I understand your feelings and I realise that there are many who do not agree with me over Iraq. I realised this as I listened to more and more people over the past months. I still believe on balance that we did the right thing, though I have been shocked to appreciate the depth of frustration among those who disagree with me. I solemnly promise to spend more time at home in contact with our own people and to debate these issues more seriously before we launch on such an endeavour again.

There is no difference in policy position in either case. But the difference to role-playing voters was significant. This laid the foundations for the reconnection or 'masochism strategy', which played a significant part in rehabilitating Blair's overall image and limiting the damage it had done to the Labour brand. The strategy was broadly successful. As Scammell (2008) observed, Labour improved its opinion poll rating over the campaign, increasing its leads over the Conservatives as the best party to deal with the issues of the economy, health and education, and Blair improved his advantage over the opposition leader Michael Howard.

This example shows there is the potential to rebrand in government, as long as politicians and their advisors continue to monitor the brand before it is too late and are prepared to listen to good strategic suggestions when they receive it – and that advice can suggest new ways to deal with old issues, such as getting out of touch. It also shows the varying fortunes of market-orientation and positive branding over time. Promise classified the three periods of the electorate's relationship with the prime minister in 1997, 2001 and 2005 in Figure 8 of their own report (Promise 2005); and these can also be linked to the Lees-Marshment POP/SOP/MOP classifications:

- 1997: 'A new dawn': Blair is eager to please, permeable; a Young Tony (market-driven as opposed to market-oriented).
- 2001: 'I know best': Blair is about conviction and is impermeable; a Tough Tony (product-oriented).
- 2005: 'Reconnection and integration': Blair attempted to have both conviction and reflection; a Mature Tony (market-oriented – comprehensively?).

Case study 8.4 discusses another question for the UK Labour Party, and indeed all parties that change leader while in power: how to reformulate the brand under the new leader, Gordon Brown, who succeeded Blair in 2007. It is often difficult for new leaders to rebrand after a particularly strong leader has gone before them, without the benefit of a period in opposition in which to rebuild. In the US, vice presidents don't always follow two-term presidents because of this, because their predecessor constrains them.

Resource-based view

Parties in government also need to maintain their party organisation outside the formal structures of power. Lynch *et al.* (2006) argue that a resource-based view (RBV) suggests parties need to maintain strong resources, such as leadership, staff, supporters, organisation, knowledge and management. If a party develops superior performance on these aspects over the long term, it can help it outperform rivals – and so ensure it has a strong basis from which to strategise and secure re-election. Parties in government often neglect their party organisation, focusing too much on daily government business, and then turn to consider re-election only to find their party organisation is in tatters. Lynch *et al.* (2006: 88) conclude that 'long-term political success requires years of resource investment by political parties . . . so that they become superior to those of their rivals.' Wiser governments will ensure the party is considered a valuable resource that can help them stay in power.

Discussion point 8.5

What does the UK Blair government case show about maintaining a responsive, market-oriented brand in power, and what difficulties and solutions does Case study 8.4 suggest for new leaders who take up office while their party is in power?

Market intelligence as consultation

In government, market intelligence can be conducted in the form of public consultation. There are many resources for this. UK Labour's Big Conversation was one example of this, but there are others that are issue- or policy-focused and they occur at all levels of government – federal, national, devolved, state, province and local. In 2008, Kevin Rudd's new Labour federal government in Australia held a 2020 summit: see Box 8.9. This was another means of gaining ideas about future product development.

Box 8.9 The Australian 2008–20 summit

The prime minister of Australia, Kevin Rudd, convened an Australia 2020 summit at Parliament House on 19 and 20 April to help shape a long-term strategy for the nation's future.

The summit brought together some of the best and brightest brains from across the country to tackle the long-term challenges confronting Australia's future – challenges that require long-term responses from the nation beyond the usual three-year electoral cycle.

To do this, the government brought together more than a thousand leading Australians to the national parliament to debate and develop long-term options for the nation across ten critical areas:

1   The productivity agenda – education, skills, training, science and innovation.
2   The future of the Australian economy.
3   Population, sustainability, climate change and water.
4   Future directions for rural industries and rural communities.
5   A long-term national health strategy – including the challenges of preventative health, workforce planning and the ageing population.
6   Strengthening communities, supporting families and social inclusion.
7   Options for the future of Aboriginal and Torres Strait Islanders.
8   Towards a creative Australia: the future of the arts, film and design.
9   The future of Australian governance: renewed democracy, a more open government (including the role of the media), the structure of the Federation and the rights and responsibilities of citizens.
10 Australia's future security and prosperity in a rapidly changing region and world.

Participants were selected by a ten-member non-government steering committee. The summit was co-chaired by the prime minister and Professor Glyn Davis, Vice Chancellor of the University of Melbourne.

This steering committee selected up to 100 participants in each of the summit areas to attend in a voluntary capacity. The participants were drawn from business, academia, community and industrial organisations and the media and included a number of individual eminent Australians. Summit participants were invited in their own right, rather than as institutional representatives from any particular organisation. Each of the ten summit areas was co-chaired by a federal government minister and a member of the steering committee.

The summit had the following objectives:

•   to harness the best ideas across the nation;
•   to apply those ideas to the ten core challenges that the government had identified for Australia – to secure our long-term future through to 2020;
•   to provide a forum for free and open public debate in which there are no predetermined right or wrong answers;
•   for each of the summit's ten areas, to produce, following the summit, options for consideration by government;

- for the government to produce a public response to these option papers by the end of 2008, with a view to shaping the nation's long-term direction from 2009 and beyond.

In providing this response, the government may accept some options and reject others – but will provide its reasons for embracing its course of action for the future. The government has no interest in a talkfest. The government's interest is in harnessing and harvesting ideas from the community that are capable of being shaped into concrete policy actions.

Government, irrespective of its political persuasion, does not have a monopoly on policy wisdom. To thrive and prosper in the future we need to draw on the range of talents, ideas and energy from across the Australian community. For too long Australian policymaking has been focused on short-term outcomes dictated by the electoral cycle. If Australia is effectively to confront the challenges of the future, we need to develop an agreed national direction that looks at the next ten years and beyond. For these reasons, the government also invited the leader of the federal opposition to participate in the summit, together with state premiers, chief ministers and their opposition counterparts.

In addition to those participating in the summit, all Australians were invited to make submissions on each of the ten future challenges. These were submitted to the Department of Prime Minister and Cabinet, which acts as the secretariat for the summit. The Rudd government believes Australians, whatever their political views, can come together to build a modern Australia capable of meeting the challenges of the twenty-first century.

Source: www.australia2020.gov.au/about/index.cfm (accessed 13 May 2008)

Government consultation can also be seen as a form of participation and takes many different forms, with varying levels of effectiveness in terms of representation of the public, effect on government decision-making and so on. UK Prime Minister Gordon Brown launched a substantial programme of citizen juries in September 2007, with the aim of producing a more effective means of consultation: see Box 8.10.

Box 8.10 UK Prime Minister Gordon Brown on citizen juries, in September 2007

The old models of consultation need radical renewal . . . in the old days when politicians went round the country, the principal method of communication was political party speeches from platforms. More recently, this country opened up to question and answer sessions, where politicians went round the country offering to do questions and then answers, and often, I admit at least in my case, the answers from the politicians were far longer than the questions. Now we need new ways and means to bring together citizens to discuss both specific challenges that need addressing, and concrete proposals that we can discuss for change . . .

So starting this week we will hold citizens juries round the country. The members of these juries will be chosen independently. Participants will be given facts and figures that are independently verified, they can look at real issues and solutions, just as a jury examines a case. And where these citizens juries are held the intention is to bring people together to explore where common ground exists . . . I also propose that representatives assembled from every constituency come together in a nationwide set of citizens juries held on one day. And these juries will look at a range of issues like crime and immigration, education, health, transport and public services . . . Citizens juries are not a substitute for representative democracy, they are an enrichment of it.

Source: www.pm.gov.uk/output/Page13008.asp (accessed 5 March 2008)

This relates to participation in politics and democratic political theory such as deliberative democracy, where consulting the public includes deliberating on the issues and will be discussed in the last chapter, on political marketing and democracy.

Discussion point 8.6

To what extent do the government intentions to consult the public, shown in Boxes 8.9 and 8.10, seem genuine? Do they manage expectations of consultation outcomes effectively?

Government marketing communications

Governments, like parties, need to engage in media management, which relates to political communication and can be carried out with or without regard to marketing. This section will discuss those aspects marketing can affect, and the differences that being in power creates.

Credibility and reputation management

Once a politician is in power, they are held more responsible for what happens and what goes wrong. Managing problems is therefore even more important, as they can damage the overall credibility image of a government, which relates to delivery and trust. In government, consultants work to maintain a leader's image, even where scandals and failures of policy occur. The same management of a politician's personal characteristics in a campaign for office can occur in power. Newman (1999: 88) observes how Bill Clinton's advisors dealt with a number of scandals during his presidency 'by carefully crafting an image of himself as leader in charge and almost above the rumour mongering of the media about his sex life'. He focused on what was important and, amazingly, he did not lose public support, despite continual criticism from the opposition.

Equally, governments and elected politicians also want to gain credit for any successes. Communication involves many of the aspects already discussed, such as delivery communication tools, rebranding a leader and refreshing the party. Wring (2005: 148–50) details how, once Blair got into government in 1997, his press secretary Alastair Campbell reorganised government communications, creating a new strategic communications unit in 1998 to co-ordinate media management from Downing Street across different government departments, alongside other units, such as media monitoring and research and information, which expanded the intelligence communication staff had to inform their work. The problem with such a strategy was that, in attempting to unify communication from government, it stifled debate and freedom within the parliamentary party, and the government earned a reputation for being more concerned with presentation than delivery (see also Scammell 1995, especially Chapter 5 on the Thatcher government, and Scammell 2003, on Blair).

Selling government policy

Another aspect to communication in government is to sell government policies, including unpopular initiatives that politicians decide are the right thing to do, once in power and after receiving more informed advice and information from the civil service and think tanks. Such initiatives can have profound effects on the way a country is run. It is not easy to ensure success, however, given the difficulties of changing public opinion, and also lobbying by interest groups or think tanks plays a greater role because there is both need and resources to provide more detailed policy legislation and implementation (see Harris 2001: 1151). In many ways they are like engineers who put the detail in to make a product work, after the initial research and design process stages; but in other cases they can block change.

One example of this is the UK Conservative government's attempt to sell privatisation of British Telecom and British Gas, previously public utilities, to raise capital and create greater efficiency in the 1980s. Allington *et al.* (1999: 637) discuss how understanding of the desires of the market was used to sell what was once a 'radical political idea' to both business and voters. Initially, the Telecom proposal faced opposition from the Labour Party, the unions and the media. Such a process, which required the city finding £4 billion for a single flotation, had also never been achieved before. In order to gain support, the following methods were used:

- communication aimed at the general public, many members of which had never been shareholders;
- appeals to individual needs and desires, showing how the public could gain from buying shares;
- emotive advertising, with positive depictions of the UK, including the white cliffs of Dover.

It was very successful, and all shares were sold easily. The campaign to privatise British Gas:

- built on the appeal to individuals with a slogan, 'Tell Sid';
- suggested the sale was good news for ordinary people, because they could share in ownership;
- encouraged people to spread the word themselves, depicting a range of people whispering 'Tell Sid' to each other.

Communication suited the market at the time, as it reflected the moods of the time, e.g. success through individual entrepreneurship and empowerment of the little guy against institutional organisations, and implied that share buying was a higher-class activity but one that was open to all.

This case suggests responsive marketing communications can be used to change opinion. Allington *et al.* (1999: 635–6) conclude that 'marketing, when employed in conjunction with other communication methods, has the power to change things and even to change the world order.' It could also be argued that privatisation met a need of the public: it generated significant resources to be used elsewhere, made previous public utilities more efficient and therefore enabled the public to pay less for better services, and so met demand rather than working against it, even if that demand was latent and not directly voiced. Additionally, there are many other cases where politicians can also choose to go against party and public opinion; aside from the Iraq war, there are other recent examples, such as Tony Blair implementing tuition fees in universities (see also Gelders and Van de Walle 2005). Some succeed, and some don't, depending on a range of factors.

Discussion point 8.7

Why do some attempts to sell initially unpopular policies work, while others don't?

Government advertising

Once parties get into power, they can employ government resources to pay for advertising. This is controversial, as it blurs the line between spending public money in the public interest and in the party's. Government advertising is where public money is used by the government to advertise something that is its policy, but it can be argued that it is in the public interest to know more about it, such as a new state welfare benefit or change in legislation, so they can take advantage of it. As the product being sold is created by the government, the argument follows that it benefits the party in power to have this communication, to remind voters of what they have done for them.

For example, in Australia, there are two main bodies responsible for government advertising: the ministerial committee on government communications (MCGC) and the government communications unit (GCU) (see www.aph.gov.au/library/pubs/rn/2003–04/04rn62.pdf for the amount spent, and www.aph.gov.au/library/pubs/rn/2003–04/04rn62.pdf for examples of government advertising campaigns in Australia 1991–2004). An information leaflet produced in June 2004 by a member of staff at the Politics and Public Administration Section, Information and Research Services in the Australia federal parliament in Canberra notes how,

> at one level, government advertising has an important democratic function. The public has a right to be informed about the programs which their taxes fund. Equally, governments have a right to establish a framework for delivering this information, subject to parliamentary scrutiny.

Box 8.11 outlines some of the issues around government advertising in Australia.

Another form of government advertising is social marketing, which aims to utilise government advertising to change behaviour in the interests of society (see, for example, Andreasen 1995, McKenzie-Mohr and Smith 1999, Kotler and Roberto 2002). This involves campaigns on issues such as drink-driving, smoking, child abuse and domestic violence, many of which can be explored online: see Box 8.12.

Understanding the consumer first is important to the success of campaigns. Anti-sunburn and skin cancer campaigns were launched in Australia and New Zealand to help combat skin cancer in the 1980s and beyond, with the slogan 'Slip! Slap! Slop!' pioneered by Victoria Cancer Council. The UK government in the United Kingdom devoloped a comprehensive health social marketing strategy in 2007. The aim is to achieve long-term behavioural change in target populations, which is not an easy task to achieve.

Another example of how social marketing can be utilised is illustrated in Canada's Aboriginal Wellness Campaign of 1995, which 'addressed tobacco, alcohol and drugs, HIV/AIDS, nutrition, substance abuse and mental health'. Through an extensive marketing campaign highlighted by a travelling exhibit, 'The Wellness Lodge', the strategy worked in partnership with aboriginal leaders and organisations from across Canada to provide culturally relevant and sensitive information in an interesting and interactive manner. Targeted to all First Nations, Métis and Inuit peoples in Canada, from toddlers to elders, the 1997 campaign placed a special emphasis on youth aged thirteen to twenty-five, continuing Health Canada's push towards preventative care. Initial feedback had shown that the campaign had reached a broad audience with encouraging results. The aboriginal youth video, *Balance,* created as part of the campaign, received an award from the American Indian Film Festival in 1997. The Wellness Lodge, through the work of many local health organisations, travelled to over twenty communities, spreading the message of the benefits

Box 8.11 Controversies and regulations for government advertising in Australia

This piece was written by Sally Young in 2005 about the state of government advertising at the time.

Big spending on government advertising is a major issue in Australia and, in recent weeks, there has been increased focus on it because of the Howard Government's controversial ads on its planned industrial relations changes. The full IR campaign has not yet started but it is estimated that, by its conclusion, it will have cost (taxpayers) at least $20 million and possibly up to $100 million. Because the advertising is coming out before the IR legislation has been passed (or even seen) by Parliament, Labor and the unions are challenging the authority of the campaign and have taken their complaint to the High Court in an attempt to try to stop the advertisements.

The IR ads are part of a much broader pattern though, through which governments increasingly use advertising as one of the key perks of incumbency to advantage them over opponents who cannot afford the same media access to get their message across.

In recent years, Australian governments at both state and federal level have dramatically increased their spending on advertising – particularly on television. The Federal Government now spends $100 million a year on advertising.

. . . The Government is sensitive because there are real concerns that it is misusing government advertising as pseudo-political advertising to shore up its re-election chances. You may recall the host of advertisements that the Government ran in the lead-up to last year's election when it advertised everything from 'strengthening Medicare' to superannuation, family tax benefits, apprenticeships, state funding, domestic violence and many other programs and policies. Now, the IR campaign has pushed the boundaries of government communication even further. Its timing, cost and content are controversial.

While communication between citizens and their governments is a crucial part of democratic discourse, unlike other traditional methods such as oratory and debate, advertising is an expensive method of communication and it only works one way – from the Government to citizens – without any opportunity for citizens to respond. Government advertising is also an incumbency benefit that, without adequate regulation, governments can misuse as a form of modern-day political propaganda. Now that the Federal Government is frequently listed as the top advertiser in Australia – outranking commercial giants such as Coles Myer, Holden and McDonald's – it is time to question how our Government chooses to communicate with us and how much that costs us (not only financially but also democratically in terms of values such as fairness, equality and competition).

Worldwide, the Australian Government is the fifth biggest spender on government ads. An extraordinary amount of public money is now being spent on advertising 'feel good' messages promoting the Government. This is possible because our government advertising regulatory system is almost non-existent. We have the weakest rules of any comparable country in the world. Unlike Canada, the United States, the United Kingdom and New Zealand, we have no guidelines or legislation prohibiting the misuse of government advertising for partisan purposes. It is vital that we adopt such guidelines and have a proper debate about government communication that looks at the issues rather than the personalities involved.

Source: Young (2005)

Box 8.12 Example social marketing campaigns to explore

There are many examples throughout the world, covered in academic textbooks but also online. Below is a sample list, which can be followed, or students can create their own with a general search.

- www.hc-sc.gc.ca/ahc-asc/activit/marketsoc/socmar-hcsc/experience_e.html
- www.toolsofchange.com/ (Canada): proven methods for promoting health and environmental citizenship.
- www.social-marketing.org/success/cs-hpylori.html (nationwide, USA): how we lost our stomach pains and regained our love for chilli.
- www.social-marketing.org/success/cs-clickit.html (State of North Carolina, USA): why North Carolina has one of the highest seat belt usage rates in the US.
- www.social-marketing.org/success/cs-massmedia.html (Honduras): Honduran mothers are mixing salt, water and sugar to fight dehydration – their leading cause of infant mortality.
- www.social-marketing.org/success/cs-ndephispanic.html (Nationwide, USA): switching languages reversed trends and increased knowledge about diabetes in Hispanic and Latino/a America.
- www.social-marketing.org/success/cs-peachcare.html (State of Georgia, USA): Georgia guarantees affordable health care for the children of working parents, and parents know about it.
- www.wwu.edu/chw/preventionandwellness/grantpages/socialmarketing.htm
- www.social-marketing.org/success/cs-stopaids.html (Switzerland): the world's longest running HIV/AIDS prevention programme succeeds by working to change both private behaviour and public attitudes.

of healthy lifestyle choices (www.hc-sc.gc.ca/ahc-asc/activit/marketsoc/socmar-hcsc/experience_e.html#Advertising, accessed 10 April 2008). Other, more recent high-profile campaigns with long-term goals include the celebrity chef campaigns to promote healthy eating at schools for children (see www.guardian.co.uk/business/2006/jun/27/supermarkets.health, for example).

Discussion point 8.7

How effective is government advertising?

When to lead, when to follow: the dilemmas facing leaders in power

The final aspect of marketing in government is that the dilemma of when to lead or when to follow public opinion becomes even more acute, faced with crisis, unexpected events and also more information than is available before election. Henneberg (2006a,b) discussed this, considering how there are two main dimensions political elites can choose from (2006a: 17):

- **They can try to lead**, knowing their political product is essentially right, so marketing, if used, is only to help fulfil a certain mission and involves convincing others of the benefits of a proposal or policy.
- **They can try to follow**, so marketing is used to guess, anticipate or analyse the demands of the market or a particular segment and create a political product that integrates market demands; so marketing is used to develop the actual political offering.

It is easier for politicians to respond to the market hypothetically when in opposition, but much harder when they are actually in power. Government involves hard choices, including yes or no decisions. Arguably, no model can state specifically when political leaders should lead against opinion and when they should heed it. Practitioner perspective 8.5, on the need for leadership in relation to market intelligence, shows these concerns.

The realities of government and the desire for political principle and achieving change mean that marketing also involves utilising communication approaches to try to present a problematic argument in the best light possible. Nevertheless, as suggested by Lees-Marshment's (2001) MOP concept, which includes product adjustment, leading and following can happen within the same government; leaders are not unidimensional. Similarly, Henneberg (2006a: 19) talks of relationship building, arguing that the relationship builder both leads and follows and develops the product, including 'brand heritage', such as ideology and belief.

Nonetheless, marketing does not remove the problem of leaders having to take decisions on key and controversial issues to which market demand may be opposed, or even unclear. Goot (2007: 48) notes how, in the US, Australia and the UK, public opinion, in terms of

---

Practitioner perspective 8.5

It may be that contract democracy and spin control have gone too far. We may well be facing a change in direction, where the people are getting tired of politicians aligning their policies with opinion polls. All political strategies are open to over-use and risk becoming caricatures of themselves. And there is little respect for politicians who simply tell people what they want to hear. Voters expect politicians to lead the field and show the way.

(Mogens Lykketoft, Minister of foreign affairs and minister of finance in the Danish Nyrup government and strategist, interviewed and quoted in Lindholm and Prehn 2007: 56)

I'm not a different human being from what I was ten years ago, but I'm a different type of politician and in the last few years I've tried to do what I really think is right, take difficult decisions on behalf of the country, that I think are in the country's long-term interests.

(Tony Blair, UK prime minister 1997–2007, *BBC Politics Show*, 15 April 2007)

I think there is a false demand for a strong leader who makes an impact and draws a line. If a leader of this kind did actually appear and said, in the manner of Moses coming down from the mountain ... 'we have thought about it, no we're going to tell you about it, and from tomorrow onwards, this is how things are going to be' the Danish people would simply refuse to have any part in it. The art is to lead the flock, but not to move so far ahead that you disappear from sight, nor disappear in it.

(Lars Lokke Rasmussen, minister of domestic affairs and health for the Fogh Government, interviewed and quoted by Lindholm and Prehn 2007: 56)

satisfaction with the leaders' (Bush, Howard and Blair) performance, grew at the beginning of the Iraq war. ICM polls in the UK saw Blair's satisfaction rating rise from 38 per cent in mid-March 2002, just after the war started, to 49 per cent in mid-April, shortly before Bush declared the mission had ended and the war was won. Howard's satisfaction rating in Newspoll figures rose from 48 to 56 per cent. Bush's satisfaction ratings, according to Gallup, stayed between 71 and 74 per cent during the war. Subsequently, however, the standing of all leaders declined, and Goot's (2007) analysis suggests that this started in the UK before accusations of the sexing-up of intelligence reports – the problem was 'the electorate's frustration, by the middle of 2003, with the progress of the war'. Changes in opinion after a decision to go to war are too late; leaders cannot just pull out once the public change its mind, however. This is the problem with government by opinion poll. This also leads us into issues of democracy, which will be discussed in the final chapter of the textbook.

Debate 8.1

Proposition: Being responsive to voter opinion when in opposition is fine, but, once in power, politicians have to decide what is right according to the information they get in government.

Summary

Marketing in government raises all of the issues of marketing in opposition, but with further complications and also new issues to consider. The main difference is the need to deliver and be seen to deliver, but there are also many forces that work against maintaining a market-orientation. If they want to be re-elected, politicians and parties have to try to rebrand and redevelop their product, which is also less straightforward than in opposition. Communication also varies once in power, as more crises emerge, but at the same time there are other resources at a government's disposal that those in opposition do not have. Such issues affect all governments around the world. The next chapter will look at how political marketing has been transferred across different countries.

ASSESSED WORK

Essays

1　'Marketing in government is a very different exercise to marketing in opposition.' To what extent is this statement true?
2　What challenges do politicians and parties face once elected in trying to deliver and to satisfy consumers they have delivered, and what tools can they use to succeed?
3　Critically discuss whether it is inevitable that political parties, despite becoming market-oriented to win an election, will in government eventually lose touch, fail to deliver and slip back into a sales-orientation.
4　'Political marketing aims to satisfy voters through delivery of a market-oriented product.' Discuss the extent to which recent empirical examples of parties in government support or contradict this statement.
5　Product redevelopment and rebranding are difficult in power. What could governments do to make this process more effective?

Applied

1   Design your own pledge card, either for if you were running for power now, or for a candidate or party you know. Justify which policies you choose to focus on, the positions and the nature of the wording.

2   Develop a political consultant's plan to (a) keep your leader in touch once they are in government, or (b) communicate delivery handling good and bad news. Consider factors such as the relationship between you and the leader, psychology, realities and pressures of the daily grind/being in office, and how the public react to leaders and delivery.

3   Carry out a search for local politicians' communication in your own country to identify any attempt to issue annual reports and critically evaluate the effectiveness of such reports. (If there is none, try examples as of April 2008 such as: www.edwarddavey. co.uk/report99.htm; www.greghands.com/NewFiles/ar06.pdf; www.timloughton.com/ timloughton_pdf/tim_loughton_annual_report_2006.pdf; www.harrietharman.org/fileadmin/ file_downloads/Annual_Report_2003-03.pdf; www.alan-whitehead.org.uk/reports/08march. html; www.stevewebb.org.uk/SW%20Report%20April%202008.pdf; www.markoaten. com/files/annual-report; www.jeremywright.co.uk/files/2007report.pdf; www.davidlammy. co.uk/sitedata/Misc/Annual-Report2007.pdf; http://walberg.house.gov/UploadedFiles/ Walberg2007AnnualReport.pdf; www.dextermaine.org/townreport/2003/senatorreport. html; and www.robhogg.org/content.asp?ID=1932&I=6226).

4   (*For marketing students*) Read literature on the factors that affect the maintaining of a market orientation in business, and cases where, losing standing, successful businesses have then lost their market share and customer base. What can we learn from this that we can apply to politics, to advise government and politicians in power?

5   Research different examples of strategy, whether in the UK or other countries. Evaluate their effectiveness.

6   Explore social marketing campaigns and evaluate the extent to which they follow marketing guidelines.

Case study 8.1 Unpredictable influences threaten government re-election: the effect of situational factors on the results of recent elections in Turkey   *Umit Alniacik*

Turkish democracy is still in progress; it has been interrupted by military interventions several times, the most recent of which took place in 1980, before the military voluntarily handed back the administration to the civilians. However, today, political parties in Turkey conduct research to find out the wants, needs and expectations of voters; to try to develop candidates and programmes that are best fitted to voters' wills; and to utilise political communication to promote themselves. Turkey's market has one key distinction: the party leader is the most important factor in the political product in Turkey, because it influences voting behaviour more than any others. When asked which party they will vote for, Turkish voters usually answer with the name of the party leader. Leaders themselves are affected by uncontrollable situational factors, which have affected the outcome and presented challenges for the governing party. The rest of the case study explores these situational factors.

1999 General elections influenced by 'soft' military intervention and a terrorist

In 1999, the coalition government of Necmettin Erbakan's Islamist Welfare Party (Refah Partisi – RP) and Tansu Ciller's True Path Party (Dogru Yol Partisi – DYP) had to resign because of the effects of a soft military intervention by the National Security Council (NSC) in a memorandum in February 1997 that had asked the government to stop its anti-laic and anti-democratic activities, and to follow the constitution and laws of the country.

First, Tansu Ciller's DYP resigned from the coalition, and the RP–DYP government collapsed. In 1998, Mesut Yilmaz's ANAP formed a coalition government with Husamettin Cindoruk's Democratic Turkey Party (Demokrat Turkiye Partisi – DTP) and Ecevit's DSP, along with the support of CHP. However, owing to malpractices, big scandals and political corruption, CHP withdrew its support from the coalition, and the government fell again. Just before the elections of 1999, Ecevit's DSP formed an interim minority government with the support of DYP and ANAP.

Despite managing to reform government amid very turbulent political times, another non-political event affected electoral fortunes. Turkey's most wanted terrorist Abdullah Ocalan, the head of the terrorist organisation PKK, was suddenly captured in Kenya under the Ecevit rule. Ecevit was presented as a 'victorious commander' by the media. This boosted Ecevit's DSP's support, and it received 22.1 per cent, while Devlet Bahceli's MHP recieved 17.9 per cent of the votes in 1999 parliamentary elections.

It is widely accepted that the main factor in Ecevit's political victory was arresting the head of the terrorists, Abdullah Ocalan, months before the election, while still prime minister of the minority government. MHP doubly benefited from the situation as it was seen as the most reasonable alternative for the right-wing (and extreme religious) voters after the soft military intervention process on 28 February. Religious–traditional constituencies saw MHP as the only alternative that could normalise the political process.

2002 General elections: the impact of economic crisis and the leader's health

Until 2002, Bulent Ecevit remained prime minister of the coalition government made up of the DSP, MHP and ANAP. However, in the elections on 3 November, no member of the coalition could pass the national threshold of 10 per cent to be able to gain power in the parliament. They were beaten by Recep Tayip Erdogan's Justice and Development Party (Adalet ve Kalkinma Partisi – AKP), which had only been established in 2001 by Erdogan and a group of 'reformist–Islamists' who broke off from the more traditional Islamist RP. AKP won a landslide victory in the 2002 elections with 34 per cent support.

The most important reason for the coalition losing power was the pressure of continuing deep economical crisis since 2001 and the prime minister's sudden health problems in the first half of 2002. AKP benefited from a strong protest vote sparked by a serious economic crisis that left about one million unemployed: insolvent craftsmen crumbled their cash registers in front of the prime minister's office. The 76-year-old Prime Minister Ecevit's deteriorating health was another unexpected issue: he was hospitalised twice and had to rest at home for weeks in May 2002. This increased fears over the fragile coalition government's future and damaged the financial markets.

Ecevit defied a growing chorus (including DSP legislators) of demands that he step down because of his poor health, but more than forty DSP legislators resigned, and the government was forced to schedule early elections for November. Erdogan's AKP won a parliamentary majority that enabled it to form a single-party government in Turkey for the first time in fifteen years, showing how unpredictable factors such as a leader's ill health can change electoral fortunes.

2007 General elections and military e-memorandum

Between 2002 and 2007, Erdogan's AKP enjoyed a strong position, achieving success in delivery on the economy. Erdogan nominated Foreign Minister and Deputy Prime Minister

Abdullah Gul as a candidate for the presidential elections in May 2007, in a bid to run both the government and the presidency. Erdogan's election campaign mainly focused on his government's impressive economic achievements when compared with the crisis situation five years ago.

However, the prospect of having an Islamist party ruling both the government and the presidency alarmed secularist establishments, and millions of Turks took to the streets in mass demonstrations against the AKP. Furthermore, first the army and then the law interfered in response to this. The army issued a statement that said:

> The Turkish Armed Forces maintain their sound determination to carry out their duties stemming from laws to protect the unchangeable characteristics of the Republic of Turkey. Their loyalty to this determination is absolute.

This was interpreted as a veiled warning that the Turkish Armed Forces stood ready to intercede in politics – military e-intervention. The country's highest court then decided that a minimum of two-thirds of the plenum (367 parliamentarians) needed to participate in the presidential elections, thus trying to force the political parties to agree on a compromise candidate.

However, Erdogan was able to regain control by being both stubborn and gaining public support overall, but it was a risky strategy. The AKP reacted by refusing to agree on a compromise candidate. Baykal's CHP boycotted the presidential election. Thus, 367 votes could not be achieved, and Gul's election was blocked. AKP called the parliamentary elections early because of this. Fortunately, AKP won a landslide victory and managed to gain 46.7 per cent of votes at the parliamentary elections on 22 July 2007, allowing it to form a single-party government, and the public authorised AKP to elect the president, too. AKP renominated Abdullah Gul for the presidency on 13 August 2007. Gul was elected as the eleventh president of the Turkish Republic on 28 August 2007.

Lessons for political marketing

Turkish government leaders faced a number of unexpected issues that influenced election outcomes. Among typical factors such as ideological concerns, commitment to the party and voter perception of the party leader, the last three general elections in Turkey revealed how unexpected developments that occur close to the elections could affect voter behaviour. Each time, the government and leaders have changed as a result. This presents a challenge for governing parties, as it is difficult to formulate and stick to an effective strategy when such events can change their standing in the political marketing. Despite the best research, it would be difficult to predict such factors that may affect the market, and elites then have to take sometimes risky decisions about how to respond.

Case study 8.2 Delivering in Greece: a threat or an opportunity for democracy?   *Iordanis Kotzaivazoglou and Yorgos Zotos*

One of the basic characteristics of politics in Greece today is the extensive use of political marketing. The phenomenon is particularly obvious – in both parties of government – during the pre-election period, although it is being used more and more extensively in governing as well. The major parties use a variety of marketing techniques. They flood the media with advertising messages, many of them negative. They strive systematically for maximum publicity. They organise rallies and meetings. They focus on the short-term expectations of the electorate and the front-page issues in the media. They aim to polarise and fanaticise. They present themselves as saviours, accusing their opponents of being incapable of governing, and try to outbid one another in promises. Their sole object is to win votes and gain or retain power. The pre-election period often seems to be an unending spiral of unrealistic pledges, while the hidden agendas make their appearance after the fact.

Greece's parties of government display more of the characteristics of the sales-oriented party than the market-oriented party (Lees-Marshment 2001). Their products are designed according to market intelligence, but they bombard the electorate with negative or alarmist messages in order to persuade voters to vote for them. Delivery fails to match promise, resulting in a high degree of voter dissatisfaction (Kotzaivazoglou and Zotos 2008).

Political marketing in Greece is basically a means of vote chasing. Its mission is confined to selling the political product, usually with no concern for ethics, the breach of faith with the voter or the day after the election.

Consequences

The way political marketing is implemented has a number of side effects for the practice of politics in the country. 'Communication logic' has superseded 'political logic' (Samaras 2003). Much of politics is now conducted by non-politicians, the spin doctors whose decisions are usually based more on impression making and communicational rather than political effectiveness.

The parties of government in Greece today have largely 'de-ideologized' (Loulis 1999: 20) or even 'depoliticized' themselves (Spourdalakis 2003: 55). They have transformed themselves from vehicles of ideology and political thinking into what Mancini has called 'communication machines' (1999: 243). Their 'policies' are general, middle-ground, fuzzy, sound-good evocations of a better future, designed to appeal to the greatest possible number, while negativism, scare-mongering, sloganeering and playing on the emotions frequently outweigh substance and dialogue.

Candidate lists are increasingly loaded with representatives of the country's 'recreational elite': athletes, actors, singers, socialites, etc. The criterion for media exposure is usually how well the candidate 'sells'. A good-looking politician is assured of publicity; the less telegenic are at a distinct disadvantage.

Campaign costs continue to mount. Those without the funds to match are usually doomed from the start. Cross-linkage between political entities and the media is a fact of contemporary government (Frangonikolopoulos 2005, Kontogiorgis 2005). Access to the media is essential: those without the appropriate media connections have little chance of success.

The result: a political system in crisis

The combination of the situation described above and the inability of the parties to govern effectively and to meet the demands of contemporary society has rendered the system dysfunctional, thus constituting a serious threat to the democratic system itself. Greek society needs and demands changes, which its political agents promise but do not implement, fearing the reaction of 'powerful minorities' and the 'political cost'. The increasing depreciation of political entities and politics in general translates into a public disgust for politics and poor turnouts at the elections (Kotzaivazoglou and Zotos 2008).

Marketing practices cannot be held entirely to blame for this situation. There are many factors involved, but in any case the problem is more with the way in which the marketing is done than with marketing itself. Other factors include contemporary social structures and values in Greece, which are in crisis, the dominance of commercial television, which has imposed a culture of image, spectacle and infotainment, the inability of the parties of government to meet today's demands, and the attitude of voters, who disregard important issues and everything beyond the boundaries of their own little world, or who act irresponsibly.

Possible approaches to a solution

The situation is dismal, and all those involved – politicians and voters, media and communications experts – bear a share of the blame. It is not, however, irremediable, but all players must assume their responsibilities.

Citizens must become more active, more informed about political affairs and less blinkered to matters outside their own concerns. Communications consultants must resist pressures for short-term results and unethical attitudes, and act in a way that combines impact with substance.

The media must practise responsible journalism. The legal framework in which they operate also needs to be clarified, and a clear distinction made between the roles of the media and those of the politicians, to prevent interlocking interests.

Finally, the parties of government, which bear the lion's share of responsibility, must stop vote chasing. Their inability to achieve real and long-term solutions to contemporary problems drives voters into the arms of the smaller parties, and may, in the future, result in new political formations. The parties of government have a duty to concern themselves more with the public interest and to forge specific ideologies and a substantive political discourse that correspond to the needs of today's Greek society.

Adoption of the marketing concept by all political entities can help achieve this. Politicians and political bodies must listen to the voters and act in a way that will satisfy their needs and wishes. The model of the market-oriented party (Lees-Marshment 2001) is a complete guide for converting voter needs and wishes into political action. Implementing the marketing concept can enable political entities to achieve long-term voter satisfaction and their own electoral success. In so doing, it also promotes the democratic polity, which is based on the will of the sovereign people.

Sources and further reading

Daremas, George (2004). 'Politics and television'. *Greek Politics Journal* (in Greek).

Frangonikolopoulos, Christos (2005). 'The mass media in Greece today: thoughts and preoccupations'. In Christos Frangonikolopoulos (ed.), *Media, Society and Politics: Role and Function in Contemporary Greece*. Athens: Sideris, pp. 13–34 (in Greek).

Kontogiorgis, George (2005). 'Corruption and political system'. In Kleomenis Koutsoukis and Pantelis Sklias (eds), *Corruption and Scandals in Public Administration and Politics*. Athens: Sideris, pp. 131–43 (in Greek).

Kotzaivazoglou, Iordanis and Yorgos Zotos (2008). 'The level of marketing orientation of political parties in Greece'. In Jennifer Lees-Marshment, Jesper Strömbäck and Chris Rudd (eds), *Global Political Marketing*. London: Palgrave.

Lees-Marshment, Jennifer (2001). 'The marriage of politics and marketing'. *Political Studies* 49(4): 692–713.

Loulis, Ioannis (1999). *Triangulation. Dominant Ideas and Political Dynamics in our Era*. Athens: Sideris (in Greek).

Mancini, Paolo (1999). 'New frontiers in political professionalism'. *Political Communication*, 16(3): 231–45.

Samaras, Athanassios (2003). *Televised Political Advertisement: A Qualitative Research on Greece*. Athens: Institute of Broadcast Media (in Greek).

Spourdalakis, Michael (2003). 'The partisan phenomenon: development and circumstance'. In Dimitrios Tsatsos and Xenofon Kontiadis (eds), *The Future of Political Parties*. Athens: Papazisis, pp. 39–63 (in Greek).

Case study 8.3 When politics becomes contractual: a case from Denmark   *Jens Jonatan Steen*

Political marketing is a fairly unknown term in Danish national politics. Traditionally, politicians had been reluctant to accept that the voters have become more critical and less recipient to political authority: the Liberal Party, *Venstre,* still had a strong ideological base, while the Social Democrats still believed in a 'natural' right to govern. However, political ideology has declined gradually since the Conservative Prime Minister Poul Schlüter in the eighties declared 'that all ideology was rubbish', and, in the 1990s, Social Democratic governments started to hire professional advisors and use opinion polls more deliberately.

The Social Democrat party and the then prime minister, Poul Nyrup Rasmussen, followed public opinion and issued a guarantee that meant that the early-retirement scheme would not be changed during his administration. This promise was broken, with the notorious reform package 'Pinsepakken' from 1998. As stated by a political commentator: 'The punishment came fast and hard; the voters ran away. Nyrup had to learn this the rough way' (Pittelkow 1998). After the breach of the pledge, which had been both advertised in national media and printed as an official guarantee, the government lost support: the Social Democrats received their lowest poll rating since 1903.

The Liberals took advantage of the loss of trust in the Social Democrats and began to focus more on delivery. The prime minister, Anders Fogh Rasmussen, argued that the party needed to 'stop talking about great and incomprehensible structural reforms and instead focus on carrying through straight political proposals, that the public are given time to comprehend.' (Larsen 2000: 160). The Liberal Party wanted to change the way modern politics was conducted, and the leader took inspiration from the UK 1997 Labour victory. Like the British Labour Party, the Danish Liberal Party was not trusted by the voters in the early 1990s. They still feared that the Liberals were liable to experiment with the basic elements of their personal welfare. This had to be changed in order to win the next general election.

The basic strategy was openly and undisguisedly borrowed from Phillip Gould and Tony Blair. Modern politics was now to be regarded as more of a contract that resembled the basic social contract of Thomas Hobbes. The aim is that the political contract will create trust and stability in a given system. The prime minister took this lesson very seriously and interpreted the British 1997 election as follows:

> During the last election Tony Blair only put out few and concrete pledges and he kept them down to the last resort. This is quite crucial. The conditions for modern politics are changing dramatically these years. Politicians who do not keep their promises are judged severely by the voters. And that is a position in which I do not wish to place myself.
>
> (Termansen 1999)

The answer to this challenge was the creation of a new *partnership with the people*. The strategy was to use a clear-cut contract to put up the concrete promises that a Liberal government would be carrying through, if the voters decided to give them the chance to run the government in 2001. While the Social Democratic Party was running on 100 different proposals, the Liberals had tuned in on six specific pledges, which they presented under trust-increasing slogans such as 'You know, we will make it happen':

1   1.5 mia. dkr extra to hospitals;
2   500 mio. dkr. extra for homecare;
3   one-year flexible maternity leave;

4   a firm and fair immigration policy;

5   a consequential judicial policy;

6   tax freeze.

The pledges followed recommendations by Phillip Gould (1998), who insisted that political promises should be small, concrete, tested and costed.

The strategy was successful in the 2001 election, where the Liberal Party and their supporters won 54.6 per cent of the vote. More interesting than the election result in itself was a survey from the Danish analysis institute, IFKA, which asked voters about their perceived trust of their politicians over a period of more than thirty years. The survey showed the highest score ever for the Liberal government of Anders Fogh Rasmussen, who gained full confidence from 54 per cent of all voters, whereas the former Social Democratic government never scored higher than 34 per cent during its nine years in government (IFKA 2005).

The strategy of contractual politics was used again in 2005, and when the Liberal government regained power again in 2007, the contractual politics played a less dominant role. But the strategy has been successful in reshaping Danish politics. The former party secretary and current minister of employment, the mastermind behind the contractual politics, described the purpose as follows:

> The contractual politics was a confrontation with the ordinary way of conducting politics. It had previously been an ideal that political parties during a campaign constrained themselves to as little as possible in order to maximize their freedom of action after the election. We had to face this way of thinking and restore the trust in the political system. There are some issues that we commit ourselves to and some issues you can measure us on.
>
> (Interview with Claus Hjorth Frederiksen 2008).

Confidence in politicians

	Don't know (%)	Very low (%)	Low (%)	Neither (%)	High (%)	Very high (%)
1999	1.8	15.8	36.0	34.0	11.5	1.3
2005	4.5	9.6	24.8	43.5	16.1	1.4

Source: IFKA (2005)

According to the table, there is a strong indication that the strategy actually served its original purpose and restored some of the population's trust in the political system. With 1,100 respondents in the survey, confidence in Danish politicians had improved 13 per cent from 1999 to 2005 (IFKA 2005: 15).

Lessons for political marketing

The recent development in Danish politics shows how the basic political philosophy is changing, and previous authority is losing its high ground. Political marketing is taking over, and the fight for trust has become vital to modern politicians, who have to demonstrate delivery on their pledges and stability in their politics in order to win the favour of the voters. Contractual politics played a less dominant role in the 2007 election, perhaps because, this time, the political contract was simply not needed. Even though the trust base can be tricky and easy to break, it seems that the Liberal government has constructed a unique position that allows them to 'kick back' and enjoy their level of trust (Lykkeberg 2007). Modern political marketing is changing the methods and principles of everyday politics. Contractual politics may be only the first of many methods to restore and rebuild trust in politicians. In the years to come, you will most likely see a growing emphasis on achievability and delivery. Politicians need to work harder – trust can no longer be taken for granted.

Sources and further reading

IFKA (2005). 'De professionelles omdømme 1999–2005'. Institut for Konjunktur-Analyse.

Gould, Phillip (1998). *The Unfinished Revolution – How the Modernisers Saved the Labour Party.* London: Little Brown.

Larsen, Thomas (2000). *I godt vejr og storm – samtaler med Anders Fogh Rasmussen*. Forlaget Gyldendal.

Lykkeberg, Rune (2007). 'Apropos: Det ligner et protestvalg'. *Dagbladet Information.*

Pittelkow, Ralf (1998). 'Store løfter dur ikke'. *Jyllandsposten.*

Termansen, Jesper (1999). 'Anders Fogh i lære hos Blair'. *Berlingske Tidende.*

Case study 8.4 After Blair . . . the challenge of communicating Brown's brand of Labour   *Jenny Lloyd*

The victory enjoyed by the Labour Party in the 1997 UK General Election was notable for more than just its landslide proportions. It marked a return to power of a political party that, for so many years, had been deemed unelectable. Exactly how and why the UK Labour Party staged such a successful return from the electoral wilderness are questions that have been widely discussed both in the media and in academe. From a marketing perspective, it is arguable that Labour's resurgence was not so much a successful repositioning exercise, as the creation of a new brand of Labour politics that offered a viable alternative to the sleaze and disharmony associated with the long-empowered Conservative Party. Its perceived newness was hugely advantageous to the party itself, as it was able to distance itself from the militants and economic mismanagement so often associated with the Labour governments of the 1970s and effectively move forward with a clean slate.

Yet, as any commercial marketer will agree, it is one thing to create a new brand, but quite another to gain acceptance in the market. Appearance is extremely important, and certainly the Labour leader Tony Blair looked quite different to the party leaders before him. Younger and more casual than the formal, statesman-like figures that the British electorate were used to, he appeared to have much in common with the 'average man in the street': a young family, a working wife, a love of modern music (indeed, he had played in a rock band at university) and support for Newcastle United Football Club. Appearance is an important differentiator in any branded sector, and politics is certainly no exception. It has long been acknowledged that voter choice can be influenced by a liking for, or an affinity to, the personal characteristics of a candidate. Therefore, an attractive and charismatic candidate is a highly persuasive brand asset.

Appearances aside, this 'new' Labour Party also differentiated itself in terms of its product. The clean slate proffered by its 'new' status allowed it to shed the weight of historical baggage and seek out the popular middle ground. It allayed the City's concerns over nationalisation with its modification of Clause IV of its Constitution and distanced itself from its traditional ties with the trade unions. Further, in contrast to its Conservative rivals, whose election platform focused upon European policy, taxation and allowances, 'New Labour' focused on issues that voters could relate to in their everyday lives: education, the National Health Service and the issue of young offenders. Finally, it promised transparency and an end to the 'sleaze' that had dogged the previous Conservative administration and tarnished the reputation of the political sector as a whole, offering hope that, in the words of their campaign anthem 'things can only get better'.

Ten years on, Tony Blair has retired from front-line British politics, and factors that originally made the recreation of the Labour brand so successful now present the greatest challenge to his successor, Gordon Brown. Both in terms of appearance and product, the clear difference that once existed between the Labour Party and the other political brands has disappeared. With the election of David Cameron and Nick Clegg as the respective leaders of the Conservative Party and the Liberal Democrats, the qualities of youth and vibrancy that so characterised the 'new' Labour brand are in danger of being eclipsed. Further, in terms of policy, all of the main parties now claim the middle ground, and voters struggle to distinguish between their respective political offerings.

Moreover, Gordon Brown is no longer in possession of a 'clean slate'. Over the course of Labour's ten years in office, while real progress has been claimed in a number of areas of key public concern, major world events, such as the terrorist attacks on New York, London and Madrid, the invasion of Iraq and the threat of international recession, questions have been also raised as to the transparency and competence of both individual ministers and, indeed, whole government departments. It is therefore the case that, while Brown is able to lay claim to some of the successes, his long-term position at the centre of government means he cannot convincingly lay blame at the door of the opposition for the failures, and any attempt to point the finger at Blair would only appear feeble.

In light of these circumstances, Gordon Brown is faced with the challenge of communicating his own 'brand' of Labour politics in a way that recaptures the imagination of the electorate and conveys a positive and distinctive position in the political market. The first step should be the effective communication of a revitalised brand proposition. Given the current trend towards personalising politics, the penchant in recent years for the media to focus on the serious, dour, even brooding side to Brown's character has the potential to be highly damaging. Therefore, the time has come to shift the focus onto other attributes, for example, sincerity and integrity: characteristics that polls have shown are rarely associated with politicians of any political party. This achieved, it will position both Gordon Brown and his party in line with particularly positive brand values.

The second imperative for Gordon Brown is the need to draw a line under the previous administration, thereby creating his own version of a 'clean slate'. This would establish a clear and positive point of difference from the product offerings of, not only the Blair administration, but also his rival political brands. There are a number of ways in which this might be achieved and, while rapid shifts in policy may not be practical, possible or even desirable, there is certainly scope to make other high-profile changes. The policy of inclusion is a good example, with past attempts to make the Houses of Parliament more representative achieving only limited success. A shift in parliamentary recruitment procedures might yield a more varied cohort with the inclusion of a requirement for a significant level of life and/or work experience outside of the 'Westminster Village'. Such an approach has the potential to spark the imagination of the electorate, as they find themselves able to identify more closely with candidates whose life experience mirrors their own. It also has the potential to counter concerns over a lack of understanding of the 'real world' so often associated with career politicians, and would support other Labour Party policies on diversity and community engagement.

Ultimately, however, the most effective way for Brown to distinguish his brand of Labour is through the tangible delivery of election promises. The political sector as a whole has long suffered from a poor reputation for trustworthiness, and any political party that actually fulfilled its commitments would be highly distinctive indeed. This being the case, Labour's position as the governing party lends it a key competitive advantage as, unlike its rivals, it has the mandate, power and resources to deliver material outcomes. To this end, campaign promises and manifesto pledges would have to be treated as sacred contracts between government and electorate, only to be broken under the most difficult of circumstances. Promises made need to be *visibly* fulfilled, leaving the voter in no doubt that, at the next election, the promises made by Gordon Brown's Labour Party would be the promises delivered. Thus, if he can achieve this, Gordon Brown will not only have created his own 'brand' of Labour politics, he will also have taken the first steps to putting a positive spin back into the political sector as a whole.

FURTHER READING

Allington, Nigel, Philip Morgan and Nicholas O'Shaughnessy (1999). 'How marketing changed the world. The political marketing of an idea: a case study of privatization'. In Bruce Newman (ed.), *The Handbook of Political Marketing*. Thousand Oaks, CA: Sage.

Andreasen, A.R. (1995). *Marketing Social Change: Changing Behavior to Promote Health, Social Development*. San Francisco: Jossey-Bass.

Arterton, Christopher F. (2007). 'Strategy and politics: the example of the United States of America'. In Thomas Fischer, Gregor Peter Schmitz and Michael Seberich (eds), *The Strategy of Politics: Results of a Comparative Study*. Butersloh: Verlag, Bertelsmann Stiftung.

Barber, Michael (2007). *Instruction to Deliver*. London: Politicos.

Boaz, Annette and William Solesbury (2007). 'Strategy and politics: the example of the United Kingdom'. In Thomas Fischer, Gregor Peter Schmitz and Michael Seberich (eds), *The Strategy of Politics: Results of a Comparative Study*. Butersloh: Verlag, Bertelsmann Stiftung.

Butler, Patrick and Neil Collins (1999). 'A conceptual framework for political marketing'. In Bruce Newman (ed.), *Handbook of Political Marketing*. Thousand Oaks, CA: Sage Publications.

—— (2001). 'Payment on delivery: recognising constituency service as political marketing'. *European Journal of Marketing*, 35(9/10): 1025–37.

Fischer, Thomas, Gregor Peter Schmitz and Michael Seberich (eds) (2007). *The Strategy of Politics: Results of a Comparative Study*. Butersloh: Verlag, Bertelsmann Stiftung.

Gelders, Dave and Steven Van De Walle (2005). 'Marketing government reforms'. In Walter Wymer and Jennifer Lees-Marshment (eds), *Current Issues in Political Marketing*. Binghamton, NY: Haworth Press.

Glaab, Manuela (2007). 'Strategy and politics: the example of Germany'. In Thomas Fischer, Gregor Peter Schmitz, Michael Seberich (eds), *The Strategy of Politics: Results of a Comparative Study*. Butersloh: Verlag, Bertelsmann Stiftung.

Glover, Julian (2006). 'Labour support at lowest level since Thatcher's last election victory'. Available online at www.guardian.co.uk (25 October 2006).

Goot, Murray (2007). 'Questions of deception: contested understandings of the polls on WMD, political leaders and governments in Australia, Britain and the United States'. *Australian Journal of International Affairs*, 61(1): 41–64.

Hamburger, Peter (2006). 'The Australian Government Cabinet Implementation Unit. In improving implementation: organisational change and project management'. ANZSOG/ANU. Available online at http://epress.anu.edu.au/anzsog/imp/mobile_devices/ch18.html (accessed 11 April 2008).

Harris, Phil (2001). 'Machiavelli, political marketing and reinventing government'. *European Journal of Marketing*, 35(9/10): 1135–54.

Henneberg, Stephan C. (2006a). 'Strategic postures of political marketing: an exploratory operationalization'. *Journal of Public Affairs*, 6(1): 15–30.

—— (2006b). 'Leading or following? A theoretical analysis of political marketing postures'. *Journal of Political Marketing*, 5(3): 29–46.

Kotler, P. and Eduardo L. Roberto (2002). *Social Marketing: Strategies for Changing Public Behavior*. New York: Free Press.

Lederer, Andreas, Fritz Plasser and Christian Scheucher (2005). 'The rise and fall of populism in Austria – a political marketing perspective'. In D. Lilleker and J. Lees-Marshment (eds), *Political Marketing: A Comparative Perspective*. Manchester: Manchester University Press.

Lees-Marshment, Jennifer (2001). *Political Marketing and British Political Parties: The Party's Just Begun*. Manchester: Manchester University Press.

—— (2008a). 'Managing a market-orientation in government: cases in the UK and New Zealand'. In Dennis W. Johnson (ed.), *The Routledge Handbook of Political Management*. New York: Routledge.

—— (2008b). *Political Marketing and British Political Parties* (2nd edn.). Manchester: Manchester University Press.

Levin, Ben (2005). *Governing Education*. Toronto: University of Toronto Press.

Lilleker, Darren (2006). 'Local political marketing: political marketing as public service'. In D. Lilleker, N. Jackson and R. Scullion (eds), *The Marketing of Political Parties*. Manchester: Manchester University Press.

—— and Jennifer Lees-Marshment (eds) (2005). *Political Marketing: A Comparative Perspective*. Manchester: Manchester University Press.

Lindholm, Mikael R. and Anette Prehn (2007). 'Strategy and politics: the example of Denmark'. In Thomas Fischer, Gregor Peter Schmitz and Michael Seberich (eds), *The Strategy of Politics: Results of a Comparative Study*. Butersloh: Verlag, Bertelsmann Stiftung.

Lynch, Richard, Paul Baines and John Egan (2006). 'Long-term performance of political parties: towards a competitive resource-based perspective'. *Journal of Political Marketing*, 5(3): 71–92.

McKenzie-Mohr, D. and W. Smith (1999). *Fostering Sustainable Behavior: An Introduction to Community-Based Social Marketing*. Gabriola Island BC, Canada: New Society Publishers.

Mehlman, Steve (2006). 'California's special election: political miscalculations and PR missteps'. *Public Relations Tactics*, 13(2): 12–13.

Needham, Catherine (2005). 'Brand leaders: Clinton, Blair and the limitations of the permanent campaign'. *Political Studies*, 53(2): 343–61.

Newman, Bruce (1999). *The Mass Marketing of Politics: Democracy in an Age of Manufactured Images*. Beverley Hills, CA: Sage Publications.

Patrón-Galindo, Pedro (2004). 'Symbolism and the construction of political products: analysis of the political marketing strategies of Peruvian President Alejandro Toledo'. *Journal of Public Affairs*, 4(2): 115–24.

Promise (2005). 'Reconnecting the Prime Minister'. Company paper, Promise UK. Available online at www.promisecorp.com.

Rothmayr, Christine and Sibylle Hardmeier (2002). 'Government and polling: use and impact of polls in the policy-making process in Switzerland'. *International Journal of Public Opinion Research*, 14(2): 123–40.

Rudd, Chris (2005). 'Marketing the message or the messenger?'. In Darren Lilleker and J. Lees-Marshment (eds), *Political Marketing in Comparative Perspective*. Manchester: Manchester University Press.

Scammell, Margaret (1995). *Designer Politics: How Elections are Won*. New York: St Martin's Press.

—— (2003). 'Citizen consumers: towards a new marketing of politics?'. In John Corner and Dick Pels (eds), *Media and the Restyling of Politics*. Thousand Oaks, CA: Sage. Available online at http://depts.washington.edu/gcp/pdf/citizenconsumers.pdf.

—— (2008). 'Brand Blair: marketing politics in the consumer age'. In D. Lilleker and R. Scullion (eds), *Voters or Consumers: Imagining the Contemporary Electorate*. Newcastle: Cambridge Scholars Publishing.

Steger, Wayne (1999). 'The permanent campaign: marketing from the hill'. In Bruce Newman (ed.), *The Handbook of Political Marketing*. Thousand Oaks, CA: Sage.

Van der Hart, Hein W.C. (1990). 'Government organisations and their customers in the Netherlands: strategy, tactics and operations'. *European Journal of Marketing*, 24(7): 31–42.

Wring, Dominic (2005). *The Politics of Marketing of the Labour Party*. Hampshire: Palgrave Macmillan.

Young, S. (2005). 'Government advertising costs us dearly'. *The Age*, 30 August. Available online at www.theage.com.au/news/opinion/sally-young/2005/08/29/1125302509121.html (accessed 10 April 2008).

9   Global knowledge transfer

This chapter will examine the way that political marketing is used across different countries, especially focusing on the role of political marketing consultants, as well as the transfer of political products and strategies. The chapter will also discuss how political marketing varies from one country to another, given the different nature of political systems, cultures and markets. It also includes a series of case studies that demonstrate how political marketing is used in different countries, as well as discussion about the democratic implications of political marketing being copied around the world.

Political marketing practitioners and consultants

Alongside the expansion of political marketing practice, there has been significant growth in the number and notoriety of practitioners offering their services to candidates and parties seeking to win election or re-election. This has been noted by political science literature (see, for example, Kinsey 1999, Thurber and Nelson 2000, Medvic 2001, Plasser and Plasser 2002, Kaid and Holtz-Bacha 2006 and Johnson 2007), but can also be linked to political marketing in particular, because consultants increasingly engage in marketing advice on aspects such as strategy. Johnson's (2007) study of professional consultants includes analysis of how consultants test public opinion, conduct opposition research and contact voters utilising market segmentation: see Table 9.1.

The growth of such consultancy work means there can be sharing of best practice, which can be learned from the consultants themselves. Medvic (2006: 20–3) interviewed consultants about campaign strategy and from this drew a number of principles:

1   The candidate is the foundation of the strategy.
2   The campaign is enhanced by data on voter attitudes and opinions; no professional campaign would develop a campaign strategy without the use of polling.
3   The issue–image divide is a false dichotomy: strategies include issues either as direct appeals to voters in terms of policy, or as a more general sign of principles and attitudes.
4   Consultants rely heavily on the 'most important issue facing the nation/state/district' question and also find ways to uncover other issues that resonate with voters but may not show up in traditional lists of problems, using their ear to the ground, experience and intuition to identify issues that may not immediately jump to the voters' minds.
5   It is virtually impossible to convince voters that their beliefs about a candidate or party are wrong; it is easier to gain influence by reinforcing what they already believe.

Table 9.1 Consultants' use of marketing

Area	What consultants do
Candidate and opposition research	• Political consultants commission research about the candidate and the opposition. • This identifies both positive and negative attributes, such as a good record of achievement, or helps inform strategies to protect the candidate. • It helped define both John Kerry and George W. Bush in the 2004 presidential election. • It is carried out by professional opposition research companies. • It can probe into personal issues, most notably when Bill Clinton stood for election in 1992 and 1996, when it uncovered alleged affairs. • Despite ethical issues, such research can help a campaign, so if it works, it is used. • It is limited to what the public will tolerate.
Testing public opinion	• Market intelligence informs strategies, positioning and communication. • It tests new ideas before launching them publicly; the public is a sounding board to keep politicians in touch. • It is used in an election campaign, policy formation and government. • Methods include focus groups, benchmark surveys, trend surveys, dial meter analysis, tracking polls. • Consultants don't just commission the research, they interpret it and use it to suggest strategies.
Market segmentation to contact voters	• It helps politicians reach the right audience with the right message. • It ensures resources are utilised most efficiently. • It involves direct mail, telemarketing and GOTV techniques. • Example: in the 2004 presidential election, Republicans divided Michigan voters into 31 political categories, noting numbers and likelihood of voting Republican in each one, such as religious Conservative Republicans, tax-cut Conservative Republicans and flag and family Republicans, anti-port, anti-terrorism Republicans, and harder to reach groups such as wageable weak Democrats.

Source: Johnson (2007)

Some consultants become more famous than others because they are associated with high-profile success and write their own accounts of their work (see the list at the end of the chapter, p. 265). Box 9.1 provides a brief profile of the most famous ones.

Plasser *et al.* (1999: 89) noted how most of these figures are from the US; they often 'receive more mass media attention than do the candidates' they advise. Key questions are how much influence they really have and what contribution they make to elections. Johnson's case study evaluates the importance of such consultants.

Consultancy across countries

Consultants travel between countries to share experiences and offer advice. In some cases, this is nothing other than exchange of ideas. In others, it becomes more wholesale transplantation of political marketing products and campaigns from one country to the next. Consultants also deliver new modes of operation to less-developed nations. A whole array of companies and consultants are found travelling to Croatia or Czech or China, to extol the latest virtues of electioneering, perhaps via the UK Westminster Foundation for Democracy, or because they are a member of the International Association of Political Consultants, or simply because they find themselves in the right place at the right time.

However, just because one marketing campaign works in one country does not mean it will work in all others. Plasser *et al.* (1999: 90–1) noted how, whereas campaigns in the

Box 9.1 Profiles of the most famous political marketing consultants

James Carville: 1992, Bill Clinton, US Democrats

Carville was the lead strategist of Bill Clinton's 1992 presidential campaign and, in 1993, Carville was named Campaign Manager of the Year by the American Association of Political Consultants. His role on the Clinton campaign was potrayed in the documentary *The War Room*. Carville has also hosted and appeared on political television shows.

Phillip Gould: UK Labour, 1997, 2002 and 2005 with Tony Blair

Gould is a former advertiser who founded his own polling and strategy company, Philip Gould Associates, in 1985, and acted as adviser to the party in the General Elections of 1987, 1992, 1997, 2001 and 2005. Gould played a significant part in helping design, form and implement 'New Labour' alongside Peter Mandelson and Alastair Campbell.

Dick Morris: 1996, Bill Clinton, US Democrats

Morris was an adviser to the first 1992–96 administration, suggesting the third-way policies of triangulation that merged traditional Republican and Democratic proposals, rhetoric and issues to achieve maximum political gain and popularity. He was campaign manager of Clinton's successful 1996 re-election bid. He then became a political journalist in print and on TV.

Robert M. 'Bob' Shrum: 2000, Al Gore's presidential bid; and Kerry's bid in 2004

Shrum was a political consultant for Democratic candidates at the presidential, congressional and gubernatorial levels, but worked on a number of failed campaigns, including Al Gore's campaign for the White House in 2000 and John Kerry's campaign for the White House in 2004.

Stan Greenberg: 1992, Bill Clinton, US Democrats

Greenberg was a political scientist who became a political consultant and worked as a pollster for Clinton in 1992 alongside Carville. Greenberg has served as pollster to President Bill Clinton and Vice President Al Gore, British Prime Minister Tony Blair, South African Presidents Nelson Mandela and Thabo Mbeki, Israeli Prime Minister Ehud Barak, German Chancellor Gerhard Schröder, Bolivian President Gonzalo Sánchez de Lozada and Austrian Chancellor Alfred Gusenbauer (see www.gqrr.com/index.php?ID=403). He is now chairman and CEO of Greenberg Quinlan Rosner and provides strategic advice and research for a range of organisations and candidates.

Lynton Crosby: John Howard, the Liberal Australian Federal Prime Minister, in 1998 and 2001; UK Conservative Party in 2005, and London Mayor Boris Johnson in 2008

An Australian consultant, Crosby engaged in various advisory jobs for ministers and the Liberal Party in the 1980s, before becoming campaign director for Howard's second victory at the 1998 Australian federal election and again in 2001. In 2002, Crosby set up Crosby-Textor with Mark Textor. In 2005, Crosby managed the Conservative Party's general election campaign in the United Kingdom, although they lost the election, but he then ran UK Conservative MP Boris Johnson's London mayoral election campaign, which won.

Mark Penn: Bill Clinton, 1996–2000; Hillary Clinton's senate campaign and US presidential nomination bid, 2007–8

Penn came to prominence as President Bill Clinton's pollster and political adviser for the 1996 re-election campaign and throughout the second term of the administration, but he also advised British Prime Minister Tony Blair's campaign to win a third term in the 2005 UK election, and

Hillary Clinton's senate and presidential nomination campaigns. He is president of the polling firm Penn, Schoen and Berland Associates and advises organisations and companies on a wide range of marketing issues. He wrote a book called *Microtrends,* which discusses the potential of small segments to make a difference to, not just elections, but different kinds of change.

Karl Rove: 2000 and 2004 US presidential elections, George W. Bush, and in government White House

Rove advised Bush on his strategy to win in 2000 and 2004, and held various White House positions, including senior advisor 2000–04 and deputy chief of staff 2004–07. Since leaving the White House, Rove has worked as a political analyst and contributor for Fox News, *Newsweek* and the *Wall Street Journal* (see www.rove.com/articles).

Source: consultants' own websites and media sites

US are 'candidate centred, money and media driven, professionalized and highly individualised', in most European countries campaigns are 'party-centred and labour intensive, receive free television time, are publicly funded, and are managed by party staff'. US-connected consultants had less feel for the importance of traditional party organisation. The firm Crosby-Textor, which worked successfully for John Howard, Australian prime minister, then travelled over to the UK to run the Conservatives' 2005 campaign. Box 9.2 discusses Crosby, the techniques he used, and some of the controversies surrounding Crosby's role in the UK 2005 campaign.

The Crosby-Textor firm also worked for the New Zealand National Party in their 2005 election, and this led to calls in the media for him to be prevented from coming into the country. Aside from the democratic concerns regarding the methods of particular consultants, such transference of consultants does not guarantee electoral success. Both the Conservatives and Nationals lost their respective elections. Indeed, some consultants advise against going into different countries: see Practitioner perspective 9.1.

Practitioner perspective 9.1

There's a rule no matter where you are that you can't make Adolf Hitler into Ghandi. You have to adapt. You can't go into a parliamentary system with a message that a candidate is independent. What you can bring is expertise in analysing a situation – what you can't bring the cultural values from own country. So you bridge the gap by:

1   relying on local expertise so you don't impose US values;
2   relying on local linguists – so you don't create problems in polling;
3   understanding the political history enough.

(Rick Ridder, international political consultant, interviewed by Jennifer Lees-Marshment 2007)

Of course, you can take techniques and you can take polling from polling techniques in America ... But ultimately though strategy is situational. I don't believe in absolute campaigning truths that travel ... what worked in one country may not work in the next ... the point of winning an election is to win the election on the basis of political projects, a set of ideas and a set of values. And they have to be distinctive to that country in so many ways.

(Phillip Gould, UK strategist, interviewed by Jennifer Lees-Marshment 2007)

Box 9.2 Lynton Crosby

Crosby . . . was summoned halfway around the world by Howard in the autumn to revive the Tories' fortunes . . . While Crosby, 48, appears to be winning rave reviews from Tory MPs and shadow ministers who were fed up with the confusion under the dual chairmanship of Liam Fox and Maurice Saatchi, questions are being raised about his track record. Few doubt his extraordinary success in shepherding John Howard, the 'dull dog' of Australia, to four consecutive general election victories. Howard himself declared: 'There's no better political strategist in Australia than Lynton Crosby.'

But much of this involved highly controversial tactics, most notably during Australia's 2001 General Elections, which will be remembered for an ugly row about a refugee ship, the Tampa. A false allegation that asylum seekers had tried to blackmail their way into the country by throwing children overboard prompted John Howard's notorious slogan in the final days of the campaign: 'We decide who will come into this country.' Wind forward four years and another Howard has just issued a call to 'limit immigration' with a quota for asylum seekers. The policy was not new but the decision to make such a sensitive subject one of the Tories' defining issues of the campaign was inspired by Crosby . . .

The Australian Labor party, whose leader, Mark Latham, resigned after another defeat at the hands of the Howard–Crosby partnership, has bitter memories of Crosby's tactics. One Labor candidate received £34,000 in damages in 1995 from Mark Textor, Crosby's business partner, and others after suggestions that she supported abortions at nine months. Textor . . . had deployed 'push polling', a US tactic of spreading damaging information about opponents under the guise of questions . . .

Labour strategists in Britain detect a repetition of these tactics. But Crosby has told a series of senior Tory MPs that he appreciates Australian politics are wholly different. His aim is to instill tight discipline, sharpen the party's national message and focus on the 50 to 80 marginal seats where the Tories have a realistic chance . . . Within days of taking over Crosby had renamed the party offices 'Conservative campaign headquarters' and introduced a daily session where the author of the best press release is invited to take a bow.

. . . Attacking the prime minister – and reeling off a series of policy initiatives – is not enough, Crosby is telling staff as he reminds them of the importance of his buzzword: values. 'People don't generally vote simply on the basis of issues,' he told a conference in Canberra last May. 'They vote as much on the values and motivation of political parties in taking a particular position on an issue . . . It is the values you communicate, and the motivation you have, that influences the way people vote.'

Source: Watt (2005)

“”

Discussion point 9.1

To what extent is the global transfer of political marketing consultations effective and democratic?

Global political marketing products

Marketing has had comparative influence on the political party product. *Global New Labour* has seen strategies copied from Clinton in the US and Blair in the UK by leaders in Germany, New Zealand, Japan and Denmark, and there has also been sharing among right-wing Conservatives (see Lees 2005, Rudd 2005 and Lees-Marshment 2008). Kevin Rudd, who won a substantial victory in the 2007 Australian federal elections, also drew ideas from Tony Blair. Case study 9.2 discusses how such a strategy was effective when used by the Danish *Venstre-Danmarks Liberale Parti* (Left-Denmark's Liberal Party).

George W. Bush's use of the market-oriented approach to win in 2000 (Knuckey and Lees-Marshment 2005) was also copied by Iain Duncan-Smith, who was leader of the UK Conservative Party from 2001 to 2003. The UK Conservatives adopted many of the concepts, such as 'No child left behind', 'Compassionate Conservatism' and focusing on the vulnerable. In 2005, the New Zealand National Party's campaign appeared very similar to that run by the Australian Liberal Party in 2004 and the UK Conservatives in 2005, in terms of its focus on right-wing and negative issues and therefore a sales-, not market-oriented, approach. Most recently, Stephen Harper, who won power in Canada in 2006, copied ideas from Howard's campaigns in Australia, with Patrick Muttart, one of Mr Harper's chief strategists, studying the 2004 victory closely. And Howard's federal party director, Brian Loughnane, was informally involved in the Conservative campaign (see Laghi 2006). Case study 9.3 explores the similarities and differences in international political marketing in the UK, US, Australia and New Zealand, as well as some of the issues it causes.

Comparative analysis of political marketing in different countries

All comparative analysis, both in marketing and politics, suggests that because of various factors – differences in the political system and nature of the market (voting behaviour, party identification and political participation, political culture, electoral system, media, etc.) – behaviour varies from one country to another. In business, companies try to understand the nature of different international marks and cultures when establishing new endeavours overseas, to ensure success. In politics, logic would suggest that such adaptability is also needed, if ideas and strategies are to be transported from one system to another (see Plasser *et al.* 1999: 91, for example). Baines (2004: 139) shows how the difference between the UK and US impacts on different marketing functions: see Table 9.2.

Table 9.2 Variances in marketing function in the UK and US

Marketing function	UK	US
Direct mail	Party function	Subcontracted to political direct mail specialists
Advertising	Subcontracted for main parties	Subcontracted
Polling	Subcontracted by major parties to pollsters	Subcontracted
Fundraising	Subcontracted to fundraisers by main parties	Subcontracted to specialist fundraisers
Opposition research	Main parties use small rebuttal units within party	Subcontracted

Studying the UK and Sweden, Strömbäck (2007) concluded that there were significant differences in the use of political marketing by parties, with Swedish parties not showing the same trend towards the market-oriented party (Lees-Marshment 2001). Accepting that systemic differences affect this, he put forward a number of predictions: see Box 9.3.

The practice of political marketing across different countries can both vary and converge in several ways, as Case studies 9.4–9.7 at the end of this chapter illustrate. Previous comparative analysis of political marketing, such as Bowler and Farrell (1992) and more recently Lilleker and Lees-Marshment (2005) identified similarities as well as differences in the use of political marketing and argued that systemic factors impacted on political marketing behaviour in the following ways:

1   A PR electoral system, by requiring coalition governments, enables smaller parties to adopt a sales-oriented approach and still have influence in coalition.
2   The power of the leader and strength of the party are also issues; some UK party leaders have tried but failed to follow a market-orientation as they are blocked by

---

Box 9.3 Propositions regarding the impact of differences between countries and between parties within countries on their likelihood to be market-oriented parties

1   Parties in candidate-centred political systems are more likely to be market-oriented than parties in party-centred political systems.
2   Parties in countries with majoritarian electoral systems are more likely to be market-oriented than parties in countries with proportional electoral systems.
3   Parties in countries where the left–right ideological dimension is of less importance in the minds of voters are more likely to be market-oriented than parties in countries where it is of major importance.
4   Parties in countries with few competing parties are more likely to be market-oriented than parties in countries with many competing parties.
5   Parties in countries with a low degree of party identification are more likely to be market-oriented than parties in countries with a high degree of party identification.
6   Parties in countries with high electoral volatility are more likely to be market-oriented than parties in countries with low electoral volatility.
7   Parties in countries with a highly commercialised media system are more likely to be market-oriented than parties in countries with a less commercialised media system.
8   Parties in countries with an adversarial journalistic culture are more likely to be market-oriented than parties in countries with a less adversarial journalistic culture.
9   Parties in countries with deep social or political cleavages are less likely to be market-oriented than parties in countries without such deep cleavages.
10 Parties in countries with an egalitarian political culture are more likely to be market-oriented than parties in countries with a hierarchical political culture.
11 Parties in countries with a high level of political distrust are more likely to be market-oriented than parties in countries with a lower level of political distrust.
12 Parties in countries with news media independent of the party-political system are more likely to be market-oriented than parties in countries where the news media form part of the party-political system.

Source: Strömbäck (2007: 87) and Strömbäck (2009)

internal culture, but in the US presidential system, where there is a separation of powers, that is not an issue.

3 The availability and regulations of funding for political parties affects their ability to conduct market intelligence and utilise professional staff.

4 Delivery may be achieved for smaller parties by delivering greater representation to their members and supporters by entering into coalition, or purely by continuing to influence government through pressure while retaining their radical character.

Overall, despite any differences, there remains a world market for political marketing; as the more famous cases such as Tony Blair in 1997 and Bill Clinton in 1992 suggest, marketing can help win elections. In response to this, consultants have become more likely to work, not just for one nation, but for several countries.

Democratic implications of international political marketing

There are obvious implications of knowledge transfer in political marketing. Is it a good thing for the world? Should political products be transported from one country to another? Can techniques developed for the US electorate be used in any political system? Or is each country so unique that we shouldn't expect, or want, to see similarity in strategy across countries? Copycat marketing can impede the creation of new ideas and solutions, but, on the other hand, policy transfer between countries has long been practised, and countries can learn from each other as to what to avoid as well as what to copy, sharing the benefits of experience and hindsight. Should political marketing consultants consider ethics?

Discussion point 9.2

Consider comparative examples of political marketing (e.g. Case studies 3.1–3.3, 5.1, 5.3, 7.2, 9.2, 9.4–9.7 and 10.2 in this book), noting differences and similarities, and consider why such convergence or divergence exists in relation to the nature of the political system and market.

Ethics and political consultants

Johnson (2007: 226) notes that, for some political consultants, ethics questions have 'no bearing on what they do'. However, he notes that the American Association of Political Consultants (AAPC), the main professional association for consultants, has a code of conduct it requires its members to sign: see Box 9.4.

There is no means to enforce the code however. Johnson (2007: 227) notes that, in a poll in 1998 called 'Don't blame us', 81 per cent said it had little or no effect on professional conduct. However, the survey also showed that respondents felt that making factually untrue statements and push polling were clearly unethical. Practice varies, and so do ethical standards.

Johnson (2007: 58) notes that opposition and candidate research 'at its worst . . . crosses the line of decency and fairness, is used ruthlessly for character assassination and becomes the indispensable weapon in gotcha campaigning', but at its best it can simply give direction, increase differentiation and build an evidence-based campaign. Johnson (2007: 227) concludes though that any real abuse in campaigns 'falls on the shoulders of the candidate' – they have the final say.

Box 9.4 American Association of Political Consultants Code of Professional Ethics

As a member of the American Association of Political Consultants, I believe there are certain standards of practice which I must maintain. I, therefore, pledge to adhere to the following Code of Professional Ethics:

- I will not indulge in any activity which would corrupt or degrade the practice of political consulting.
- I will treat my colleagues and clients with respect and never intentionally injure their professional or personal reputations.
- I will respect the confidence of my clients and not reveal confidential or privileged information obtained during our professional relationship.
- I will use no appeal to voters which is based on racism, sexism, religious intolerance or any form of unlawful discrimination and will condemn those who use such practices. In turn, I will work for equal voting rights and privileges for all citizens.
- I will refrain from false or misleading attacks on an opponent or member of his or her family and will do everything in my power to prevent others from using such tactics.
- I will document accurately and fully any criticism of an opponent or his or her record.
- I will be honest in my relationship with the news media and candidly answer questions when I have the authority to do so.
- I will use any funds I receive from my clients, or on behalf of my clients, only for those purposes invoiced in writing.
- I will not support any individual or organization which resorts to practices forbidden by this code.

Source: www.theaapc.org/about/code/ (accessed 16 April 2008)

Discussion point 9.3

Zanu PF, Robert Mugabe's party in Zimbabwe, employed professional PR help between the first and second presidential elections. Should marketing consultants be prepared to help any political leader, regardless of their ideology and democratic and civil rights practices?*

Our brand is crisis

In 2002, a team of strategists from the American political consultant firm Greenberg Carville Shrum, including James Carville and Jeremy Rosner, advised a campaign for presidential candidate Gonzalo Sanchez de Lozada (or Goni for short) in Bolivia, an economically depressed country in South America with a long history of political chaos. This was depicted by a fly-on-the-wall documentary by Rachel Boynton called *Our brand is crisis*. It showed how the team of consultants was almost 'imported' into South America

---

* I am grateful to the anonymous reviewer who suggested this discussion point.

Discussion point 9.4

Johnson (2007: 86) concludes that:

> it is no wonder that many decent and honorable civic-minded individuals refuse to run for elective office. They know that the moment their names surface as possible candidates, the opposition party, a potential primary opponent, or even a freelance investigator will be digging through public records, compiling information on business and personal matters, and searching vast electronic databases.

Does it matter that some political marketing consultant practices may be considered unethical?

to help revitalise the image of the president, Sanches de Lozada, who had become very unpopular between 1993 and 1997, to help him be re-elected for a second time. The country faced economic crisis, and it was not easy to rebrand Goni. The opposition on the left, Evo Morales, was previously a leader of the coca leaf-growers' union and was Brazil's first indigenous president and he presented strong competition. Goni was seen as arrogant in contrast, as seen from results of focus groups and poll numbers. The campaign tried to reduce the election to a simple brand. Goni barely won the election, with just 22.5 per cent of the vote and, once in office, remained stubbornly out of touch with the general needs of the market. His term ended with large-scale demonstrations and riots (see www. ourbrandiscrisis.net/).

The case provides a fascinating insight into how advisors work, the use of focus groups and polls to create a strategy, as well as potential ways to reform a poor image, but particularly in a global context. It raises many issues of the transplantation of US techniques and approaches into emerging democracies in particular and highlights concerns about political marketing transfer without adaptation. Strategists import more than just campaigning advice, because Goni was a western-educated wealthy businessman who privatised Bolivia's economy and created social security; and they support his aim to reinstitute capitalisation. As one reviewer said:

> [The] film sheds light on the political machinery that renders their goals – and intentions – largely impossible despite some brilliant salesmanship. It's a lesson that touches the raw nerve of America's, and Americanization's, basic dilemma in the 21st Century. As much as the United States and certain business interests want it otherwise, the globalization game gets messy in the details – the transposition of our economic framework and/or government to an entirely different culture and society can't possibly be smoothed over by clever television commercials and confetti. I would point to similar current examples – ones even more violent and bloody – but the lesson becomes disturbingly clear upon a viewing of 'Our Brand,' in which Boynton's images speak it as viscerally as possible.
>
> (Rowin with Koresky and Wisniewski 2006)

The results of the election and subsequent events in the country raise many issues.

Global political marketing

Lilleker and Lees-Marshment (2005) suggested a number of democratic concerns arising from their study. In relation to ideology, the Brazilian PT found themselves under attack for weakening their ideology and seeking compromise over issues; this has also occurred in Peru and the USA, where parties have been criticised and been described as 'swinging like a pendulum' as public opinion changes. With delivery, expectations commonly far exceed reality, and public demands may simply not be able to be met within the political environment in which politicians govern. The integration of public opinion into political policy design can cause problems: the weak political culture in Peru, for example, means people may be less able to articulate their wants and desires than those in established democracies. They may also be seeking a certain type of leadership, as opposed to being able to offer a shopping list of political outcomes. Even in well-developed nations, there is a risk of developing an 'undeveloped' or weak product if there is a complete reliance on public opinion; parties benefit from the anchorage of a core of constraints, based upon ideology, that will allow the party to develop solutions and allow the electorate to be aware of what the party stands for.

They also concluded that world leaders around the globe are facing issues such as: the rise of the political consumer; delivery; internal implementation; maintaining a market-orientation in government; and developing policies that will satisfy the needs of the country in the long term while maintaining popular support necessary to stay in power in the short term. Political marketing has perspectives on all of these. Potentially, political marketing could help leaders and parties respond to this twenty-first-century development. While the potential remains, it is unlikely that political marketing knowledge transfer will halt and will instead develop further over time, as more and more lessons from both study and practice are learned and shared across different countries in the world. Overall, it raises many practical as well as ethical debates.

Debate 9.1

Proposition: A political product designed for one market cannot just be taken and transferred to another country – political marketing has to be adapted.

Summary

Political marketing is clearly a global activity, with tools and concepts being used in political systems around the world, and practice in all areas of political marketing being shared between parties in different countries, aided by utilisation of the same consultants. There remain, however, questions as to the effectiveness of the transference of global political marketing techniques and products from one country to another. As with other marketing activities, political marketing knowledge transfer also raises ethical and democratic questions, depending on how it is practised. Political marketing's potential influence on the democratic process is enough to raise both interest and concern. The next and final chapter will consider political marketing and democracy.

ASSESSED WORK

Essays

1   To what extent have political leaders copied strategies, products and campaigning techniques from each other?
2   How effective are political marketing strategies that work across different countries?
3   To what extent do comparative examples of political marketing (e.g. Case studies 3.1–3.3, 5.1, 5.3, 7.2, 9.2, 9.4–9.7 and 10.2 in this book) show differences or similarities from one country to another?
4   How accurate are Strömbäck's (2007) propositions regarding the impact of differences between countries and between parties within countries on their likelihood to be market-oriented parties? Illustrate your answer with empirical examples.
5   To what extent is political marketing an effective and appropriate approach for all parties in any country?

Applied work

1   Identify and critically analyse the practitioner perspective on marketing consultants, conducting interviews with practitioners and asking them about three areas: (a) their influence and effectiveness; (b) what methods they prefer; and (c) their impact on democracy.
2   Choose one of the following consultant positions: (a) strategist, (b) pollster, (c) press secretary, or (d) advertiser, and develop a political marketing plan for what you would advise a current political leader to do over the next twelve months, taking into account factors such as their goals, position in the electoral cycle, constraints, likely crisis, potential positives, nature of the leader his or herself, how to manage markets (e.g. party, other MPs, media, the public, civil service).

Case study 9.1 Top down or bottom up?   *Dennis W. Johnson*

For several decades now, American presidential, statewide and even many important local election campaigns have been managed by a cadre of political professionals. Around five to seven thousand such professionals help candidates navigate the pitfalls and opportunities of modern elections. Nearly all consultants are unknown to the public. In the 2008 presidential race, for example, few Americans could name the principal consultant for Barack Obama, Hillary Clinton or John McCain.

One cardinal principle in political management has been that the campaign must be controlled from the top down. This means that consultants, working on behalf of their candidate clients, try their best to control the campaign. On a campaign bulletin board, James Carville, the lead consultant for Bill Clinton's successful 1992 presidential bid, famously wrote: 'It's the economy, stupid'. In his own inimitable way, Carville was exerting one of the key elements of professional campaigning: message discipline. Campaigns need to focus on the issues that help them gain footing with voters, and consultants also want to define and frame the race in terms most favourable to their candidate. Obama became the *change* candidate; Clinton, the *experience* candidate; and McCain, the *national security* candidate. Candidates do not want to be defined or framed by their opponents or outside forces.

Top down campaigning means the candidate (and consultants) strategically will decide which areas of the country (or state) to visit, whom to meet, what messages to articulate, how to spend limited campaign funds, and a whole host of other issues. The campaign manager will have to juggle competing internal demands: the direct mail consultant wants money for campaign brochures, the volunteer co-ordinators are pleading for more help, while the telemarketing firm insists that the best way to contact voters is through telephone calls. Many a campaign has fallen apart because of internal bickering. The real battle, of course, is supposed to be against the opponent and the opponent's allies. Those allies might be labour unions, the political parties, interest groups cobbled together specifically for this one election cycle, or politically savvy bloggers.

During the first eight years of this century, we have been hearing about another kind of campaigning: bottom up. It is the idea that campaigns should be guided by, and directed by, what happens at the grass-roots level, and should not be controlled and manipulated from the top. This has been best exemplified by the Democratic presidential primary in 2003–04, with the candidacy of former Vermont governor Howard Dean. The campaign decided to listen to what voters wanted first and created the first blog site for an American presidential candidate; it also teamed up with a website called Meetup.com, which linked like-minded Dean supporters with each other. Suddenly, enthusiastic supporters of Howard Dean, who had never met each other before, were meeting in over a thousand homes and community centres throughout the country, sharing their enthusiasm and, in many cases, willingness to volunteer and help the campaign with both their ideas and their shoe leather. Through the Internet, new supporters identified themselves and, through Meetup.com, coalesced into groups. The other revolutionary aspect of Dean's campaign was the incredible ability to raise campaign funds, in small dollar amounts, through the Internet. The Dean campaign astounded his rivals by raising millions of dollars overnight, thanks to online donations.

Dean's campaign manager, Joe Trippi, boasted that American campaigns had entered into a new era, writing a book called *The Revolution Will Not Be Televised: Democracy, the Internet, and the Overthrow of Everything*. Others joined in, including pioneer bloggers Jerome Armstrong and Markos Moulitsas Zuniga, who wrote *Crashing the Gate: Netroots, Grassroots, and the Rise of People Powered Politics*. It was a jolt of reality, however, when Dean was easily beaten in the first Democratic caucus by Massachusetts Senator John Kerry, despite the presence of thousands of Dean supporters pounding on doors of Iowa Democrats. They were beaten, ironically, in part by the old-fashioned weapon of television advertising.

But the long-anticipated online communication revolution had just begun. The 2008 presidential primaries, with the Democratic contests the most interesting, tightly fought and longest in memory, launched a whole new set of online possibilities. By 2007, political blogging had matured, with hundreds of voices from all sides of the ideological spectrum putting in their two cents. Social networking – through Facebook, MySpace and other sites – now replaced Meetup.com as the way for like-minded citizens to get together. Online fundraising soared. More than ever, campaigning had entered the digital age.

Top down or bottom up? Has the traditional, top-down campaigning been replaced? No, it hasn't, but it has had to adapt to new challenges. Have bloggers and social networkers, Internet activists and others crashed the gate? There have been some successes for online activists, they are a definite factor at all levels of elections, but certainly no gates have been crashed.

Ironically, professional campaigners have been listening to people in campaigns for at least sixty years now. Private pollsters, hired by campaigns, have been telling candidates what people want, fear, think, who they prefer and who they don't. Pollsters have developed sophisticated, scientifically validated survey research techniques that assure impartiality and accurate results. Bloggers may think they are the voice of the people and have to be taken seriously. They are a voice, but hardly a representative voice. Bloggers are self-selective: they want their voices heard and want others to hear them. Smart, professionally run campaigns will pay attention to outside blogs and bloggers, but also will have their own site and designated blog-masters, who keep content fresh and on message, and who can quickly reach out to refute rumours or attacks.

All major presidential campaigns now have a director of electronic media: someone (or a whole unit of people) who updates the campaign website; co-ordinates and sends out campaign emails; updates the campaign blog and monitors and contributes to outside blogs; connects the campaign with other websites, including social network sites; and aggressively uses the Internet to solicit campaign funds. All these tools and tasks were available for the 2008 presidential primary candidates, and two candidates took particular advantage. Ron Paul, the seventy-two-year-old former congressman, with quirky libertarian ideas, drew enormous amounts of money to his campaign via the Internet and some excitement from voters (although hardly enough to register many delegates), but did not have the campaign structure and direction to capitalise on his popularity. Barack Obama's campaign set the gold standard for online communications through his inventive emails, excellent website filled with policy and other information, his integration of social networking and particularly his ability to solicit funds online. Obama's campaign has made giving money so easy that all one has to do is type 'Obama' into a major search engine, such as Google, and up pops an ad from the Obama campaign. Two more clicks, and the donation can be made.

The key ingredients, however, have to be there: exciting candidates with exciting ideas. That's why Howard Dean, in 2004, Ron Paul, in 2007, and Barack Obama were so successful. Their energy and ideas fuelled an Internet boom.

Professional campaigns will remain top down. There are so many things that can go wrong, so many forces tugging at the campaign, that there must be control. The smart campaigns, however, will adjust and co-opt new electronic communication tools. Ironically, the more blogging, external independent groups, social networking and others join in through electronic sources, the greater the need for control. Message discipline, focus, clarity, definition – all are required in a modern campaign, and only professionals can give it.

Case study 9.2 Learning from the master: the impact of New Labour on political parties in Denmark   *Robin T. Pettitt*

The main British parties, i.e. Labour and the Conservatives, are often seen as pioneers in political marketing in Europe, sometimes learning from their more 'advanced' cousins in the United States. This is something that the Labour Party in its 'New Labour' incarnation under the leadership of Tony Blair took to new heights, resulting in massive electoral successes, at least for a while.

What is interesting about the example of New Labour is not only how it learned from Bill Clinton and the New Democrats, but how other European parties in turn have learned from the example of New Labour. One example is the Swedish *Moderata Samlingspartiet* (Moderate Unity Party), a centre-right party, which in 2003 became *Nya Moderaterna* (New Moderates). Another example is the Danish *Venstre-Danmarks Liberale Parti* (Left-Denmark's Liberal Party). *Venstre*, meaning left, has its origins in the late nineteenth century as a liberal agrarian party and, until the rise of the Social Democrats, was the main opposition to the Conservative Party, originally called *Højre* (right). It is *Venstre* that will be the main focus of the following. *Venstre* is an example of a party that has very clearly and successfully been inspired by the New Labour model.

Venstre has struggled with the Danish Conservative Party for the role of the main centre-right party, and the Social Democrat Party has long enjoyed the position as the biggest party. Throughout most of the 1980s and the early 1990s, *Venstre* was the junior coalition partner in a string of Conservative-led governments, the last of which was forced out in 1993 after a scandal. In the early 1990s, *Venstre* regained the position as the largest opposition party and, in 2001, the party not only took the lead in a centre-right coalition, it also deposed the Social Democrats as the largest party, a position they had held since 1924. In 2005, the *Venstre*-led government was re-elected, the first time in the past century a *Venstre* government has survived its first meeting with the voters. In 2007, the government won yet another election. The party's leader and prime minister, Anders Fogh Rasmussen (commonly referred to as Fogh), has thereby secured himself a place in Danish political history as *Venstre*'s most successful leader.

A significant part of Fogh's success can be found in his willingness to learn the lessons of political marketing from New Labour. Fogh had a reputation as the party's leading neo-liberal, best exemplified by his 1993 book *Fra Socialstat til Minimalstat* (*From a Social State to a Minimal State*), which was a strong call for rolling back the state on Thatcherite lines. In 1998, after the right wing's second successive defeat, Fogh was made leader of *Venstre* and soon set about modernising the party. The main impetus to this modernisation came after Fogh read Philip Gould's (in-)famous book on the making of New Labour, *The Unfinished Revolution: how the modernisers saved the Labour Party*. Inspired by the example of New Labour, Fogh reformed *Venstre* on similar lines. The similarities with Blair and New Labour are manifold. However, one issue will serve to illustrate the similarities between the transformations of the two parties. This issue is the attitude the two leaders have to traditional ideologies.

In 2005, Fogh said:

> Modern people are tired of being put into old-fashioned political boxes. *Venstre* is today a broadly based party with voters in all groups ... People do not think in terms of classes anymore but insist on being allowed to make the decisions that affect their lives by themselves. People no longer accept politicians saying 'we know what is best for you' ... We live at the beginning of the twenty-first century and I believe that ... the answers to society's problems are not the same as the answers at the beginning of the twentieth century.
>
> (www.information.dk/print/118060)

The same year, Blair said:

> In the late twentieth century, the world had changed, the aspirations of the people had changed; we had to change. .... Today is not the era of the big state, but a strategic one: empowering, enabling, putting decision making in the hands of people, not government . . . Political parties love to tie themselves up in doctrine. They develop comfort zones. Policy becomes ideology, sometimes theology. To challenge it is heresy; to agree it is a sign you belong. But real people in the real world think instinctively, free from doctrine. Not free from values, but free to apply them differently in different times. New Labour reconnected us to them.
>
> (www.guardian.co.uk/uk/2005/sep/27/labourconference.speeches)

The success of the Gould approach is clear. Obviously, there is more to it than following what it says in Gould's book, but there is little doubt that learning the lessons of New Labour created the foundations for the successes since 2001.

The need for global political marketing

A further lesson to be draw from Denmark is what happens when the potential of political marketing is ignored. The Social Democrats were well aware of the successes of New Labour and the background of those successes, but did not act on that knowledge. The result has been three serious election defeats and the worst results at the polls for decades. The Social Democrats did eventually realise the need for change, as exemplified by the election of the centre-seeking Helle Thorning-Schmidt in 2005. Thorning-Schmidt has close ties with central figures in New Labour (and is married to former Labour leader Neil Kinnock's son) and has tried usurping the centre ground from *Venstre*. The new approach is illustrated in the similarities between her rhetoric and that of both Fogh and Blair. In a speech immediately prior to her being elected leader, she said:

> Let me say it to you straight: this is not about class struggle. This is not about some people being forced to sell their labour to the owners of the means of production. We might as well put these Marxist slogans away ... Regardless of how many borrowed clothes they [the right-wing parties] try to dress up in it shall always be us who are the broadly based party gathering together people in our society.
>
> (www.u-landsnyt.dk/indhold.asp?ID=5339&mode=Nyhed)

However, the more centre-seeking leadership did not succeed in reversing the electoral fortunes of the Social Democrats. Indeed, the result was a further decline for the Social Democrats. There are many reasons for this, not least a resurgence of the far left picking up votes from the now more centrist Social Democrats. However, what this shows is that the Social Democrats were not able to pick up the crucial centre votes, despite their renewed centrist orientation. What this suggests is that, when two parties are struggling over the centre ground, voters cease to look for policy differences and start looking for personalities or dissatisfaction with the incumbents as the main reasons to switch their votes. Thorning-Schmidt's leadership, especially at the beginning, has been marred by an aura of inexperience and a lack of visibility in the media. In addition, the government has yet to outstay its welcome or make any really major mistakes.

The case of Denmark therefore seems to suggest that, with two centre-seeking, market-oriented parties, what makes the difference is popular perception of the party's image and competence. It also suggests that successful use of political marketing, especially oriented towards capturing the middle ground, depends partly on the middle being vacated by the competition. Once occupied, it can be very difficult to recapture, unless the competition relinquishes it or is damaged by perceptions of incompetence or lack of strong leadership.

Case study 9.3 International political product marketing   *Jamie Turner*

Similar marketing strategies have been employed, with varying degrees of success, in elections since the 1990s in the United Kingdom, United States, Australia and New Zealand. This case study details some of these similarities, considering the reasons for their relative success and what lessons they have for political marketing.[1]

The essential aim of a political campaign is to offer voters a product that has sufficiently wide appeal. Three distinctive products have been transferred between countries. The first originates from the 1992 campaign of President Bill Clinton. Advisers who worked on Clinton's campaign then assisted Tony Blair and his party in the design of the product that won them the 1997 British election. The 'New Labour' product straddled the divide between traditional left and right and accepted market forces as fundamental to the economic system. It retains a centre-left approach to health and education, but was accompanied by a healthy dose of conservatism on issues such as crime, welfare and tax. Both Blair and Clinton promised to 'get tough' on crime and engage in 'welfare to work' type benefit reform. During the 2007 Australian election, Kevin Rudd borrowed from Blair's book, reassuring voters of his economic conservatism by stating, 'I have never been a socialist and I never will be a socialist' (quoted in Keenan 2007). Rudd promised tax cuts almost as large as the coalition's, a welfare package premised on the need for 'mutual obligation', and an 'education revolution' had been given similar prominence by Tony Blair in 1997. In New Zealand, Helen Clark and her Labour party took advice from UK Labour strategist Alastair Campbell. Clark has, at successive elections, promised strong investments in health and education in conjunction with a 'tough' stance on crime and, by late 2007, tax cuts.

The 'Compassionate Conservative' product was evident in the George W. Bush campaign of 2000. This product differed from the 'New Labour' product in that it must balance maximising voter appeal with maintaining traditional support on the centre right rather than left. The essential characteristic is the inclusion of a set of policies that make the party and its candidates seem more caring and inclusive. The Bush product included policies on tax designed to appeal to traditional Republicans, but was balanced with strong commitments to health, social security and ensuring no child is 'left behind' in education. The UK Conservative Party borrowed the latter phrase directly from the Republicans in 2003 and set about showing concern for lower-income communities. Under the leadership of David Cameron since 2005, the Tories spoke of the need to strengthen public services, ensure social justice and maintain a clean environment. In New Zealand, the National Party, under John Key's leadership, took advice from David Cameron, producing a product that balances strong advocacy for tax cuts with concern for a growing 'underclass' and the environment.

The third recurring product is 'Crosby-Textorism', after the Australian Liberal Party pollsters, Lynton Crosby and Mark Textor. This involves a more confrontational style of politics, based on right-wing-flavoured populism. A good example of this product is provided by the 2001 Australian election in the wake of the *Tampa* incident, when John Howard capitalised on anti-asylum sentiment by proclaiming that 'we will decide who comes to this country and the circumstances in which they come'. The UK Conservative Party took advice from Crosby at the 2005 election, running a similarly emotive campaign primed against asylum seekers and immigration. Don Brash and his National Party also took Crosby's advice for the 2005 New Zealand election, running a campaign emphasising the importance of 'mainstream values'.

The success of the Crosby-Textor product in Australia at the 2001 election must, however, be understood in context. First, public anxiety over immigration had been cultivated by the leader of the One Nation Party, Pauline Hanson. It is also arguable that Australians possess relatively conservative attitudes on issues of race and immigration (Jackman 1998). The Crosby-Textor product, in this context, was therefore relatively market-oriented. These circumstances were not present in the UK and New Zealand when the major centre-right party in each imported the Crosby-Textor product and lost their respective elections. The failure of the product to achieve the same level of success in these two countries can therefore be attributed to a failure to use market intelligence optimally. It supports political marketing theory to the extent that it shows that the optimal product is developed by responding to the specific voters to which you are selling it, not by importing a product that constitutes an optimal response to voters in another country. The latter constitutes a sales-orientation: market intelligence is still valued, but only for its ability to assist in selling the product to be imported, rather than determining whether it is optimal.

Lessons for political marketing

Copying a product that has been successful elsewhere has also been unsuccessful where, in the course of its implementation, internal marketing has been neglected. Naturally, those who are members or core supporters of a political party tend to be individuals with strongly ideological views. Sudden changes in the product of a party that are seen as a departure from ideology therefore have the potential to alienate such people, resulting in reduced support. The failure of the Compassionate Conservative product when implemented by the UK Conservatives under William Hague and Iain Duncan-Smith for 2000–04 can be attributed to the fact that the wider party was uncomfortable with the direction these leaders wanted to take them in. David Cameron has similarly struggled to keep those ideologically Conservative satisfied, including MP Quentin Davies, who resigned from the party in 2007 claiming that its sense of mission had been replaced by a PR agenda. Kevin Rudd has also created dissatisfaction among those on the traditional left of the ALP, who have accused him of merely being an echo of John Howard. Helen Clark and John Key, however, have not experienced similar problems. This is potentially owing to the fact that they are constrained from shifting too far from their ideological homes by the electoral system. Under MMP in New Zealand, it is easier for a minor party to convert votes taken from the left or right flanks of a major party into parliamentary seats than it is, for example, under FPP in the UK. These examples support political marketing theory by highlighting the relationship between the level of change the imported product constitutes and the internal marketing required.

Sources and further reading

Goldman, Peter and Tom Mathews (1992). 'Manhattan Project 1992'. *Newsweek*, November 1992: 40–5.

Keenan, Elizabeth (2007). 'Australia's new order', *Time*, 47, 3 December 2007: 24–31.

Luntz, Frank (2007). 'It's Cameron's political language that is doing for Brown', *The Spectator*, 24 February 2007: 14–15.

Jackman, Simon (1998). 'Pauline Hanson, the mainstream, and political elites: the place of race in Australian political ideology'. *Australian Journal of Political Science*, 33(2): 111–12.

New Zealand Herald (2007). 'Rudd momentum stirring déjà vu'. Wednesday 7 November 2007, available online at www.nzherald.co.nz/topic/story.cfm?c_id=467&objectid=10474421 (accessed 17 April 2008).

Note

1 This case study and the idea of global transfer of political marketing product and strategies originates from Jennifer Lees-Marshment's teaching and guidance in a political marketing course at Auckland University in 2007.

Case study 9.4 Political marketing in the rise and fall of Taiwan's New Party   *Dafydd J. Fell*

In the summer of 1993, a group of middle-ranking politicians from Taiwan's ruling party, the Kuomintang (KMT), formed the Chinese New Party (NP). At the time, few expected the party to make a major impact on the party system. However, it became the island's first significant third party, winning numerous parliamentary seats from the KMT and threatening its majority status. Nevertheless, from 1997, the NP declined. This case examines the role played by the NP's marketing strategies in its sudden rise and subsequent fall.

Taiwan developed from a one-party authoritarian state to an electoral democracy in the 1990s. The formation of opposition parties was legalised in 1989, and the first democratic, multi-party parliamentary elections were held in 1991 and 1992. In 1996, the first direct presidential election took place. However, in 1993, the party scene was still dominated by the KMT and the first real opposition party, the Democratic Progressive Party (DPP). Traditional European left–right cleavages are not dominant in this new democracy. Instead, the four dominant issues contested have been: (1) the pace and contents of democratic reform; (2) a national identity spectrum of Chinese unification versus Taiwan independence; (3) political corruption; and (4) the scope of the welfare state.

The NP was able to make its mark on Taiwan's party politics by learning from the mistakes of previous challenger parties and its ability to exploit a clear gap in the political market. At the time of formation, the NP was undoubtedly what Lees-Marshment calls a product-oriented party, laying out its core party policies and just assuming that voters will realise its ideas are the best. This initially enabled the NP to gain a core support base of voters disillusioned with the KMT's betrayal of core party values. Then in the mid 1990s, the NP was able expand beyond its initial support base by making a transition to becoming a sales-oriented party, in which it attempted to persuade voters to buy a political product that was based on the party's own core values, but also combined these appeals with innovative policy proposals based on extensive market research. However, a change in the NP's factional balance of power meant that, from the late 1990s, the party reverted to an ideologically oriented POP, contributing to its electoral demise.

The religious and social democratic parties' appeals had limited impact owing to the failure of their policy products to attract a core support base. In contrast, the NP took quite a nationalistic approach, with heavy emphasis on attacking the two main parties for promoting Taiwan independence, and it made extensive use of Chinese nationalist symbols. For instance, it chose yellow for its party flag owing to the colour's Chinese nationalist symbolism. The NP tapped into the widespread disillusionment among many KMT supporters over the party's shift to the centre on the identity spectrum. The party also created a very positive public image, as its founders were group of middle-aged, highly educated and articulate politicians. They were able to attract the financial and human resources needed for electoral campaigns. Although it only won a limited number of local election seats in its first two elections of 1993 and 1994, the NP had crossed the threshold to becoming a relevant party.

The next stage in the NP's development came in the mid-1990s, when it won significant numbers of seats in parliamentary elections. It went from almost nothing to 13 and 14 per cent of seats in the legislature and National Assembly, respectively, largely at the expense of the KMT. The key to the NP's success was broadening its appeal by its understanding of urban public opinion, especially in northern Taiwan and the major cities. The party began stressing popular issues, such as anti-corruption and a five-day working week. It also claimed to be the party of the ordinary city dweller. Moreover, it identified issue areas ignored by the two mainstream parties, such as welfare for the handicapped and closer economic integration with the People's Republic of China (PRC). Therefore, it was able to appeal to urban middle-class voters dissatisfied with the KMT but uncomfortable with what many viewed as the extremist and violent DPP.

However, by 1997, there were cracks in the NP product. Unity was destroyed in a series of high-profile public rows among the party's leading figures, and the party's appeal was limited to multiple-member district parliamentary elections and then mainly in the urban north. The party support base was vulnerable to supporters returning to the KMT once the party appeared to be returning to party orthodoxy, and, in 1998, many NP supporters returned to vote KMT, and the NP suffered a severe erosion of seats.

It is heatedly debated whether or not the NP's decline was avoidable. In 1997, a group of party reformers proposed taking the party towards the centre on national identity to enable the party to expand its support base, while, in 1995, another leader made proposals for greater emphasis on rural issues, such as farmers' welfare, to attract rural voters. In both cases, these initiatives were rejected by the party's founders as going against party ideology. Instead, from 1998, the party shifted to the far right on national identity, as the party became dominated by extremists. This meant that the party was moving in the opposite direction to public opinion, which was shifting to the centre left. Thus the NP made a transition from being a SOP in the mid 1990s to a POP by the late 1990s. This process continued through to the 2000 presidential election, as moderates left the party, and the party's electoral fortunes continued to worsen.

The NP's development since 2000 is the best Taiwanese model for political suicide in its marketing approach. The NP went from 5 per cent of seats in 1998 to being almost completely wiped out in the 2001 parliamentary election. The shift to becoming a pure POP after 1999 can be explained by changes in the party's internal power structure and the overall political environment. First, the broader appeals of the 1990s were dropped; instead, the party focused exclusively on attacking Taiwan independence, calling for closer integration with the PRC and appealing to Chinese nationalist symbols. For instance, in 2001, the NP held the first party-to-party negotiations with the Chinese Communist Party and called for unification under a model close to the PRC's one-country, two-systems model that is in use in Hong Kong. Such Chinese nationalist sentiments had been in steep decline since the early 1990s, so, by dropping its social appeals and taking more radical positions, the NP was appealing to a shrinking market.

As in the past, the NP continued to nominate very well-educated candidates with clean reputations; however, as critical as its poor issue strategies was its failure to adjust its product to suit the new post 2000 party system. After 2000, the centre right of Taiwanese politics became crowded, as the KMT reverted to party orthodoxy, and the People First Party appeared as a strong party, with a popular leader and an image similar to that of the NP. Rather than trying to move to the centre (as party reformers had attempted in 1997), the party shifted to the far right on national identity. This contributed to the party's disastrous results in 2000 and virtual disappearance in 2001.

Sources and further reading

Fell, Dafydd (2005). *Party Politics in Taiwan*. London: Routledge.

—— (2005). 'Success and failure of new parties in Taiwanese elections'. *China: An International Journal*, 3(2) (September): 212–39.

Rawnsley, Gary (2006). 'Democratization and election campaigning in Taiwan: professionalizing the professionals'. In Katrin Voltmer (ed.), *Mass Media and Political Communication in New Democracies*. London: Routledge, pp. 133–51.

Case study 9.5 Ideology matters: how political marketing influences the preparation process of election campaigns at Germany's federal state level   Melanie Diermann

This case explores whether, and, if so, in which way, German parties at the state level adapt marketing propositions in the preparation process of their election campaigns. It does so by investigating whether political actors accept that the concept of political marketing can be used for analysis, planning, realisation and control of success, for example in matters of political campaigning (Oellerking 1988: 16), so that they consider the voter's expectation in all steps of campaign development. Campaigns were analysed in the light of three possible ideal alternatives: product-oriented, sales-oriented or marketing-oriented (Lees-Marshment 2001), which are mainly based on the expectations of the potential voters. The case focuses on Germany's federal states, rather than just the national arena, which other political marketing literature considers. For this analysis, the preparation process of election campaigns considering the state election of 2005 in North Rhine-Westphalia (NRW) was selected, and the campaigns of all four member parties of the NRW state parliament were analysed.

Methodological approach

This analysis focuses on the period of campaign preparation regarding the state election in 2005, considering the question: how far it can be shown that NRW state parties adapt marketing propositions. Therefore, guideline-based expert interviews were recorded in all party headquarters, each with the person who had most responsibility regarding the campaign preparation process. Questions were asked about six areas, with areas 1–5 being implicit, while area 6 was explicit:

1   Campaign communication: how significant was the value of voters' expectations regarding the planning process of campaign communication?
2   Candidate selection: how significant was the value of voters' expectations regarding the candidate selection process?
3   Issue selection and positioning: how significant was the value of voters' expectations regarding the phase of programme definition?
4   Campaign distribution: how significant was the co-ordination process of the campaign components and resources?
5   Segmentation and targeting: was the campaign designed in a regional and target-group-specific way?
6   Explicit approvement of political marketing: does political marketing as a leading strategy for the process of campaign preparation matter in an explicit way?

The interviews were interpreted with qualitative content analysis, and it was asked whether the parties acted in a marketing-oriented, sales-oriented or product-oriented way in each of the six areas; the interviews were then collated to provide an overall result.

Appraisal of findings

All in all, the results show a broad distribution: see Table 9.3. In three of four cases, an (pro rata) implicit adaptation of marketing propositions was seen for areas 1–5. In area 6, which contained the direct confrontation with marketing terms and explicit questions regarding the importance of political marketing for the process of campaign preparation, there was also evidence for marketing adaptation, but not as clearly or consistently, suggesting some parties have ethical scruples about using marketing strategies.

Regarding the results overall, political marketing was adopted by the parties with differences in terms of orientation between the analysed parties: see Table 9.4. For the left-liberal Green Party, it can clearly be said that the campaign preparation process was more product-oriented. The results for the social democratic SPD suggested elements of MOP behaviour alongside SOP, especially regarding the implicit dimensions, while marketing adaptation in an explicit way was denied. For the liberal FDP and the conservative CDU, again adaptation of more market-oriented tendencies could be seen in the implicit areas. For the conservative CDU, this result was also reflected in the explicit area.

Conclusion

Overall, parties with more conservative ideologies seem to be more susceptible to marketing approaches (see Huber and Inglehart 1995 or Pappi and Shikano 2004). While the left-wing Green Party denied using marketing in an implicit and explicit way, the Social Democrats and

Table 9.3 Patterns of leadership, characterising the preparation process of election campaigns facing the state election in NRW, 2005

	Social Democrats (SPD)	Conservatives (CDU)	Green Party (Grüne)	Liberal Party (FDP)
1 Campaign communication	Marketing-oriented	Marketing-oriented	Product-oriented to sales-oriented	Marketing-oriented
2 Candidate selection	Marketing-oriented	Marketing-oriented	Product-oriented to sales-oriented	Sales-oriented to marketing-oriented
3 Issue selection and positioning	Marketing-oriented	Marketing-oriented	Product-oriented to sales-oriented	Marketing-oriented
4 Campaign distribution	Sales-oriented to marketing-oriented	Marketing-oriented	Product-oriented to sales-oriented	Marketing-oriented
5 Segmentation and targeting	Marketing-oriented	Marketing-oriented	Sales-oriented	Marketing-oriented
6 Explicit approvement of marketing aspects	Sales-oriented	Marketing-oriented	Product-oriented to sales-oriented	Sales-oriented

Table 9.4 Patterns of leadership regarding the campaign preparation process ahead of the NRW state election in 2005

Party	Patterns of leadership
Social Democrats (SDP)	Sales-oriented to marketing-oriented
Conservatives (CDU)	Marketing-oriented
Green Party (Grüne)	Product-oriented to sales-oriented
Liberal Party (FDP)	Sales-oriented to marketing-oriented

the liberal FDP also denied using marketing explicitly, but showed usage of marketing implicitly; the conservative CDU was much more positive towards market-oriented behaviour in all six areas.

This case study suggests there could well be other reasons than financial ones that make a party use marketing strategies within the campaign preparation process. Particularly with regard to the specific party ideology, these results show interesting correlations; left-wing ideology seems to cause a sceptical position with regard to political marketing strategies, while conservative and liberal ideologies seem to be correlated with a friendlier point of view concerning political marketing. These findings also agree with more general research results of party professionalisation, which also show a correlation between adaptation of professionalisation steps and Conservative Party ideology. Furthermore, this case study, as well as other research results found by the author (Diermann *et al.* 2007, Diermann and Korte 2007), shows that marketing-specific wording has in fact entered party headquarters. Nevertheless, these results also point out that this does not automatically mean a consistent, systematic or explicit application of the whole marketing framework, seen as a leadership strategy. Instead, marketing strategies seem to be applied in a more implicit and intuitive way, especially when the specific party ideology offers latitude for economic adaptations. Regarding further research, these findings advise taking a more detailed look at the (implicit) marketing mechanisms concerning the processes of decision-making in party headquarters, instead of searching for an (explicit) marketing orientation in the retrospective.

Sources and further reading

Diermann, Melanie (2007). *Politisches Marketing*. Marburg, Germany: Tectum Verlag.

—— and Karl-Rudolf Korte (2007). 'Im Südwesten nichts Neues?' In Josef Schmid and Udo Zolleis (eds), *Wahlkampf im Südwesten: Parteien, Kampagnen und Landtagswahlen 2006 in Baden-Württemberg und Rheinland-Pfalz*, Münster, Germany: LIT Verlag, pp. 66–87.

——, Moritz Ballensiefen and Karl-Rudolf Korte (2007). 'Alles Marketing oder was?! Betrachtung zweier Wahlwerbesports von SPD und CDU aus dem Bundestagswahlkampf 2005 unter Marketingaspekten'. S.101–128. In Andreas Dörner and Christian Schicha (eds), *Politik im Spot-Format Politische Werbung – ein Überblick*. Wiesbaden, Germany: VS Verlag für Sozialwissenschaften.

Huber, John and Ronald Inglehart (1995). 'Expert interpretations of party space and party locations in 42 societies'. *Party Politics*, 1(1): 73–111.

Lees-Marshment, J. (2001). *British Political Marketing and Political Parties*. Manchester: Manchester University Press.

Oellerking, Christian (1988). *Marketingstrategien für Parteien. Gibt es eine Techonolgie des legalen Machterwerbs?*. Frankfurt/Main: Lang Verlag.

Pappi, Franz Urban and Susumu Shikano (2004). 'The positions of parties in ideological and policy space: the perception of German voters of their party system'. Arbeitspapiere Mannheimer Zentrum für Europäische Sozialforschung, Mannheim, Germany.

The author would like to thank Professor Dr Rüdiger Schmitt-Beck for his support during this project.

Case study 9.6 How are Macedonian parties oriented?

Gordica Karanfilovska

The Republic of Macedonia is a young democracy that has passed through many significant political and economic processes since its independency in 1991. Several periods can be recognised and clarified according to the Lees-Marshment classification of product-, sales- and market-oriented behaviour of political parties.

The process of pluralism and liberalisation in the country in the fields of politics and the economy brought new values, behaviour, communication and structural organisation in the political parties of the country. The voter became a subject upon whom great attention was focused to meet his or her needs and wishes. Many techniques were used to find the best approach in order to satisfy him/her. The government, which adopted market-oriented behaviour, has led the country into a period of stabilisation and maturity. It is known that Macedonia is moving in the right direction by the confirmation of public opinion.

Nature of the market in the Republic of Macedonia

The Republic of Macedonia has a parliamentary democracy, with a multi-party system; it elects a national president every five years, and the government is chosen from the party or parties that has/have a majority in the assembly (*Sobranie*) elected every four years. The first multi-party elections in the Republic of Macedonia took place in September 1990.

Political parties as a *spiritus movens* of political processes contribute to the development of parliamentary democracy in the country. The Communist Party of Macedonia with its old ideology has passed through a process of reformation and has given birth to new parties, which have acquired new names. Brand new parties without any previous political experience came into the political market. The process of liberalisation in the economy brought a market-oriented economy, while the process of pluralisation has put many of the Macedonian politicians in a new position called political pluralism. The country's main political divergence is based on political views held by the largely ethnically based political parties representing the country's ethnic Macedonian majority and Albanian minority.

Many politicians did not have any previous experiance and have had to adjust to a new market, whereas before there was the only governing political party that had never been questioned. Now, in terms of competitiveness, they are facing a 'marketing shock'. Political marketing was at first only understood as advertising, with the focus on political communication. However, more recently it has been used in a planned marketing strategy for election campaigns, with greater utilisation of public opinion research agencies and focusing on the voter in political planning.

International political marketing training

The international community was quick to offer advice and experience to the new democracy, such as the Institute for Democracy, Solidarity and Civil Society, International Republican Institute, National Democratic Institute for International Affairs, OSCE-Office for Democratic Institutions and Human Rights. The table below shows examples of activities such as conferences, study visits, training courses, seminars and discussion programmes organised for the largest social democratic-oriented political parties in Macedonia: the Social Democratic Union of Macedonia (SDSM) and the Democratic Union for Integration (DUI).

Year	Themes
1998	Democracy, public relations, tolerance, building civil society, party programme and media
1999	Modern social democracy, ethnicity and civil society, use of language and education in multi-ethnic society, political institutions in divided societies
2000	Women in politics, local politics and political parties, youth, political system and corruption, youth, democracy and politics, organisation and democracy, organisational management in the party
2001	Political education
2002	Discussion programmes of German MPs with Macedonian politicians, forum on current political topics
2003	Political management, introduction of parliamentary democracy, political analysis, political communication, course for promising politicians, organisational management and pre-electoral campaign
2004	Political system and elections in Macedonia, organisation und methodology of political communication, course for promising politicians, follow-up of the promising politicians 2003 – study visit to Brussels and Strasburg
2005	Course for promising politicians, discussion programmes with representatives from EU countries and MPs from the Macedonian parliament, political organisation and communication, political management and its implementation in local self-government
2006	Course for promising politicians, study visit to the Slovenian and to the Austrian parliaments, communication and public relation skills, political communication – responsibilities and leadership

Periods of Macedonian life characterised with a certain model of political behaviour

The nature of the market has inevitably affected how political marketing has been used. Macedonian political parties passed the three models of behaviour by implementing the marketing concept in order to be more in touch with the people.

- **Stage of understanding of political marketing**: The beginning of the constitutive period (1991) was characterised by the start of transition and radical changes in the political and economic systems, such as the constitution of: the state, parliament, assembly, political parties, army, public services, judiciary system, local self-government, diplomatic mission, birth of new media, liberalisation of the market, process of privatisation etc. In this period, seen also as a period of transition, we can understand what political marketing means and recognise a five-stage (product design, communication, campaign, election, delivery) marketing process of the *product-oriented party*. The electorate and the parties were faced with a completely new political and economic situation. Parties proposed the best considered by them as crucial for the constitution of an independent country.
- **Stage of political marketing implementation**: This stage came in symbioses with the period of building civil society and decentralisation. The latter was characterised by continuation of transition, reinforcement of the fundamental elements of democracy and implementation of the processes of (de)centralisation. Using market intelligence, parties make an effort to understand voters' needs and, using the latest advertisement techniques, they endeavour to persuade them in what they want to offer to the voters. In this period, the marketing process is recognisable as and through the *sales-oriented behaviour* of parties.
- **Stage of managing the crucial period, using political marketing**: Political marketing played one of the main roles when the country went through a period of insecurity in transition (2001–03), characterised by making the effort to lead Macedonia out of civil war. Receiving the Balkans' influence on the political processes in the country with young parliamentarian democracy was a big challenge to continue building the country's 'career'. All political parties were confronted with the instability of the country and with the mission to bring peace back. For the first time, the Macedonian government recognised the need to have a spokesperson in its own structure. After the parliamentary election in 2002, the government introduced the position and the responsibility of a spokesperson who articulated that the state's institutions are more interested in communication with the voters and vice versa. Parties' *sales-oriented behaviour* was strongly visible in their attempt to have a positive influence through communication that was well planned and organised. This has been shown to have resulted in peace, achieved by all political participants in the country and supported by international communities.
- **Stage of growth in the use of political marketing**: This stage appears alongside the period of consolidation of democracy (2004–05) in the country. It was characterised by the continuation of the reform processes in Macedonia; by the introduction of a new goal in the state's diary with regard to the process of EU integration; communication with EU institutions; implementing EU policy; NATO integration processes; more understanding on the subject of political marketing, management and elections in Macedonia, etc. With certainty, we can say that it is not a coincidence that consolidation of democracy was an end product of the *market-oriented behaviour* of the parties. The voters' demands were identified using many polls, surveys and focus groups. Many products were designed to suit demands, bring satisfaction and create a path for the country to enter the European family.

- **Stage of maturity in use of political marketing**: Maturity contains the end and the beginning. The stage of maturity is concomitant with the period of maturation and stabilisation of the country (2006 to the present). In fact, the stage can be observed in the beginning of the end of the 'early transition' of the country and in the course of the *market-oriented behaviour,* which is the driving force for Macedonia's future. Becoming a member of the EU and NATO is one of the indispensable, key components of the agenda of the country. From the results of using polls, surveys and focus groups that evaluate voters' satisfaction concerning certain processes or activities, it is easy to comply with the voters' demands and create a policy for governing or strategy to run a political campaign.

Figures from the survey done on behalf of UNDP, from 2001 until 2007 (from Bilali *et al.* 2007), support the argument that the *market-oriented behaviour* of the parties has initiated the consolidation of democracy and the period of maturation and stabilisation of the country. This period is recognised by the voters: 'for the first time, those who consider that Macedonia is taking the right direction (45.3 per cent) are more numerous than those who think the opposite is true (39.7 per cent)' (p. 23). The policy of any government, including the Macedonian government, that is created by market-oriented behaviour brings hope instead of disappointment, because its focus is to serve citizens. Data suggested that the government's approach to carrying out policies was in tune with the voters' needs: 'after the elections in 2006, there has been an increase in the trust in the Government' (Ivanov 2007). The government focused on the issues citizens cared most about, such as improvement of the economy and decrease in unemployment; reduction of poverty; prevention of corruption and crime; and EU and NATO membership.

Conclusion

This case study showed how Macedonian political parties passed through experiences of product-, sales- and market-oriented behaviour, despite the country being a new democracy. In the beginning, political marketing was understood as an advertisement to make a trendy appeal or to attack political opposition. Nevertheless, later on it became the main source for parties to alter and amplify their behaviour, membership, organisational structure, leadership and policy.

Furthermore, the market-oriented behaviour of the parties had a crucial role in leading the country from a period of insecurity and transition into a period of consolidation and preparation for new challenges in the European family. Macedonian political parties were open to collaborate and learn from countries with much more experience of democracy and political marketing. Therefore, they successfully met the demands of the voters, giving them top-priority attention. In the future, Macedonian parties must strengthen their own human resources in the knowledge of political marketing and management. This is how they will gradually leave the infancy stage in which they were mainly supported by international organisations and strive towards the right direction of the country's development.

Sources and further reading

Bilali, M., L. Georgieva, G. Ivanov and V. Uzunov (2007). 'Early warning report' (Internet). Skopje, UNDP. Available online at www.undp.org.mk/datacenter/files//files07/EWR0607ENG.pdf (accessed 9 October 2007).

Chebotarev, A. (2007). Email to: Karanfilovska, G. Subject: Chebotarev. 7 September 2007.

Ivanov, G. (2007). Email to: Karanfilovska, G. Subject: UNDP. 18 September 2007.

Mihajlovski, S. and D.M. Verigic (1998). 'Multiparty elections in Republic of Macedonia. Skopje'. (In Macedonian) Institute of Sociological, Juridical and Political Research.

Trajkovska, N. (2007). Email to: Karanfilovska, G. Subject: Fw: Request for list of trainings_Gordica. 4 September 2007.

Case study 9.7 The 'party of power' in Russian politics
Derek S. Hutcheson

Russia's party system has suffered throughout the post-communist period from a lack of institutionalisation. Nonetheless, although the menu of parties on offer at successive elections has varied, there has been a clear trend away from programmatic parties towards more amorphous 'parties of power' – relatively ideology-free, 'virtual' parties, whose sole unifying policy is support for the presidential administration and government.

'Parties of power' have been successive political structures formed *from within* by the entrenched establishment to consolidate and legitimise its rule through party façades. Their party platforms have lacked ideological foundation, and their identities have been defined through market-oriented, media-driven television campaigns to position themselves within gaps in the electoral market (hence the Sarah Oates' (2006) description of them as 'broadcast parties'). These virtual structures have in turn been given a public face through the presence of prominent national politicians, regional governors and numerous middle-ranking state officials in the party's regional leadership organs.

The pro-Kremlin parties' early attempts to use 'marketing' in the mid 1990s focused too much on the outputs – professional-looking advertisements – and neglected real marketing features such as product assessment and product adjustment in the 'inputs'. As a result, a sales-oriented approach was inadvertently adopted that sought to sell unpopular government policies and leaders to a sceptical electorate, rather than reflect its aspirations. The situation has reversed since 1999, and the 'party of power' has been the dominant electoral form in the second decade of Russian independence in legislative and other elections.

The success of the 'parties of power' is based on a variety of factors, not least of which is the tremendous administrative capital advantage that comes with the backing of the federal and regional administrations, domination of television news coverage and the reflected popularity of a popular president. At a marketing level, however, the 'product' has evolved within these parameters. In this brief examination, we focus on the segmentation, product design and product adjustment phases of the last three national parliamentary elections to the state Duma.

In 1999, Unity was one of a number of 'parties of power' hastily formed by competing elite groups. Rather than reuse a sales-oriented approach to sell unpopular government policies, the liberal 'brand' was attached to a smaller, pro-presidential organisation, the Union of Rightist Forces, which ultimately gained 8.5 per cent of the vote. Unity, on the other hand, targeted centrist non-ideological voters – a potential 35 per cent of the electorate, according to New Russia Barometer VIII. Formed a matter of weeks before the election in an attempt to slow the momentum of the rival Fatherland-All Russia movement, it sought to de-emphasise ideology and was careful to avoid creating a 'product' on which its delivery could be tested. Its main weakness – potential association with the unpopular Yeltsin and the oligarch-dominated Kremlin 'Family' – was neutralised by fronting the campaign with new and apolitical figures, combined with the implicit backing of the popular new prime minister, Vladimir Putin. Its platform, such as existed, was to emphasise a strong, safe and non-corrupt Russian state, tapping into the popularity of the war in Chechnya. This image was encapsulated by images of its three non-political leaders in action, its very vague adverts and its use of the traditional Russian bear as its emblem. By and large, it succeeded unexpectedly in targeting the middle voter: it was striking how similar its ultimate voter profile was to that of the Russian electorate as a whole.

For the 2003 state Duma election, some product adjustment was required. Unity and Fatherland-All Russia merged in 2001 to form a coherent pro-presidential party called United Russia, with a more extensive infrastructure, and the target on this occasion was to form a parliamentary faction that would control the Duma for the next four years. Once again, the Kremlin segmented its electorate: this time it focused on creating a 'virtual' left-wing party, Motherland, to draw communist voters, leaving United Russia to target the centrist and centre-right electorate. The party platform was again vague, and the main 'product' was its support for Vladimir Putin. As such, it attempted to cultivate itself as the party of a vaguely defined national interest, and its branding effectively conflated its identity with that of the state itself: the bear image was retained, and there was constant use of the Russian national flag and a stylised map of the country on almost all party literature. It made rhetorical and historical links with Russia's pre-Soviet history, and saturated the country with Putin's fairly nondescript pun on the party name that 'together we will make Russia strong and united' (although his backing was in a private capacity, and he was not officially a party member or on its list).

The success of this strategy meant that it was further developed for 2007. For the third election in a row, the essential elements remained the same, but the 'product' – Putin's now explicit support – was further developed. The focus of its once again vague programme was on 'continuing the course of Putin'; indeed, it sought to redefine the election as 'a national referendum on Putin', whose name featured in the title of the party's manifesto, and who was referred to as the 'national leader'. This attempt to polarise the electorate carried the subliminal message that anybody not voting for it was voting against the 'national leader' and, by implication, being unpatriotic. The segmentation strategy was slightly less assured on this occasion: after attempting in the pre-election months to build up a centre-left partner for United Russia called 'Fair Russia', aimed once again at siphoning off communist voters, Putin's decision to head the United Russia party list himself left its partner to carry out the difficult balancing act of being 'in opposition to the ruling liberal United Russia party but supportive of Vladimir Putin'. Nonetheless, the overwhelming success of United Russia itself compensated for this.

The success of the 'party of power' model in the last decade gives several important indications. The rise of United Russia (and other satellite 'parties of power') has been reinforced by the consolidation of the elite, such that 'administrative resources' in Russian election campaigns have become a unipolar resource. United Russia's primary advantage, as Putin himself has noted, is that it is 'close to the power structures', even though it lacks firm ideological principles.

The 1990s showed, however, that being close to power does not, in itself, guarantee success if the product is not designed properly. In other words, a 'party of power' cannot be created without effective segmentation and targeting of the electoral middle ground. The twin strategies of segmenting the potential electorate – using newly established satellite parties to target ideologically driven voters and leaving the electoral middle ground to the main 'party of power' – and designing the project around a president and platform that seek to be above politics have served the Kremlin well in the first decade of the twenty-first century.

Sources and further reading

Hale, Henry E. (2006). *Why Not Parties in Russia? Democracy, Federalism and the State.* Cambridge: Cambridge University Press.

Hutcheson, Derek S. (2003). *Political Parties in the Russian Regions.* London/New York: Routledge Curzon.

—— (2006). 'How to win elections and influence people: the development of political consulting in post-communist Russia.' *Journal of Political Marketing,* 5(4): 47–70.

Oates, Sarah (2006). *Television, Democracy and Elections in Russia.* London/New York: Routledge Curzon.

Overloot, Hans and Ruben Verheul (2000). 'The party of power in Russian politics'. *Acta Politica,* 35: 123–45.

Wilson, Andrew (2005). *Virtual Politics.* New Haven/London: Yale University Press.

FURTHER READING

Baines, Paul (2004). 'Marketing the political message: American influences on British practices'. *Journal of Political Marketing*, 4(2/3): 135–62.

Bowler, Shaun and David M. Farrell (eds) (1992). *Electoral Strategies and Political Marketing*. Hampshire: Macmillan.

Boynton, Rachel (2005). *Our Brand Is Crisis*. Boynton Films; or (2006) Kock Lorber Films. DVD, ISBN 1–4172–0108–8.

Cotrim Maciera, Josiane (2005). 'Change to win? The Brazilian Workers' Party's 2002 General Election marketing strategy'. In Darren G. Lilleker and Jennifer Lees-Marshment (eds), *Political Marketing: A Comparative Perspective*. Manchester: Manchester University Press.

Fell, Dafydd and Isabelle Cheng (2007). 'Testing the market-oriented model of political parties in a non-Western context: the case of Taiwan'. Paper presented at the 4th ECPR General Conference, Pisa, 6–8 September 2007. Section: 'Professionalisation of Campaigning and Political Marketing Panel: Political Marketing Strategy'.

Hutcheson, Derek S. (2007). 'Political marketing in Russia in the era of managed democracy'. Paper presented at the 4th ECPR General Conference, Pisa, 6–8 September 2007. Section: 'Professionalisation of Campaigning and Political Marketing Panel: Political Marketing Strategy'.

Ingram, Peter, and Jennifer Lees-Marshment (2002). 'The Anglicisation of political marketing: how Blair 'out-marketed' Clinton'. *Journal of Public Affairs*, 2(2): 44.

Johnson, Dennis (2001). 'Perspectives on political consulting'. *Journal of Political Marketing*, 1(1): 7–22.

—— (2007). *No Place for Amateurs* (2nd edn). New York: Routledge.

Kaid, Lynda Lee and Christina Holtz-Bacha (eds) (2006). *The Sage Handbook of Political Advertising*. London: Sage.

King, Desmond and Mark Wickham-Jones (1999). 'From Clinton to Blair: the [US] Democratic (Party) origins of welfare to work'. *Political Quarterly*, 70(1): 62–74.

Kinsey, Dennis F. (1999). 'Political consulting: bridging the academic and practical perspectives'. In Bruce Newman (ed.), *A Handbook of Political Marketing*. Thousand Oaks, CA: Sage.

Knuckey, Jonathan and Jennifer Lees-Marshment (2005). 'American political marketing: George W. Bush and the Republican Party'. In D.G. Lilleker and J. Lees-Marshment (eds), *Political Marketing in Comparative Perspective*. Manchester: Manchester University Press.

Kotzaivazoglou, Iordanis and Yorgos Zotos (2007). 'Political marketing in Greece and the level of marketing orientation of Greek parties'. Paper presented at the 4th ECPR General Conference, Pisa, 6–8 September 2007. Section: 'Professionalisation of Campaigning and Political Marketing Panel: Political Marketing Strategy'.

Laghi, B. (2006). 'How Harper fashioned his lead'. *The Globe and Mail*. Accessed from www.theglobeandmail.com/servlet/story/RTGAM.20060107.wxharper07/BNStory/specialNewTory2006/ on 6 May 2008.

Lederer, A., F. Plasser and C. Scheucher (2005). 'The rise and fall of populism in Austria – a political marketing perspective'. In D.G. Lilleker and J. Lees-Marshment (eds), *Political Marketing: A Comparative Perspective*. Manchester: Manchester University Press.

Lees, C. (2005). 'Political marketing in Germany: the case of the SPD'. In D.G. Lilleker and J. Lees-Marshment (eds), *Political Marketing: A Comparative Perspective*. Manchester: Manchester University Press.

Lees-Marshment, Jennifer (2001). *Political Marketing and British Political Parties: The Party's Just Begun*. Manchester: Manchester University Press.

—— (2008). 'Comprehensive political marketing: global political parties, strategy and behavior'. In Adrian Sargeant and Walter Wymer (eds), *Non-Profit Marketing Companion Text*. New York: Routledge.

——, Chris Rudd and Jesper Strömbäck (eds) (2009). *Global Political Marketing*, London: Routledge.

Lilleker, Darren and Jennifer Lees-Marshment (eds) (2005). *Political Marketing: A Comparative Perspective*. Manchester: Manchester University Press.

Marland, A. (2005). 'Canadian political parties: market-oriented or ideological slagbrains?'. In Darren Lilleker and Jennifer Lees-Marshment (eds), *Political marketing: a comparative perspective*. Manchester: Manchester University Press.

McGough, S. (2005). 'Political marketing in Irish politics: the case of Sinn Féin'. In Darren Lilleker and Jennifer Lees-Marshment (eds), *Political Marketing: A Comparative Perspective*. Manchester: Manchester University Press.

Medvic, Stephen K. (2001). *Political Consultants in US Congressional Elections*, Parliaments and Legislatures Series. Columbus: Ohio State University Press.

—— (2006). 'Understanding campaign strategy "deliberate priming" and the role of professional political consultants'. *Journal of Political Marketing*, 5(1/2): 11–32.

Patrón-Galindo, P. (2005). 'The re-launch of the APRA party: the use of political marketing in Peru in a new political era'. In Darren Lilleker and Jennifer Lees-Marshment (eds), *Political Marketing: A Comparative Perspective*. Manchester: Manchester University Press.

Plasser, Fritz (2000). 'American campaign techniques worldwide'. *Harvard International Journal of Press/Politics*, 5(4): 33.

—— Christian Scheucher and Christian Seft (1999). 'Is there a European style of political marketing? A survey of political managers and consultants'. In Bruce Newman (ed.), *A Handbook of Political Marketing*. Thousand Oaks, CA: Sage.

—— and Gunda Plasser (2002). *Global Political Campaigning. A Worldwide Analysis of Campaign Professionals and Their Practices*. Westport, CT: Praeger.

Róka, Jolán (2004). 'Forming political cultural and marketing strategies in a central-European setting'. *Journal of Political Marketing*, 3(2): 78–108.

—— (2005). 'Turnout and its strategic political marketing implications in Hungary during the 2004 European Parliamentary Elections'. *Journal of Political Marketing*, 4(2): 169–75.

Rowin, M.J. with M. Koresky and C. Wisniewski (2006). 'Anger management: Rachel Boynton's "Our brand is crisis"', 27 February 2006, available online at www.indiewire.com/movies/2006/02/anger_managemen.html (accessed April 2008).

Rudd, Chris (2005). 'Marketing the message or the messenger?'. In Darren Lilleker and J. Lees-Marshment (eds), *Political Marketing in Comparative Perspective*. Manchester: Manchester University Press.

Strömbäck, Jesper (2007). 'Antecedents of political market orientation in Britain and Sweden: analysis and future research propositions'. *Journal of Public Affairs*, 7(1): 79–90.

—— (2009). 'A framework for comparing political market orientation'. In Jennifer Lees-Marshment, Chris Rudd and Jesper Strömbäck (eds), *Global Political Marketing*. London: Routledge.

Sussman, Gerald and Lawrence Galizio (2003). 'The global reproduction of American politics'. *Political Communication*, 20(3): 309–28.

Thurber, James and Candice Nelson (eds) (2000). *Campaign Warriors: Political Consultants in Elections*. Washington, DC: Brookings.

Watt, N. (2005) 'The Guardian profile: Lynton Crosby'. *The Guardian*, 28 January. Available online at www.guardian.co.uk/politics/2005/jan/28/uk.conservatives (accessed 16 April 2008).

Work by practitioners themselves

Gould, Philip (1998). *The Unfinished Revolution: How the Modernisers Saved the Labour Party*. New York: Little Brown.

Morris, Dick (1998).) *Behind the Oval Office: Getting Re-elected Against All Odds*. New York: Renaissance Books.

Penn, Mark with E. Kinney Zalesne (2006). *Micro-Trends: The Small Forces Behind Tomorrow's Big Changes*. New York: Twelve, Hachette Book Group.

Shrum, Robert (2007). *No Excuses: Concessions of a Serial Campaigner*. New York: Simon & Schuster.

Stephaneopoulos, George (1999). *All Too Human: A Political Education*. New York: Little Brown.

Trippi, Joe (2004). *The Revolution Will Not Be Televised: Democracy, the Internet, and the Overthrow of Everything*. New York: Regan Books.

10 Political marketing and democracy

Political marketing is an approach that politicians, parties and governments can use to attain, increase and maintain support from the public in order to gain or retain power in office. It includes a range of activities, including orientations; market intelligence to understand, predict and identify the market; product development strategies and positioning; internal marketing approaches; communication and campaigning; and marketing once in government. Marketing can be used simply to inform communication and presentation of the political product and potentially affect the outcome of elections; furthermore, it can be used to inform the nature of that political product and influence government policy and legislation. This raises concerns about its impact on democracy. Political marketing has profound ramifications for the political system from a normative, ethical or democratic perspective. This chapter will explore all of the issues: first, the problems with political marketing; and, second, the potential of political marketing.

Problems with political marketing

Political marketing leads to the end of ideology

The first major concern with political marketing is that it will lead to the end of ideology. Ideology is like an applied philosophy: it puts forward an idea of how things should be. It provides a framework of principles from which policies can be developed. In political parties, ideology is intended to provide an enduring, long-standing source of ideas for policy. Savigny (2006: 83) notes how ideology 'plays a significant role in the political process', because values and beliefs 'about the proper distribution of resources, and what a society should look like, underpins the notion of politics'. Practitioner perspective 10.1 highlights the importance of values and conviction in politics.

In practice, many concerns were raised with the way UK New Labour, in 1997, was seen as a vacuous product, lacking distinction and having abandoned many of Labour's long-standing policies or beliefs on issues such as public spending and tax. Lees-Marshment and Lilleker (2001) examined the extent to which New Labour was a party with values or a skilfully manufactured entity designed to win elections, by considering the history of the party as well as its behaviour in 1997. They note how Blair even addressed this in a party election broadcast on 27 May 2001, noting how he was often criticised for lacking principles. Blair was criticised by academics, media and comedians for lacking ideas and having overridden his party's traditional values in order to lead it to electoral success in 1997. The 1997 manifesto clearly stated New Labour to be 'a party of ideas and ideals but not of outdated ideology'. They suggest that, despite the changes made under Blair to policy and the apparent newness of the policies, not all ethos – i.e. Labour's sense of historical identity

Practitioner perspective 10.1

The message is simple. Political marketing is important and is certainly no threat to the democratic process. It is simply that it will not prove effective unless it is founded on substance . . . Political parties cannot just become marketing exercises even if they wish to. Ultimately it will fail because the public won't wear it . . . there will always be a market for conviction in politics.

(David McLetchie, leader of the Scottish MSP Conservatives, 1999–2005, debate on political marketing and democracy, Aberdeen, 2002)

I think you got to look at . . . whether or not one makes decisions on sound principles, or whether or not you rely upon polls and focus groups on how to decide what the course of action is. We don't stick our finger in the air trying to figure out which way the wind is blowing. I do what I think is right for the American people.

(George W. Bush, then candidate for president, in the first presidential debate as reported in *New York Times* 3 April 2002: A21)

developed through tradition and experience – was removed. Marketisation was more a development and updating of the party than an outright rejection of the party's past, even if the phrase 'New' Labour was used to appeal to concerned voters who wanted a different future from the party. Blair did integrate elements of Labour ideology such as neo-liberalism, communitarianism and socialism, while policy was developed to suit the reality of changing circumstances, such as capitalism, but with a Labour approach such as social justice.

Discussion point 10.1

To what extent did Blair's New Labour succeed in integrating ideology into the market-oriented product in 1997?

However, there is no doubt that, within some parties, the tension between doing what is right and winning election persists, and marketing, by informing product development in response to market demands, exacerbates this and alongside it a feeling that something may be lost in the attempt to respond to the market, or segments of it, to win control of government.

Political marketing imposes an ideology of marketing itself

Savigny (2006) argues that the rise of political marketing has led political parties to adopt the ideology of marketing itself. She contends that, as political marketing is based on the

Debate 10.1

Proposition: Political marketing leads to the end of ideology.

analogy that 'parties behave as businesses, voters as consumers, all operating in a political market place', and this in turn is based on the managerialist, rational-choice, neo-classical economic perspective, this introduces such concepts into the political sphere (2006: 83). Furthermore, political marketing analysis carries certain assumptions into analysis that raise a number of issues (Savigny 2006: 26 and 33–4):

1   there is an assumption of rationality;
2   there is a perception that preferences are fixed, transitive, expressed and identifiable;
3   it endorses a positivist epistemological position of rational choice theory;
4   placing the consumer/voter at the centre of the political process improves the quality of democracy;
5   by providing the consumer with a product they want, the process is responsive to consumer demand, which makes politicians more accountable;
6   there is a reciprocal and dynamic relationship between parties and voters;
7   it only considers consumer wants and needs in order to achieve organisational goals, not those of the consumer;
8   it neglects to consider how the organisation manipulates the preferences of the consumer.

Indeed, marketing itself has become an ideology in politics, and such issues were shown in the 2005 UK election: see Case study 10.1.

Segmentation targets only certain groups

One of the problems with using market segmentation is that it enables, and arguably encourages, politicians to target certain groups whose support they need – rather than represent the public as a whole. Steger (1999: 680) argues that local political marketing by Congressional members means in the US:

> representation of the public interest more generally occurs as a side effect of, or an externality to, the exchanges between politicians and their constituencies . . . legislators are disproportionately attentive and responsive to those subsets of society that contribute most heavily to their re-election.

This is problematic from a normative democratic perspective that considers the ideal of egalitarianism. Savigny (2007) argued that this happened in the UK, when New Labour conducted and responded to focus groups from certain segments of the population, so that the party was only listening to certain groups in society – 'Tory switchers' – who were not representative of the electorate at large. Similarly, Lilleker (2005a) observed how 'segmentation of the market and targeting of communication are to some extent responsible for causing a division in society: those to whom politics belongs and those whom politics has abandoned.'

Political marketing alienates internal supporters

As well as market segmentation encouraging responsiveness to one section of society at the risk of others, political marketing can lead to a neglect of internal supporters. Lilleker (2005a) argues that UK New Labour lost volunteers because its promises became more oriented 'towards the middle-class swingers, rejecting working-class based politics'. Such concern for traditional supporters tends to be restricted to developed democracies where there are established ideological traditions. In some cases, party members play a significant

---

Discussion point 10.2

To what extent does using market segmentation give more voice to one section of society than another?

---

role in internal party democracy, participation, policy-making and campaigning. They therefore develop loyalty and attachment to a party and what it stands for. They participate because of a 'belief in a common societal goal' (Lilleker 2005b: 571). Political marketing can change internal power: as strategists, together with the leadership, determine policy direction in relation to market intelligence, this 'can leave ordinary members feeling alienated' (Lilleker 2005b: 573) if they see no response to their demands within that product development process. In the UK Labour case, Lilleker (2005b) found that members felt there had been a lack of consultation and they had been disenfranchised.

Political marketing focuses on short-term benefit

Political marketing can encourage more focus on short-term solutions – what the market wants for the next electoral period, rather than what is right for the country in the long term. The market-oriented concept of political marketing may conflict with the need for long-term solutions, especially in areas such as the environment. There may be a conflict between immediate consumer wants and the long-term welfare of citizens. Responsible marketing should be more concerned with quality of life in the long term rather than the short term.

Polling and marketing undermine creativity and new ideas

Excessive following of public opinion can also undermine creativity in policy development. As Paleologos (1997: 1184) argues: 'Herein lies the depressing and harsh reality of a poll-driven society. This is what it means for each and every one of us. Such a society ignores creativity. It overlooks new ideas. It prohibits change and true reform.'

Paleologos (1997: 1184) argues that polling is unlikely to uncover new ideas. Even if an individual 'had a great idea or plans for a new policy, it would never get picked up or recognised in the analysis', because there has to be a certain number expressing that idea.

Even market-oriented politics, which isn't purely about just following voters, may prevent emergence of new policies that at first seem controversial, but are a necessary part of society's development, and therefore reduces participation and deliberation. Washbourne (2005) argues that:

> what is missed out is the idea of public discussion and debate being central to, even representative of, politics. CPM's (Comprehensive political marketing's) replacement of (some part of) public discussion by polls and focus groups bypasses democratic politics rather than engages it . . . it also neglects the complex role that debate plays in the origins of people's political ideas, identities and even (recognition of their) interests.

Paleologos (1997: 1187) also noted the need to maintain a public sphere: 'a society that has no public sphere risks loss of any sense of itself as a true collective, replete with shared problems, dreams, opportunities, and viewpoints.' Case study 10.2 raises issues as to whether a MOP strategy encourages ignorance of more difficult, controversial issues.

Political marketing places too much trust in public opinion

Often, political marketing is seen as arguing that politicians need to pay too much attention to the needs of public opinion. The problem with this is the issue of how the public forms its opinion, and also how it articulates it. Lane (1996: 40–5) argues that such theory assumes individuals have certain abilities, such as how to advance their interests through public policies and how to monitor the performance of incumbents on matters related to the individual's own interests. However, individuals may not be able to do this in practice. Demands are not unitary and need to be divided into wants, desires, interests and needs. Marketing can encourage a neglect of the real needs of the population. Voters may never gain enough understanding of the implications of policy choices. Lane (1996: 47–9) notes that, compared with political elites, the mass public is generally:

1   less interested in politics and less likely to discuss politics;
2   less supportive of open discussion of conflicting opinion and more willing to forbid discussion of policy issues considered to be sensitive;
3   less tolerant and more punitive towards disliked groups;
4   less likely to support legal due process for people accused of crimes;
5   morally more rigid, conventional and moralistic, and more ready to make categorical moral judgements;
6   more nationalistic and less international in outlook;
7   less able to weigh the costs of policies supported;
8   likely to display the instability and inconsistency of mass opinion in the face of counterarguments.

Many arguments have been made that the public can't decide key questions: see Box 10.1.
    However, marketing suggest that elites pay more attention to their markets, including citizens, professionals, informed activists and new members. Furthermore, attention can include disagreeing with different views; what matters is listening and responding in some form, rather than slavishly following public opinion.

Political marketing restricts effective leadership

In their acceptance speech for the nomination to run for the 2000 US presidential election, both Bush and Gore tried to argue they did not, and should not, use polls in decision-making: see Practitioner perspective 10.2. The political elite can be considered better qualified to make decisions about what the people need and should be given.

Practitioner perspectives 10.2

The presidency is more than a popularity contest. It's a day to day fight for people. Sometimes you have to choose what's difficult or unpopular.

(Gore, acceptance speech, DNC, 17 August 2000)

I believe great decisions are made with care, made with conviction, not made with polls, I do not need to take your pulse before I know my own mind.

(Bush, acceptance speech, RNC, 3 August 2000)

Box 10.1 Objections to the general public making political decisions

The central questions of politics, the nature of punishment, the organisation of health and education, foreign relations and the formation of law cannot be settled on the basis of consumers' expression of wants.

(Walsh 1994: 68)

Politicians are there, or ought to be there, to do what is right by their country. They ought to have the courage of their convictions to do what is right and then they ought to employ the means available to put over that message and explain effectively why those policies are in the interests of the nation. If all we do is reduce politics to the art of analysing public opinion and going for that which is possible, then all we shall have is a bunch of measly, incompetent, useless followers.

(Bernard Ingram, former press secretary to Prime Minister Margaret Thatcher, in a debate held at the House of Commons in 2003. *Journal of Public Affairs*, 4(3))

Voters are promiscuous and rationally irresponsible in the range of inconsistent views they hold at any one time, and rarely think about long-term policy consequences in ways that politicians and their advisors are required to do.

(Coleman 2007: 181)

Asking the general population to vote effectively on certain subjects raises a number of complex issues ... the general public may hold views which are considered by policy-makers to be unacceptable in society.

(Scrivens and Witzel 1990: 11)

Pandering to the prejudices of the majority might herald a tyranny of the ill-formed. Capital punishment, forced repatriation and other lowest common denominator issues could become important if marketing research showed a short-term benefit in courting them.

(Smith and Saunders 1990: 298)

This does raise profound questions. The delegate theory of representation argues that it is better for each person to decide what is best for him or herself. Market economics supports this approach: the model assumes, in a perfect market, that demand creates supply until demand is satisfied. Nevertheless, in practice, there are a number of problems with this (Lane 1996: 37–8):

1 Politics separates benefits from costs, so only society rather than the individual considers the costs and benefits.
2 Demands are often voiced by political elites before the market raises them.
3 Decision-making in politics is very different to economics; the individualistic assumption does not apply well in politics.
4 The concept of the common good in politics includes market externalities and ideals and the needs of those without purchasing power.

Political marketing, by encouraging politicians to over rely on market intelligence results, can be seen to undermine leadership. Paleologos (1997: 1183) argues that 'polling today ... harms our democracy ... Politicians are unwilling to take important leadership risks when immediate electoral gratification is so starkly visible.' Even in power, leaders are constrained: Newman (1999: 41) noted how Bill Clinton's desire to introduce legislation to protect homosexuals in the military was prevented by strong opposition:

> Herein lies the dilemma facing political leaders, who want to be responsive to the needs and desires of the citizenry. Even though leaders strongly believe in pushing through certain legislation, the cost to them in their approval ratings might be so great that they simply retreat from their positions.

Some issues may be less suitable for determination by public opinion than others (see Murray 2006). Kaufmann (2004: 32) noted how, in the US debate in 2002–03 on the decision to go to war with Iraq, a number of factors prevented effective discussion taking place, in a way that meant the public were less able to develop effective opinions, including:

1   The ability of the White House to control the release of intelligence information.
2   The authority advantage of the presidency in national security policy debates.
3   The failure of countervailing institutions – mainly the press, independent experts and opposition parties – on which the marketplace of ideas theory relies to combat threat inflation.
4   The crisis atmosphere created by the shock of September 11.

Not only is leadership sometimes justified for the good of the country or the world, forgetting principles can also lose an election. Morris (2002) argues that Al Gore lost the 2000 presidential election against George W. Bush precisely because he did not stand up for the ideal he really believed in. Morris (2002: 76) observed how Gore was a true believer in the need to take action to protect the environment: 'even when polls said the public wasn't ready for a serious focus on the issue, he continued to study, ponder, and act when he could to save the planet.' In his earlier political career, he was ahead of his time; a bid to win the Democratic presidential nomination in 1988 focused on the environment met with ridicule; the *New York Times* said he was esoteric, and his own party also reacted negatively: 'Gore came to realise that his environmentalism wasn't selling' (Morris 2002: 78).

Discussion point 10.3

The easy thing to do, frankly, is to hit the button on exactly what the public wants to hear ... The responsibility, though, in the end, particularly in the case of war, is to do what I believe to be the right thing for the country. I can't do it simply on the basis of the number of people who demonstrate, or on the basis of this opinion poll or that opinion poll. You've got to do, on an issue like this, what you genuinely believe to be right for the country, and then pay the price at the election if people disagree with you.

(Tony Blair, *Tony and June*, Channel 4, 30 January 2005)

To what extent do you agree with Tony Blair? Do the public not consume war enough to be informed enough about the complexities of international relations, war strategy, the realities of the battleground and the interplay of global forces to make the right decision?

He doubted his own political judgement, and that trying to do something the market did not want at that time was not going to work. Morris (2002: 79) quotes Gore as saying in retrospect that:

> I began to doubt my own political judgement, so I began to ask the pollsters and professional politicians what they thought I ought to talk about. As a result, for much of the campaign I discussed what everybody else discussed . . . a familiar list of what the insiders agree are the issues.

In 2000, Gore was over-cautious about focusing on his own issue, knowing the problem of ignoring issues people care most about before campaigning begins. However, by putting the environment on the back burner, he lost his traditional supporters in the process. Morris (2002: 83) quotes *Time* magazine as saying in 2000:

> His strategists figure, quite right, that he can't be elected President solely as Mr. Environment and Technology . . . If all this means that Gore will soft pedal his signature cause, climate change . . . that's bad for the earth and unworthy of a politician who has a record for being principled and decisive.

Morris (2002: 86–7) argues that, had Gore stuck to his environmental principles, he could have gained secure support from environmentally conscious voters, and the young especially, and implemented an activist agenda, and sometimes the politicians rely too much on experts, and experts stick to the conventional wisdom too much. Leaders have always been constrained by the market, but perhaps even more now they are so acutely aware of public opinion and receive advice from consultants.

Demand exceeds capabilities

The problem with markets is that, in most cases, demand always exceeds expectations. The use of political marketing raises expectations. This is the problem with delivery, as noted in the chapter on marketing in government. Even when they are satisfied, they then want more. In his last party conference speech in 2006 Tony Blair noted:

> I spoke to a woman the other day, a part-time worker, complaining about the amount of her tax credit. I said: Hold on a minute: before 1997, there were no tax credits, not for working families, not for any families; child benefit was frozen; maternity pay half what it is; maternity leave likewise and paternity leave didn't exist at all. And no minimum wage, no full time rights for part time workers, in fact nothing. 'So what?', she said 'that's why we elected you. Now go and sort out my tax credit.'

Discussion point 10.4

To what extent can politicians decide for themselves when to follow their own convictions and focus on a new issue? Could an advisor guide them so they are never too soon, but also never too late, to raise a change-the-world position?

Sales-oriented marketing gives undue power to extremist political parties

Marketing techniques such as segmentation and targeting enable parties to concentrate their efforts and can help smaller parties and new candidates gain support, and power, in a shorter period of time. While this can be seen as beneficial, it can also be problematic where extremist parties utilise marketing to increase their support: see Case study 10.3.

Global political product marketing

As the previous chapter on global knowledge transfer showed, increasingly political leaders get their ideas for strategy and product development from other countries, resulting in significant similarity between campaigns around the world. This can reduce the potential for new policy and product development, resulting in inertia and, overall, a lack of responsiveness to changing market demands.

Political marketing causes declining turnout

Lees-Marshment and Lilleker (2005) argued that the sudden fall in turnout in the UK 2001 election suggested that, although in theory the dominance of the MOP approach should lead to a higher level of interest from the voter, in 2001 participation fell. The greater the use of targeted marketing techniques, such as voter segmentation, the more likely it is that non-target groups are demobilised, so political marketing could cause the problem. However, it is reasonable to note that there are many other potential reasons for low turnout, all unrelated to the use of political marketing.

Parties in government are more likely to descend into a SOP than maintain a MOP

Marland's (2005) case study of Canadian parties in 2000 showed that, if the governing party is the only MOP, with the competition adopting less responsive strategies, then there is little pressure for that organisation to remain market-oriented. Similarly, Lees (2005) noted that, despite market-oriented behaviour in 1998, once in power the SPD moved away from the MOP strategy, because it was constrained by the SPD's record in government. Change was easier in opposition than in government. Furthermore, Marland (2005) argued that marketing can become very negative: 'an environment of multiple sales-oriented parties may turn nasty . . . Market intelligence is not used to primarily identify benefits for electors, but also to identify negative messages that can be used as part of a conflict marketing strategy . . . resulting in lower trust in politicians, and increasing numbers of dissatisfied electors.' The longer that a government is not challenged by another MOP, the further it can descend into a SOP or even POP, and the less democratic accountability exists for its decision-making.

Consumerism threatens the notion of citizenship and equality

As explored in Chapter 1, consumerism can threaten values associated with citizenship. Aberbach and Christensen (2005: 234) noted that 'neo-liberal reforms have a market logic that downplays or even disregards the legal and moral aspects of citizenship that were emphasised in the republican (and what we have also called the collective) concept of the citizen role.' Treating voters as consumers does not guarantee equality. Consumer and customer concepts ignore the big issues of politics, such as distribution of power, fairness and social justice (Aberbach and Christensen 2005: 236).

Consultation does not always lead to responsiveness in government

As noted in Chapter 4, many studies of consultation by governments raise concerns about the degree to which it is genuine, affects decision-making and promotes positive participatory democracy. For example, Needham (2002) studied the impact of the 1997 UK Labour government's requirement of local councils to introduce consultation as part of 'Best Value' and found that there were many barriers to councils actually responding to the findings of consultation, such as time and resources. Consultation was not necessarily genuine: 'consultation may therefore be used to garner support for a pre-agreed policy or to discredit opposition forces' (p. 707). Needham's study of Oxford city council found a number of problems with practice, including:

- Public input was limited to a short session.
- Bulky material was given out that was not comprehensible to public.
- Most consultation was conducted in survey form, measuring current performance, not what the public would like to see happen.
- Cost limited the methods used and their impact: 'a planning for real exercise on a deprived housing estate generated creative ideas but no money was available to implement them' (p. 710).

Cheeseman and Smith (2001)'s study of the Australian government's consultation about defence in June 2000 found similar problems. Government goals were not genuine consultation but more to persuade the public to agree with proposals to legitimise government policy. Meetings were only two hours, which was not enough time to talk. They lacked real debate, and discussion was unconstructive and superficial. Participation was biased towards male, middle-aged citizens. The formal nature of the meetings was intimidating to participants. The end results were what the government had aimed for from the beginning, i.e. an increase in defence spending (see also Rowe and Shepherd 2002, Culver and Howe 2004). These are just two of many examples where consultation can fall down on its promise to enhance democracy. Overall, there are a number of concerns with the impact of political marketing on democracy (see also Henneberg 2004).

Potential of political marketing

Political marketing will make politics more responsive

The main argument in favour of political marketing is that, by ensuring politicians are more aware of public opinion, it will encourage greater consideration of the public's views and reduce elite domination of the political process. This is true of all countries: Lilleker (2005b: 570) observed how even 'in nations where the party structure is weak, and democracy is not fully embedded, the design of party policy around voter groups' needs and wants may underpin the development of democracy.' Lees-Marshment (2001a and 2008) has argued that the market-oriented party holds the potential to make politics more democratic in several ways: see Box 10.2.

Political marketing places citizens first, and so could improve the representative function of a political system and democracy as a whole. Doulkeri and Kotzaivazoglou (2006)

Box 10.2 Potential gains from the political marketing approach

1 Getting politicians to listen and understand the market more effectively.
2 Enabling effective targeting, not just of majorities, but also minorities.
3 Making government focus more on actual delivery rather than rhetorical promises.
4 Elevating the citizens' position in the political process.
5 Raising the game of competition if both parties are responsive.
6 Developing a more mature relationship with the electorate, where political consumers are active players in the political system, understand the complexities of government, and move away from demanding to helping create government.

Source: Lees-Marshment (2008: 273–4)

argued that political marketing can also create more effective communication between government and citizens. With regard to the Iraq war, some argue the war was an example of where, if leaders had followed the public, the policy decision would have been more successful. Kaufmann (2004: 5) explains that:

> The logic of the marketplace of ideas in foreign policy is based on the proposition that median voters have strong incentives to scrutinise expansionist arguments and reject those that seem to serve only narrow interests or risk weakening, rather than strengthening, national security . . . a robust marketplace of ideas ensures thorough policy debate, making it unlikely that median voters will be persuaded by arguments that cannot withstand independent evaluation.

Although, in the 2002–03 US debate over going to war with Iraq, this failed to happen, had the public been less subject to elite influence and more powerful, then the war may have been prevented.

Political marketing does not mean the end of ideology

Theoretically, political marketing may not lead to a reduction in ideology. Lees-Marshment (2001a: 1) argues that parties 'no longer pursue grand ideologies, fervently arguing for what they believe in and trying to persuade the masses to follow them. They increasingly follow the people.' The market-oriented party concept could be interpreted as encouraging parties to abandon all ideology in favour of developing a product to suit the market. However, Lees-Marshment argued that the MOP concept allowed room for ideology: political marketing is 'not all about following focus groups . . . Responsiveness does not equate with just doing what the market wants. It can mean not making any change at all – judgment is required alongside consideration of members, ideology, MPs and the realities of government and

" " Discussion point 10.5

To what extent does the market-oriented party concept include ideology as part of the political marketing process? Try to think of any successful parties or politicians that have won elections while maintaining a distinct ideology.

what is feasible financially' (2008: 21). The specific stage-three product adjustment and internal reaction analysis within it call for changes to be made in response to party ideology and history, to create a distinctive product from that of the competition and ensure effective implementation. For example, in 1999, Helen Clark in New Zealand combined targeting of the middle classes with welfare policies to suit the lower-income, working-family supporters. George W. Bush's presidential campaign in 2000 focused on education, a policy area designed to appeal to Democrat voters, but did so with the 'Compassionate Conservatism' theme – a Republican approach to traditional Democrat or liberal issues (Knuckey and Lees-Marshment 2005).

Marketing tools can be used to enhance democracy

While the previous chapters have noted many problems, in practice, with tools such as push polling, this depends on how they are used. For example, segmentation can be used to reach hitherto ignored groups in society. It can be used to identify and help politicians understand the concerns of smaller groups, which might otherwise be neglected, such as those less likely to vote and those who don't normally participate in consultation; and mechanisms and services can be developed to target them and help their involvement in the political process. As Davidson (2005: 1190) noted, there is an argument that, 'where levels of party identification and trust in the political system as a whole are in decline, simplistic categorizations of voters is an inadequate response.' Segmentation of the pensioner or retiree market has shown significant variation in the needs of those who have retired. Emerging minorities may be found earlier, because of organisations using market segmentation, than if they were just left to grow over time until they were powerful and established enough to get their issues placed on the agenda.

Voters are not fools

As noted in previous chapters, many practitioners argue that voters are not fools and can make good choices. Mark Penn (2007: xii) argued that V.O. Key's 1960 book *The Rational Voter*, which argued that 'voters are not fools', was 'not only sound' but 'should be the guiding principle of understanding the trends we see in America and around the world.' Penn argues that 'people have never been more sophisticated, more individualistic or more knowledgeable about the choices they make in their daily lives' (p. xii).

Room for political leadership

Listening to voters, in whatever form, does not mean politicians have no role to play, or that there is no room for passion in politics. Market intelligence can be used in many different ways: 'presidents can use polls to determine how to explain and present already determined proposals and policies to the public' (Jacobs and Shapiro 2000a: 13). The Lees-Marshment (2001a) sales-oriented party notion suggests there is room to use marketing to help persuade people of elites' point of view without changing the product. Parties can and do adopt this approach to electioneering, as we have seen in this book. Goot (1999) detailed how an Australian party was able to use polling to inform its desire to implement an unpopular policy – selling off the publicly owned phone company Telstra. Pre-decision-making polling suggested the party would lose votes with the privatisation policy. However, market intelligence also suggested two ways to make the proposal more attractive: it showed strong public concern with public debt and the environment. Howard therefore announced that funds from such a sale would go towards reducing the public debt and environmental projects, and the proposal therefore appealed to voters concerned about the environment. Goot concludes that it was not true 'that on every issue, or even on all the important ones, polling necessarily commits politicians to the position of the median voter. Had Howard simply followed the polls, he would not have pushed for privatisation' (1999: 237). Therefore Goot (1999: 215) concludes that market intelligence 'may be just as effective as a means of working out how to galvanise support, neutralise opposition or convert those who might otherwise be reluctant to see things the party's way.' Goot also makes a pertinent point (1999: 237):

> Typically, though not invariably, those who attack poll-driven policies are less concerned with how the policies are derived than the substance of the policies; the poll-driven decisions they dislike are derided, not the poll-driven decisions they like.

A market-orientation allows room for judgement; it is not just about following public opinion. Leadership can be integrated within political marketing, as the Promise work on reconnecting Tony Blair for the 2005 election suggested with its proposal for a Mature Tony, including both conviction and reflection. Henneberg's (2006a,b) concept of a relationship builder also includes both leading and following. Jacobs and Shapiro (2000a: 11) argue that 'neither moral leadership nor prospects for leadership in general will end with the rise of polling and other means to listen to public opinion.' The conducting and consideration of market intelligence do not mean leaders follow or rely on it. Murray's (2006: 495) study of the Reagan presidency concluded that, while some party-driven issues were sidelined, and changes were made if too much opposition was encountered, this did not mean it was all about following the market:

The Reagan White House appears to have used survey data to locate the overlap between its political agenda and the current tides in public opinion and to thereby identify political opportunities where it could accomplish some of its ideological goals and satisfy some of its partisan constituents, while staying within broad constraints established by the majority opinion.

There is room for leadership alongside listening: see Practitioner perspective 10.3.

Marketing members as well as voters

Political marketing need not alienate internal supporters, even MOP-type strategies. Even in the US, where party affiliation is traditionally seen as weaker, and there is no formal

Practitioner perspective 10.3

Listening to Britain . . . is about the Conservative Party listening to the people of Britain . . . it is not about writing the next manifesto by opinion polls. Nor does it mean abandoning our principles . . . *A car company developing its next model will consult and listen to its potential customers about transportation needs. But it won't ask them to design the engine or tell them the principles of engineering.* Likewise, we should listen to people about their needs and concerns. But we must then develop policies to meet those needs based on the basis of Conservative principles.

(Peter Lilley, a UK Conservative MP, *Statement on Listening to Britain,*
Information from the Conservative Party, 14 July 1998)

membership, candidates for the presidency reflect the need to gain internal party support during the primary process. Knuckey and Lees-Marshment (2005) showed how George W. Bush was forced to respond to internal supporters during his bid for nomination in 1999–2000. When he lost the first-in-the-nation New Hampshire primary to Senator John McCain, a right-wing conservative, he adjusted his product to increase his own conservative credentials in order to obtain support McCain might otherwise take away from him. He temporarily replaced the 'Compassionate Conservative' slogan with 'A Reformer with Results' and stressed traditional conservative Republican themes, emphasising his belief in limited government.

Continued marketing can help government stay in touch or reconnect

Despite earlier predictions that marketing was only suitable to opposition, consideration of Helen Clark's third government in New Zealand and Blair's bid to win for a third time in 2005 indicated that marketing can be utilised by long-term governments. The work by Promise to reconnect Tony Blair, utilising innovative market intelligence methods to uncover potential positive changes that could be made as part of a rebranding exercise, shows how marketing can be used in government to bring leaders back in tune with public opinion, increasing democracy.

Marketing can help new democracies

Cotrim Maciera, in her study of Brazil concludes that, 'in the 21st century, considering the Brazilian case, the idea that political parties should design their product to suit the voters' preferences may be seen as a proof of democratic maturity' (Cotrim Maciera 2005). Similarly, Patrón Galindo's (2005) study of Peru suggests that, while APRA utilised market-oriented concepts, it played an effective role in helping represent citizen needs, despite their traditional inability to do so. Political marketing can help support new democracies.

Branding integrates ideology

Branding, a new area of political marketing, could help restore ideological elements that some commentators fear have been lost. Lilleker (2005a) adapted Kapferer's (1997) pyramid model of brand identity to politics: see Box 10.3.

Lilleker (2005a) argues that UK New Labour did not change the kernel or core concepts. Changes to Clause IV had symbolic significance, but little practical impact on policy; indeed, changes to the kernel were not necessary, because Labour's ideological kernel was aligned with current market demands for supporting the public sector. The changes that did occur were largely within the area denoted as 'promises' by Kapferer, not a redefinition of its ethos.

Box 10.3 The Lilleker three-sphere model of a political party brand

1 Inner kernel: history, traditions and ethos of the party; its roots and history.
2 Middle layer: core concepts – policy constraints that cannot be altered.
3 Outer sphere: the public representation of the other two spheres; how the kernel and core concepts are communicated to the potential consumer.

Source: Lilleker (2005a)

E-marketing offers the potential for more effective consultation and discussion

Geiselhart *et al.* (2003) observed a number of examples in Australia where governments had used websites to promote consultation and involvement. For example, Moreland City Council in Melbourne provided a webpage called *Moreland chat* that enabled citizens to participate in live discussions with elected representatives. Such consultation and public sphere-type discussions are also engaged in by non-governmental organisations. Geiselhart *et al.* (2003: 226–7) provide a few examples:

- www.onlineopinion.com.au/: a not-for-profit e-journal that aims to provide a forum for public social and political debate about current Australian issues.
- www.notgoodenough.com: NGE provides customers with an online space to seek advice, share experiences and learn accordingly. This is done at Gripe HQ discussion forums and through the Have Your Say box.

Geiselhart *et al.* (2003: 229–30) suggest this is a positive potential change and that, 'from a theoretical perspective, there is growing awareness that political models developed in the eighteenth century are giving way to a new paradigm ... The new models recognise and harness diversity and pluralism as micro-drivers of democracy.' Similarly, Morison and Newman (2001) argued that 'the possibilities that a more thoughtful engagement with the new technologies offers accord very well with a range of approaches within recent political theory which suggest ways in which traditional democracy can be renewed' (p. 177). Online could create a new public sphere 'where discourse, opinion forming and, indeed decision taking, can take place on a basis of real equality and participation' (p. 179). Technology could improve consultation by identifying issues of importance to the public, through online discussion, where topics are set by the citizens, not researchers as in focus groups, ensuring early public input before plans are fixed and providing feedback once policies are implemented: see Box 10.4.

Morison and Newman (2001) explain that computer software can be developed to enable this, with facilities such as support negotiation, structure arguments and shared mental models; a system called IBIS, which maps out arguments on an issue, has been used in Germany in experiments in environmental decision-making.

Political marketing and deliberative democracy

Like e-marketing, empirical studies of consultation in practice also affirm the positive potential for consultative methods. Cheeseman and Smith (2001) argue that the Australian government could have used polls, public debates and informal outreach groups to target minorities, and consultation could be continual, not a one-off. Culver and Howe's (2004) study of a Canadian city's consultation argued that it did succeed in encouraging citizen participation; at the end of the process, both officials and participants wanted more consultation, and elites were open to new methods in which more people might participate in future. The potential of marketing lies in the most basic of its foundations: the marketing concept. This is all about responsiveness; using market intelligence to better understand the market; and ideas about how to design a product, thinking from the consumer perspective rather than that of the elite politician. Such a concept could be allied, not with delegatory democracy, but with a newer political theory, deliberative democracy. Box 10.5 on this offers some initial thoughts.

Box 10.4 Morison and Newman's model of deliberative decision-making for computer support

1 Open discussion
- people get familiar with each other;
- discuss issues of concern;
- explain their own needs and listen to others' needs;
- do not set out propositions and solutions as yet (otherwise they end up arguing about the first two solutions proposed, ignore other possibilities and put themselves into a win/lose bargaining mode);
- agree on the key issues to be discussed further.

2 Structured problem solving
- participants start to explore the issues;
- they identify many possible solutions, by brain-storming or other exercises to enable consideration of non-obvious solutions;
- they consider how well these alternatives meet their needs and others' needs, considering the pros and cons where one side is required to argue the other side's case;
- they try to modify and synthesise the options into ones that meet the most important needs of the group.

3 Evaluation and choice
- sometimes stage 2 produces a plan agreeable to all. In some societies, such as Canadian Indians or Koori, where they are experienced at deliberation, discussion continues until this happens;
- where this doesn't, different options can be presented that may benefit some more than others, so they need to be evaluated and choices made;
- evaluation and choice may involve independent mediators who combine options into a list to choose from; participants then evaluate them through a deliberative process leading to a voting system, and the consensors pick the options with the most consensus support.

4 Implementation
- the top choices are then worked into a workable plan by participants, consensors or planners, civil servants, elected officials or other decision-makers;
- citizens then give feedback on practical consequences of the plan, providing early warning of unintended consequences, and identify issues to go into the 'Open discussion' stage again.

Source: Morison and Newman (2001: 182–3)

Summary

Political marketing clearly has both potential limitations and potential benefits for democracy. There are many significant concerns with the notion, both in theory and practice. These will develop over time as political marketing study and behaviour develop. Problems with political marketing can stem from the way it is used – its practical application – in certain situations. But it nevertheless highlights many different issues. There is, as yet, no clear

Box 10.5 Reconciling political marketing MOP theory with deliberative democracy: initial conceptual thoughts

Jennifer Lees-Marshment and Stephen Winter[1]

Market-oriented political marketing suggests political elites should listen and respond to the public when deciding what policy to adopt and implement. However, academics and practitioners criticise the idea of consulting the public, on grounds of their ignorance, selfishness and other factors. Nevertheless, governments increasingly use various forms of consultation. Although the motives of such consultation may vary, from genuine belief in its potential to improve services and policy to the desire to appear to be consulting, another question is whether recent theories of market-oriented parties from political marketing, and deliberative democracy from political theory, can be synthesised to offer both a more effective framework for consulting the public in both theoretical and practical terms.

Market-oriented political marketing: our interpretation

Market-oriented governments (Lees-Marshment 2001a), by integrating public input into their behaviour, consider public demand before political product design. Responsiveness to public demand is supposed to consider needs as well as wants, and long-term not just short-term opinion. Responding to public opinion is supposed to occur alongside professional judgement, internal party views and the need to take account of governing realities so that promises are achievable, as well as consideration of the market support and competition.

Government consultation

As well as parties seeking to win elections, governments engage in more public forms of market intelligence. This is generally called consultation, but has the same intention as market intelligence: to understand, predict and identify public behaviour. It can also be seen as a form of participation, in different forms at different levels of government. It does, of course, have varying levels of effectiveness in terms of representativeness of the public and effect on government decision-making. However, government consultation also raises concerns. Only certain segments of society are likely to participate – e.g. the educated middle class, with time – which marginalises sections of society. It does not always follow scientific principles of market research. Methods used do not ensure objective opinion, nor take into account the voter's level of knowledge, nor offer enough debate.

Deliberative democracy

Deliberative political theory offers suggestions for enhancing democracy and a more just and democratic way of responding to pluralism. It is focused on deliberation rather than voting and emphasises citizen involvement in a political process. It considers opinion and will-formation before voting and can be an expansion of representative democracy, indeed the res publica itself, beyond just interest aggregation. Deliberative theory suggests a range of methods including citizen juries, national deliberation days, local parliaments, neighbourhood initiatives, citizen panels and so forth. Deliberative democracy resists representative tendencies towards elite judgement and decision-making – decision-making is a result of citizen action. It is not the same as direct democracy or delegatory democracy. Deliberative mechanisms offer further strengths in facilitating the efficacy of local knowledge and, where training or information is provided, may mitigate some of the weaknesses in mass public knowledge and understanding compared with elites.

Deliberative theory of politics may therefore offer greater insight into how governments can consult the public and make that consultation more worthwhile, both theoretically and in terms of practice. It offers potential solutions to the weaknesses of the MOP.

Note

1   These ideas emerged in discussion with the author's colleague, Dr Stephen Winter, at Auckland University.

Discussion point 10.6

To what extent does deliberative democracy offer a more effective way to consult the public within a market-oriented framework?

answer to whether political marketing is good for democracy or not. Perhaps the final concern about political marketing should be this: as Newman (1999: 141) notes, *'caveat emptor* – let the buyer beware'. To a significant extent, any problems with political marketing are as much the responsibility of the market to which it adheres as of the political elites who seek election within it.

Debate 10.2

Proposition: Political marketing is good for democracy.

ASSESSED WORK

Essays

1　Outline and critically evaluate criticisms of political marketing.
2　How can a political leader know when to lead against opinion and when to follow it, whether in their party or country?
3　'In an age in which politicians win elections by inventing beliefs they have never really held, Gore stands out as an anomaly: a passionate ideologue who lost by dropping his signature issue – the environment (Morris 2002: 75)' Critically evaluate the validity of this assertion as to why Gore lost the 2000 US presidential election.
4　What methods of consultation will facilitate the most effective dialogue, e.g. could parties and government borrow from local government, or are they already doing so but with what effect? (The policy commissions using consultation from independent experts under Cameron are one example; Labour supporters' network another.)
5　'The responsibility . . . in the case of war, is to do what I believe to be the right thing for the country. I can't do it simply on the basis of . . . this opinion poll or that opinion poll. You've got to do, on an issue like this, what you genuinely believe to be right for the country, and then pay the price at the election if people disagree with you' (Tony Blair, UK prime minister, 2004). Discuss the extent to which war and international relations can be subject to a market-orientation.
6　To what extent could market-oriented political marketing, a recent theory of empirical party behaviour, be allied to deliberative democracy, a modern addition to political theories of democracy?

Applied

1　Interview local politicians about their views on political marketing and democracy and assess in relation to your understanding of both political marketing theory and practice.

Case study 10.1 Ideology, political marketing and the 2005 UK election　*Heather Savigny*

Ideology refers to a unified, internally consistent and coherent set of values and beliefs. Alongside a normative aspect, ideology has a functional role in that it is coherent and can also provide a set of guiding strategies. In politics, ideology refers to a set of unified, inherently political judgements and ideas, for example, conservatism, liberalism and socialism, and functionally provides for a vision of what society should be like. In marketing, ideology is important for its functional and directive role. Leading marketing scholars, such as Kotler, claim that, for marketing to succeed, marketing must be adopted as a 'mindset': that is, practitioners must believe in marketing in order to implement it effectively. The idea is, then, that it is marketing itself that forms a guiding and functional ideology. Political ideology, rather than being a guiding philosophy for the behaviour of political parties, has been viewed as only one part of a broader set of branding, selling and marketing strategies (see Savigny 2008). Political ideology has been replaced by marketing ideology as the driving motivation for action in politics. This case study explores this proposition with reference to the electoral strategies of the British Labour and Conservative Parties in the 2005 UK General Election and draws out some of the key areas of concern for the democratic process.

Disenfranchising the electorate?

At national level, both Labour and the Conservatives ran broad campaigns, distinguished by differences in style rather than substantive distinctions in policy. There was a lack of debate at national level, and both parties appealed to a relatively prosperous middle class, so the campaign focus was on key voters in marginal seats who were able to influence the outcome of the election. Sophisticated marketing strategies and technologies enabled both Conservatives and Labour to, first, bypass the traditional media and, second, identify key strategic voters who comprised only 2 per cent of the electorate (Wintour 2005). Therefore, there was only a small section of the population whose vote 'mattered'. If parties target their attention to strategically important voters, does it matter if the rest of the polity don't participate?

Negative campaigning

The emphasis on the use of marketing strategies themselves was reinforced by coverage in the media. The Conservatives took advantage of this and successfully dominated the national media campaign. Initially, this was with their highly populist, Saatchi-created, 'Are you thinking what we're thinking?' campaign. Heavily advised by Australian strategist, Lynton Crosby (known for his willingness to 'go negative'), the Conservatives continued their populist campaigning, focusing on immigration. Both parties engaged in highly negative campaigning throughout. This negativity was also seen in the advertising process. Labour again employed Trevor Beattie of TBWA (responsible for controversial FCUK and Wonderbra ads), who created the highly contentious and negative 'flying pigs' ad. One of the key issues here, then, is to what extent does this negative campaigning simply aid political consciousness and awareness, enabling voters to distinguish between competing parties. Or, does it have the opposite effect and disillusion voters about their politicians, adding to their loss of faith and trust in the political process and leading to a lack of willingness by the public to participate in politics?

Centre-ground competition and consensus

Alongside negativity at national level, the campaign was also characterised by minor stylistic differences, and little in terms of policy differentiation. There was fundamental agreement by both parties over basic political issues that reached the agenda, such as the economy, health, crime and immigration (and also those that did not reach the agenda, for example Europe and environmental issues). While there were many similarities at national level, and consensus on issues that would reach the campaign agenda, there was also agreement on those that wouldn't. Further, in a move echoing Labour's modernisation strategies of the 1990s, the Conservatives agreed to retain key planks of Labour policy, including independence for the Bank of England and a commitment to a minimum wage, and agreed to match Labour spending plans on health and education.

The generality and similarity of their campaigning were evidenced again, for example, by both parties' appeal to broad cross-sections of the electorate, with the use of sound bites such as 'hard-working families'. This phrase was widely used by both parties (as was done by Kerry and Bush in the 2004 US election) and had been market-tested in focus groups. Both parties relied heavily on this style of nondescript rhetoric to characterise the kind of person that they were seeking to identify with. It could be argued this represented the parties' own perception of the existence of very little ideological difference between them. Competition and discussion occurred around a narrow centre ground, given the limited issues on the agenda, and focused on the minutiae of policy. The consequence was an election campaign, at national level, characterised by differences in imagery rather than substantive political/ideological distinctions. One of the issues for consideration here is: is it problematic if there is little substantive difference between the two parties?

Marketing as an ideology?

The extensive employment of marketing strategies and technologies, at both national and local level, by both parties suggests their belief in the primacy of marketing as a driving force in the political process. Neither the Labour nor Conservative campaign was characterised by a desire to effect broader structural or ideational change; instead, they were both premised upon an underlying acceptance of neo-liberalism, evidenced in the intensive usage of marketing, and narrow competition around similar party policy platforms.

The use of marketing in politics is nothing new, and what this case study of the 2005 election provides is an up-to-date snapshot of contemporary UK campaign behaviour (see also Savigny 2005, Lilleker *et al.* 2006). The identification of marketing during the 2005 election campaign reveals a continuation of the use of marketing an underlying ontological and ideological commitment to the primacy of markets and marketing. This suggests that marketing did indeed become a mindset.

While political ideology may perform a similar function to marketing (in that it provides an underlying guiding philosophy), there is a significant difference between marketing and political ideology. Marketing is concerned to evoke a response for organisational benefit. Political ideology is a set of guiding principles as to the manner in which society *should* be organised. The eagerness of both parties to focus on marketing strategies and techniques at the expense of political debate implies real problems for the political process. Choice in electoral competition and the opportunity to participate are key components of a healthy democracy. The less the public are presented with a choice and engaged in democratic dialogue, the greater the potential for disengagement.

Sources and further reading

Harris, P. and D. Wring (2001). 'Editorial. The marketing campaign. The 2001 British General Election'. *Journal of Marketing Management*, 17: 909–12.

Lilleker, D., N. Jackson and R. Scullion (eds) (2006). *The Marketing of Political Parties. Political marketing at the 2005 British General Election.* Manchester: Manchester University Press.

Savigny, H. (2005). 'Labour, political marketing and the 2005 election: a campaign of two halves'. *Journal of Marketing Management,* 21(9–10).

—— (2008). *The Problem of Political Marketing.* New York and London: Continuum.

Wintour, P. (2005). 'Campaign planners buy into supermarket tactics'. Available online at www.spinwatch.org

Case study 10.2 Political marketing in the 2006 Canadian federal election: delivering citizen or party needs and wants? *Daniel J. Paré*

According to the Lees-Marshment framework, MOPs are defined as seeking to obtain and understand public concerns *a priori* as a basis for designing their product offering (i.e. policy platform, party and leader image). MOPs do not 'attempt to change what people think, but to deliver what they need and want.' But is this really the case? The evidence from recent elections in Canada suggests that things may not be quite as they seem.

Between June 2004 and January 2006, Canadian voters were twice called upon to elect a new government. In the 2004 campaign, the governing Liberal Party retained power but lost its parliamentary majority in the wake of a $100 million sponsorship scandal, or Adscam. Eighteen months later, in 2006, Canadians returned to the polls and elected the Conservative Party of Canada as a minority government, bringing twelve years of Liberal rule to an end. So what led to this turnaround in the electoral fortunes of the Conservative Party?

The issue for the Conservatives between the two elections was the need to develop a unified voice and a co-ordinated policy platform and, more importantly, to gain sufficient credibility among the Canadian electorate to be seen as a viable option to form a government. Three aspects of their activities suggest at least a partial shift towards the adoption of a market-orientation approach aimed at securing electoral victory.

First, the gathering and analysing of market intelligence to develop a product offering reflecting the concerns and priorities of specific segments of the Canadian electorate (e.g. soft conservatives and soft liberals) was a key component of the reconstruction process undertaken by the Conservative Party in the wake of its election defeat. In March 2005, more than one year after the party had been formed, the Conservatives held their first National Policy Convention, at which they released the Party's 2005 *Policy Declaration,* structured around five valence issues that market intelligence had identified as being of particular importance to Canadian voters: political accountability, health care, crime/security, tax relief and childcare. This moved the party away from issues that had previously 'allowed their opponents to label the Conservatives as extreme and accuse them of harbouring hidden agendas' (Ellis and Woolstencroft 2006: 65). It balanced the demands and priorities of its target audience and those of party members and linked the issues to specific policies that were easy to communicate and understand. Market intelligence also was used to develop a strategy for communicating this policy platform to voters. Demographic analysis of the party's core supporters enabled resources to be focused on the most receptive segments of the electorate. Market intelligence helped develop a 'campaign that could 'narrowcast' rather than 'broadcast' (Marzolini 2006: 258).

The second component of the party's reconstruction focused on rebranding Stephen Harper's leadership into that of a 'friendly, nice guy' image. In the 2004 election, the Liberals portrayed him as a 'scary' individual with a hidden right-wing agenda. In the province of Québec, where in 2004 the Conservatives had failed to win any seats, the rebranding exercise was closely tied to the Liberal sponsorship scandal and the subsequent Gomery Commission that had Québec as its epicentre. These events allowed the Conservatives to seize upon and reinforce popular dissatisfaction with the Liberals in Québec by giving greater precedence to the Québec electorate's concerns and by working towards improving Mr Harper's French language skills.

In their media and communication strategy, the Conservatives sought to frame themselves as speaking on behalf of Canadian citizens, with a policy platform focusing on valence issues, which meant debate focused on 'which party has the best solution to the problem or, more frequently, which party leader can most competently deal with it' (Clarke *et al.* 1996: 110). Communication was also more cohesive and disciplined, avoiding the problems of 2004, when candidates voiced inflammatory and socially conservative messages that detracted attention away from the party's central message. Candidates focused on the main elements of the party's 2006 platform. The party also took the strategic decision to convey one policy announcement per day, which portrayed the Conservatives as being policy-driven and continually back-footed the Liberals throughout the campaign. The Conservative Party received considerably more positive media coverage and public opinion support (see Blake *et al.* 2006).

The Conservative victory in the 2006 election suggests that the market-oriented activities underpinning the party's reconstruction enabled it to revise its product offering, with short-term and personal-gain proposals, in areas such as national unity, social policy and economic policy, that were aimed at appealing directly to the demands of voters (Pammett and Dornan 2006). It also struck a balance between the interests of specific segments of the Canadian electorate (i.e. the desire for efficiency, accountability and direct benefits, without a radical ideological shift) and the interests of internal party supporters. It also conveyed an image of credibility and ability to deliver.

Lessons for political marketing

There are two key lessons for political marketing that can be drawn from the 2006 Canadian federal election. The first is that there are obviously other factors that went into the election result, as the Conservatives only managed to win a mandate to form a minority government, and the result may represent more of a strategic defeat for the Liberal Party in government. Second, it must be noted that the Conservative Party's market-oriented shift towards the centre of the political spectrum appears, foremost, to reflect strategic considerations aimed at avoiding engagement with contentious policy considerations that appeal directly to contending social values. As a result, it is far from clear whether the 2006 election outcome means that the Canadian electorate is getting what it needs and wants, or whether the more market-oriented change in party behaviour reflects, foremost, a strategy aimed at enabling the Conservative Party to get what *it* needs and wants.

Note

This case study draws from a full, peer-reviewed article in the *Canadian Journal of Communication*, 2008, 33(1): 39–63.

Sources and further reading

Blake, A., A. Maioni and S. Soroka (2006). 'Just when you thought it was out, policy is pulled back in'. *Policy Options*, 27(3): 74–9.

Clarke, H.D., A. Kornberg, T. Scotto and J. Twyman (2006). 'Flawless campaign, fragile victory: voting in Canada's 2006 federal election'. *PS: Political Science & Politics*, 39(4): 815–19.

——, J. Jenson, L. LeDuc and J.H. Pammett (1996). *Absent Mandate: Canadian Electoral Politics in an Era of Restructuring*. Toronto: Gage Educational Publishing.

Clarkson, S. (2006). 'How the big red machine became the little red machine'. In J.H. Pammett and C. Dornan (eds), *The Canadian General Election of 2006*. Toronto: Dundurn Group, pp. 24–57.

Ellis, F. and P. Wollstencroft (2006). 'A change of government, not a change of country: the Conservatives and the 2006 election'. In J.H. Pammett and C. Dornan (eds), *The Canadian General Election of 2006*. Toronto: Dundurn Group, pp. 58–92.

Marland, A. (2003). 'Political marketing in modern Canadian federal elections'. Paper presented at the Canadian Political Science Association Conference, Dalhousie University, Halifax, 30 May to 1 June.

—— (2005). 'Canadian political parties: market-oriented or ideological slagbrains?'. In D.G. Lilleker and J. Lees-Marshment (eds), *Political Marketing: A Comparative Perspective*. Manchester: Manchester University Press, pp. 59–78.

Marzolini, M. (2006). 'Public opinion in the 2006 election'. In J.H. Pammett and C. Dornan (eds), *The Canadian General Election of 2006*. Toronto: Dundurn Group, pp. 253–82.

Pammett, J.H. and Dornan, C. (2006). 'From one minority to another'. In J.H. Pammet and C. Dornan (eds), *The Canadian General Election of 2006*. Toronto: Dundurn Group, pp. 9–23.

Turcotte, A. (2006). 'After fifty-six days . . . the verdict'. In J.H. Pammet and C. Dornan (eds), *The Canadian General Election of 2006*. Toronto: Dundurn Group, pp. 283–303.

Case study 10.3 Political marketing, democracy and terrorism: Ireland highlights the dangers   *Sean McGough*

Democracy rests upon voter participation, and thus marketing is a vital key to listening to the voter, transforming that knowledge into a political strategy, winning power and converting the market demands of the majority of the people into democratic government. However, in the age of increasingly more sophisticated political extremists and the search by terrorists for political power at any costs, the danger of political marketing becoming a tool to subvert democracy and replace the consensus of the majority by the tyranny of a fundamentalist minority is a problem that society must now address. This case looks at Northern Ireland, which presents complex politics whereby the IRA and Sinn Féin are seen by many Republican Irish men and women as the legitimate government of Ireland, but through its own acts of war and the general international consensus of democratic states, the link between the IRA and Sinn Féin, and thus the relationship between their political strategies and terrorism, is unavoidable.

The 'war on terrorism'

In the 'age of Al Qaeda', the threat of terrorism to democracy has never been greater. However, the IRA demonstrated that the strategies of terrorism need not be confined to the use of political violence, and that a ballot box in one hand and an Armalite in the other could reflect a more modern way of achieving power than only through force of arms. Regardless of the political legitimacy of Sinn Féin, the example of how to merge together the armed struggle and the quest for political power is one that has readily been taken up by even the most extremist Islamic fundamentalists groups and rests clearly on the convergence of three interlinking forces:

1   the military discipline, dedication and order of the terrorist army;
2   these combined then with the illegal and legal strategies and tactics to gain legitimate political power; and
3   these factors merged with the business methods of marketing.

The aim is not to gain democratic power but power enjoyed when in an oligopolistic position, or even a virtual total monopoly of power, where all competitors are found to be terminally weakened by their inability to compete with the market leader's competitive advantages.

History

The 'troubles' in Ireland stretch back centuries and culminated in the civil rights protests of the 1960s, which eventually coalesced around demands for the ending of the British occupation of Northern Ireland. By the 1980s, the forefront of this campaign against British and Protestant Unionist rule was the Irish Republican Army and its then relatively weak political face, Sinn Féin. The IRA realised that victory in the war against the British would better result from a combination of armed force and politics. Indiscriminate, civilian-affecting bombings were now avoided, as the IRA and the political leaders of Sinn Féin co-ordinated political marketing within the decision-making structures of the IRA Army Council, and a campaign began of achieving the objectives of the 'struggle' through the democratic process. Political marketing could be effectively used as a weapon of persuasion, targeted not only at the voters but the at the British public and government, by demonstrating the legitimacy, inevitability and support for the political demands of the armed struggle. Political marketing can help activate a minority of voters into the kinds of numbers that can achieve dominance in the face of a political system crippled by an increasing number of non-voters.

Political marketing training and the election campaign

The first stage in utilising marketing was training. All those involved in the political campaign received training, often in military-style settings that never left the learners in doubt as to the 'struggle' they were part of. Whether it was in a training camp or in a local party headquarters, the images on walls, bookshelves and general surroundings were punctuated by the armed and uniformed 'volunteers' contribution to the 'struggle'. The trainees, from serving army volunteers to community helpers and political activists of all levels, were part of an organised and disciplined system of education in democratic political activism. Classes in the history, politics and philosophy of Irish Republicanism were undertaken on the same basis as any other form of vocational training. 'Graduates', destined to be election 'doorknockers', speakers at rallies, flag-bearers at marches and peaceful protestors at each and every photo opportunity, were required not only to take the classes, but also to demonstrate a tested level of success at understanding and reflecting on the lessons learned in training. Most of all, they were all expected to have understood and be able to reiterate the party line on everything from freedom from the British occupation to Sinn Féin's position on non-faith schools, the collection of rubbish bins and care policies for the elderly. Consistency in delivering a party message that reflected unity and direction was believed to be an essential aspect of setting the Sinn Féin 'product' apart from its competitors. Once an initial, trained party team was ready, it was then incorporated into a highly organised marketing campaign that introduced its own particular 'spin' on what constituted a 'good' political marketing strategy; and discipline was maintained through constant central management and regular retraining and new training classes.

Segmentation, market intelligence, GOTV and local delivery

From the outset, research was the basis of all political marketing of the party. Planning was essential, and research was systemised, with election areas divided into streets, houses and individual voters. Workers co-ordinated in delivering the party message, while also reporting back to the centre any comment, action or evidence of political usefulness to the campaign centre. Streets were divided into mapped areas, with constant updates on each area and regular meetings to discuss findings and reactions to be co-ordinated to the party's central message and strategy in the light of the market/voters' responses.

Communication was sales-oriented: the message was constrained by the historical certainty of Republican ethics and nationalist desires, but its presentation could be altered in response to the market reactions fed back to the centre by party activists. The communications back to the leaders also enabled them to target precisely their resources. Voters needed to be attracted and activated to actually turn vocal support into physical votes, and this meant that voter complaints had to be addressed, transport difficulties for the elderly solved, community projects supported, and the campaign to be seen as a market-driven strategy. The Sinn Féin Party was seen as a party of the people and for the people.

The candidates were to demonstrate a willingness to represent the voter, whether or not they were elected, and the actual election campaign was designed on a fifty-two weeks a year promise, with Sinn Féin presented as being different to the 'others' in its willingness to actually deal with problems of the community and take an active part in community projects before, during and after the election. So effective was this policy that Protestant, Unionist/Loyalist residents in areas close to, or in, a Republican area who wanted their bins emptied, a road mended or a complaint addressed by their political representative, would secretly contact Sinn Féin for help because 'they [Sinn Féin] got things done'.

Overall, lessons of 'armed struggle' were directly applied to the political marketing strategy, with intelligence networks utilised effectively to understand each and every voter. The discipline and order of the army was equally applied to the election worker, while the Green Book regulations and philosophy were adapted to formulate a voter-friendly message designed to win democratic power through peaceful means rather than seize it through violence and terror. The outcome was an increased voter turnout and success on each and every election. The support for the moderate nationalist party, the SDLP, declined in the face of such political efficiency on the part of Sinn Féin.

Conclusion

Although political marketing can help make democracy more effective, there is clearly an opportunity here for extremists to achieve a 'fair' advantage but use it in an undemocratic manner. Although the example here is of a former terrorist-linked party contributing towards a conflict resolution process by demonstrating its political and democratic effectiveness and, eventually, even leading to the surrender of arms by its own military 'army', the same tactics have the potential to allow groups such as Al Qaeda to gain a democratic position with clear intentions of eventually subverting that democracy for fundamentalist and oppressive aims. The extremists may gain far more advantages through democracy than they ever did through the bomb and the bullet.

FURTHER READING

Aberbach, Joel D. and Tom Christensen (2005). 'Citizens and consumers'. *Public Management Review*, 7(2): 226–45.

Baines, Paul and Robert M. Worcester (2005). 'When the British 'Tommy' went to war, public opinion followed'. *Journal of Public Affairs*, 5(1): 4–19.

Banker S. (1992). 'The ethics of political marketing practices, the rhetorical perspective'. *Journal of Business Ethics*, 11(11): 843–8.

Cheeseman, Graeme and Hugh Smith (2001). 'Public consultation or political choreography? The Howard Government's quest for community views on defence policy'. *Australian Journal of International Affairs*, 55(1): 83–100.

Coleman, Stephen (2007). 'Review'. *Parliamentary Affairs,* 60(1): 180–6.

Collins, Neil, and Patrick Butler (2003). 'When marketing models clash with democracy'. *Journal of Public Affairs*, 3(1): 52–62.

Cotrim Maciera, J. (2005). 'Change to win? The 2002 General Election PT marketing strategy in Brazil'. In D. Lilleker and J. Lees-Marshment (eds), *Political Marketing: A Comparative Perspective*. Manchester: Manchester University Press.

Culver Keith and Paul Howe (2004). 'Calling all citizens: the challenges of public consultation'. *Canadian Public Administration*, 47(1): 52–75.

Davidson, Scott (2005). 'Grey power, school gate mums and the youth vote: age as a key factor in voter segmentation and engagement in the 2005 UK General Election'. *Journal of Marketing Management*, 21(9/10): 1179–92.

Doulkeri, Tessa and Iordanis Kotzaivazogolou (2006). 'Political marketing and democracy: does political marketing strength or threaten democracy'. Paper presented to the UK Political Studies Association.

Edwards, George C. (2003). *On Deaf Ears: The Limits of the Bully Pulpit.* New Haven, CT: Yale University Press.

Geiselhart, Karin, Mary Griffiths and Bronwen FitzGerald (2003). 'What lies beyond service delivery – an Australian perspective'. *Journal of Political Marketing*, 2(3/4): 213–33.

Goot, Murray (1999). 'Public opinion, privatization and the electoral politics of Telstra [Australia]'. *Australian Journal of Politics and History*, 45(2): 214–38.

Heater, Derek (2004). 'The political citizen'. In Derek Heater, *Citizenship*. Manchester: Manchester University Press.

Henneberg, Stephan (2004). 'The views of an advocatus dei: political marketing and its critics'. *Journal of Public Affairs*, 4(3): 225–43.

—— (2006a). 'Strategic postures of political marketing: an exploratory operationalization'. *Journal of Public Affairs*, 6(1): 15–30.

—— (2006b). 'Leading or following? A theoretical analysis of political marketing postures'. *Journal of Political Marketing*, 5(3): 29–46.

Jacobs, Lawrence R. and Robert Y. Shapiro (2000a). 'Polling and pandering'. *Society*, 37(6): 11–13.

—— and —— (2000b). *Politicians Don't Pander: Political Manipulation and the Loss of Democratic Responsiveness*. Chicago, IL: University of Chicago Press.

Kapferer, Jean-Noel (1997). *Strategic Brand Management*. London: Kogan Page.

Kaufmann, Chaim (2004). 'Threat inflation and the failure of the marketplace of ideas: the selling of the Iraq War'. *International Security*, 29(1): 5–48.

Knuckey, J. and Jennifer Lees-Marshment (2005). 'American political marketing: George W. Bush and the Republican Party'. In D. Lilleker and J. Lees-Marshment (eds), *Political Marketing: A Comparative Perspective*. Manchester: Manchester University Press.

Lane, Robert E. (1996). 'Losing tough in a democracy: demands versus needs'. In J. Hayward (ed.), *Elitism, Populism and European Politics*. Oxford: Clarendon Press.

Lees, C. (2005). 'Political marketing in Germany: the case of the SPD'. In D. Lilleker and J. Lees-Marshment (eds), *Political Marketing: A Comparative Perspective*. Manchester: Manchester University Press.

Lees-Marshment, Jennifer (2001a). *Political Marketing and British Political Parties*. Manchester: Manchester University Press.

—— (2001b). 'The political marketing revolution'. Paper presented to the PSA. Available online at www.psa.ac.uk/journals/pdf/5/2004/Lees-Marshment.pdf.

—— (2008). *Political Marketing and British Political Parties* (2nd edn). Manchester: Manchester University Press.

—— and Darren Lilleker (2001). 'Political marketing and traditional values: "Old Labour" for "new times"?'. *Contemporary Politics*, 7(3): 205–16.

—— and —— (2005). 'Political marketing in the UK: a positive start but an uncertain future'. In D. Lilleker and J. Lees-Marshment (eds), *Political Marketing: A Comparative Perspective*. Manchester: Manchester University Press.

Lilleker, Darren G. (2005a). 'Political marketing: the cause of an emerging democratic deficit in Britain?'. In W. Wymer and J. Lees-Marshment (eds), *Current Issues in Political Marketing*. Binghamton, NY: Haworth Press.

—— (2005b). 'The impact of political marketing on internal party democracy'. *Parliamentary Affairs*, 58(3): 570–84.

McGough, S. (2005). 'Political marketing in Irish politics: the case of Sinn Féin'. In D. Lilleker and J. Lees-Marshment (eds), *Political Marketing: A Comparative Perspective*. Manchester: Manchester University Press.

Marland, A. (2005). 'Canadian political parties: market-oriented or ideological slagbrains?'. In D. Lilleker and J. Lees-Marshment (eds), *Political Marketing: A Comparative Perspective*. Manchester: Manchester University Press.

Morison, John and David R. Newman (2001). 'On-line citizenship: consultation and participation in new labour's Britain and beyond'. *International Review of Law Computers and Technology*, 15(2): 171–204.

Morris, Dick (2002). *Power Plays: Win or Lose – How History's Great Political Leaders Play the Game*. New York: Harper.

Murray, Shoon-Kathleen (2006). 'Private polls and presidential policymaking: Reagan as a facilitator of change'. *Public Opinion Quarterly*, 70(4): 477–98.

Needham, Catherine (2002). 'Consultation: a cure for local government'. *Parliamentary Affairs*, 55(4): 699–714.

Newman, Bruce I. (1999). *The Mass Marketing of Politics*. Thousand Oaks, CA: Sage.

Paleologos, David A. (1997). 'A pollster on polling'. *American Behavioral Scientist*, 40(8): 1183–9.

Palmer, Jerry (2002). 'Smoke and mirrors: is that the way it is? Themes in political marketing'. *Media, Culture and Society*, 24(3): 345–64.

Patrón Galindo, Pedro (2005). 'The re-launch of the American Popular Revolutionary Alliance'. In D. Lilleker and J. Lees-Marshment (eds), *Political Marketing: A Comparative Perspective*. Manchester: Manchester University Press.

Penn, Mark with E. Kinney Zalesne (2007). *Micro-Trends: The Small Forces Behind Tomorrow's Big Changes*. New York: Twelve, Hachette Book Group.

Rowe, Rosemary and Michael Shepherd (2002). 'Public participation in the new NHS: no closer to citizen control?'. *Social Policy and Administration*, 36(3): 275–90.

Savigny, Heather (2004). 'Political marketing: a rational choice?'. *Journal of Political Marketing*, 3(1): 21–38.

—— (2005). 'Labour, political marketing and the 2005 election: a campaign of two halves'. *Journal of Marketing Management*, 21(9/10): 925–41.

—— (2006). 'Political marketing and the 2005 election: what's ideology got to do with it?'. In D. Lilleker, N. Jackson and R. Scullion (eds), *The Political Marketing Election? UK 2005*. Manchester: Manchester University Press.

—— (2007). 'Focus groups and political marketing: science and democracy as axiomatic?'. *The British Journal of Politics and International Relations*, 9(1): 122–37.

—— (2008). *The Problem of Political Marketing*. London: Continuum.

Scammell, Margaret (2003). 'Citizen consumers – towards a new marketing of politics?'. In John Corner and Dick Pels (eds), *Media and the Restyling of Politics*. Available online at http://depts.washington.edu/gcp/pdf/citizenconsumers.pdf.

Scrivens, Ellie and Morgan Witzel (1990). 'Editorial'. *European Journal of Marketing*, 24(7): 5–14.

Smith, Gareth and John Saunders (1990). 'The application of marketing to British politics'. *Journal of Marketing Management*, 5(3): 295–306.

Steger, Wayne (1999). 'The permanent campaign: marketing from the hill'. In Bruce Newman (ed.), *The Handbook of Political Marketing*. Thousand Oaks, CA: Sage.

Valdez Zepeda, Andrés, (2005). 'Marketing and democracy'. In *Mercado y Democracia. La política en la era moderna*. México: Instituto Electoral del Estado de Chihuahua, Chapter 1.

Walsh, Kieron (1994). 'Marketing and public sector management'. *European Journal of Marketing*, 28(3): 63–71.

Washbourne, Neil. (2005). '(Comprehensive) political marketing, expertise and the conditions for democracy'. Paper presented at the PSA/PMG Conference.

Weissberg, Robert (2002). *Polling, Policy and Public Opinion: The Case Against Heeding the Voice of the People*. Basingstoke: Palgrave Macmillan.

Index